THE LANGUAGE ANIMAL

The Language Animal

The Full Shape of the Human Linguistic Capacity

CHARLES TAYLOR

THE BELKNAP PRESS OF HARVARD UNIVERSITY PRESS

Cambridge, Massachusetts, and London, England

2016

Library of Congress Cataloging-in-Publication Data

Taylor, Charles, 1931– author.

The language animal : the full shape of the human linguistic capacity / Charles Taylor.

    pages cm

  Includes bibliographical references and index.

  ISBN 978-0-674-66020-5 (alk. paper)

  1. Language and languages—Philosophy.   2. Linguistics—Philosophy.   3. Cognition.

I. Title.

  P107.T39 2016

  401—dc23

                                2015034224

To my grandchildren
Francis and Annik
Alba and Simone
Sabah and David

Contents

Preface

This is a book about the human linguistic capacity. In it I attempt to show that this is more multiform than has usually been supposed. That is, it includes capacities for meaning creation which go far beyond that of encoding and communicating information, which is too often taken as its central form.

My inspiration has been the views on language developed in the 1790s in Germany, the time and place where what we think of as German Romanticism flowered. The main theorists I have drawn on are Hamann, Herder, and Humboldt—hence my name for the theory I have taken from them, the "HHH".

The contrast case to this outlook is one which developed in the great thinkers of early modernity, rationalist and empiricist, which were also responsible for the modern epistemological theories which grew out of, and sometimes partly against, the work of Descartes. The main early figures in this tradition which I cite here are Hobbes, Locke, and Condillac. Hence the shorthand title "HLC".

This theory seems impossibly unsophisticated to thinkers in the twentieth and twenty-first centuries, influenced as we have all been by Saussure, Frege, and to some extent Humboldt. But certain of its key assumptions have survived into analytic post-Fregean philosophy, as well as some branches of cognitive theory.

So an important part of my task in this book has been to refute the remaining fragments of the legacy of the HLC, by developing insights out of the HHH. The result (I hope) is a much more satisfactory, and therefore varied (if less tidy), account of what the human linguistic capacity consists in.

My original intention in embarking on this project was to complement this development of the Romantic theory of language with a study of certain strands of post-Romantic poetics, which I see as closely linked. I started on this in the late 1980s and early 1990s, and in face of numerous self-interruptions, I have only got as far as completing the first part, plus a scattering of studies which could help constitute the second.

I have therefore decided to publish this book on the linguistic capacity, and to continue my work on the Romantics in order to complete the second part (I hope), as a companion study to this one. I will from time to time in this book indicate what that second study may contain. But I hope that this work will be sufficiently interesting on its own to justify its separate publication.

I have greatly benefitted from discussions with a host of thinkers, mainly from the network around the Centre for Transcultural Studies, in particular, Akeel Bilgrami, Craig Calhoun, Dilip Gaonkar, Sean Kelly, Benjamin Lee, and Michael Warner.

I would also like to thank Muhammad Velji for his great work in helping to prepare the manuscript for publication, and in pointing out lacunae that needed filling, particularly in finding adequate English translations of quotes in other languages, not to speak of other improvements; finally I owe him thanks for drawing up the index.

THE LANGUAGE ANIMAL

PART I

Language as Constitutive

1

Designative and Constitutive Views

1

How to understand language? This is a preoccupation going back to the very beginning of our intellectual tradition. What is the relation of language to other signs? To signs in general? Are linguistic signs arbitrary or motivated? What is it that signs and words have when they have meaning? These are very old questions. Language is an old topic in Western philosophy, but its importance has grown. It is not a major issue among the ancients. It begins to take on greater importance in the seventeenth century, with Hobbes and Locke. And then in the twentieth century it becomes close to obsessional. All major philosophers have their theories of language: Heidegger, Wittgenstein, Davidson, Derrida, and all manner of "deconstructionists" have made language central to their philosophical reflection.

In what we can call the modern period, from the seventeenth century, there has been a continual debate, with philosophers reacting to and feeding off each other, about the nature of language. I think we can cast light on this debate if we identify two grand types of theory. I will call the first an "enframing" theory. By this I mean that the attempt is made to understand language within the framework of a picture of human life, behavior, purposes, or mental functioning, which is itself described and defined without reference to language. Language is seen as arising in this framework, which can be variously conceived as we shall see, and fulfilling some function within it, but the framework itself precedes, or at least can be characterized independently of, language.

The other type of theory I want to call "constitutive". As this word suggests, it is the antitype of the enframing sort. It gives us a picture of language as making possible new purposes, new levels of behavior, new meanings, and hence as not explicable within a framework picture of human life conceived without language.

These terms mark a major issue at stake between the two theories. But as it turns out, they are divided on a number of other major questions, and the two approaches can be contrasted on a number of other dimensions as well, and so they are sometimes referred to as the "designative-instrumental" and the "constitutive expressive" theories respectively. And besides this, they even end up differing on the contours and limits of what they are trying to explain, viz., language; as well as on the validity of atomistic versus holistic modes of explanation. They belong, in fact, to very different understandings of human life. But we have to enter the labyrinth at some point, and I will do so at first through this contrasting of enframing versus constitutive, and gradually connect up with the other dimensions of controversy later.

2

The classical case, and most influential first form of an enframing theory, was the set of ideas developed from Locke through Hobbes to Condillac. I have discussed this in "Language and Human Nature."[1] Briefly, the Hobbes-Locke-Condillac (HLC) form of theory tried to understand language within the confines of the modern representational epistemology made dominant by Descartes. In the mind, there are "ideas". These are bits of putative representation of reality, much of it "external". Knowledge consists in having the representation actually square with the reality. This we can only hope to achieve if we put together our ideas according to a responsible procedure. Our beliefs about things are constructed; they result from a synthesis. The issue is whether the construction will be reliable and responsible or indulgent, slapdash, and delusory.

Language plays an important role in this construction. Words are given meaning by being attached to the things represented via the "ideas" which represent them. The introduction of words greatly facilitates the combination of ideas into a responsible picture. This facilitation is understood in

1. See Charles Taylor, *Human Agency and Language: Philosophical Papers 1* (Cambridge: Cambridge University Press, 1985), 215–47.

different ways. For Hobbes and Locke, they allow us to grasp things in classes, and hence make possible synthesis wholesale where nonlinguistic intuition would be confined to the painstaking association of particulars. Condillac thinks that the introduction of language gives us for the first time control over the whole process of association; it affords us "dominion over our imagination" [*empire sur notre imagination*].[2]

The constitutive theory finds its most energetic early expression in Herder, precisely in a criticism of Condillac. In a famous passage of the treatise on the *Ursprung der Sprache,* Herder repeats Condillac's fable—one might say "just so" story—of how language might have arisen between two children in a desert.[3] He professes to find something missing in this account. It seems to him to presuppose what it's meant to explain. What it's meant to explain is language, the passage from a condition in which the children emit just animal cries to the stage where they use words with meaning. The association between sign and some mental content is already there with the animal cry (what Condillac calls the "natural sign"); the pre-linguistic infants, like other animals, will cry out in fear when they are faced with danger, for instance. What is new with the "instituted sign" is that the children can now use it to focus on and manipulate the associated idea, and hence direct the whole play of their imagination. The transition just amounts to their merely tumbling to the notion that the association can be used in this way.

This is the classic case of an enframing theory. Language is understood in terms of certain elements: ideas, signs, and their association, which precede its arising. Before and after, the imagination is at work and association takes place. What's new is that now the mind is in control. Thus the cry of fear can be used to communicate the presence of danger to another, as a voluntary and not just a reflex action; as a way of designating danger, it can be used in reasonings about the antecedents and consequences of certain forms of threat.

This control itself is, of course, something that didn't exist before. But the theory establishes the maximal possible continuity between before and after. The elements are the same, combination continues, only the direction changes. We can surmise that it is precisely this continuity which

2. See Thomas Hobbes, *Leviathan,* ed. Michael Oakeshott (Oxford: Blackwell, 1989), 20; John Locke, *An Essay Concerning Human Understanding,* ed. P. H. Nidditch (Oxford: Clarendon Press, 1975), 3.3.2; Étienne Bonnot de Condillac, *Essai sur l'Origine des Connaissances Humaines* (Paris: Vrin, 2014), 1.2.4.45–46.

3. Johann Gottfried Herder, *Über den Ursprung der Sprache,* in *Johann Gottfried Herder's Sprachphilosophie,* ed. Erich Heintel (Hamburg: Felix Meiner, 1960), 12–14.

gives the theory its seeming clarity and explanatory power: language is robbed of its mysterious character and is related to elements that seem unproblematic.

Herder starts from the intuition that language makes possible a different kind of consciousness, which he calls "reflective" [*besonnen*]. That is why he finds a continuity explanation like Condillac's so frustrating and unsatisfying. The issue of what this new consciousness consists in and how it arises is not addressed, as far as Herder is concerned, by an account in terms of preexisting elements. That's why he accuses Condillac of begging the question. "The Abbot Condillac . . . had already presupposed the whole of language as invented before the first page of this book" [*Der Abt Condillac . . . hat das ganze Ding Sprache schon vor der ersten Seite seines Buchs erfunden vorausgesetzt*].[4]

What did Herder mean by 'reflection' [*Besonnenheit*]? This is harder to explain. I have tried a reconstruction in "The Importance of Herder."[5] We might try to formulate it this way: prelinguistic beings can react to the things which surround them. But language enables us to grasp something *as* what it is. This explanation is hardly transparent, but it puts us on the right track. To get a clearer idea we need to reflect on what is involved in using language.

You ask me what kind of shape this is, and I say "a triangle". Let's say it is a triangle. So I get it right. But what's involved in getting it right in this sort of case? Well, it involves something like knowing that 'triangle' is the right descriptive term for this sort of thing. Perhaps I can even tell you why: "see, the thing is bounded by three straight sides". But sometimes I recognize something and I can't say very much if anything about why. I just *know* that that's a classical symphony we're hearing. Even in this case, however, I acknowledge that the question "why?" is quite in order; I can imagine working further on it and coming up with something, articulating what underlies my confidence that I've got it right.

What this brings out is that a certain understanding of the issue involved is inseparable from descriptive language, viz., that the word can be right or wrong, and that this turns on whether the described entity has certain characteristics. A being who uses descriptive language does so out of a sensitivity to issues of this range. This is a necessary proposition. We would

never say that a being like a parrot, to whom we can attribute no such sensitivity, was describing anything, no matter how unerringly it squawked
out the "right word". Of course, as we prattle on, we are rarely focusing on
the issue of rightness; we only do so when we get uncertain and are plumbing
unexplored depths of vocabulary. But we are continuously responsive to
rightness, and that is why we always recognize the relevance of a challenge
that we have misspoken. It's this nonfocal responsiveness which I'm trying
to capture with the word 'sensitivity'.

So language involves sensitivity to the issue of rightness.[6] The rightness
in the descriptive case turns on the characteristics of the described. We
might call this "intrinsic rightness". To see what this amounts to, let's look
at a contrast case. There are other kinds of situations in which something
we can roughly call a sign can be rightly or wrongly used. Suppose I train
some rats to go through the door with the triangle when this is offered as
an alternative to a door with a circle. The rats get to do the right thing.
The right signal behavior here is responding to the triangle positively. The
rat responds to the triangle door by going through it, we might say, as I
respond to the triangle by saying the word.

But now the disanalogy springs to light. What makes going through the
door the right response to the triangle is that it's what brings the rats to
the cheese in the end-chamber of the maze. The kind of rightness involved
here is one which we can define by success in some task, here getting the
cheese. Responding to the signal plays a role in completing the task, and
that's why there's a "correct use" of the signal. But this is a different kind
of rightness from the one involved in aligning a word with the characteristics of some described referent.

But, one might object, doesn't the rat do something analogous? Doesn't
it recognize that the triangle indicates "cheese"? It is after all responding
to a characteristic of the triangle door, even if an instrumental one. The
rat, we might say, aligns its action with a characteristic of this door, viz.,
that it's the one behind which the cheese always is. So perhaps we might
better "translate" his understanding by saying that the triangle indicates

6. This point is really another facet of the central intuition which underlies post-Fregean philosophy. This intuition was common to a number of different philosophers at the end of the nineteenth century and the turn of the twentieth; not only Frege and Russell, but also Husserl and
Meinong. The idea was that language, and the logical relations it allows, cannot be captured by an
empirical science, like psychology, because it involves crucial issues of validity [*Geltung*]. The "psychologism" of John Stuart Mill and other theorists of the nineteenth century who tried to reduce
logic to psychology was roundly rejected.

"rush through here". But this shift in translation alerts us to what is wrong with this assimilation. There are certainly characteristics of the situation in virtue of which "rush through here" is the right response to a triangle on a door. But getting the response right has nothing to do with identifying these characteristics or any others. That's why the question, under what precise description the rat gets it right—"that's where the cheese is", or "where reward is", or "where to jump", or whatever—is pointless and inapplicable.

What this example brings out is the difference between responding appropriately in other ways to features of the situation, on one hand, and actually identifying what these features are, on the other. The latter involves giving some definition, some explicit shape, to these features. This takes us beyond merely responding to them; or, otherwise put, it is a further response of its own special kind. This is the response we carry out in words. We characteristically define the feature in applying the word, which is why this application must be sensitive to issues of intrinsic rightness, to the fact that the word applies *because* of the defined features, else it is not properly a word.[7]

By contrast, let's call what the rat responds to a 'signal', marking by this term that the response involves no definition of features, but rather rushing through to reward. Otherwise put, where responding to a signal plays a role in some task, correct signal behavior is defined by success in that task. Unless this success is itself defined in terms of getting something intrinsically right—which is not the case for winning through to cheese—correct response to the signal need involve no definition of any particular characteristics; it just involves reacting rightly, and this is compatible with recognizing a whole host of such characteristics, or none at all: the rat just knows to rush through here; it knows from nothing about descriptions and qua what it should rush it.

The rightness involved in description is crucially different. We can't just define it in terms of success in some task—unless we define this task itself

7. Nothing in our experience really corresponds to the wordless world of the rat. But we do have experiences which illustrate what it is to take the further step beyond inarticulate action. We are sometimes asked to articulate just what we have been responding to, for instance, what angers us in a person's demeanor, or why we find some scene pleasing. Being able to say something gives an explicit shape to features which were all undefined, molding our feelings and behavior. This alters our stance toward these features, and often opens up new possibilities for us. I repeat: this example is not intended to offer insight into the world of animals, because much of our world is already articulated, even when we are not focally aware of it. I will touch on this below.

in terms of what I called above intrinsic rightness. In other words, intrinsic rightness is irreducible to what we might call task rightness simpliciter: the account in terms of some task only works for language if we have already incorporated intrinsic rightness in our success criteria.[8]

We might make this distinction in another way, in terms of notions of "awareness". For a nonlinguistic animal A, being aware of X consists of X's counting in shaping A's response. A characteristically responds to X in a certain way: if X is food, and A is hungry, A goes for it, unless deterred; if X is a predator, A flees; if X is an obstacle, A goes around it, and so on. By contrast, linguistic awareness of X can't be reduced to or equated with its triggering a particular response, or range of responses, in certain circumstances. We could think of this as an awareness which is independent from, or can sit alongside of, response triggering. But it would be better to say that awareness involves a new kind of response, linguistic recognition, which cannot be reduced to or equated with any behavioral response.

We can have this linguistic awareness even while inhibiting our standard behavioral response (I can see that you're a dangerous character, but I stop myself fleeing); or even if I make this response, linguistic recognition involves something more than so responding. Of course, other animals can also have behaviorally inert awareness of some normally arousing object if the conditions aren't right: the animal sees prey, but it is replete, and doesn't react. But in the analogous human case, there will normally be the response I'm calling linguistic recognition.

This linguistic awareness is of a different kind than the response-triggering mode; it's a more focused awareness of this object, as rightly called W. It involves a kind of gathering of attention which Herder describes as "reflection", or *"Besonnenheit"*, in the passage in which he introduces this term.[9]

8. The above contrast between people describing and rats in mazes might be thought to be skewed by another obvious disanalogy between the two cases, that the person describing is emitting the signals, and the rat is only responding to them. But consider this case: certain birds are genetically constituted so that when one sights a predator it cries out, and all flee. There is a "right use" of this signal—one could imagine a case of a bird with damaged vocal cords who emitted the wrong sound, with disastrous consequences. But there is likewise no answer to the question, what precise "translation" to give to the cry: "hawk!", or "predator!", or "skedaddle!", or whatever.

9. "The human being demonstrates reflection when the force of his soul operates so freely that in the whole ocean of sensations which floods the soul through all the senses it can, so to speak, separate off, stop, and pay attention to a single wave, and be conscious of its own attentiveness. The human being demonstrates reflection when, out of the whole hovering dream of images which proceed before his senses, he can collect himself into a moment of alertness, freely dwell on a single image, pay it clear, more leisurely heed, and separate off characteristic marks for the fact that this is

To return to our example above of the rats learning how to get to cheese, we can see the possible ambiguity in the use of expressions like "knows that this is the proper door to rush through". Applied to the rat in the above example it can just mean that it knows how to respond to the signal. But in another context, we might mean something like "knows how to apply the description 'the proper door to rush through' correctly". The point of the above discussion is to show that these are very different capacities. Having the first capacity doesn't need to involve aligning any signs with reality on grounds of the features this reality displays; having the second essentially consists in acting out of sensitivity to such grounds. In the second case a certain kind of issue must be at stake, animating the behavior, and this may be quite absent in the first.

A confusion between these two bedevils a number of discussions about animal behavior, most notably the controversy about chimp "language". We can prescind from all the arguments whether the chimps really always sign in the appropriate way, concede the case to their protagonists, and still ask what is going on here. That an animal gives the sign 'banana' only in the presence of bananas, or 'want banana' only when it desires one, doesn't by itself establish what is happening. Perhaps we're dealing with a capacity of the first kind: the animal knows how to move its paws to get bananas, or attention and praise from the trainer. In fact, the sign is aligned with an object with certain features, a curved, tubular, yellow fruit. But this doesn't show that that's the point of the exercise; that the animal is responding to this issue in signing.

But only in the latter case would the chimps have "language" in something like the sense we do. In the former, we would have to see their signing behavior as more of a piece with the clever instrumental performances that we know chimps can master, like manipulating sticks, and moving boxes around to get at things out of reach, which Köhler described.[10] One

---

that object and no other." Johann Gottfried Herder, "Treatise on the Origin of Language," in *Herder: Philosophical Writings*, trans. Michael N. Forster (Cambridge: Cambridge University Press, 2004), 87 [*Der Mensch beweist Reflexion, wenn die Kraft seiner Seele so frei wirkt, daß sie in dem ganzen Ocean von Empfindungen, der sie durch alle Sinne durchrauscht, eine Welle, wenn ich so sagen darf, absondern, sie anhalten, die Aufmerksamkeit auf sie richten und sich bewußt sein kann, daß sie aufmerke. Er beweist Reflexion, wenn er aus dem ganzen schwebenden Traum der Bilder, die seine Sinne vorbeistreichen, sich in ein Moment des wachen sammeln, auf einem Bilde freiwillig verweilen, es in helle, ruhigere Obacht nehmen und sich Mermale absondern kann, daß dies der Gegenstand und kein andrer sei*]; Herder, *Ursprung*, 24.

10. Wolfgang Köhler, *The Mentality of Apes* (London: Kegan Paul, Trench and Tubner, 1925). There is a tendency to react to any sophisticated signaling behavior by animals which seems to ap-

kind of achievement need be considered no more properly "semantic" than the other.

Whereas to be sensitive to the issue of intrinsic rightness is to be operating, as it were, in another dimension. Let me call this the "semantic dimension" (or more broadly, the "linguistic dimension"—I shall discuss the relation between these two in section 3). Then we can say that properly linguistic beings are functioning in the semantic dimension. And that can be our way of formulating Herder's point about "reflection". To be reflective is to operate in this dimension, which means acting out of sensitivity to issues of intrinsic rightness.

---

proach features of human language as an indication that these animals have already made up part of the gap, and are on the road to language. But many such steps can be made, whether in the "wild" or as a result of human training, without reducing the crucial distinction that Herder identified. Vervet monkeys have not just one alarm call, but three, discriminated to leopards, eagles, and snakes respectively; these each trigger off an appropriate reaction by those that hear them—climbing into trees (for leopards), and racing out of trees (for eagles). But these are simply innate responses; there is no call to speak of "reference" here, even though evolution has given these monkeys a very refined and sophisticated signaling system. Again, Duane Rumbaugh and Sue Savage-Rumbaugh trained chimps to manipulate a computer keyboard with simple lexigrams on the keys. But instead of just, say, pressing the key for banana, and getting a banana, they had to learn a combination. There were not only "object" lexigrams, like "banana", "juice", but also "verb" lexigrams, like "give". The chimps got the banana only if they pressed the combination: "give" + "banana". This was understandably very hard for the chimps to learn, and the series of trials confused them for a long time. One time in pressing "banana", they got a banana; the next time (when they failed to combine it with "give"), they didn't. But eventually two chimps, Sherman and Austin, mastered it. So have the chimps mastered the combinatorial feature of human language, whereby we put together verbs and object terms? It depends on whether we think that the Herder feature is present here that the chimps are responding to intrinsic rightness, or simply task rightness. Nothing else in their behavior indicates the former. This seems to be Merlin Donald's conclusion after examining the research in this area. "In some ways, apes have come close to symbolic cognition as individuals, but they have failed completely on the cultural side of the equation. Despite the brilliant efforts of researchers such as the Rumbaughs and many others before them, apes continue to use symbols only for a pragmatic personal agenda." Donald, "The Central Role of Culture in Cognitive Evolution: A Reflection on the Myth of the 'Isolated Mind,'" in *Culture, Thought and Development*, ed. Larry P. Nucci et al. (Mahwah, NJ: Lawrence Erlbaum Associates, 2000), 30. Or again, "the use of signing by apes is restricted to situations in which the eliciting stimulus, and the reward, are clearly specified and present, or at least very close to the ape at the time of signing." Donald, *Origins of the Modern Mind* (Cambridge, MA: Harvard University Press, 1991), 152. Above all, "it is generally acknowledged that [chimpanzees and gorillas] are able to use symbols, in the critical sense that they can use them as substitutes for their referents. . . . But they are incapable of symbolic invention; and therefore have no natural language of their own" (ibid., 160). And a fortiori, crucial features of the human infant's learning of language are absent, like pair bonding, the invention of new words, celebratory rituals of sharing. I return to these features below in discussing human ontogeny. All this points to the conclusion that in learning to use signs, apes are responding to species of task rightness, and not to the intrinsic rightness which defines the semantic dimension. For further discussion of these phenomena, see Terence Deacon, *The Symbolic Species* (New York: W. W. Norton, 1997), chapters 2 and 3. For the interesting work of the Rumbaughs, see also Stanley Greenspan and Stuart Shanker, *The First Idea* (Cambridge, MA: Da Capo Press, 2004), chapter 3.

3

Herder's theory of language is holistic in the way that the traditional view he was criticizing was not. Indeed, it is holistic in more than one way; but at the moment I want to stress that one cannot enter the linguistic dimension by the acquisition of a single word. Entering this dimension, being able to focus on objects by recognizing them, creates, as it were, a new space around us. Instead of being overcome by the ocean of sensations as they rush by us, we are able to distinguish one wave, and hold it in clear, calm attention. It is this new space of attention, of distance from the immediate instinctual significance of things, of focused awareness, as I described it above, which Herder wants to call "reflection".[11]

This is what he finds missing in Condillac's account. Condillac does have a more sophisticated idea of the move from animal to human signs than Locke. Animals respond to natural and "accidental" signs (e.g., smoke is an "accidental" sign of fire, and clouds of rain). Humans have also "instituted" signs. The difference lies in the fact that by means of these latter humans can control the flow of their own imagination, whereas animals passively follow the connections which are triggered off in them by the chain of events.[12]

There is obviously some link between Herder's description of our interrupting the "ocean of sensations" and this Condillaquian idea of taking control. But what is still missing in the French thinker is any sense that the link between sign and object might be fundamentally different when one crosses the divide. It is still conceived in a very reified way, typical of the followers of Locke, a connection which is there in a thing-like fashion, such that the only issue allowed is whether it drives us or we drive it. Condillac belongs to the mode of thought which conceives language as an instrument, a set of connections which we can use to construct or control things. The point of language is to give us *empire sur notre imagination*."[13] Locke is the great source of this reifying language. He often uses images of construction out of materials when speaking of the mind.[14] That a wholly different issue about rightness arises escapes him.

To raise this issue is to swing our perspective on language into a quite new angle. But this issue is easy to miss. Condillac was unaware that he had

11. Herder, *Ursprung*, 24–25.
12. Condillac, *l'Origine des Connaissances*, 1.1.4.45.
13. "dominion over our imagination"; ibid., 1.2.4.45–46.
14. See Locke, *Essay*, 2.2.2.

left anything out. He wouldn't have known where Herder was "coming from", just as his heirs today, the proponents of chimp language, "talking" computers, and truth-conditional theories of meaning, find the analogous objections to their views gratuitous and puzzling. That is why Herder stands at a very important divide in the understanding of language in our culture.

To appreciate this better, let's examine further what Locke and Condillac were missing, from Herder's standpoint. Their reified view of the sign didn't come from their taking the external observer's standpoint on language, as the people I have just described as their heirs do in our day. On the contrary, they wanted to explain it very much "from the inside", in terms of the agent's experience of self. They weren't trying out a behaviorist theory à la Skinner, in which linguistic rightness played no role. Rather they assumed this kind of rightness as unproblematically present. People introduced signs to "stand for" or "signify" objects (or ideas of objects), and once instituted these plainly could be rightly or wrongly applied. Their "error" from a Herderian perspective was that they never got this constitutive feature into focus.

This failure is easy, one might almost say natural, because when we speak, and especially when we coin or introduce new terms, all this is in the background. It is what we take for granted or lean on when we coin expressions, viz., that words can "stand for" things, that is, that there is for us such a thing as irreducible linguistic rightness. The failure is so "natural" that it has a venerable pedigree, as Wittgenstein showed in introducing a passage from Augustine as his paradigm for this mistake.

What is being lost from sight here is the background of our action, something we usually lean on without noticing. More particularly, what the background provides is being treated as though it were built in to each particular sign, as though we could start right off coining our first word and have this understanding of linguistic rightness already incorporated in it. Incorporating the background understanding about linguistic rightness into the individual signs has the effect of occluding it very effectively. As the background it is easy to overlook anyway; once we build it into the particular signs, we bar the way to recognizing it altogether.

This is a fault of any designative theory of meaning. But the reification wrought by modern epistemology since Descartes and Locke, that is, the drive to objectify our thoughts and "mental contents", if anything made it worse. The furniture of the mind was accorded a thing-like existence, something objects can have independent of any background. The occluding of the background understanding of the linguistic dimension by incorporating it into reified mental contents prepared the way for an elision of it altogether in those modern behaviorist and semi-behaviorist theories which try to explain thought and language strictly from the standpoint of the external observer. The associations of thing-like ideas were easily transposed into the stimulus-response connections of classical behaviorism. An obvious line of filiation runs from Locke through Helvétius to Watson and Skinner.

In this context, we can see that any effort to retrieve the background had to run against the grain of this important component of modern culture, the epistemology which was most easily associated with the scientific revolution. In fact, some of what we now recognize as the most important developments in philosophy in the last two centuries have been tending toward this retrieval, culminating in the twentieth century in different ways in the work of Heidegger and Wittgenstein, to name the most celebrated variants. If I consider Herder a hinge figure, it is because he had an important place as one of the origin points of this counterthrust, in particular in relation to our understanding of language. This is not to say that he went all the way to this retrieval. On the contrary, as we shall see later on, he often signally failed to draw the conclusions implicit in the new perspective he adopted; but he did play a crucial role in opening this perspective.

There have been two very common, and related, directions of argument in this counterthrust, both of which can be illustrated in Herder's views on language. The first consists in articulating a part of the background in such a form that our reliance on it in our thought, or perception, or experience, or understanding language, becomes clear and undeniable. The background so articulated is then shown to be incompatible with crucial features of the received doctrine in the epistemological tradition. We can find this type of argument with Heidegger, Wittgenstein, and Merleau-Ponty in the twentieth century. But the pioneer in this kind of argument, in whose steps all the others have followed, is Kant.

The arguments of the transcendental deduction can be seen in a number of different lights. But one way to take them is as a final laying to rest of a certain atomism of the input which had been espoused by empiricism. As this came to Kant through Hume, it seemed to be suggesting that the original level of knowledge of reality (whatever that turned out to be) came in particulate bits, individual "impressions". This level of information could be isolated from a later stage in which these bits were connected together, for example in beliefs about cause-effect relations. We

find ourselves forming such beliefs, but we can, by taking a stance of reflexive scrutiny which is fundamental to the modern epistemology, separate the basic level from these too hasty conclusions we leap to. This
analysis allegedly reveals, for instance, that nothing in the phenomenal
field corresponds to the necessary connection we too easily interpolate
between "cause" and "effect".[15]

Kant undercuts this whole way of thinking by showing that it supposes,
for each particulate impression, that it is being taken as a bit of potential
information. It purports to be about something. This is the background
understanding which underpins all our perceptual discriminations. The
primitive distinction recognized by empiricists between impressions of sensation and those of reflection amounts to an acknowledgment of this. The
buzzing in my head is discriminated from the noise I hear from the neigh-
boring woods, in that the first is a component in how I feel, and the second
seems to tell me something about what's happening out there (my neighbor
is using his chain saw again). So even a particulate "sensation", really to be
sensation (in the empiricist sense, that is, as opposed to reflection), has to
have this dimension of "aboutness". This will later be called "intentionality",
but Kant speaks of the necessary relation to an object of knowledge. "Now
we find that our thought of the relation of all knowledge to its object carries with it an element of necessity" [*Wir finden aber, dass unser Gedanke
von der Beziehung aller Erkenntniss auf ihren Gegenstand etwas von Notwen-
digkeit bei sich führe*].[16]

With this point secured, Kant argues that this relationship to an object
would be impossible if we really were to take the impression as an utterly
isolated content, without any link to others. To see it as about something is
to place it somewhere, at the minimum out in the world, as against in me, to
give it a location in a world which, while it is in many respects indeterminate
and unknown for me, cannot be wholly so. The unity of this world is presupposed by anything which could present itself as a particulate bit of
"information", and so whatever we mean by such a particulate bit, it
couldn't be utterly without relation to all others. The background condition
for this favorite supposition of empiricist philosophy, the simple impression,

15. David Hume, *An Inquiry Concerning Human Understanding*, ed. Tom L. Beauchamp (Oxford: Oxford University Press, 1999), chapter 7.

16. The reference in the by now canonical form is to A 104 of the first edition of Kant's *Kritik der
reinen Vernunft*, in the Berlin Academy edition, in *Kants Werke, vol. IV* (Berlin: Walter de Gruyter,
1968). For English version see *Immanuel Kant's Critique of Pure Reason*, trans. Norman Kemp
Smith (London: Macmillan Education, 1989), A 104.

forbids us giving it the radical sense which Hume seemed to propose for it. To attempt to violate this background condition is to fall into incoherence. Really to succeed in breaking all links between individual impressions would be to lose all sense of awareness of anything. "These perceptions would not then belong to any experience, consequently would be without an object, merely a blind play of representations, less even than a dream" [*Diese <sc. Wahrnehmungen> würden aber alsdann auch zu keiner Erfahrung gehören, folglich ohne Objekt und nichts als ein blindes Spiel der Vorstellungen, d.i. weniger als ein Traum sein*].[17]

So Kant by articulating the background understanding of aboutness sweeps away the empiricist atomism of experience. I want to suggest that Herder does something analogous. By articulating the background understanding of the linguistic dimension, he also undercuts and transforms the designative theory of language dominant in his day. And to make the parallel closer, one of the features swept away is precisely its atomism, the view that language is a collection of independently introduced words. I will return to this shortly.

The second main direction of argument in the counterthrust to Cartesianism or empiricism has been the attempt to place our thinking in the context of our form of life. The original early modern epistemologies gave a notoriously disengaged picture of thinking.[18] This was no accident. The foundationalist drive, the attempt to lay bare a clear structure of inference on the basis of original preinterpreted bits of evidence, pushed toward a disengagement from embodied thinking, and the assumptions buried in everyday custom.[19] The move toward a more situated understanding of thinking is evident enough in the work of Wittgenstein and Heidegger. But Herder is one of its pioneers. He constantly stresses that we have to understand human reason and language as an integral part of our life form.

---

17. Ibid., A 112.

18. See, for instance, Elizabeth Anscombe, who argues, "Can it be that there is something that modern philosophy has blankly misunderstood: namely what ancient and medieval philosophers meant by practical knowledge? Certainly in modern philosophy we have an *incorrigibly contemplative conception of knowledge.*" Anscombe, *Intention,* 2nd ed. (Cambridge, MA: Harvard University Press, 1963), 57, emphasis added.

19. For the suspicion toward unthinking custom, see Locke, *Essay,* 1.2.22.6. I have discussed this connection between disengagement and modern epistemology at greater length in "Overcoming Epistemology" in *Philosophical Arguments* (Cambridge, MA: Harvard University Press, 1995), 1–19; in *Sources of the Self* (Cambridge, MA: Harvard University Press, 1989), chapter 9; and in "'Lichtung' or 'Lebensform': Parallels between Wittgenstein and Heidegger" in *Philosophical Arguments,* 61–78.

They cannot be seen as forming a separate faculty which is just added on to our animal nature "like the fourth rung of a ladder on top of the three lower ones." We think like the kind of animals we are, and our animal functions (desire, sensibility, etc.) are those of rational beings: "in every case the whole, undivided soul takes effect" [*überall . . . wirkt die ganze unab-geteilte Seele*].[20]

These two directions, retrieving the background and situating our thinking, are obviously closely interwoven. In fact, it is the firm belief in situated thinking which leads Herder to his articulation of the linguistic dimension. Just because he cannot see language/reason as a mere add-on to our animal nature, he is led to ask what kind of transformation of our psychic life as a whole attends the rise of language. It is this question to which "reflection" is an answer. To see our thinking as situated makes us see it as one mode among other possible forms of psychic life. And it is this which makes us aware of its distinctive background.

It is by embarking on these two related directions of argument that Herder brings about a rotation of our thought about language, so that we see it from a new angle. A good illustration of this is Herder's grasp of holism. One of the most important, and universally recognized, consequences of Herder's discovery was a certain kind of holism of meaning. A word only has meaning within a lexicon and a context of language practices, which are ultimately embedded in a form of life. Wittgenstein's is the most celebrated formulation of a thesis of this kind in our day.

This insight flows from the recognition of the linguistic dimension as Herder formulated it. Once you articulate this bit of our background understanding, an atomism of meaning becomes as untenable as the parallel atomism of perceptions does after Kant. The connection can be put in the following way:

To possess a word of human language is to have some sense that it's the right word, to be sensitive, we said above, to this issue of its irreducible rightness. Unlike the rat who learns to run through the door with the red triangle, I can use the word 'triangle'. That means that I can not only respond to the corresponding shape, but can recognize it as a triangle. But to be able to recognize something as a triangle is to be able to recognize other things as nontriangles. For the description 'triangle' to have a sense

---

20. Herder, "Origin of Language," 83; Herder, *Ursprung,* 21.

for me, there must be something(s) with which it contrasts; I must have some notion of other kinds of figures. 'Triangle' has to contrast in my lexicon with other figure terms. But in addition, to recognize something as a triangle is to focus on a certain property dimension; it is to pick the thing out by its shape, and not by its size, color, composition, smell, aesthetic properties, etc. Here again, some kind of contrast is necessary.

Now at least some of these contrasts and connections we have to be able to *articulate*. Someone can't really be *recognizing* 'triangle' as the right word if they have absolutely no sense of what makes it the right word; for instance, if they don't even grasp that something is a triangle in virtue of its shape, not its size or color. And one cannot have any sense of this, if one cannot say *anything* whatever, even under probing and prompting. There are cases, of course, where we cannot articulate the particular features peculiar to something we recognize, for example a certain emotional reaction to something, or an unusual hue. But we know to say that it is a feeling or a color. And we can state its ineffability. The zone where our descriptions give out is situated in a context of words. If we couldn't say any of this: even that it was a feeling, couldn't even say that it was indescribable, we couldn't be credited with linguistic consciousness at all; and if we did utter some sound, it couldn't be described as a word. We would be out of the linguistic dimension altogether.[21]

In other words, a being who just emitted a sound when faced with a given object, but was incapable of saying why, that is, showed no sign of having any sense that this is the (irreducibly) right word, other than emitting the sound, would have to be deemed to be merely responding to signals, like the animals I described earlier. (Think of the parrot.)

What flows from this is that a descriptive word, like 'triangle', couldn't figure in our lexicon alone. It has to be surrounded by a skein of terms, some which contrast with it, and some which situate it, place it in its property dimension, not to speak of the wider matrix of language in which the various activities are situated where our talk of triangles figures: measurement, geometry, design; and where description itself figures as one kind of speech act among others.

This is what the holism of meaning amounts to: that individual words can only be words within the context of an articulated language. Language

21. Ludwig Wittgenstein, *Philosophical Investigations,* trans. G. E. M. Anscombe (Oxford: Blackwell, 1997), 93.

is not something which could be built up one word at a time. Mature linguistic capacity just doesn't come like this, and couldn't; because each word supposes a whole of language to give it its full force as a word, that is, as an expressive gesture which places us in the linguistic dimension. At the moment when infants start to say their "first word", they are certainly on the road to full human speech, but this "first word" is quite different from a single word within developed speech. The games the infant plays with this word express and realize a quite different stance to the object than the adult descriptive term. It's not a building block out of many of which adult language is gradually built. I shall return to this below.

But this exactly was the error of the traditional designative view. For Condillac, a one-word lexicon was quite conceivable. His children acquire first one word, then others. They build language up, term by term. That's because Condillac ignores the background understanding necessary for language; rather, he builds it unremarked into the individual words. But Herder's articulation of the real nature of linguistic understanding shows this to be impossible. Herder rightly says in the passage I quoted earlier that Condillac presupposes "*das ganze Ding Sprache.*"[22]

This expression seems happily to capture the holistic nature of the phenomenon. And yet, here too, Herder disappoints in the conclusions he actually draws in his passage on the birth of language. His "just so" story after all tells us of the birth of a single word. And at the end of it, he unfortunately throws in the following rhetorical question: "What is the whole of human language but a collection of such words" [*was ist die ganze menschliche Sprache als eine Sammlung solcher Worte*]?[23] And yet I'd like to credit him again with putting us on the track to holism. Not only because it is clearly implicit in what he did articulate; but also because he himself made part of the mediating argument.

He sees that the recognition of something as something, the recognition which allows us to coin a descriptive term for it, requires that we single out a distinguishing mark [*Merkmal*]. The word for X is the right word in virtue of something. Without a sense of what makes it the right word, there is no sense of a word as right. "Distinctly in an immediate way, without a distinguishing mark? No sensuous creature can have outer sensation in this way, since it must always suppress, so to speak destroy, other feelings, and

---

22. "the whole of language."
23. Herder, "Origin of Language," 89; Herder, *Ursprung,* 25.

must always recognize the difference between two things through a third thing" [*Deutlich unmittelbar, ohne Merkmal? so kann kein sinnliches Geschöpf ausser sich empfinden, da es immer andere Gefühle unterdrücken, gleichsam vernichten und immer den Unterschied von zweien durch ein drittes erkennen muss*].[24]

So Herder's articulation of the linguistic dimension, properly understood, and as he began to work it out, shows the classical designative story of the acquisition of language to be in principle impossible. This story involves in a sense a deep confusion between the mere signal and the word. For there *can* be one-signal repertoires. You can train a dog to respond to a single command, and then add another one, and later another one. In your first phase, whatever isn't your one signal isn't a signal at all. But there can't be one-word lexica. That's because getting it right for a signal is just responding appropriately. Getting it right for a word requires more, a kind of recognition: we are in the linguistic dimension.

The holism of meaning has been one of the most important ideas to emerge from Herder's new perspective. Humboldt took it up in his image of language as a web.[25] And it took its most influential form early in the last century in the celebrated principle of Saussure: "in language there are only differences without positive terms" [*dans la langue il n'y a que des différences sans termes positifs*].[26] What this slogan means is that we can't understand linguistic meaning as an alignment of sounds (words) and things; rather we align differences in sound with differences in signification. So in English the distinction in sound between "b" and "p" yields in a given context the distinction in sense between "but" and "put". In other words, a term gets its meaning only in the field of its contrasts. In this

---

24. Herder, "Origin of Language," 89; Herder, *Ursprung*, 25.

25. "Language can be compared to an immense web, in which every part stands in a more or less clearly recognizable connection with the others, and all with the whole. Whatever his point of departure, man always makes contract in speaking with a merely isolated portion of this fabric, but invariably does so instinctively, as if everything this one portion must necessarily agree with were simultaneously present to him at the same moment." Wilhelm von Humboldt, *On Language: The Diversity of Human Language-Structure and Its Influence on the Mental Development of Mankind*, trans. Peter Heath (Cambridge: Cambridge University Press, 1988), 69. [*Man kann die Sprache mit einem ungeheuren Gewebe vergleichen in dem jeder Teil mit dem anderen und all mit dem ganzen in mehr oder weniger deutlich erkennbaren Zusammenhange stehen. Der Mensch berührt im Sprechen, von welchen Beziehungen man ausgehen mag, immer nur ein abgesonderten Teil des Gewebes, tut dies aber instinktartig immer dergestalt, als wären ihm zugleich alle, mit welchem jener einzelne notwendig in Übereinstimmung stehen muß, in gleichen Augenblick gegenwärtig*]; Humboldt, *Schriften zur Sprache*, ed. Michael Bühler (Stuttgart: Reklam 1995), 65.

26. Ferdinand de Saussure, *Course in General Linguistics*, trans. Wade Baskin (New York: Columbia University Press, 2011), 120; Ferdinand de Saussure, *Cours de Linguistique Générale* (Paris: Patot, 1978), 166.

form, the principle has achieved virtually universal acceptance. It is an axiom of linguistics.

Humboldt's image of the web brings out the fact that our grasp of any single word is always situated within our grasp of the language as a whole, and the multiple rules and connections that define it. So when we coin a new verb, and by adding "-ed" put it in the past tense, everyone understands what is being said; and thus also, we have for any word some notion of how it relates to others, for instance, what combination with others in a proposition would make sense, as we see from the paradigm of absurdity which Chomsky made widely familiar: "colorless green ideas sleep furiously". In another famous image, Humboldt likens the mention of a word to the touching of a note in a keyboard instrument. This resonates through the whole instrument.[27]

But perhaps its most powerful application in philosophy is in the work of late Wittgenstein. Wittgenstein's devastating refutation of "Augustine's" designative theory of meaning constantly recurs to the background understanding which we need to draw on to speak and understand. Where the traditional theory sees a word acquiring meaning by being used to name some object or idea, and its meaning as then communicated through ostensive definition, Wittgenstein points out the background of language which these simple acts of naming and pointing presuppose.[28] Our words only have the meaning they have within the "language games" we play with them, and these in turn find their context in a whole form of life.[29]

This holism of meaning is inextricably connected to the fact that human beings as linguistic animals also live in a bigger world, which goes beyond

27. Humboldt, "Schriften zur Sprache," 138–39.

28. See, for instance, Wittgenstein, *Philosophical Investigations,* 92.

29. There is an important link between this holistic point and that which Brandom makes central in *Making It Explicit: Reasoning, Representing, and Discursive Commitment* (Cambridge, MA: Harvard University Press, 1994) and other works. Brandom rejects the atomism of the empiricist tradition, that one could first take in one piece of information, and then another, then link them, and see the correlation; and hence make inferences. This process doesn't make sense for Brandom. How could we take in an isolated piece of information? What sense could we make of such an isolated bit of information? Well what sense *do* we make of it? Elder says: "go, Scout, and see if there are any tiger tracks." Scout comes back: "Elder, I saw a paw track in the sand!" That's a particulate bit, but it makes sense here within our whole general grasp of our situation, which includes forest, tigers, the consequent danger of being eaten, our collaborative efforts to avoid this and other dangers, and so on. This bit is relevant because it will license multiple inferences, practical and factual. Included among the former would be here: "Let's not go there now." So Brandom's opening move in *Making It Explicit* is absolutely crucial. He dethrones representation as the primary building block of thought and language. What is crucial is inferences.

the episodic present. Their present experience is accompanied invariably by the sense that it was preceded by a personal and social history; that it will be followed by a future; and that what happens in their immediate predicament takes place in a broader context of space. Indeed, we can say that humans live not only in the immediate situation, but also in a vast cosmos or universe, stretching out in time and space from our momentary surroundings. The further reaches of this cosmos may have been more conjectured or imagined than known for much of human history, the product of myth and wild surmise; but this larger context is inescapable.

But the broader context is also social: we live among relatives, and in a village, perhaps also a nation. Within these contexts, familial or societal, we interact with people through different roles; we carry on different activities, which create different contexts. All this is captured in language, for instance the language of kinship, that of the different political and social positions—police officer, doctor, president; that of different activities and spheres—like the political, the economic, the religious, entertainment, and so on. It is not just that these roles, spheres, relations wouldn't be possible without language (I will return to this point later on). It is also that the holism of language means that we cannot but have a sense of how these roles and spheres are meant to relate to each other: how some are distinct from others, for example parent and child; or a context of serious negotiation versus one of play, or work as against recreation, and so on. To learn the language of society is to take on some imaginary of how society works and acts, of its history through time; of its relation to what is outside: nature, or the cosmos, or the divine.

But my principal point here is not that these words for roles, relations, activities, spheres, allow each of these severally to be part of our world, but rather the holistic point that our language for them situates them in relation to each other, as contrasting or alternating, or partially interpenetrating. To grasp them in language *is* to have some sense of how they relate. This relationality may be more or less articulate in one or other of its aspects, may be more or less clearly defined. But some sense of it is always present in human life qua linguistic.[30]

This is part of what Heidegger wanted to evoke in his famous phrase about language as the "house of being". A house is an environment in which

---

30. See the interesting discussion on language and "lexification" in Robert Pogue Harrison, *The Dominion of the Dead* (Chicago: University of Chicago Press, 2003), chapter 5.

things are arranged by our action and design, different rooms for different uses, for different people, or different times; or for storing different kinds of things; and the like. So the way in which the language we speak at a given time relates things, disposes of them, is seen as a kind of active arrangement. Such a relating is essential to language.[31]

But what gives especial force to this image is our seeing this disposition as one of different human meanings. Our sense of the meanings of things in their different dimensions is carried in our language. But what might make us uneasy with this expression is the fact that we have developed uses of language which allow description and explanation of things which are no longer characterized in terms of human meaning: paradigmatically, post-Galilean natural science. As one activity among many, this is within the "house", but as a vision of reality it takes us beyond the "house"; it presents a universe which is "unhoused" in any arrangements of human meanings.

So as human beings we live inescapably in a larger social, and even cosmic, context. The reflection seems obvious that only beings with language can live in this kind of context, because it takes language to have an idea, however wild, of what doesn't and cannot impinge on our immediate situation. But the real point is that as linguistic, we cannot but so live in a wider world.

This holism of language has another facet. To have linguistic awareness is to be constantly encountering its limits. We know that we can say certain things easily. For instance, we can answer certain questions right off: "when did you last see him?"—"yesterday"; "what kind of a tree is

---

31. Possessing a language is having a liminal sense of a great constellation of such ordered distinctions, some already articulated for us, some not yet expressed: kinds of animals; kinds of furniture; houses/stores/office blocks; then inside (buildings in general) versus outside; field/forest; then also bigger domains: living/inanimate; on earth/in the sky; now/past/future. Then there is the social domain: kin versus others; various social roles. Then there is the domain of feelings: liking/disliking, love/indifference; pride/shame, and the like. Then there are the grammatical forms and combinations: things and their properties, as above; objects and processes, agents and actions. The liminal access to these distinctions underpins my capacity to speak, and helps constitute my sense of this capacity; that is, my sense of what I can say, and what is (as yet) beyond my ability to articulate. I can tell you that that picture is of a storm at sea, but I can't find a way of describing the conflicting emotions it arouses in me. Different languages and cultures carry with them different such constellations of distinctions; each proposes its own order, its own way of "housing" Being, to use Heidegger's metaphor. And at the same time, each of these orders evolves and changes, and in the present language there are always hints and reminders of its past. Some terms have an archaic ring to them; some modes of address have a formality and solemnity which is inseparable from their venerable origin in earlier times (Your Majesty, Your Honor). See the discussion in John Richardson, *Heidegger* (New York: Routledge, 2012), chapter 8.

that?"—"an oak". But sometimes when people ask: "why did you do that?", or "what were you feeling?", or "why do you dislike that painting?", we can be at a loss. In these cases, part of the problem may be our own (often motivated) opaqueness to ourselves. But it can be that we just lack the terms. The city dweller might even be at a loss if asked what kind of tree he's standing under.

We not only have this sense of what we can and cannot (easily) say; we are often motivated to extend our range of articulacy. We might get the city dweller interested in examining leaf forms, kinds of bark, and so on, so that he would easily come to distinguish oaks from elms. Or we might be induced to a more self-transformative reflection, and come to a deeper understanding of our motives, our affinities and repugnances. Expanding articulacy can regestalt our experience in a rather minimal way by learning to distinguish elms and oaks, but more profoundly when we come to distinguish different kinds of love and what they involve and hence come to read our relationships and their tensions and conflicts in a quite different fashion.

This kind of change is analogous, on a more abstract and objectified level, to our changing our mode of scientific enquiry by shifting paradigms. Here it's not just a matter of adding words, but of taking on new models, and recognizing previously unseen patterns.

Self-understanding, and human understanding in general, can also be enhanced by coming to recognize new models; and that is why literature is such a source of insight. Balzac in *Les Chouans* paints a portrait of a miser [*avare*] through a chain of actions, words, and responses which reveal the pattern of obsession which defines this type for him.[32]

Humboldt shows the importance of this boundary between the sayable and what lies beyond, as well as our recurrent desire to push this boundary back, and expand our zone of articulacy. On a more banal level, we are often forced to find new words for what we have to say, as when our interlocutor says: "I can't understand you, can you explain it differently?" But Humboldt sees us as pushed further, to open up to speech areas which were previously ineffable. Certainly poets are embarked on this enterprise: T. S. Eliot speaks of "raids on the inarticulate."[33] Humboldt, for his part, posits a drive [*Trieb*] "to couple everything felt by the soul [mind] with a sound"

32. Honoré de Balzac, *Les Chouans* (Paris: Gallimard, Folio Classique, 1972), 240–56.
33. T. S. Eliot, "No. 2: East Coker," in *Four Quartets,* section 5.

[*alles, was die Seele empfindet, mit dem Laut zu verknüpfen*].[34] I will return to this drive, and the ways in which we make inroads into the hitherto unsayable, in Chapter 6.

4

But we need to extend somewhat our notion of the semantic dimension. In fact, we should speak now of the linguistic dimension, because the semantic is only one of the facets or uses of language. Above I was speaking of descriptive rightness. But we do more things in language than describe. There are other ways in which a word can be "*le mot juste*". For instance, I come up with a word to articulate my feelings, and thus at the same time shape them in a certain manner. This is a function of language which cannot be reduced to simple description, at least not description of an independent object. Or else I say something which reestablishes the contact between us, puts us once again on a close and intimate footing. We need a broader concept of intrinsic rightness than just that involved in aligning words with objects.

We can get a more general description if we recur to a contrast I made above. The correct response to a signal for a rat trained in a maze was defined, I said, by success in some task. Let's use the word 'sign' as a general term which can apply indiscriminately to this kind of case as well as to genuine uses of language. Then we can say that functioning with signs lies outside the linguistic dimension wherever the right response is defined simply in terms of what leads to success in some nonlinguistically defined task. Where this account is not sufficient, the behavior falls within the dimension.

Rats responding to triangles, and birds responding with cries to the presence of predators, meet this criterion. An account in terms of a simple task suffices. Where it fails to, we enter the linguistic dimension. This can happen in two ways. First the task itself can be defined in terms of intrinsic rightness; for instance, where what we are trying to do is describe some scene correctly. Or else, where the end is something like articulating our feelings, or reestablishing contact, the failure occurs at another point. As goals, these don't on the face of it seem to involve intrinsic rightness.

---

34. Humboldt, "On Language," 157; Humboldt, "Schriften zur Sprache," 146. This is the drive to produce what Merleau-Ponty describes as "*paroles parlantes*"; see note 39.

But the way in which the correct sign behavior contributes to fulfilling them does.

Thus when I hit on the right word to articulate my feelings, and acknowledge that I am motivated by envy, say, the term does its work because it is the right term. In other words, we can't explain the rightness of the word 'envy' here simply in terms of the condition that using it produces; rather we have to account for its producing this condition—here, a successful articulation—in terms of its being the right word. A contrast case should make this clearer. Say that every time I get stressed out, tense and cross-pressured, I take a deep breath, and blow it explosively out of my mouth, 'how!' I immediately feel calmer and more serene. This is plainly the "right sound" to make, as defined by this desirable goal of restored equilibrium. The rightness of 'how!' admits of a simple task account. It's like the rat case and the bird case, except that it doesn't involve directing behavior across different organisms, and therefore doesn't look like "communication". (But imagine that every time you feel cross-pressured, I go 'how!', and that restores your serenity.) That's because we can explain the rightness simply in terms of its bringing about calm, and don't need to explain its bringing about calm in terms of rightness.

This last clause points out the contrast with 'envy' as the term which articulates/clarifies my feelings. It brings about this clarification, to be sure, and that's essential to its being the right word here. But central to its clarifying is its being the right word. So we can't just explain its rightness by its de facto resolving, say, the state of painful confusion I was in. You can't simply make this de facto causal outcome criterial for its rightness, because you don't know whether it's clarifying unless you know that it's the right term. Whereas in the case of 'how!', all there was to its rightness was its having the desired outcome; the bare de facto consequence is criterial. That's why normally we wouldn't be tempted to treat this expletive as though it had a meaning.

Something similar can be said about my restoring the intimacy between us by saying "I'm sorry". This was "the right thing to say", because it restored contact. But at the same time, we can say that these words are efficacious in restoring contact because of what they mean. Intrinsic rightness enters into the account here, because what the words mean can't be defined by what they bring about. Again, we might imagine that I could also set off a loud explosion in the neighborhood, which would so alarm you that you would forget about our tiff and welcome my presence. This would then be, from a rather cold-blooded, strategic point of view, the "right move". But the explosion "means" nothing.

What this discussion is moving us toward is a definition of the linguistic dimension in terms of the (im)possibility of a reductive account of rightness. A simple task account of rightness for some sign reduces it to a matter of efficacy for some nonlinguistic purpose. We are in the linguistic dimension when this kind of reduction cannot work, when a kind of rightness is at issue which can't be cashed out in this way. That's why the image of a new "dimension" seems to me apposite. Sometimes the rightness is a matter of correct description, and then we can speak of the "semantic" dimension. But linguistic rightness is more multifaceted than can be captured by semantics alone.

To move from nonlinguistic to linguistic agency is to move to a world in which a new kind of issue is at play, a right use of signs which is not reducible to task rightness. The world of the agent has a new axis on which to respond; its behavior can no longer be understood just as the purposive seeking of ends on the old plane. It is now responding to a new set of demands. Hence the image of a new dimension.[35]

Condillac as we saw missed this dimension. And what perhaps contributed to this occlusion was his starting point in his account of the origin of language. His explanation begins with "natural signs", things like cries of pain or distress. Their right use in communication could only be construed on the simple task model. Language arose supposedly when people learned to use the connection already established by the natural sign, between say, the cry and what caused the distress, in a controlled way. The "instituted sign" is born, an element of language properly speaking. Herder, as we just saw, cannot accept that the transition from prelanguage to language consists simply in a taking control of a preexisting process. What this leaves out is precisely that a new dimension of issues becomes relevant, that the agent is operating on a new plane. Hence in the same passage in which he declares Condillac's account circular, Herder reaches for a definition of this new dimension, with his term 'reflection'.

On my reconstruction, Herder's 'reflection' is to be glossed as the semantic (and more generally, the linguistic) dimension, and his importance is that he made this central to any account of language. Moreover,

---

35. Hence also my use of the word 'intrinsic'. This is a dangerous word, which triggers often unreflective reactions from pragmatists, non-realists, and other such idealists. Its point here is simply to serve as an antonym to 'capable of reductive explanation'.

Herder's conception of this dimension was multifaceted, along the lines of the broad conception of rightness above. It didn't just involve description. Herder saw that opening this dimension has to transform all aspects of the agent's life. It will also be the seat of new emotions. Linguistic beings are capable of new feelings which affectively reflect their richer sense of their world: not just anger, but indignation; not just desire, but love and admiration. For human beings an emotional response is inseparable from a certain characterization of the situation which elicits it. But linguistic beings can be sensitive to distinctions which are lost on prelinguistic animals. Important among these are distinctions involving moral or other values. Prelinguistic animals treat something as desirable or repugnant by going after it or avoiding it. But only language beings can identify things as *worthy* of desire or aversion. For such identifications raise issues of intrinsic rightness. They involve a characterization of things which is not reducible simply to the ways we treat them as objects of desire or aversion. They involve a recognition beyond that, that they *ought* to be treated in one or another way. So we may ascribe anger to a nonhuman animal, but indignation requires the recognition that the object of our ire has done something wrong, unconscionable. To admire someone is more than being impressed by them, it is experiencing them as having exceptional virtues, or achievements.

Being in the linguistic dimension not only enables a new kind of awareness of the things which surround us, but also a more refined sense of human meanings, and hence a more complex gamut of emotions. And in this domain, unlike in that of purely external objects, a changed or clarified understanding of meanings will mean a changed or clarified emotion. That is why, in my example above, when I come to see that I am actuated by envy, my feelings characteristically change.

The linguistic dimension also made human agents capable of new kinds of relations, new sorts of footings that they can stand on with each other, of intimacy and distance, hierarchy and equality. Gregarious apes may have (what we call) a "dominant male", but only language beings can distinguish between leader, king, president, and the like. Animals mate and have offspring, but only language beings define kinship. And it is obvious that our understanding of footings and relations, like our vocabulary of feelings, is deeply intricated in our grasp of value, moral or other.

This discussion brings us back to the central thesis that I want to draw out of Herder, the one that justifies the label 'constitutive'. I have been arguing above that operating in the linguistic dimension is an essential condition of counting as a being which uses language in the full sense. No language without linguistic dimension of irreducible rightness. But the crucial Herderian thesis also inverts this relation: no linguistic dimension without language. This may seem a trivial consequence of the way I have set up this discussion. If we define the linguistic dimension as sensitivity to certain issues concerning the (intrinsically) right use of *signs,* then it follows tautologically that it requires language to be.

But the point I'm trying to make here goes well beyond tautology. The claim is that our sensitivity to these issues of rightness arises out of and along with our ability to express it. This sensitivity is articulated in certain responses, including the various uses of words and articulate speech; but also, as we shall discuss more fully below, gesture, mimicry, the fashioning of images and symbols, and the like. This range of expressive activities, as we can call them, serves not only to communicate this sensitivity to others. The articulation serves just as much and equiprimordially to realize this sensitivity in ourselves. This is at the core of Herder's "expressivism".

Here he inaugurates a theme which has been developed in recent times by Merleau-Ponty. In his chapter on language in *La Phénomènologie de la Perception,* Merleau-Ponty focuses on what seems the mystery of new expression, and the creation of new meanings. We see what happens with gestures. A new gesture, or a style of moving and acting in our surroundings, can express and thus reveal the possibility of a new way of being, conferring new meanings on the things which surround us. There might be someone whose whole stance, way of looking, way of responding to the scene expresses a sensitivity to the beauty in the fine detail of this landscape, or flower bed, or building. This might be our introduction to this kind of sensibility as a human possibility. On the other side, we have a man whose whole demeanor expresses bluff, no-nonsense concern for the business at hand; and this might also be our introduction into this stance as a possibility.

We can see here how new gestures can express by enacting new ways of being, and make visible new significances that things can have for us. The necessary condition for this innovation is that we and our teachers in each such case are familiar with a certain "vocabulary" of gestures and meanings, against the background of which these new meanings emerge.

Merleau-Ponty want us to see language innovation as fundamentally continuous with gestural invention of this kind, and of the same order. A new expression reveals a new way of inhabiting the world, and the new significances which this way responds to. A metaphor like Mallarmé's "the sky is dead" [*le ciel est mort*][36] opens for us a new significance of our world and the desolate response which it provokes. Or as Merleau-Ponty puts it: "Speech is a gesture, and its signification is a world" [*la parole est un geste et sa signification un monde*].[37] Or a few pages later: "we must begin by placing thought back among the phenomena of expression" [*il faut commencer par replacer la pensée parmi les phénomènes d'expression*].[38]

These innovations then take their place among the sedimented meanings which will enable us to grasp other innovations. These original creations are examples of "*une parole parlante*", as against "*une parole parlée*".[39]

Seeing the linguistic dimension as constituted by expression came naturally to Herder. It emerged from his understanding of linguistic thought as situated, which we discussed in the previous section. Reflection arises in an animal form that is already dealing with the world around it. Language comes about as a new, "reflective" stance toward things. It arises among our earlier nonlinguistic stances toward objects of desire, or of fear, or to things which figure as obstacles, supports, and the like. Our stances to these things are literally bodily attitudes or actions on or toward objects. The new stance can't be in its origins entirely unconnected with bodily posture or action. But it can't be an action just like the others, whose point is definable outside the linguistic dimension. It has to be seen rather as an "expressive" action, one which both actualizes this stance of reflection, and also presents it to others in public space. It brings about the stance whereby we relate to things in the linguistic dimension.

Speech is the expression of thought. But it isn't simply an outer clothing for what could exist independently. It is constitutive of reflective, that is, linguistic thought, of thought which deals with its objects in the linguistic dimension. Later we can detach our thinking over some of its extent from public expression, and even from natural language. But our power to function in the linguistic dimension is tied for its everyday uses, as well as its origins, to expressive speech, as the range of actions in which it is not only communicated, but realized.

36. From the poem "L'Azure."

37. Maurice Merleau-Ponty, *Phenomenology of Perception*, trans. Donald A. Landes (New York: Routledge, 2012), 190. Maurice Merleau-Ponty, *La Phénoménologie de la Perception* (Paris: Gallimard, 1945), 214.

38. Merleau-Ponty, *Phenomenology*, 196; Merleau-Ponty, *Phénoménologie*, 222.

39. Landes translates these terms as "speaking speech" and "spoken speech". See Merleau-Ponty, *Phenomenology*, 202; Merleau-Ponty, *Phénoménologie*, 229.

This doctrine is obviously contested, first by those who have remained tied to the "intellectualism" of the old disengaged epistemology, but also surprisingly enough by some thinkers who have explicitly built on post-Herderian themes, for instance Jacques Derrida.[40] It has, however, been central to those who have tried to give a picture of human agency as embodied.[41] But can we attribute it to Herder? One can contest this, because Herder himself doesn't seem to take the point in the very passage about the birth of language I quoted above. Instead of stressing the crucial role of overt expression, he speaks of the recognition of the animal through a distinguishing mark as the discovery of a "word of the soul" [*Wort der Seele*]. The new mark is, indeed, a sound, the bleating, but it can become the name of the sheep, "even though [the human's] tongue may never have tried to stammer it."[42]

Nevertheless, I want to see the origin of this idea in Herder, not just because it so obviously flows from his concern to situate thought in a life form, but because he himself stresses elsewhere (including elsewhere in this same work) the importance of speech and vocal expression for the human life form.[43]

This substantive point about language is an answer to the question of whether things can have this meaning for us without (real, spoken, enacted)

40. See, for example, *De La Grammatologie* (Paris: Éditions de Minuit, 1967). Derrida's almost obsessive attempt to deny altogether any special status whatever to speech in the human language capacity raises the question whether he doesn't have more in common with the Cartesian tradition than he would like to admit. "*L'écriture*" and "*la différance*", while embedded in culture (or constitutive of it), are peculiarly disembodied functions. See also *L'Écriture et la Différance* (Paris: Le Seuil, 1967).

41. See Merleau-Ponty, *Phénoménologie*.

42. Herder, *Ursprung*, 24–25.

43. See, for instance, "How singular, that a moveable breath of air should be the sole, or at least the best, medium of our thoughts and perceptions! Without its incomprehensible connexion with all the operations of our [soul] which are so dissimilar to it [this breath] these operations would never have taken place.... A people have no idea for which they do not have a word: the liveliest imagination remains an obscure feeling, til the mind finds a character for it. And by means of a word incorporates it with the memory, the recollection, the understanding, and lastly the understanding of mankind, tradition: a pure understanding, without language, on Earth, is an utopian land." Johann Gottfried Herder, *Outlines of a Philosophy of the History of Man*, trans. T. Churchill (London: Luke Hansard, 1803), 420. [*Wie sonderbar, dass ein bewegter Lufthauch das einzige, wenigstens das beste Mittel unsrer Gedanken und Empfindungen sein sollte! Ohne sein unbregreifliches Band mit allem ihm so ungleichen Handlungen unsrer Seele wären diese Handlungen ungeschehen ... Ein Volk hat keine Idee, zu der es kein Wort hat: die lebhafteste Anschauung bleibt dunkles Gefühl, bis die Seele ein Merkmal findet und es durchs Wort dem Gedächtnis, der Rückerinerung, dem Verstande, ja endlich dem Verstande der Menschen, der Tradition einverleibt; eine reine Vernunft ohne Sprache ist auf Erden ein utopisches Land*]; Herder, *Ideen zur Philosophie der Geschichte der Menschheit* (Berlin: Michael Holzinger, 2013), book 9, chapter 2.

language. And the Herderian answer is "no". Contemporary philosophers are familiar with this thesis, and with arguments for it, most notoriously perhaps from Wittgenstein. These arguments are sometimes construed as deployed from an observer's perspective: how could you tell for any creature you were studying whether it was defining features or attributing properties, as against just treating things functionally in relation to simple ends, unless this being had language?[44] But Wittgenstein actually uses it at a more radical level. The issue is not: how would some observer know? But how would the agent itself know? And what sense would there be in talking of attributing properties if the agent didn't know which? Wittgenstein makes us sensible of this more radical argument in *Philosophical Investigations* I.258 and following: the famous discussion about the sensation whose occurrences the subject wants to record in a diary. Wittgenstein pushes our intuitions to the following revelatory impasse: what would it be like to know what it is you're attending to, and yet be able to say absolutely nothing about it? The answer is, that this supposition shows itself to be incoherent. The plausibility of the scenario comes from our having set it up as our attending to a *sensation*. But take even this description away, leave it absolutely without any characterization at all, and it dissolves into nothing.[45] Of course, something can defy description; it can have a je ne sais quoi quality. But this is only because it is placed somewhere by language. It is an indescribable *feeling*, or *experience*, or *virtue*, or whatever. The sense of being unable to say wouldn't be there without the surrounding sayable. Language is what constitutes the linguistic dimension.

We could sum up the point in this way. Herder's analysis establishes a distinction between (Ro) the case where an agent's (nonsemantic) response to an object is *conditional* on its having certain features, and/or *because* of certain features (the rat rushes the door when this has a triangle on it, because this has been paired with reward), and (Rs) the case where the agent's response consists (at least partly) in *identifying* the object as the locus of certain features. It is Rs that we want to call responding to a thing

44. Mark Okrent offers an argument of this form in *Heidegger's Pragmatism* (Ithaca, NY: Cornell University Press, 1988), chapter 3.
45. "And it would not help either to say that it need not be a *sensation*; that when he writes 'S', he has *something*—and that is all that can be said. 'Has' and 'something' also belong to our common language.—So in the end when one is doing philosophy one gets get to the point where one would like just to emit an inarticulate sound." Wittgenstein, *Philosophical Investigations*, I.261 [*Und es hülfe auch nichts, zu sagen: es müsse keine Empfindung sein: wenn er 'E' schreibe, habe er Etwas—und mehr könnten wir nicht sagen. Aber 'haben' und 'etwas' gehören auch zur allgemeinen Sprache.—So gelangt man beim Philosophieren am Ende dahin, wo man nur noch einen unartikulierten Laut ausstossen möchte*].

as that thing. Once these two are distinguished, it is intuitively clear that Rs is impossible without language. This is what Wittgenstein's example shows up. He chooses an exercise (identifying of each new occurrence whether it is the same as an original paradigm) which is inherently in the Rs range, and we can see straight off that there is no way this issue could even *arise* for a nonlinguistic creature.

This in turn throws light on the other facets of the linguistic dimension. Consider the case of strong value mentioned above. What would it be to have such a sense without language? It can't just consist in certain things being very strongly desired. There has to be the sense of their being worthy of this desire. The motivation has a different quality. But how would the distinction of quality stand out for the creature itself from differences of force of desire? We can't just say: because its reaction would be different. This is, of course, true as far as it goes. A difference of reaction may be at a certain stage the only way a moral distinction is marked. But then the distinction must be carried in the kind of reaction, for example one of shock, or horror, or awe and admiration. But consider what we mean by a reaction of horror. It doesn't just mean a negative one, even strongly negative. There is only horror when the reaction expresses a recognition that the act was heinous or gruesome. But how can a creature distinguish the heinous or gruesome from the merely (in a nonmoral sense) repugnant, unless it can identify the act *as* heinous? How does it have a sense of *transgression,* unless it had language or some way of *expressing* its experience of the heinous?

The impossibility of an external observer's knowing really turns on something more radical, the impossibility of the creature's being in the linguistic dimension without language. This is the crux of Herder's thesis, that language is constitutive of reflection. And at the same time, this shows how a constitutive theory of language breaks out of the bounds of the enframing. We can't explain language by the function it plays within a pre- or extralinguistically conceived framework of human life, because language through constituting the semantic dimension transforms any such framework, giving us new feelings, new desires, new goals, new relationships, and introduces a dimension of strong value. Language can only be explained through a radical discontinuity with the extralinguistic.

Of course, this argument of Wittgenstein may be taken as showing only that an agent must have some grasp of an articulated language, even if it only an intramental grasp, if he/she is to make sense of these distinctions; whereas Herder's expressivism asserts the necessity of a behaviorally enacted language in words and deeds. The necessity of this latter has to be shown in order to clinch Wittgenstein's argument against the possibility of a private language. The basic thesis is a genetic one, that we could never have the silent, monological, inner language if we hadn't first acquired the language capacity in its expressed-enacted form. I will return to this below.

5

Let's pause for a minute and take stock of how far we have traveled. I started off with the contrast between an enframing and a constitutive theory of language; and I identified the constitutive view in terms of Herder's notion of "reflection", the background understanding inseparable from language that the terms we use are (intrinsically) "right". Our first examples were drawn from the field of ordinary description, the characterization of independent objects, but we very soon saw that this understanding of intrinsic rightness operates way beyond this sphere. There is also the domain where we find terms for "objects" which are not independent of their designation: for instance our feelings and emotions, which are sometimes transformed when we find a more penetrating or insightful language to describe them.

Then there are the uses of language wherein we establish (or rupture) intimacy, communication, concord with others, as in my example above where I say "I'm sorry" to heal the breach between us. This is, on the surface, a descriptive statement, and if it didn't correspond sincerely to how I feel, it would probably fail its purpose; but this purpose is not to describe accurately, but to bring about something, reconciliation. There is a quasi-ritual element here; and to do what it's meant to do, it's not sufficient to feel contrite; I have to *say* it, to *express* contrition. I want to change the (at present bad) footing we're on with each other, and restore harmony. We're in the domain that is often identified as "pragmatic", as against "semantic".

This domain is frequently transformed, made more conscious and refined, by description at a new level. We not only rupture and then restore intimacy by the things we say, but we reflect on and give names to these footings and their makings and breakings. We speak of a relation of "harmony", or "intimacy", or "concord", and we give a name to the act of restoring concord by saying, for example, "I'm sorry"; we speak of "apologizing". We step to the "meta" level and describe what we're doing. We can call the vocabulary we deploy here, following Silverstein, "metapragmatic".[46] Then, of course, we can sometimes restore harmony by saying "I apologize", which again looks like a self-description, but which everyone recognizes as a "performative".

We see something similar with the whole range of footings that come about in human culture, those of intimacy and distance, or those of hierarchy and equality, those of kinship and outsider; and the whole range of more officially codified footings which constitute our polity, economy, and civil society. And we see that these are constituted partly through ritual expressions, and then in their more refined regions through (metapragmatic) descriptions; like 'president', 'prime minister', 'CEO', 'director of department', and so on.

And in the example above of our moral discriminations, we can see that these are constituted in part through expressive reactions (horror at this dastardly act, beaming admiration for that heroic deed), and on the metalevel by descriptive terms like 'moral', 'aesthetic', 'etiquette', which are paradigms of domains which are not independent of the way they are characterized in language.

We have tumbled outside the range that enframing theories were designed to deal with, which was very much that of the descriptive coding and communication of information, particularly useful in a scientific context, and that of exchanging orders and recommendations for action, and engaging in common deliberation. And it is indeed, very obvious that language enables a more refined coordination of action, as well as rational deliberation, and the acquisition of knowledge which can help us decide what to do. Encoding states of affairs, either which exist, or which we might want to bring about, is obviously central to these purposes. But once we lose sight of the language-constituted background which enables these activities, once we just take it as given, it is easy to slide into seeing our emotions, footings, normative understandings as well as simply given, as it were, in the nature of things.

Reciprocally, once we come to see how language can help constitute our emotions, footings, norms, we are cured from a narrow view of the func-

46. See, for instance, Michael Silverstein "Metapragmatic Discourse and Metapragmatic Function," in *Reflexive Language: Reported Speech and Metapragmatics,* ed. J. Lucy (Cambridge: Cambridge University Press, 2001), 33–58.

tions of language as encoding information. A difference about the nature of linguistic meaning rapidly escalates into wider questions about the shape, scope, and uses of language. This wider set of issues was decisively put on the agenda by Wittgenstein, notably in his *Philosophical Investigations*. His protest against the construal of all subject-predicate sentences on the model of descriptive attribution took the form of a demand to recognize a plurality of "language games", which operate on different logical "grammars". He sought to undo the overshadowing of all other uses on behalf of the information-sharing, instructional, deliberative uses which are central to post-Fregean philosophy, the (much more sophisticated) twentieth-century successor of the HLC. This hegemony still seems to hold in the most refined versions of this philosophy, for example with Robert Brandom. I will discuss this below.[47]

6

Herder has provided my paradigm of a constitutive theory of language. Let's now look a bit further at the ramifications and developments of this kind of theory since Herder.

Herder's constitutive theory gave a creative role to expression. Views of the HLC type related linguistic expression to some preexisting content. For Locke, a word is introduced by being linked with an idea, and henceforth becomes capable of expressing it.[48] The content precedes its external means of expression. Condillac develops a more sophisticated conception. He argues that introducing words ("instituted signs") allows us to discriminate more finely the nuances of our ideas because it gives us greater control over the train of thoughts. This means that we identify finer distinctions, which we in turn can name, which will again allow us to make still more subtle discriminations, and so on. In this way, language makes possible science and enlightenment. But at each stage of this process, the idea precedes its naming, albeit its discriminability results from a previous act of naming.

Condillac also gave emotional expression an important role in the genesis of language. His view was that the first instituted signs were framed from natural ones. But natural signs were just the inbuilt expressions of

47. See Chapter 4.
48. See Locke, *Essay,* 3.2.2.

our emotional states, animal cries of joy or fear. That language originated from the expressive cry became the consensus in the learned world of the eighteenth century. But the conception of expression here was quite inert. What the expression conveyed was thought to exist independently of its utterance. Cries made fear or joy evident to others, but they didn't help constitute these feelings themselves.

Herder develops a quite different notion of expression. This is in the logic of a constitutive theory, as I have just described it. This tells us that language constitutes the semantic, and more broadly, the linguistic dimension, that is, that possessing language enables us to relate to things in new ways, for example as loci of features, and to have new emotions, goals, relationships, as well as being responsive to issues of strong value. We might say: language transforms our world, using this last word in a clearly Heidegger-derived sense. That is, we are talking not of the cosmos out there, which preceded us and is indifferent to us, but of the world of our involvements, including all the things they incorporate in their meaning for us. 'Meaning' is being used in the phenomenologically derived sense introduced above. Something has meaning for us in this sense when it has a certain significance or relevance in our lives. *So much is standard English.* The neologism will consist in using this as a count noun, so that we can speak of the different ways that things are significant as different "meanings", or speak of a new form of significance as "a new meaning".[49]

Then we can rephrase the constitutive view by saying that language introduces new meanings in our world: the things which surround us become potential bearers of properties; they can have new emotional significance for us, for example as objects of admiration or indignation; our links with others can count for us in new ways, as lovers, spouses, or fellow citizens; and they can have strong value.

But then this involves attributing a creative role to expression. Bringing things to speech can't mean just making externally available what is already there. There are many banal speech acts where this seems to be all that is involved. But language as a whole must involve more than this,

---

49. Okrent, "Pragmatism," uses the happy expression "meaning-subscript-h" to carry this sense, contrasting it with "meaning-subscript-i" to carry the familiar sense where we want to talk about the meaning of a word. This is an excellent way to avoid confusion. But I don't know how to manipulate subscripts on this computer, and so I'm going to take a chance, a well-warranted risk considering the phenomenologically sophisticated audience I'm writing for here. I hope the context will always make clear which sense I mean.

because it is also opening possibilities for us which wouldn't be there in its absence.

The constitutive theory turns our attention toward the creative dimension of expression, in which, to speak paradoxically, it makes possible its own content. We can actually see this in familiar, everyday realities, but it tends to be screened out from the enframing perspective, and it took the development of constitutive theories to bring it to light.

A good example is the "body language" of personal style. We see the leather-jacketed motorbike rider step away from his machine and swagger toward us with an exaggeratedly leisurely pace. This person is "saying something" in his way of moving, acting, speaking. He may have no words for it, though we might want to apply the Hispanic word 'macho' as at least a partial description. Here is an elaborate way of being in the world, of feeling and desiring and reacting, which involves great sensitivity to certain things (like slights to one's honor: we are now the object of his attention, because we unwittingly cut him off at the last intersection), and cultivated-but-supposedly-spontaneous insensitivity to others (like the feelings of dudes and females), which involves certain prized pleasures (riding around at high speed with the gang) and others which are despised (listening to sentimental songs); and this way of being is coded as strongly valuable; that is, being this way is admired, and failing to be earns contempt.

But how coded? Not, presumably in descriptive terms, or at least not adequately. The person may not have a term like 'macho' which articulates the value involved. What terms he does have may be woefully inadequate to capture what is specific to this way of being; the epithets of praise or opprobrium may only be revelatory in the whole context of this style of action; by themselves they may be too general. Knowing that X is "one of the boys" and Y is a "dude" may tell us little. The crucial coding is in the body expressive language.

The biker's world incorporates the strong value of this way of being. Let's call it (somewhat inadequately, but we need a word) 'machismo'. But how does this meaning exist for him? Only through the expressive gesture and stance. It's not just that an outside observer would have no call to attribute machismo to him without this behavior. It is more radically that a strong value like this can only exist for him articulated in some form. It is this expressive style that enables machismo to exist for him, and more widely this domain of expressive body language is the locus of a whole host of different value-coded ways of being for humans in general. The expression makes possible its content; the language opens us out to the domain of meaning it encodes. Expression is no longer simply inert.

But when we turn back from this rather obvious case to the original description case, which was central to HLC theories, we see this too in a new light. Here too expression must be seen as creative; language opens us to the domain it encodes. What descriptive speech encodes is our attribution of properties to things. But possessing this descriptive language is the condition of our being sensitive to the issues of intrinsic rightness which must be guiding us if we are really to be attributing properties, as we saw above. So seeing expression as creative generates Herder's constitutive theory as applied to descriptive language.

This illustrates the inner connections, both historical and logical, between the constitutive theory and a strong view of expression. Either the espousal of the first can lead one to look for places where expression obviously opens us to its own content, which we will find in this domain of body language, and with emotional expression generally. Or else, the sense that expression is creative, which will likely strike us if we are attending closely to the life of the emotions, will lead us to revise our understanding of the much-discussed case of description. In the case of Herder, the connections probably go in both directions, but if anything the second is more important than the first. The major proponents of the HLC were all rationalists in some sense; one of their central goals was to establish reason on a sound basis, and their scrutiny of language had largely this end in view. The proto-Romantic move to dethrone reason, and to locate the specifically human capacities in feeling, naturally led to a richer concept of expression than was allowed for in Condillac's natural cries, which were quite inert modes of utterance. From the standpoint of this richer notion, even the landscape of descriptive speech begins to look very different. But whatever the direction of travel, a road links the constitutive insight with the strong view of expression, so that the alternative to the enframing theory might with equal justice be called the constitutive-expressive.[50]

---

50. Charles Guignon has used the term 'expressive' for this view on language, in specific application to Heidegger. See his "Heidegger: Language as the House of Being" in *The Philosophy of Discourse: The Rhetorical Turn in Twentieth-Century Thought, Vol. II*, ed. Chip Sills and George H.

Being constitutive means that language makes possible its own content, in a sense, or opens us to the domain it encodes. The two cases we have just looked at: bodily expression and ordinary description, seem to involve somewhat different forms of this.[51] In the latter case, language gives us access in a new way to a range of preexisting things. We identify them *as* what they are; they show up for us as loci of features. In the machismo case, we feel more tempted to say that something new comes into existence through expression, viz., this way of being which our biker values. Prior to the coinage of this range of expression, this life ideal didn't exist.

The parallel between the two cases is that in both language makes possible new meanings. In the descriptive case, the new meaning is just things showing up *as* something. This also involves a new way of being in the world for us. Reciprocally, the bodily gesture case involves more than a new way of being; machismo also makes preexisting things show up in new ways, for example we show up as dudes. So each involves, as it were, two dimensions: (1) a new manner of disclosure of what in a sense already exists (that is, identity propositions hold between items under previously available descriptions and items described in newly accessible ways), and (2) a new manner of being, or a new human possibility. We might call these two dimensions respectively, the accessive (1) and the existential (2).

The difference between the two kinds of case lies in the balance of significance. Some new uses of language (e.g., a more rigorous scientific discourse) seem mainly significant because of their accessive dimension; others, like our bodily expression case above, seem important because of their existential innovations.

But it is not true, of course, that descriptive language invariably fits in the first category, while expressive gesture makes up the second. Many uses of descriptive language have primordially existential import.

This is already true of words identifying things of strong value, for example the terms 'macho' and 'dude' in the above example. Insofar as the

---

Jensen (Portsmouth, NH: Boynton/Cook, 1992), 171–77. It follows from the above that this is just as legitimate a term as 'constitutive', or the double-barreled combination.

51. It will undoubtedly seem strange to many readers that I am treating bodily expression, as well as description, as part of "language". And in fact, expressive constitutive theories are led to see the two as linked, and to see the phenomenon to be explained, the human linguistic capacity, as involving a range of "symbolic forms", and not just what we think of normally as "speech".

biker isn't totally inarticulate (and how could he be, being human?), terms like this will also, along with body language, help existentially constitute his way of being. But this is also true of the language of social positions and relations. Distinctions like friends/lovers, or king/president/leader, define a space of possibilities within a given culture. This space is not the same from culture to culture, which is why translation is often hazardous (Greek *'philia'* is only approximately rendered by English 'friendship'). These terms have helped constitute the existential possibilities for a given society.

Then there are the languages of the self. I have tried to show how the language of inwardness, for instance, and the peculiar form of moral topography it lays out, is connected in the modern West with certain moral ideals and certain notions of identity.[52] But such locations as "inner depths" wouldn't be immediately comprehensible to people in some other cultures. Language is helping to shape us here.

This can be made sense of in the light of the earlier account of descriptive language. It allows us to locate features, as I put it. New descriptive languages lay out new topographies, a new disposition of places. But humans as self-interpreting animals are partly constituted by their own self-descriptions. And so a new topography of the self cannot but have existential import.

So language is existentially constitutive in more than its expressive modes. These are essential, as we shall see more clearly below, but when we look at the way in which new human meanings come to exist for us, we see an interweaving of the expressive and the descriptive. Certain meanings enter our world in the course of early training simply through our being taught to express them in our bodily behavior. We can imagine that our biker learnt this macho style through watching, imitating, alternatively being laughed at and praised, and then eventually being accepted into the gang by his older brother and companions. Of course, he learnt it partly through verbal exchanges, for instance when he was put down for behaving "like a girl", or a sissy. But all these words would have remained opaque, if he hadn't picked up the personal style which made sense of them.

This kind of learning obviously plays an important role in human life, the more crucial the earlier we go back in our development as children.

52. See Taylor, *Sources.*

Bourdieu speaks of our learning meanings, for instance values and norms, through embodied enactment as the acquisition of a "habitus". The habitus is a "system of durable and transposable dispositions";[53] that means, dispositions to bodily comportment, say, to act, or to hold oneself, or to gesture in a certain way. A bodily disposition is a habitus when it encodes a certain cultural understanding. The habitus in this sense always has an expressive dimension. It gives expression to certain meanings that things and people have for us, and it is precisely by giving such expression that it makes these meanings exist for us.

Children are inducted into a culture, are taught the meanings which constitute it, partly through inculcating the appropriate habitus. We learn how to hold ourselves, how to defer to others, how to be a presence for others, all largely through taking on different styles of bodily comportment. Through these modes of deference and presentation, the subtlest nuances of social position, of the sources of prestige, and hence of what is valuable and good, are encoded.

> Adapting a phrase of Proust's, one might say that arms and legs are full of numb imperatives. One could endlessly enumerate the values given body, made body, by the hidden persuasion of an implicit pedagogy which can instil a whole cosmology, through injunctions as insignificant as 'sit up straight' or 'don't hold your knife in your left hand', and inscribe the most fundamental principles of the arbitrary content of a culture in seemingly innocuous details of bearing or physical and verbal manners, so putting them beyond the reach of consciousness and explicit statement.

> [On pourrait, déformant le mot de Proust, dire que les jambes, les bras sont pleins d'impératifs engourdis. Et l'on n'en finirait pas d'énumérer les valeurs faites corps, par la transsubstantiation qu'opère la persuasion clandestine d'une pédagogie implicite, capable d'inculquer toute une cosmologie, une éthique, une métaphysique, une politique, à travers des injonctions aussi insignifiantes que 'tiens-toi droit' ou 'ne tiens pas ton couteau de la main gauche' et d'inscrire dans les détails en apparence les plus insignifiants de la « tenue », du « maintien » ou des « manières » corporelles et verbales les principes fondamentaux de

53. See Pierre Bourdieu, *Le Sens Pratique* (Paris: Editions de Minuit, 1980), 88.

l'arbitraire culturel, ainsi placés hors des prises de la conscience et de l'explicitation.][54]

This is one way in which norms and rules can exist in our lives, as "values made flesh". Of course, it is not the only way. Some rules *are* formulated expressly, say "honor your elders". And of course, there are always *some* injunctions given, such as "*tiens-toi droit*"[55] or "don't speak like that again to Grandma, or I'll whack you!" But even with express norms, where the point is formulated (in this case, honoring elders), these are in close interrelation to our habitus. The two normally dovetail, and complement each other. Bourdieu speaks of habitus and institutions as "two modes of objectification of past history" [*deux modes d'objectivation de l'histoire passé*].[56] The latter are generally the locus of express rules or norms. But rules aren't self-interpreting; without a sense of what they're about, and an affinity to their spirit, they remain dead letters, or become a travesty in practice. This sense and this affinity can only exist where they do in our unformulated, embodied understanding. They are in the domain of the habitus, which is "a practical sense which reactivates the sense objectified in institutions" [*comme sens pratique opère la "reactivation" du sens objectivé dans les institutions*].[57]

When the young learn to show respect for their elders, they really grasp this point, even if they can't articulate it in words; they learn you might say to embody this point, not just a set of movements, but also the spirit they express. That is why we can outrageously show disrespect by just "going through the motions", or by ironically exaggerating our bow. And that is why teenagers who have attained to a certain articulacy can enrage their parents, saying with faux innocence, "speak like what to Grandma?" This is more effective a goad if the parents are less articulate, and have trouble explaining the point.

We might say that they learn to embody the point; or to enact it bodily. But this doesn't mean that articulating this point makes no difference. On the contrary, to bring the value, or good or norm, to speech makes it exist for us in a new way. It comes into focus for us. It acquires

54. Pierre Bourdieu, *The Logic of Practice,* trans. Richard Nice (Cambridge: Polity Press, 1990), 69; Bourdieu, *Pratique,* 117.

55. "sit up straight."

56. Bourdieu, *Practice,* 57; Bourdieu, *Pratique,* 95–96.

57. Bourdieu, *Practice,* 57; Bourdieu, *Pratique,* 96.

clarity for us, and sometimes as a result has greater force. This in turn can bring about two kinds of reactions. On one hand an articulated good can work on us more powerfully, and motivate us more than before; on the other, getting clear on what is involved here may make it possible for us to break away from it, and repudiate a value which we had learnt to embody.

We might thus learn a new norm in two stages, at first through being trained to embody it expressively (bowing to elders), and later through hearing explicit rules. This corresponds to the two stages of pragmatics discussed in the previous section: first we establish ways, one might say rituals, of, for example, restoring intimacy. And then we can bring these to focal attention by introducing metapragmatic terms, like 'apologize'.

So while some new coinages in language have mainly accessive importance—they open a new range of phenomena to us, for instance terms to classify animals or trees—others, which articulate meanings, have existential import. And we acquire the range of meanings which make up our world through an interplay of embodied expression, and of articulation. (As to take up the example of the previous section, when I articulate my feeling as one of envy.)

Instead of speaking of "embodied expression", we might say "enactment".[58] We learn first to enact certain meanings, and then we may learn to describe them. Both are necessary, but it seems clear that there is a certain ontogenetic primacy of the former. Our first introduction to crucial human meanings, as infants, has to be enactive. We learn a certain embodied language of love, or of strife and complaint, of pleading and pouting, and the rest. Enactment has to come first; on this basis, we can learn to use certain words and phrases like 'love', 'being good' or 'being naughty', later on 'being fair', 'being kind', and so on. And this first vocabulary forms the basis for further, deeper articulations. Enacted meaning provides the context within which articulated meanings can arise and be understood.

We might return here to the discussion of section 3, where I made a clear distinction between making it up to you by saying "I'm sorry", and strate-

---

58. The reference here to the theories of Evan Thompson and others is deliberate. I see a connection between their understanding of meanings as finding their evolutionary origin in enactment and my assertion of the primacy of enactment in the case of our human meanings. See Thompson, *Mind in Life: Biology, Phenomenology, and the Science of Mind* (Cambridge, MA: Harvard University Press, 2010).

gically getting you to return to me by causing an explosion which frightens you. The rightness of "I'm sorry" consists in its expressing-by-portraying my contrite condition; and this is what wins you back and dissolves your anger.

But how about if I say nothing, just come back to you with a soulful look, holding out a bouquet of flowers? Well, maybe we can forget the flowers, which have become symbols of love and love-offering; I just have a soulful and pleading look. Aren't we getting close here to certain animal species? For instance, a baboon may mollify another angry one by initiating a grooming ritual. This is the "right thing" for the timid baboon to do, but does this rightness consist in anything else than its producing this result? Can we make a distinction here between what is in the linguistic dimension and what isn't?

We might be tempted to answer no. But then what about my soulful look? The problem seems here that my look just enacts contrition and desire to be readmitted to your good graces; there is no element of portrayal, as there is with "I'm sorry".

But the fact is, with humans, enacting a meaning lies fully within the linguistic dimension. In the following sense, that enacting/expressing can help constitute a meaning which wasn't in our world before. We have just seen several examples of this.

This shows how my trying to heal the breach between us by my soulful look stands apart from baboon grooming. What separates it is the way in which our lives have been shaped by expressed meanings (here my contrition and yearning for return) which have also been defined and constituted in and by their expression. So this look is right, not just task-strategically (winning you back); in fact, it is only right task-strategically through being right expressively, that is, it belongs to the range of expression which helps constitute this meaningful human stance of contrition and yearning. Moreover, and not surprisingly, like other modes of constitutive human language, this kind of look and the meanings it expresses will vary subtly or widely from society to society and culture and culture—even in our rapidly changing age, from decade to decade, as lovers of interwar movies can attest.

7

I distinguished in the last section two ways in which language can open us to new possibilities, the accessive and the existential. In the first case, we sense that language is enabling us to have "reflective" awareness of what previously was there (by, for instance, distinguishing more clearly the species of animals in our environment). In the second, we see that language (in some broad sense) is opening us to new human meanings, new existential possibilities.

Now linguistic constitution in this existential sense seems to proceed along two tracks, which sometimes are interwoven but which can be notionally distinguished. In one we are given a new way of describing, or a new model for understanding, our human condition and the alternatives it opens for us; and through this we come to see and perhaps embrace a new human possibility. We may come to this existential insight through meeting, or hearing about, some paradigmatic figure (the Buddha, St. Francis), or by reading a book about ethics or the meaning of life, or (more often) through reading a novel or seeing a film. (In this last case, the experience can consist in a sort of encounter with a—fictional—paradigmatic figure [Levin, Zossima]). In all these cases, the impact can be described as a regestalting of our world and its possibilities, which opens a new (to us) way of being. So we can speak here of a regestalting constitution.

We can sometimes win through to this regestalting on our own, where under the pressure of some quandary, or difficult decision, we come to see our possibilities in a new light (and this may then retrospectively connect up with something we read or encountered earlier, which is now itself reassessed in the light of our new insight). In whatever way, regestalting offers us new terms or models to understand our lives.

The other track through which new existential possibilities emerge is what I called above "enactment", and a good example is the case of the biker (or the first to initiate this kind of machismo). New existential possibilities which emerge through enactment are often not simply individual styles, but ways of being together (which the machismo of the bikers also is). There is in any culture a range of footings we can be on with each other: intimate or formal, deferential or egalitarian, narrowly functional (clerk and customer meeting in the store) or open-ended (striking up a conversation in a pub); and there are in addition a range of institutional relations (bureaucrats meeting citizens, MPs in relation to constituents, etc.). These are usually constituted through enactment, and moreover, they are often in continual reshaping and reformulation as they are enacted in daily life. (This is perhaps particularly true of contemporary society.)

We can see from this how there are a variety of contexts in which there can be a "right word" (or expression, or gesture). There can be a correct use of a word as a description of an independent reality through a vocabulary which gives us access to the domain ("that's a triangle"). And there can be the great skill of a novelist in evoking a fictional reality which gives us insight into new possibilities. And then there can be the right word (gesture, tone of voice) which inaugurates an enacted relation; or damages it, or restores it when damaged (as when I say "I'm sorry" in my earlier example); and there are a host of other cases, or uses of language, or language games to adopt Wittgenstein's usage.

Attributing features is only one of the things we do in language, and not the most "primordial". Our speech or expressive behavior can also disclose the true order of things, cosmic or social; or the order of our feelings and desires; it can be appropriate or inappropriate to one or other of these orders; or it can disturb or help reestablish some such order; it can create harmony or disharmony between us; and so on through a large range. The linguistic dimension opens us to a family of modes of intrinsic rightness, which can't simply be modeled on descriptive rightness as their paradigm. Rather, as we shall see, the language games of descriptive adequacy can only arise against a rich background of other modes of rightness. These relate, as we shall see below, to the range of activities which form the essential matrix within which language (including that of disinterested description) can alone arise, the "forms of life" which sustain it.

I have been distinguishing two dimensions of disclosure, two ways that new words, expressions, or ways of acting can extend our grasp of things in the world, or human life. I called these the accessive and the existential. But there is another way that a distinction can be drawn. We could speak of different facets of the constitutive power of language. One might be described as general: our possession of language allows us to have a "reflective" awareness of the world and ourselves, which becomes greater the more articulate we manage to be. This general function relates closely to what I've been calling the accessive.

But alongside this, there are particular ways in which certain expressions or enactments open us to certain meanings and ways of being, and thus widen the range of what is possible for us—as our imagined innovative biker disclosed machismo as a possible way of life. And here we are fully in the domain of the existential.

I want to treat, in Part II of this study, two such particular modes of constitution, which make possible respectively, what I want to call human meanings and footings. I will explore these in detail in Chapters 6 and 7.

8

We started off distinguishing "enframing" from "constitutive" theories of language, and we took this up by examining the battle between the classical early modern theory from Hobbes, Locke, and Condillac (the HLC view) and the critique which thinkers of the German Romantic generation, principally Hamann, Herder, and Humboldt (which I will call the HHH view) leveled against this theory. Seen in the light of this critique, one could describe the alternatives as a "designative-instrumental" approach versus one which was "expressive constitutive".

But the discussion began to open other issues between the two views. One concerned the scope of language. The HLC tended to concentrate on spoken or written words as offering the means of describing the world, but the HHH, stressing the constitutive power of expression, also brings in forms of enactive meaning, like gesture, stance, body language, claiming that the interaction of these with descriptive meanings makes it impossible to understand these latter on their own.

We saw above how enacted meanings, as in the case of the biker, can be the basis of the later introduction of descriptive terms, like 'macho' (assuming, perhaps a little condescendingly, that the biker hadn't yet coined a term for his style of being); and also how the imparting of a culture and way of life reposes both on the inculcation of habitus and the internalization of rules.

But perhaps more tellingly, full linguistic activity involves *enacted* meanings as well as meaningful speech. The primary locus of language is conversation, and the original locus of this is in face-to-face encounters. But setting up these requires not just word utterance but also body language, eye contact or its absence, tone of voice. It depends on these what kind of contact is set up in the conversation, what the footing is on which the partners stand.

Then, secondarily, the contact can be truncated: in one way, just to voice contact when we speak on the phone. Or in another way, we can also "converse" in epistolary exchange, which sheds enactment in mutual presence, but keeps some shadow invocation of it—it is least clearly *addressed* ("Dear Henry"). Then we can move to written text, often not expressly addressed, although sometimes prefaced, and with occasional outbursts of, "dear reader"; all the way to terse annunciation: "Trespassers will be prosecuted."

But why think of this as full action being truncated *down*, rather than minimal information-coding-and-imparting being *added to*, so that one *rises*, through address and mutual presence, to full speech action?

Because we cannot but enter speech through full action, and then only later learn to function with truncated forms. We couldn't learn to write a treatise before we learnt to converse. Any doubts one might entertain on this score will be dispelled in Chapter 2.

In fact, one facet of the constitutive power of language lies precisely in discourse, in the way we set up or challenge and modify footings through exchange, independently of, though later transformed by, the names we give them. The way in which finding a descriptive term can change a footing reflects the other major facet of linguistic constitution, the way in which articulate expression changes human meanings. I will explore the power of discourse below in Chapter 7.

And so our two theories are driven even further apart: they disagree on what needs to be explained under the heading of language. And this disagreement will get even wider as the discussion proceeds, and we begin to look at the place of art, literature, music, dancing, in relation to linguistic competence; can a line be drawn between these and language in a narrower and more conventional sense? Or is our explicandum rather indissociably the full range of what Cassirer called the "symbolic forms"?

A second new issue is that of holism. We already saw this in connection with the Herder-Humboldt view of language as a web, the inconceivability of linguistic terms being invented just one by one. On this issue the original HLC notion of the primacy of the individual word has been irremediably relegated by the work of Frege (showing the primacy of the sentence), and that of Saussure (on the primacy of difference over positive terms). But perhaps all the implications of this relegation have yet to be appreciated by contemporary heirs of the HLC.

And in addition, there is another kind of atomism in our tradition, which needs to be overcome by a corresponding holism; not just the atomism of the word, but that of the individual subject of language. The HLC theory was thoroughly monological. What needs to be recognized is the primacy of communication, of the dialogical. The thinkers of the HHH all saw that the primary locus of language was conversation. Language doesn't just develop inside individuals, to be then communication to others. It evolves always in the interspace of joint attention, or communion. It is this holism that I want to expound in Chapter 2.

2

How Language Grows

So Herder inaugurates, or at least strikes a blow for constitutive theories in his critique of Condillac. But the irony is (and critics of this view of Herder as innovator, such as Hans Aarsleff,[1] have not failed to point this out) that Herder, while ridiculing Condillac's explanation of the origin of language, hardly does any better himself at this task. His "just so" story has a human suddenly coining a term for sheep on becoming aware of a criterial property of animals of this species, their bleating. So the first inventor of language suddenly expresses this insight (to himself) with the phrase (addressed inwardly to the sheep): "you are the bleating one" [*du bist das Blöckende*]; he says this to himself because Herder speaks of this "first word" as a "word of the soul" [*Wort der Seele*].

The purely inward and monological nature of this operation goes against insights that Herder has (about the gestural and dialogical nature of language) in other places in his work. But apart from this, Herder's great step, which was to point to the new dimension of reflection [*Besonnenheit*] doesn't itself answer Condillac's question. The ridicule comes at Condillac's assumption (typical of enframing theories), that the first step into language

---

1. See Hans Aarsleff, *From Locke to Saussure: Essays on the Study of Language and Intellectual History* (Minneapolis: University of Minnesota Press, 1982). Aarsleff's dismissal of Herder as an innovator is a good illustration of how easily the two sides in the debate can talk past each other. If we take no account of Herder's shift in perspective, then he can indeed seem to be recapitulating a number of themes from Condillac, while confusedly protesting his disagreement with him.

was small and thus unproblematic. They just had to come to use a reactive (natural) sign as a word for what provoked it (an instituted sign), says Condillac—as though this wasn't a huge leap. Understanding a sign as a word for something supposes that one is in the linguistic dimension, and the issue is, how did this change come about? That's the challenge for an account of the origin of language, and Condillac is just ducking it; hence the ridicule. Herder doesn't do better on the positive task, but at least he has clarified the explanandum, viz., the arising of a linguistic dimension in the world of some hominids.

Well how do you explain this rise? This is not easy, and will perhaps never be satisfactorily accomplished, if only because we'll never be able to recover the exact sequence of events way back in prepaleolithic times. But we can make some more or less well-motivated surmises, and can thus give some idea of the paths by which speech entered our repertory.

In this we are helped by what can be studied by us, namely, the growth of the language capacity in ontogenesis. Let's turn to this.

2

So let's look at the ontogenesis of language, in order to get a new angle on what human language consists of. The first obvious fact is that children can only become speakers by being taught language. That is, they have to pick up language from a community or family which is taking care of them, its members talking to each other, and talking to them. Without this, the human capacity for language remains without effect. The children can't speak, as we see occasionally with "feral" children, who have been brought up by animals; and moreover they lack all the capacities which go along with language. The famous memoirs of Helen Keller testify to the extraordinary leap in understanding and other possibilities that went along in her case, with the first introduction to language.[2] Or the language capacity can fail to develop, or develop in truncated ways, if in some way the child's ability to communicate with others is impaired, in conditions frequently described with the word 'autism'.

But beyond this general condition on acquiring language, it appears as well that children most effectively acquire new words in actual conversa-

2. See the discussion of the Helen Keller in Merlin Donald, *A Mind So Rare: The Evolution of Human Consciousness* (Cambridge, MA: Harvard University Press, 2001), 232–50.

tion with parents or other caregivers. Here the word 'conversation' may be too weak. The exchanges in question are bouts of shared attention, often of a quasi-ritualistic kind, in which child and parent are concentrated on the same game or activity; and the new word introduced is the word for the salient common focus of this activity, for instance 'dolly', if we're playing with a doll, or 'swing', if we're together on the swing. These repeated moments of common focus are what Bruner calls "formats", in which parent and child engage together, either in a task, such as getting dressed or bathing, or just in play. They bring about the commonly focused attention without which learning wouldn't take place.[3]

A crucial part of children's introduction to speech comes through this kind of conversational exchange. But this type of common focus is in fact built up well before the child is ready to speak. In the first year more or less, before language acquisition starts, child and parent have already been bonding, largely through rituals of this sort, what some writers have called "protoconversations"; where parent and child smile at each other, gurgle together, the parent playfully pretending to bite hands or feet, soothing the child's pain, rocking and singing her to sleep, and so on.

Indeed, this kind of bonding is essential to the child's development, even her physical growth. Utterly deprived of this kind of emotional connection to a caregiver, as in certain orphanages, children wither. A fortiori, this contact is essential to her emotional development. Indeed, contact rapidly comes to be intensely desired by the child, and hence becomes the focus of her early emotional life.

But the exchanges also give this life its shape. In responding to the child's needs, for food, for relief from pain, for loving contact, the parent is helping her identify her wants, and how they can be fulfilled. What would otherwise turn into emotional storms of frustration are given a definite purpose and a recognizable remedy.[4] The parent gives to the child a kind of protointerpretation of her desires, a grasp of what is distressing her, and how relief can come. Indeed, we might say that this mastering of explosive emotions through giving them a shape is achieved first by the parent-child

---

3. Jerome Bruner, *Child's Talk: Learning to Use Language* (New York: Norton, 1983).

4. Stanley Greenspan and Stuart Shanker, in their interesting book *The First Idea: How Symbols, Language, and Intelligence Evolved from Our Primate Ancestors to Modern Humans* (Cambridge, MA: Da Capo Press, 2004), speak of "catastrophic feeling states", often involving a sense of being overwhelmed, which "are part of a primitive perceptual motor level of central nervous system organization" (28). Their point is that we have to learn to give shape to these, and hence to tame them. See also 202–3.

dyad, and only subsequently comes to be part of the child's repertory alone.

This shaping applies not just to organic needs. The child also craves closeness, sharing; and in her interchange with the parent, she can more and more come to see that this is what she wants, and in what rituals of sharing it can be assuaged or fulfilled. She learns a gestural language of love, of desiring-without-having, and then recovering; and this conditions her further development. In the absence of this protointerpretation, the child is liable to explosive desires and emotions which are deeply disturbing, and yet shapeless, that is, without clear outlet, or hope of fulfillment; and which generally end up after blowing themselves out in apathy and despondency.[5] Of course, this foreshadows an experience which we can have much later in life, for instance in unstructured and confused longing; but our ability or inability to cope with this is probably shaped and influenced by these experiences of infancy.

This early sharing and emotional bonding is essential for human development, not only for language.[6] But we can already see a direct link with language. Greenspan and Shanker claim that achieving some kind of sense of the shape of one's emotions is an important condition for being able to grasp concepts later on. This is partly for the obvious reason that everything the child learns is closely interwoven to his emotional life, in particular to her need for contact and sharing.[7] The actual learning of words arises in the charged context of the "formats" I described earlier. Emotional confusion can lead to a weak grasp on certain (what we think of as) purely descriptive concepts later on.[8]

In fact, the clean separation of empirical experience from its emotional meaning for us is something we only achieve in growing up. And even then, it is never complete. Indeed, in certain domains, it would be disastrous to try. Knowing when you have gone too far in your critical remarks, when

5. Bruner, *Child's Talk*.

6. The evolution of humanity seems to have involved, already with earlier hominid species like Homo erectus, the development of strong, continuing affective bonding between all members of the tribe, and not just between mother and infant during the first months or years. See Sarah Hrdy, *Mother and Others: The Evolutionary Origin of Mutual Understanding* (Cambridge, MA: Harvard University Press, 2009); and Lenny Moss, "From a New Naturalism to a Reconstruction of the Normative Grounds of Critical Theory" (forthcoming).

7. Greenspan and Shanker, *First Idea*, 50. They speak of the child's "double-coding" of experience, that is, both "according to its physical and emotional properties."

8. Ibid., chapter 11. They point to research showing that some autistic children have only a fragile, overrigid grasp on descriptive concepts; they have trouble generalizing freely.

you are close to someone, where you are going to hurt their feelings, all require a kind of sensitivity which draws on our feelings in the situation. One can argue that ethical knowledge is of this nature.[9] We may need to separate our perceptions of others from some of our emotions in order to act ethically, for instance from our envy, jealousy, or our intense need for attention; but acting rightly requires that we see them in another emotion-constituted frame, for instance as needy beings striving to maintain integrity, or as beings with inherent dignity.[10]

But the fundamental point that emerges from the ontogenesis of language is that it can only be imparted from within relations of shared emotional bonding, what we might call "communion". Language cannot be generated from within; it can only come to the child from her milieu—although once it is mastered, innovation becomes possible. The young child grasps a word that is proffered to her from the parent. She has to catch on to and follow the communicative intent of the adult.

Michael Tomasello, for instance, makes this ability to grasp the communicative intentions of others the crucial new capacity which allows human children, and not animals, even advanced primates, to become language users. Chimps, he argues, and other higher mammals, can identify their conspecific's ordinary intentions; can see that this one is seeking food, the other is preparing to attack; but only humans can see that another wants to communicate something.

The crucial advantage of the human child is that she is capable of a superior "theory of mind" of her conspecifics. The young chimp can copy the useful tricks of her elders (older chimp turns over a log and scoops up the insects; baby chimp knows to look under logs in future). But the human infant can grasp the communicative intent behind a word, and imitate the communicative act of the parent. Apes by contrast have real trouble understanding our communicative, or information-providing, intentions, even when we're trying to train them to use sign language.[11]

9. See Nigel DeSouza, "Pre-Reflective Ethical Know-How," *Ethical Theory and Moral Practice* 16, no. 2 (2013): 279–94; see also John McDowell, "Virtue and Reason," in *Mind, Value and Reality* (Cambridge, MA: Harvard University Press, 1998), 50–73.

10. See Iris Murdoch, *The Sovereignty of Good* (London: Routledge and Kegan Paul, 1970); Martha Nussbaum, *Upheavals of Thought: The Intelligence of Emotions* (Cambridge: Cambridge University Press, 2001).

11. Michael Tomasello, *The Cultural Origins of Human Cognition* (Cambridge, MA: Harvard University Press, 1999), 101–2.

This is the crucial difference which sets humans off on the road to language, and hence to the possibility of cultural evolution, which surges forward incomparably faster than organic evolution, since cultural evolution is "Lamarckian": advances of one generation can be handed on to the succeeding ones. But even the most advanced apes don't really teach each other in this sense, that is, communicate something through the intention to communicate.[12]

Tomasello is undoubtedly on to a crucial point here, but I would prefer a slightly amended formulation. To speak of "perceiving communicative intentions" still partakes too much of the monological framework which has dominated too much psychology for too long, whereby we take the individual subject as our starting point, and ask whether and in what mode he can recognize other agents.

But the crucial human difference is rather that language transmission occurs in a context of intense sharing of intentions between the bonded pair. What indeed, happens in the early formats is that we focus on the doll together. It has become an object "for us", and not just for you and for me. Its being an object for each of us is quite different from its being "for us", even if we add that each of us knows that the other is aware of it. There are such awkward situations in social life, where you know that I'm embarrassed and I know you know, and you know that I know, and so on, but still we keep it out of any common focus of attention. It is this guarded state of affairs which is broken through when I make an open avowal. Now my reaction is something *for us*.

Starting a conversation always has this basic effect. We are together in the Metro in July; we are all suffering from the heat, and we all know that everyone else is too; but then you break the silence, and say something like: "Whew, it's hot", perhaps with an exaggerated wiping movement of your brow. This predicament is now something shared. Indeed, we could say that much of the point of most conversations is not the information exchanged, but precisely the sharing.[13]

I have leapt ahead to the adult predicament, but this is no misstep, because the link between language and sharing is a basic feature, which starts at the beginning and continues throughout life. It starts at the beginning, because the very first formats which precede and prepare the

12. Ibid., 34–36.
13. Bronislaw Malinowski, *Argonauts of the Western Pacific: An Account of Native Enterprise and Adventure in the Archipelagoes of Melanesian New Guinea* (London: Routledge and Kegan Paul, 1922).

ground for imparting language create this intense common focus, which makes the sense of the new word unambiguous and clear. There are well-known Quinean worries about the indeterminacy of reference, as where you observe the native informant saying "gavagai" when the rabbit jumps out, and you ask: does this mean "rabbit", or "furry animal", or "moving object", or whatever? But these only apply to this situation where I am simply an observer, trying to pick up the language, or where there is no way of reaching a common understanding (at this stage) about the context (perhaps this is part of a rite which has no analogue in my culture). But we cannot see the acquisition of our first language in anything like this framework. It is rooted in common attention.

This is what Tomasello calls "joint attentional frames",[14] or "referential triangles",[15] where two speakers share the same reference. These are not the product of a deeper "theory" of mind; they are the source out of which any such theory might be drawn. But this ability is a human primitive. Not to have it, as with severely autistic children, is to be in dire straits.

That is why grasping the word spoken by the parent is followed by role reversal, where the child uses the word herself. This recapitulates on a higher level the earliest formats where I stick out my tongue and my baby imitates me. This is how we enjoy this game together.

In a more recent book, Tomasello argues on the basis of his research that the ability to enter into joint attention frames is a condition for infants even communicating with others by pointing, as against just making the pointing gesture (something which emerges at around twelve months); and a fortiori for their learning language.[16] The higher apes can grasp often each other's intentions, and can see what others perceive or can't perceive, but this joint attention escapes them.[17]

---

14. Michael Tomasello, *Constructing a Language: A Usage-Based Theory of Language Acquisition* (Cambridge, MA: Harvard University Press, 2003), 22.

15. Tomasello, *Human Cognition,* 62.

16. Michael Tomasello, *Origins of Human Communication* (Cambridge, MA: MIT Press, 2008), 139–44.

17. Ibid., 172–85. There seems to be a growing consensus among writers on human evolution that joint attention and empathy have been crucial to the development of our species. See also Melvin Konner, *The Evolution of Childhood* (Cambridge, MA: Harvard University Press, 2010), chapter 19; and Hrdy, *Mother and Others,* 9–11. What seems to me a parallel point is made by Alison Gopnik in her interesting recent book, where she identifies a kind of empathy which can "dissolve the boundaries between the self and others." *The Philosophical Baby: What Children's Minds Tell Us about Truth, Love, and the Meaning of Life* (New York: Farrar, Strauss and Giroux, 2009), 208.

The kind of mutual knowledge which arises from joint attention, where not just you know and I know, but it is understood between us that we know together, is crucial to the sort of common ground which alone makes possible a great deal of human communication, both gestural and linguistic.[18]

Of course, in sharing a (to the child) new word together within such a mutual format, we nevertheless have quite different perspectives on it. For one, the adult, it is one element in a rich vocabulary, for the other, the child, it is a new revelation on its own. This common space is traversed by the sense that it abuts something far richer and deeper on the side of the adult, which is only dimly sensed by the child. This is the basis of Vygotsky's "zone of proximal development", which I will return to shortly.

The matrix of language is conversation, and this remains so throughout human life. The famous line from Hölderlin captures this: "Since a conversation we are / and hear from one another" [*Seit ein Gespräch wir sind / und hören voneinander*].[19] The "we" here is we humans, as essentially linguistic beings. Language comes to us through exchange, and this is the primary locus where it is maintained, altered, and renewed.

This is reflected in certain prominent features of language, notably the difference in persons. A pure system of recorded descriptions has only a use for the third person, "he/she/it" and "them". But all languages have ways of marking the speaker and the addressee, be it pronouns like "I" and "you", or other markers. Speaking normally requires that we set up the dyad (or larger circle of communicators), establish who is talking with whom, and certain key indexicals which fix reference, like "here" and "there" (or in the tripartite German distinction "*hier*", "*da*", "*dort*"), are anchored in relation to this established frame. "Here" usually designates somewhere close to us who converse, while "there" points us to somewhere more distant (German "*da*"), or altogether absent from our scene (German "*dort*"). But the anchoring can also work differently: our conversation can, as it were, take us together to the place of which we are speaking, Paris for instance; and then I might say: "here café life thrives". But in this case, too, the reference is anchored in the dyad, in the place that our conversation has situated us imaginatively.

<hr />

18. Tomasello, *Human Cognition,* chapter 3. What we know together can also be described as "wholly overt", or "mutually manifest" (ibid., 91).

19. Friedrich Hölderlin, "Versöhnender der du nimmergeglaubt." See Friedrich Hölderlin, *Poems and Fragments,* trans. Michael Hamburger (London: Routledge and Kegan Paul, 1966), 428.

Tenses situate the events we are talking about in relation to us who speak. The perfect ("George has come" [or "is come", in more correct English]) sets the event as something just completed now; the aorist ("George came") leaves it in an indefinite past.[20]

The primacy of conversation is also reflected in our notion of a language, as something normatively shared. Some have argued that what is primary is the idiolect, my peculiar language, and that the notion of a language, such as English, French, or Turkish, gets a purchase because (for good and obvious reasons) idiolects of people who live together tend to resemble each other. But we oughtn't to think of them as something like species, with their own natures, as it were. This idea quite naturally occurs from the monological perspective, where we think of language as something an individual picks up from watching the behavior of others. On this view, language exists primarily in individual minds. As Locke saw it, a word only means something because it is associated with an idea of that thing. And this association occurs in individuals. So languages are ultimately individual: "Each man hath so inviolable a liberty to make words mean what he pleases."[21] Davidson seemed to have followed him in this.

But this distorts the reality. From the very beginning, the child is trying to reproduce the word that is addressed to her. She's struggling to imitate "our" word, or "the" word. Parents are often moved, and even repeat back, childish attempts which distort, but children usually don't take this as normative and come quickly to grasp the right form. Indeed, they may even resent longer-term attempts by parents to hold on to their childish words. Language from the beginning has normative forms, lexical and grammatical, and they define "the" language.

But this doesn't mean that there is no place for the notion of idiolect. On the contrary, our grasp of language is complex, as complex as conversational exchange. We use "the" language, but we use it differently; we come at it, as it were, from different directions. This sense of the difference of perspective is essential to normal conversation. We try to put things in

---

20. Émile Benveniste, *Problèmes de Linguistique Générale*, vol. 1 (Paris: Gallimard, 1966), chapters 18 and 19; see also Michael Silverstein, "Metapragmatic Discourse and Metapragmatic Function," in *Reflexive Language, Reported Speech and Metapragmatics,* ed. J. A. Lucy (Cambridge: Cambridge University Press, 1993), 33–58.

21. John Locke, *An Essay Concerning Human Understanding,* ed. P. H. Nidditch (Oxford: Clarendon Press, 1975), book 3.

a way which our interlocutor can grasp. Children are on to this it very early; they formulate things differently for different interlocutors.[22]

It is this understanding of different perspectives which makes possible what Vygotsky called the "zone of proximal development" (ZPD). The child grasps a word; this is "our" word, or "the" word; but she also senses that the adult has a deeper grasp, and a wider use. The nearer reaches of this deeper grasp are on the edge of her awareness, as it were. These nearer reaches constitute the ZPD. We can speak of "proximal development" here because the child is on the threshold of this zone, and therefore adults can bring her across by interacting with her within this zone. All along the zone is sustained by her sense that there is something more to learn here. But this also means that the zone is sustained by the good pedagogical sense of the teacher, who has to have her own sensitive grasp of where the child is, of what the object commonly focused on means to her.[23]

In fact, this sense that there is more to the words we use than we grasp never really leaves us, even as adults. We speak standard English, and yet there are hundreds of more or less specialized, or archaic, or high literary terms which exist for us in potential ZPDs. I have some sense of what a "quark" is, but enough to know that I lack the kind of understanding which would give me a real grasp. Unlike the child, I may not be pressing to advance into this zone, but nevertheless I have a sense of "the" meaning of 'quark' which is distinct from the fuzzy things that I can say about it.[24]

Vygotsky's younger compatriot, Mikhail Bakhtin, developed a fuller and more nuanced picture of a language and its many differently situated interlocutors. His notion of "heteroglossia" points to the coexistence within (what is normatively understood as) one language of several different registers and styles. Some of these distinguish people of different classes; the accents and vocabularies of "toffs" are different from those of workers, although they frequently have occasion to speak to, and can understand, each other. Some differences are related to different occasions; you don't speak in a tavern with friends the way you do on a more formal occasion, and you will speak differently again in Parliament. We individually may not

22. Tomasello, *Human Cognition,* 166–74.

23. "Pedagogy requires not only some form of mimetic skill, but the ability of the adult to sense what the child can, and cannot, learn—in other words, to judge the ZPD." Merlin Donald, *Origins of the Modern Mind* (Cambridge, MA: Harvard University Press, 1991), 177.

24. This is the purport, I believe of Tyler Burge's excellent discussion of the person who says to her doctor, "I have arthritis in my thigh." See "Individualism and the Mental," *Midwest Studies in Philosophy* 4, no. 1 (1979): 73–121.

use all these registers, but we understand them, and we see them as different speaking situations, or different modes of interlocution, which belong to the same intercommunicating whole. This awareness of different kinds of speakers and modes of speech is built in to our grasp of "the" language we speak through the complementary understanding that "a" language is always being spoken by many differently situated interlocutors.

Something structurally similar occurs in bi- or multilingual contexts, where our notion of "the" language doesn't really apply. Many more people have lived and now do live in such contexts than are dreamed of in modern nations where a single language has become the norm for everyone. But in such stable multilingual situations, the relations between registers I have been describing holds between languages: I may only use one or a restricted few, but I am able to understand the whole range, and communication takes place across the whole population.

And in similar fashion, even in a monolingual society there is a place here for idiolects, idiosyncrasies of speech that are the property of a group, or even one individual, and that others recognize as characteristic of him or them. This is the basis of another Bakhtinian concept, that of "ventriloquation". In irony or parody, I can take on the "voice" of another. Perhaps Aunt Mabel has a favorite expression, describing many young ladies as "*nice* girls". This expression is redolent of Aunt Mabel's view of the world and of female excellence. I can use it parodically to other members of my family or circle, and say "Anne is a *nice* girl", whereby I convey something very subtle and complicated in a simple expression (Anne has the qualities that Aunt Mabel calls "nice", but that to us are less than admirable). My communicative intent is fulfilled by caroming off Aunt Mabel's "voice".

A similar kind of ventriloquation can occur between the different social and regional styles which make up a language's heteroglossia, as when a New Yorker pronounces a word in a Texan drawl, in ironic or parodic relation to another "voice".

So a basic truth about human ontogeny is that we acquire language in exchange. But as I argued in the first section, acquiring language involves not just taking hold of a new tool; it also changes our world, and introduces new meanings into our lives. In Chapter 1 I described these crucial changes as linked to our having a sense of the "right word" or expression, in different senses of "right": for instance, the descriptive rightness of a word, or the normative rightness of a certain way of acting. Linguistic beings have another sense of the "right move" than we can attribute to animals, even those that learn to make rather impressive distinctions. "Rightness" for an animal is task rightness, whereas in the case of human language it involves something more, expressive rightness, or else descriptive rightness.

How do these senses of rightness arise in the child's acquisition of language? When the child learns to say "dolly", or "more", she unquestionably uses these words on occasion to request (that I pick up the dolly, or that I go on feeding her porridge). So we might be tempted to think that the rightness involved here is simply task rightness ("more" is right because it gets additional spoonfuls of porridge). But it is plain that this is not all that is going on. Small children, as Tomasello puts it, not only utter "imperatives", but also "declaratives".[25] Sometimes, they just seem to be offering a running commentary on what is going on: "Munchy climb", "doggy gone".

What makes these the right words? Not the adult sense of descriptive rightness, which is backed by awareness of criteria (even if I don't myself have a good grip on these, as with 'quark'). Rather what we have here is a kind of ritual rightness. These "declaratives" are vehicles of sharing. The child who announces "doggie gone" is initiating, or prolonging and intensifying, a sharing of attention with the adult; and of course, in this she is imitating the adult who from way back has been initiating such shared attention by (among other gestures and actions) using words ("see the doggie?"). Words enable the creation of communion by other means (means that are new for the child, though not for the adult). It prolongs and intensifies communion.

That's why I speak of ritual rightness. "Doggie gone" is the right word to establish, prolong, or intensify communion around this fact, that the dog has gone out; as "Munchy climb" does around the fact that the child can climb and is now climbing into her chair. We have already moved quite out of the animal zone, and have entered the domain of human language. As Tomasello puts it, even apes raised in human environments, although

---

25. Of course, these "declaratives" are less like adult assertions than they are rituals of communion. This close connection between language and communion is fundamentally what separates humans from other species. Curiously, there is a feature of human language on which chimps seem farther from us than more fully domesticable animals like dogs and horses. I mean the way that language creates a kind of bond, of common understanding between those who share it. As Vicki Hearne has pointed out, something similar to the human-human bond gets set up between a dog and its trainer, a rapport we don't seem to be able to establish with chimps: the adult Washoe was no friend of her human caretakers, as Hearne tellingly describes. See her *Adam's Task: Calling Animals by Name* (New York: Knopf, 1987).

they learn a lot, cannot learn this: "for example, basically all their productions 'of signs' are imperatives, to request things, to the neglect of the declarative sharing of information."[26]

This is, as it were, the toehold that intrinsic (non-task-defined) rightness first gets in human ontogeny. But it doesn't stop there. Requests and commands in both directions help to enrich the pool of potential "declaratives", which eventually culminates in the standard capacity to make assertions. This is the capacity to operate with formulations of propositional content, so as to use them in speech acts of assertion, as well as of requests, commands, and questions. This is the direction which ends up with fully developed descriptive rightness.

But at the same time the language capacity develops in another direction. The work that I described above as protointerpretation, originally carried out in close communion with the parent, goes on in other forms. This is the task of defining and redefining our desires and longings in order to be able to live with the pattern of fulfillments and frustrations we undergo. This turns out to be an unending human task, which in its later modes we could describe as: finding the meanings which can make sense—bearable sense—of our lives.

But this begins by calling forth another dimension of portrayal, which we might call mimicking. For instance, a child may come to terms with a shaking experience, like being spanked by her father, through reenacting the scene between herself and her doll. Or children may among themselves reenact a scene between their parents. "Mimetic games are universal in human youth culture, often help to define roles, especially gender roles, and can be played even in the absence of language."[27]

This dimension, making sense of through portraying, also underlies the human love of stories, which arises very early in human life, and never ends.

Then there is a third direction. The child not only learns the right words, she also learns the right behavior. This normative dimension incorporates in human life a sense of strong evaluation; what is right is intrinsically right, and not just because it is very much desired. But then this strong normativity also has to be made sense of, just as my desires do. It has to be made sense of in general, but also we crave making livable sense of it; that is, one that doesn't condemn me and my desires unbearably.

26. Tomasello, *Constructing a Language*, 290.
27. Donald, *Modern Mind*, 174.

This calls into being another dimension of portrayal, whereby human societies develop a sense of the whole order in which they are set, social, and also inevitably also cosmic. This is the domain of ritual, myth, and eventually also theology or philosophy, often informed by "science", in whatever way this is defined in the society concerned. This defines the global religio-metaphysical culture into which children are inducted.

3

All of which suggests another model of the genesis of the sense of self. One of the baleful features of the modern epistemology which stems from Descartes is its monological character. We start off with an awareness of the self, albeit in a very simple form from the beginning, for instance in our desires, or cravings. We come then to perceive others, and eventually to build some kind of intersubjective world with them. This has been very influential; we can see it even with figures who are as distant from Descartes in other respects as Freud.

It has long been recognized that this monological starting point has been a crippling assumption, and attempts have been made to overcome it. One of the most important and influential can be found in the philosophy of George Herbert Mead, who has been taken up by a number of contemporary thinkers.[28] But one can argue that even Mead's break with the monological has been insufficiently radical. Mead utterly rejects the model that each mind is like "a prisoner in a cell", communicating with others through indirect means (like taps in the wall).[29] His alternative is to see each one of us as formed through our relations to significant others. The sense I have of myself as a stable character, in Meadian terms, my sense of myself as "me", is formed through the internalization of others' expectations. The different "me's" which arise from interaction with different significant others must eventually "be synthesized into a unitary self-image. If this synthesis is successful, then there originates the 'self' as a unitary self-evaluation and orientation of action." This self is not just an introjected

---

28. See G. H. Mead, *Mind, Self and Society: From the Standpoint of a Social Behaviorist*, ed. Charles W. Morris (Chicago: University of Chicago Press, 1934), and Hans Joas, *G.H. Mead: A Contemporary Re-examination of His Thought* (Cambridge, MA: MIT Press, 1985). Among important contemporary thinkers influenced by Mead are Joas himself, as well as Jürgen Habermas: see his *Theory of Communicative Action Vol. 2: Lifeworld and System: A Critique of Functionalist Reason*, trans. Thomas McCarthy (Boston: Beacon Press, 1985).

29. See Joas, *Mead*, 115.

dummy, but is "flexible and open to communication with a gradually increasing number of partners. Simultaneously, there develops a personality structure that is stable and certain of its needs."[30]

Now certainly this is a step forward. While the standard, Cartesian-derived monological approach puts self-awareness prior to our eventual access to an intersubjective world, Mead sees the building of the "me" as occurring *alongside* the opening of this access, and, through the same process, the internalization of the other's view and expectations of me. But we could take a further step. We could not just cancel, but invert the Cartesian priority; we could see self-awareness as emerging out of a prior intersubjective take on things. And this is precisely what the notion of communion that was developed in the previous section would suggest.

What the child is first inducted into is first understood not as the parent's view, or her own view, but what for her is "the" view of the world, which is being imparted along with the language, the view developed within the ambit of an emotion-infused joint attention, which I have been calling "communion". The dominant emotions, of course, vary from occasion to occasion, but we are still far from a disinterested registering of neutral facts. Later, the child will begin to sort out how she stands in and relates to this common view, and the differences between her standpoint and those of others. What she comes to understand as her own take is a precipitate out of the original joint attention, or communion between caregiver and infant. Alison Gopnik seems to suggest this in chapter 5 of her very perceptive book.[31] Experiments show that very young children don't have what she calls "autobiographical memory", memories which they recognize as what happened to their earlier selves. "They don't experience their lives in a single timeline stretching back into the past and forward into the future. They don't send themselves back and forward along this timeline as adults do, recapturing for a moment this past self who was the miserable loser or the happy lover, or anticipating the despairs and joys of the future."[32]

Similarly, they lack "executive control". Although "they can plan for the immediate future, they don't seem to anticipate their future states." "For three-year olds these events aren't organized into a single timeline, with memories in the past and intentions in the future (and fictions

30. Ibid., 118–19.
31. Gopnik, *Philosophical Baby*.
32. Ibid., 153.

and fantasies off to one side). And children may not have the experience of a single inner executive."[33]

But these things, autobiographical memory, executive control, a single timeline that I can remember and narrate in the past and that "leads my life" into the future, are key elements of what we ordinarily understand as the self.

Of course we talk, and quite rightly, about the experiences of a baby. We try to describe what he is going through. But these experiences are not his in the sense that they are or could be self-attributed. The ontogenesis of the self is what takes us from this initial condition to the single timeline we can narrate and decide (at first only within rather narrow limits) how to continue.

This argument may seem suspect. Are we not just moving the goalposts, introducing another sense of the term 'self-awareness', which just *makes* it true that common experience, shared in conditions of joint attention or communion, precedes the constitution of the self? Yes, we are, but this seems justified. The original wordless experiences of the newborn infant is so unlike the later linguistically constituted human identity that we can't understand them as differing only in some quantitative dimension: for instance, that the latter takes in more or more complex objects. The goalposts *ought to* be moved.

But perhaps I am moving them too far; we can trace the constitution of the self back before the important change that Gopnik identifies here. An earlier stage on the way might be when the child insists on doing things her way, or doing things herself, the "Munchy climb" stage I mentioned earlier. But however far back we push it, the development of the self comes after the constitution of the common world of joint attention. Within this common world, we are at first immersed in a view on things that is unattributed. Developing a fuller sense of self requires that we sort out that there are different perspectives, and that things may look different to others. (Piaget's overcoming "egocentrism".)

This order of stages seems indicated by experiments where you show children boxes which seem to contain smarties, but when you open them contain (disappointingly) pencils. Then other children are brought in, presented with the boxes, and before they open them, the first gang are asked what these new children think are in the boxes. The five year olds said

33. Ibid., 153–54.

"smarties" (those poor kids are in for a disappointment), but the three year olds said "pencils".[34]

So there are good reasons to go the whole way, and invert the traditional priority of self over intersubjectivity. The latter, what we called communion, comes first. This perspective has two great advantages not only over the monological one, but even over Mead's middle solution. First, it gives its due to the extraordinary human capacity for, and hunger for, communion. From the earliest days, this is essential to human flourishing, even to survival. And secondly, it recognizes the crucial feature of the human self, which is inseparably and irrevocably a particular take on a common linguistically constituted world.

So the maturing human self emerges out of shared take on "the" world, through a gradual and growing sense that my take is different from yours. We grow toward a complex, two-level understanding. There is still the one world, "the" world, but we live out different perspectives on it.

With the recognition of different perspectives comes the awareness that we have different "takes" on our world, different ways of judging, aspiring, hoping within it. Some of these may have previously existed, and only now come to light; some arise through autonomous development away from the original common understanding. And with this may come mutual opacity, alienation, a sense of mutual misunderstanding, between parents and children, for instance.

And this can (but alas, doesn't always) motivate attempts to negotiate a recovery of some common agreed take on the relationship, and the meanings which are central to it. These are what we might call "restorative conversations". This gives sense to another reading of Hölderlin's famous dictum, quoted above (section 2): "since a conversation we are". This not only points to the beginnings of speech in communion, but also to the "we" of communion, which needs recurrently to be recovered out of alienation and division by such restorative exchanges.

4

We can see how the different kinds of rightness emerge out of the original chrysalis of parent-child communion. These are the modes of rightness

34. J. Perner, S. Leekham, and H. Wimmer, "Three-Year-Olds' Difficulty with False Belief: The Case for a Conceptual Deficit," *British Journal of Developmental Psychology* 5 (1987): 125–37.

which emerge in ontogeny. But perhaps we could get further insight into these and their relations if we considered phylogeny, the evolutionary development of humans with language. Or rather, we might say that undoubtedly real knowledge about how humans evolved would be an immense help here. Our problem is that we largely lack that, and are forced to rely on hunches and deductions from indirect evidence, archaeological, and to some extent comparative (with extant ape populations).

Nevertheless some surmises can perhaps be made which might be helpful, and I'd like to enter into a brief consideration of some of these.

For my purposes I'd like to take up the extremely interesting (and to my mind generally convincing) conjectures of Merlin Donald, in his attempt to reconstruct the evolution of the human mind.[35]

Donald proposes three facets of our human capacity as a language and cultural species. These might be thought to represent stages in early hominid development, but this is merely conjectural in our present state of knowledge (and may always remain so). What is clear is that all three facets are present in human language at whatever stage of our development, even though the forms they take, their mutual relations and their relative importance, even extending to dominance, vary from culture to culture.

The first facet is the "mimetic". Mimesis in Donald's sense isn't simply imitation, but imitation with a representative intent. This is a capacity we all still have and use, but it is particularly evident in children. The case I cited above of the child coming to terms with the spanking she has received by reenacting it with her doll is a good example of what he means. This repetition of the original, somewhat traumatic, event would fail of its purpose if it didn't in some sense recall and reenact it.

Mimesis was a crucial capacity in human development because it enabled us to model reality in a quite new way; and thus to model new realities. For instance, it allowed for an understanding of the society as a whole, as against the kind of grasp which apes appear to have of their social milieu, which is largely a matter of grasping dyadic relations: who is the mate of whom, who is dominant over whom, who will retaliate if you attack X, and so on.[36] By contrast, "Mimetic skill, extended to the social realm, results in a collective conceptual 'model' of society, expressed in common ritual and play, as well as in social structure. Social roles, in a complex society, can only

35. Donald, *Modern Mind* and *Mind So Rare*.
36. Donald, *Modern Mind*, 157, 174.

be defined with reference to an implicit model of the larger society. Mimetic representations would thus be tremendously important in building a stable social structure."[37] We might add that these skills also allow us to model society's place in nature. We need only think of the prehunt rituals, in which someone puts on antlers, and plays the role of the deer.

The capacity for mimesis also goes along with two other modes of imitation: one is for exact imitation, even repeated attempts to replicate someone else's action exactly, which we need to learn skills under the guidance of another person; the second is what one might call conforming, or enacting imitation, as when we learn the right behavior. We might recur here to our example in Chapter 1 of bowing to the elders in respect, which we learn partly by, say, copying older siblings.

The difference between this conforming enactment and what we have been calling mimesis is that the latter is meant to copy something, not to be the real thing. But when I learn to bow I am enacting respect; this *is* (part of) the "real thing", that is, the unfolding of social order in social life. On the other side, the difference from exact imitation, as when I learn how to shoot with a bow, is that I have not just learned to make a certain kind of movement, but to give expression to a social meaning of normative import.

In a sense, the modeling which is mimesis and that which is conforming enactment can in different ways offer access to the same model of order, in one case by representing it, in another by playing my part in it. In the first case, there is "reference" to something else in the obvious sense that a representation always does this; but in the conforming act, there is another kind of "reference"; this act of respect makes sense in the light of its relation to the whole order, as a way of enacting/upholding the proper role of the elders and their wisdom. That's why the act has to be understood as expressive, as carrying a meaning.

But this distinction that I have been making, while it appears exclusive to us moderns, is not necessarily so. These two modes of access to order can merge. This they do in ritual. Ritual can be both a reenactment of something (the Canon of the Mass in relation to the Last Supper), and also an effecting and enactment of what is represented (the transformation of bread and wine into the Body and Blood of Christ). The two modes of access to a higher order come together here. I want to return to ritual below.

37. Ibid., 173.

But for the moment, I will point out that simple mimesis very often involves departure from strict imitation. And in this form it plays an important role as an adjunct to speech. In the example I invoked above, when you open the conversation in this stifling room by saying "Whew! It's hot", you accompany that with a gesture of wiping your brow. But such gestures are often schematic and/or exaggerated. It may not be a gesture like a real brow wiping, undertaken with maximum economy, but I will probably "ham it up" to get my point across.

The tremendous advantage of this move to the development of society is evident. It allowed us to build more complex societies, to give them a stable structure over time, with a set of recurring practices, with more complex skills and collective actions (like the hunting together, chasing horses over a cliff, evoked by Steven Pinker[38]), with rudimentary tools, and above all with the ability to hand on, through what we can now call our "culture", the advances we have made to the next generation, thus unleashing the Lamarckian evolution which has characterized the lightning (in evolutionary terms) progress of the human race.

As Donald puts it elsewhere, "from the relative anarchy of ape social groups came toolmaking industries, fixed campsites, complex group routines regulating fire use, more efficient hunting and gathering techniques, and a variety of customary expressions that served to maintain an enduring collective memory for what worked."[39]

The next facet that Donald posits is the "mythic". This involves the development of what we normally think of as language. I don't mean just vocalizations, because mimesis can also have an auditory dimension and also because language in the mythic dimension isn't necessarily vocal. It usually is for human beings, but it can use other media, as the American Sign Language signing system testifies.

I think that the crucial feature that Donald identifies here is the ability to make defined assertions. Making an assertion means picking out a referent and attributing something to it: "The cat is on the mat"; "rabbits eat lettuce". To see the difference from simple mimesis, let us imagine the following scenario. After (too many) glasses of wine, toward the end of the office party, in a game of disordered charades, I agree to "do" the boss. I strut around with a self-important air, radiating disdain for my surround-

38. See Steven Pinker, *The Language Instinct: How the Mind Creates Language* (New York: William Morrow, 1994), 17.
39. Donald, *Mind So Rare*, 273.

ings, and a sense of my own superiority. Later in conversation with a colleague he says to me "you really got the boss's number; he really is stuck up, he sees us as unwashed peasants".

So we have two "formulations" of the boss's character. The advantage of the first, mimetic, one is (obviously important in this context) deniability. "But Boss, that's not what I meant at all! It's all a terrible misunderstanding". This probably won't save me, but the possibility of weaseling out is there, which it wouldn't be if some snitch who heard me concur in my colleague's remark now denounces me.

This points up the difference: the verbal formulation here is much less ambiguous. It clearly identifies who was meant (the referent), and asserts that something was attributed to him. On the model F(a), we could say: 'stuck up, sees us as unwashed peasants (Boss)'. Of course, we often try our best to wiggle out of things with language; we use "weasel words". But the point is that the whole medium lends itself to demands for clarification: whom exactly are you talking about? What exactly are you saying?

It is in the nature of the terms of descriptive language—let's call them "words", even though the same point applies to a language of gesture—that their use can always be challenged as not "right" by a range of alternatives, for which it is claimed that they are more descriptively adequate. And so, as Donald puts it, "the use of the word reflects the process of sorting out the world into categories, of differentiating the things that may be named. The term 'definition' is a particularly elegant invention in this regard: symbols 'define' the world (rather than vice versa). Previously fuzzy properties become sharper after symbolization."[40]

Within the mythic dimension, these critical, reflexive potentialities of language remain relatively underutilized. They depend on our developing a number of forms of metadiscourse, of speech about speech, which allow for critical refinement, challenge, and change. The first important uses of language in this stage include narration as a prominent element (and this remains central to the ordinary, as against serious technical and theoretical, life of people today[41]).

And among narrations, a crucial one is myth; hence Donald's name for this facet. But the domain of myth, however much it may undergo later

---

40. Donald, *Modern Mind,* 218–19.
41. I will develop this further in Chapter 8.

analysis by modern scholars, following Vladimir Propp,[42] resists the analytic turn. Actual mythic recitation has no room for metadescriptions. Myth offers an integrative form of thought, in which what we define as elements are given meaning in wholes. Many myths, as we identify them, exist in several redactions and variants. Obviously each telling served a purpose, and this contextual purpose could fashion it afresh.

One basic purpose of myth was to make sense of ritual. Myth and ritual have always been closely linked. In a sense, we have here the same kind of complementarity I noted above between conforming enactment and mimesis proper: they offer alternative modes of access to the presumed order that is realized in one and portrayed in the other. Only moving from mimesis to myth takes us into the realm of linguistic narration, with the clarifying or disambiguating consequences I illustrated in my office story above.

But this type of complementarity can nevertheless still exist between myth and ritual, as we see in many early societies, one in which each is needed to clarify or disambiguate the other. That is because myth has its own polysemy. This comes not just from the many variants, but from the uncertainty of reference of its constitutive symbols.

In a later age, when myth coexists with theoretical modes of speech, its assertions will be downgraded, considered as irremediably indefinite, and not to be taken "literally", serving as illustrative image for people who already have some theoretical grasp of the matter—even if the myth may be thought to probe farther than we can go in theoretical speech.

So we get the role attributed to mythical images in, say, Plato's *Republic*. Socrates admits that he cannot tell us more in the theoretical-assertive mode he has been using, where each description is challenged for its descriptive adequacy, about the crucial features of the order he has been laying bare, viz., the Idea of the Good. So we are offered a set of images, some of which resemble myths, especially the story about the Cave. These are self-consciously introduced as not true assertions; one couldn't stand by each one of their formulations in the face of critical comparison with alternatives for their descriptive accuracy. But they can suggest in the way that images do.[43]

42. Vladimir Propp, *Morphology of the Folktale,* trans. Laurence Scott, 2nd ed. (Austin: University of Texas Press, 1968).

43. Plato, *The Republic,* book 6.

However, in the ages before the theoretical (which represents Donald's third facet) comes to dominate, myth doesn't stand in an inferior position. Its uncertainties are sufficiently compensated for by ritual; just as, in return, what ritual is about is clarified in myth.

The complementarity of ritual and myth has often been proposed, but with a primacy given to ritual; on this view myth comes after.[44] But whatever the truth is about this, we can explain the complementarity through the relation of both to an enframing understanding of order.

I borrow from the discussion in Roy Rappaport's very interesting book, *Ritual and Religion in the Making of Humanity*.[45] Rappaport sees original rituals as related to an overarching order of the world, we might say the cosmos. He uses the word that came to be applied in Hellenic culture, '*Logos*'; but similar notions exist in the *Ma'at* of the Egyptians, the *Rta* of Vedic Hindus, and in other cultures. This order is normative; it is the "true" order, not just in the sense that a description of the cosmos in its terms would be "true" in the normal sense; but in the deeper sense that this is the right order; this order follows a plan which it itself dictates, as it were. So it is true also in the sense that we say of someone that he or she is a "true patriot", or a "true friend".

But at the same time, the order can suffer deviations, falsehoods, in a certain sense "lies". It is normative, but not always integrally realized. We humans can be responsible for some of these deviations, and hence also for undoing these deviations. And one of the ways in which we can bring about this repair is through ritual. The accounts vary a lot between conceptions of order. In some extreme cases, the order itself may be in danger of disintegrating, and our ritual action may help renew it (as with the Aztecs' fifty-two-year cycle, which required action on their part at the end to ensure that a new cycle started). But in this case, we could argue that there is a more encompassing metaorder which makes it the case that the encompassed order is vulnerable and fragile, and can only continue under certain ritual conditions.

Or else, at the other end, all that we can damage, and hence have to repair, is our own connection to this order, which we have broken through our fault. But this connection, this inclusion of us, is also something

44. Robertson Smith, *Lectures on the Religion of the Semites,* 2nd ed. (London: Adam and Charles Black, 1894).

45. Roy A. Rappaport, *Ritual and Religion in the Making of Humanity* (Cambridge: Cambridge University Press, 1999).

normatively demanded by the *Logos,* and hence we are, through restoring contact, "repairing the world". (This reminds us of the Hebrew phrase used by the Kabbalists, "*tikkun olam*".)

The actions and words of ritual frequently have an iconic or symbolic relation to what they are trying to effect, or to the order they are meant to repair, but the crucial point about them is that they are performatives, they help to bring about what they (at least in part) represent.[46] And so, for all the elements of portrayal that they incorporate, they are examples of an enactment of order. They merge conforming enactment and portrayal, be it mimetic or linguistic. But because the elements of portrayal are scattered and enigmatic, myth can help to explain the nature of the order they restore; while at the same time, what is enigmatic in myth can be rendered more concrete through the restorative action of ritual.

Of course, the inadequacies of both on this score are what eventually motivates the move to a new kind of discourse, the theoretical discourse of (in this case of the *Logos*) Greek philosophy and theology. And it is of course from this latter discourse that our term 'logos' has been borrowed; as indeed, all the terms that we now use to talk *about* this complementary relation are and must be terms of theoretical discourse, with all the potential distortive consequences that this may bring.

Ritual, myth, and philosophy/theology then form a kind of triangle of what may be felt as complementary discourses/practices, but there seems to be an instability here: theory tends to destabilize, even perhaps undermine the other two.

Which brings us to the phase of human history where Donald's third facet, the "theoretic", becomes hegemonic. The developments of this phase have two aspects: first, we see the emergence of the new modes of discourse which allow us to take a critical stance toward the modes of mythic culture. These enabled meta- or second-order discourse, assessing and altering earlier ways of talking and thinking. The most famous mode for us in Western civilization was the invention of Greek philosophy, the original matrix for the whole range of academic disciplines, natural science, or social science or humanities in the West. But there were other modes, most notably (if we remain within Greek culture) rhetoric, originally the study

---

46. Stanley Tambiah makes this point about the performative nature of rituals in his *Magic, Science, Religion, and the Scope of Rationality* (Cambridge: Cambridge University Press, 1990), 58. I will discuss further the performative dimension of discourse in Chapter 7.

of how to make convincing speeches in the legislative and judicial bodies of the polis. (We have to acknowledge here one of the sources of contemporary "humanities"; this didn't grow from "theory" alone.) And then as we move to other cultures we find analogous discourses, either critical of myth, or offering "deeper" meanings for it, couched in a language of assertions, analogous to philosophy and theology in the Western tradition.

The second aspect was the development of various forms of external memory, from the original recording of commercial transactions on tablets, to the introduction of alphabets, to the writing of elaborate treatises and works of literature, to the constitution of libraries, to the electronic revolution of our own times.

It is clear that these two changes go together. The new metastances were basically what we usually describe as analytical; they eventually brought forth the building of doctrine we call "theory". If we distinguish, following Jerome Bruner,[47] two broadly different modes of thinking that we can still access today: narrative and logico-analytic, then the transition we are now looking at challenged the dominance of the first, and forced it to yield hegemony to the second. We still have a place for narrative in human life (how could it be otherwise?), and even in the academy (the study of literature), but in science, technology, law, government and administration, the logico-analytic dominates. Now clearly, this explosive growth of theory could never have come about without an equally impressive expansion of external memory, from writing to the Internet.

Let me quote from Donald's description of the transition: "The major products of analytic thought . . . are generally absent from purely mythic cultures. A partial list of features that are absent include: formal arguments, systematic taxonomies, induction, deduction, verification, differentiation, quantification, idealization, and formal methods of measurement. Argument, discovery, proof and theoretical synthesis are part of the legacy of this kind of thought. The highest product of analytic thought, and its governing construct, is the formal *theory*, an integrative device that is much more than a symbolic invention: it is a system of thought and argument that predicts and explains. Successful theories often convey power."[48] This change could only come about through an externalization of thought:

47. Jerome Bruner, *Actual Minds, Possible Worlds* (Cambridge: Cambridge University Press, 1986). Tambiah, *Magic, Science, Religion,* develops a similar distinction, drawing on Gregory Bateson, Suzanne Langer, Freud, and others (93).
48. Donald, *Modern Mind,* 273–74.

What was truly new in the third transition was not so much the nature of basic visuocognitive operations as the very fact of plugging
into, and becoming part of, an external symbolic system. Reading,
for example, is a very distinctive mode of knowing, one that raises
disturbing questions about the true locus of human memory. Moreover, theoretic culture broke with the metaphoric style of meaning in
oral-mythic culture. Where narrative and myth attribute *significances,*
theory is not concerned with significance in the same sense at all.
Rather than modeling events by infusing them with meaning and
linking them by analogy, theory dissects, analyzes, states laws and
formulas, establishes principles and taxonomies, and determines
procedures for the verification and analysis of information. It depends for its advanced development on specialized memory devices,
languages, and grammars.[49]

5

After this rapid overview, we might ask how the variety of "symbolic forms"
which we have deployed in this story of Donald's three facets, and the shifts
in hegemony among them, relates to the kinds of "rightness" we can identify today. Alongside descriptive rightness, which I will return to shortly
below, we identified in the first chapter expressive or enactive rightness
(what the young men have who have internalized the body habitus of
respect for elders, what the macho biker has in his body language of
coolness and swagger). This kind of behavior, which I called "conforming
enactment", belongs properly to the mimetic facet of human culture.
This may sound strange in the case of the biker, because he probably thinks
of himself at some level as not conforming to the norms of "society",
and in important ways he is right about this. But he is conforming to a
model which he and other contemporaries have devised, by modifying
existing languages of bodily expression. The crucial point is that this
style is not elaborated in descriptive language, nor in mimetic representation, or artistic portrayal; it arises purely in the enacting of certain
meanings which it expresses.

---

49. Ibid., 274–75; Donald develops his view of theoretic culture in chapter 8. See also *Mind So
Rare*, chapter 8 and 343, note 307; where he shows the link between literacy and "decontextualiza-
tion" and "objectification".

But inevitably, within this style, certain kinds of portrayal arise. There will be a certain way of talking about, describing and relating stories about, different kinds of people; certain descriptive terms, carrying admiration or anger or dismissive contempt will be used. There may even develop rituals; and then also stories which explanatorily relate to the rituals in the way that myths do to the rituals of earlier societies.

So there are analogies with earlier times. We may even say that many of the earlier forms remain very much alive, even though they are now embedded in a largely linguistic-theoretical culture. Mimesis plays an important part in our lives, fitting in as an accessory to speech. Mimetic gestures give force and vivacity to our words. Sometimes they play off against them in irony, as when I say: "he thinks Saddam Hussein colluded with Al-Qaeda", while at the same time circling my index finger around my temple (a gesture indicating folly), or I follow my sentence with "Duh", and an expression of dense stupidity.

And needless to say, we are still deeply invested in rituals and ceremonies in which the life of our society is made real to us, such as national holidays, funerals of famous people, like Princess Diana or Pope John Paul II.

But the rise of theoretical culture has modified the gamut of forms. Our understanding of descriptive rightness has been transformed by the development of theoretic culture. These changes are marked by a set of distinctions, which play a crucial role in our thinking, but didn't exist in earlier cultures. The first is that between literal and metaphorical. Metaphorical assertions may also be true, but they often don't carry the alethic weight of literal assertions. These latter are often thought to record the state of things exactly, instead of hinting at it through suggestive images. For some important writers whose thought contributed to the Enlightenment, men like Hobbes, Locke, Bentham, it was necessary in serious matters to eschew metaphor altogether, lest one be dangerously misled.

A second important distinction is that between the natural and the supernatural. Serious, literal assertions about the natural order, or events within it, are often capable of exact verification; whereas what is claimed about some reality beyond this: God, or angels, or spirits, or Karmic order, is by its very nature hard to establish; and indeed, some people disbelieve altogether in such alleged realities.

And then there is myth, which as we saw gets relegated to a new category; not really of proper assertions, but of potentially revealing images.

This dovetails into the new distinction between "literal" and "metaphorical" or "poetic" truth. Myth is now at best relegated to the second category.

And this gives rise to a third form of rightness which I will discuss more fully in Chapter 6, the kind enjoyed by works of art, including fictional narrations, like novels. They can be seen as "right", even as truth-bearers; but similarly to the demoted myth of Plato's thought, they can't be thought of as assertions. The fiction is made up of assertions, of course, which are in a new category, neither true nor false, but fictional. But the vision which the whole book carries, like that of Dostoevsky's *Devils,* can be seen as true, indeed as truth of the deepest and most important type; but this truth is not asserted but portrayed.

This relegation of myth was a perhaps inevitable consequence of theoretic culture. And we can see it happening early on. I mentioned Plato's use of myth in *The Republic.* But these creations of his own follow a withering criticism (especially in book 3) of the myths current in the culture, which formed the basis for tragedy. These portrayed the gods in ways which Plato deemed totally unworthy of the divine, as beings capable of unbridled desire, or of outbursts of uncontrollable grief. Such things had to be censored.

But another recourse for those in the Hellenistic period who judged the behavior of gods immoral and unworthy was allegorization. One could save the myths as sources of moral-theological insight by seeing them as allegories with a moral message. This involved marking a clear distinction between the surface content and the real underlying doctrinal claim. This distinction was foreign to the original mythic culture. Not that people earlier would have held to what we now call the "literal" truth of the myth. Rather it was understood that myths also hinted at things that weren't fully said, that much was hidden as well as revealed, and that myth was irreducibly polysemic. But the whole brace of modern distinctions that I've been talking about here: literal/figurative, natural/supernatural, myth/underlying meaning, mythical/historical, were absent from the scene. The progressive impingements of these distinctions is what in the end had to challenge and frequently destabilize the triad of ritual, myth, philosophy/theology, as I mentioned above.

The undermining of myth, and the enthroning of literal assertions about the natural order, has helped to create this third category of rightness, which I will call "portrayal", and which is paradigmatically exemplified in certain works of art. But our contemporary views on this have also been shaped by the thinkers of the Romantic generation, who wrote in the wake of Goethe, Hamann, and Herder. I will return to them in Chapter 6.

The upshot of all this is that there is a new way of presenting the order of things, even the true order, but it is distinct from the way we do this in philosophy or theology. It is not asserted in the way that their truths are, although they may draw heavily on the presentations of art. But the novel, for instance, is a different kind of "symbolic form", one which offers portrayals which are not assertions; which "presents" rather than "represents" reality (in German one might say they offer a "*Darstellung*", not a "*Vorstellung*").[50] Novels are not rituals either, so of the original trinity they are closest in analogy to myth; except that they exist in the theoretical age, with all its constitutive distinctions, and not in the original mythical culture.

Ritual has also suffered some dislocation in the theoretic age. The very idea of cosmic order, which we referred to above with Rappaport's term '*Logos*', has been rendered close to unthinkable by the natural/supernatural distinction. Francis Oakley, in his discussion of the history of monarchy, speaks of an " 'archaic' mentality that appears to have been thoroughly monistic, to have perceived no impermeable barrier between the human and divine, to have intuited the divine as immanent in the cyclic rhythms of the natural world and civil society as somehow enmeshed in these natural processes, and to have viewed its primary function, therefore, as a fundamentally religious one, involving the preservation of the cosmic order and the 'harmonious integration' of human beings with the natural world."[51] Human agents are embedded in society, society in the cosmos, and the cosmos incorporates the divine. What have been described as the transformations of the Axial Age tended to break this chain at least at one point, if not more.[52] Oakley argues that the break point which was particularly fateful for our development in the West was the rupture, as it were, at the top; the Jewish idea of (what we

50. Of course, the novel contains assertions; but these are about the "world of the novel". What it offers as insight into our (real) world takes the form of portrayal. See Chapter 6, sections 7 and 8.

51. Francis Oakley, *Kingship: The Politics of Enchantment* (Oxford: Blackwell, 2006), 7. Robert Bellah makes a fundamentally similar point, I believe, in his recent paper "What Is Axial about the Axial Age?," *Archives Européennes de Sociologie* 46, no. 1 (2005): 70: "Both tribal and archaic religions are 'cosmological', in that supernature, nature and society were all fused in a single cosmos."

52. See, for instance, S. N. Eisenstadt, ed., *The Origins and Diversity of Axial Age Civilizations* (Albany: State University of New York Press, 1986); see also Bellah, "Axial Age."

now call) creation ex nihilo, which took God quite out of the cosmos, and placed him above it. This meant that potentially God can become the source of demands that we break with "the way of the world"; that what Rémy Brague refers to as "the wisdom of the world" no longer constrains us.[53]

But this notion of Creation also led, through the theological controversies of the Late Middle Ages, to the clear distinction of natural from supernatural, whereby the former is seen as an order which can be explained, at least at its own level, on its own terms. Later, the tremendous success of post-Galilean natural science entrenched this picture of the natural order.

This clear demarcation makes it harder and harder to think of the old unified cosmos of gods and humans. But this was the original place of ritual action. Of course, ritual performatives recur within the theology of a Creator God, as we see with the Mass. But the foregrounding of a causal efficacy within the natural order, which we have achieved through technology, and which is quite distinct from ritual efficacy, has made it easier and easier to dismiss the latter.[54]

Of course, there are parallels. For instance, certain moves are performative within the legal order. "I pronounce you guilty", or "I pronounce you man and wife", said by a judge, sends one person to jail, and confers on a couple the legal status of married spouses. There is no cosmic involvement; all that is presupposed here is the legal order in which such moves figure. This is not altogether free of paradox. This can arise when we try to think of how the legal order came to be. If a move only has force within such an order, how about the move(s) which set this order up?

The most widespread general concept of this original move in the modern West is the social contract. The theoretical formulations we still rely on were first put forward in the seventeenth century. The original formulation envisages separate individuals coming together and making an agreement to form a political society. But when a new beginning has to be made in our day, what often happens is the calling of a constitutional conven-

---

53. Oakley, *Kingship*. See also Rémy Brague, *La Sagesse du Monde* (Paris: Fayard 1999), 219–39.

54. So much so, that modern scholarship has had great difficulty understanding ritual in non-Western societies, as Tambiah shows in *Magic, Science, Religion*, chapters 1–3. It has frequently either been construed as a quite misguided early attempt at technological control (Sir James Frazer, Sir Edward Tylor), or as a sort of way of working on ourselves and/or our social relations (Émile Durkheim).

tion, whose members are elected. These write a constitution, which may also be put to a referendum.

The paradox-creating and perhaps also subversive question is: what legalizes the first move? Why should the decision of, say, three hundred elected deputies *count* as a decision of the people to live under the régime they choose? And even if it is ratified by a referendum, in the light of the individualist presumption of the social contract theory, why should this decision bind me as an individual?

There is undoubtedly a "bootstrapping" element involved in modern constitution making, and there has been ever since the founding of the United States. This point has often been made. The U.S. Constitution can be seen as a long performative in which a collective subject, identified in the beginning as "We, the people of the United States", declares the constitution in effect. Logically, this agent should preexist in order so to act; but in fact it only comes into existence through the constitution. It decrees its own existence.

But in the original notion of the social contract, there was something resembling earlier ideas of cosmic order, or perhaps better, an order created by a cosmos-transcending God, viz., the notion of natural law. In the Grotian version, an agreement of individuals to found a political society was valid because of the preexisting natural law principle "compacts are to be honored" [*pacta sunt servanda*]. In Locke's formulation, the human race already has been constituted as a community under the natural law which binds them as creatures of the same God.

Although many modern Westerners can't accept these doctrines, some shadow of them still remains in an understanding which is difficult to articulate, but has something like this form: the rules and norms of human rights and democracy are the finest creations of a civilization which itself expresses the best of our normative being, and as such has a claim on us. Because whatever our metaphysical beliefs we tend to treat human rights as though they exercised such a claim. Hence the widespread idea that we can overrule such a fundamental norm of the international order as state sovereignty in order to prevent grievous violations of these rights.

But generally, in our disenchanted world, the original sense of ritual as performative within a larger order tends to slide out of public space, giving way to legal procedure on one side, which is performative within a context of positive law; and mere ceremony on the other, which is in a sense ritual without performative force. Ceremonies abound, of commemoration, or celebrating important dates. Human life is inconceivable without them. But the performative dimension seems to have withered. It consists often of nothing more than a rededication to our nation or cause. The effect is intrapsychic, or at best social. It alters nothing in the order of things.

Or at least, this is the way things tend to appear to us. The real continuing importance of ritual is worth further exploration. I will return to this in Chapter 7.

3

Beyond Information Encoding

1

In the first chapters, I have been expounding the constitutive-expressive view of language, descended from Hamann, Herder, and Humboldt (the HHH), which arose to challenge the dominant Hobbes-Locke-Condillac (HLC) view in the late eighteenth century. In the succeeding chapters I want to argue out my case for the superiority of the HHH. This will involve looking at the HLC in greater detail.

But at this stage it might be useful to see the overall shape of the issue between the two theories. These two theories basically concern the nature of the human capacity for language; the HHH view contends that the rival outlook offers a too narrow picture of this capacity. Without doubt, the HLC has fixed on and given some analysis of one important use of language. But this is just, and could only be, one province in a larger country. So my aim here will be draw a summary sketch of the wider terrain, and of the connection between the different provinces; a basic road map, one might say. Later I will try to fill in some of the landscape.

But if this criticism is right, how can we explain the surface plausibility of the HLC? I think this plausibility comes from a too narrow focus on certain uses of language, what Wittgenstein called a too narrow diet of examples. The power of the HLC comes from its concentration on description, and most often the description of independent objects (as against, for instance, self-description); and even more from the paradigm status of science in our culture, which involves description and explanation in terms that have been purged of purpose, and in general of "human meanings" (a term which I will explain below).

Perhaps 'description' is not the best term. Hobbes and Locke speak of the value of words as "marks" or "notes" of our thoughts, and also of their utility for communicating these thoughts. Perhaps we might formulate their view of the primary use of language as the encoding of our thoughts, or of information, which both allows us to have these thoughts more clearly in view, and also to present them to others. Beyond that Hobbes recognizes secondary purposes, such as expressions of hostility, many of which are very damaging.

Putting the emphases on this function of encoding makes sense of certain facets of the post-Fregean philosophy of language which was dominant in twentieth-century analytic philosophy, and which I will try to explain further in Chapter 4. This takes account of the fact that we do more with language than describe things; we also, for instance, ask for information, and give orders. Along with the information-imparting sentence: (1) "George has come home", we have the information-requesting (2) "has George come home?", as well as the imperative (3) "George, come home!" These speech acts, of differing illocutionary force, share a common core, or "propositional content", a combination of reference and predication, which attributes having come home to George. (1) Asserts that this is so, (2) asks whether it is, (3) commands that it come about.

The important linguistic feat here, one might think, that which allows all three speech acts to take place, is the encoding. Nonlinguistic animals, one might argue, may make analogues of all three acts—alpha male thumps his chest (assertion: "I'm the top chimp here", or perhaps command plus threat: "get out or I'll beat you up"); and one can perhaps see analogues of a request for information: "are there ants under that log?" It's the step into language that makes the difference with humans, and this mainly consists in the ability to encode propositional content.

And this way of thinking could be extended to cover other kinds of speech acts, like promising, suggesting, requesting aid, and so on. These also incorporate propositional content. I can promise to bring it about that George come home, ask you to do so, suggest this to George, and the like.

Of course this very "excarnate" way of thinking of language as encoding reflects what I called an "enframing" theory in Chapter 1; that is, language doesn't alter the basic purposes of the creatures possessing it, but provides other means to encompassing the same ends. This issue posed in these terms is still far from clear. But we can get it better in focus in two ways. One is to examine the question of the continuity between humans and other "higher" species. To what extent can we understand the goals they pursue as identical to ours, with the differences lying in the means used? Or to what extent can we understand their key capacities as fundamentally the same, with the differences merely being quantitative? One dimension which encourages a continuity view is that of instrumental ingenuity. As we look at the higher mammals, and particularly other primates, we see steady progress in this: chimps which can stand on boxes, and use sticks to knock down desirable fruit. There are even birds who can put nuts in situations in which they will be cracked open. Perhaps human intelligence is just a further stage in this progression, a greater quantity of the same ability rather than a capacity of a different kind?

To the extent that this continuist perspective seems correct to you (and that depends in part on what you feel about reductive explanations), the development of language may not seem such a big deal. Human intelligence may appear simply as a supreme degree of instrumental ingenuity. Our technology will seem a more significant achievement of the same basic capacity that the chimpanzee shows when it knocks the banana down with the stick. And the advance of humans over these primates will likely be seen to reside in our expanded abilities to code and manipulate information.[1]

OK perhaps for technology, but what about science? The desire to grasp the universe at it really is? The kind of thing Aristotle meant when he said: "all human beings desire to know"?[2]

And how about moral standards? The principles of justice? The search for virtue? Or again, what to say of aesthetic standards: the principles of beauty, and the like?

There are reductive accounts that would make these appear continuous. In favor of these one might argue: perhaps the phenomenology is misleading and even pure science is really driven by the technological imperative.

---

1. Lenny Moss comments on this tendency among some cognitive theorists to understand the specifically human capacities in terms of our superior information-processing abilities, and the corresponding hope that we can produce machines which can match our achievements. This seems to ignore utterly the role of affect and affective bonding in the evolution of humanity. "From a New Naturalism to a Reconstruction of the Normative Grounds of Critical Theory" (forthcoming). See also his "The Hybrid Hominid: A Renewed Point of Departure for Philosophical Anthropology," in *Naturalism and Philosophical Anthropology: Nature, Life, and the Human Between Transcendental and Empirical Perspectives*, ed. Phillip Honenberger (New York: Palgrave Macmillan, 2015).

2. These are the famous opening lines of Aristotle's *Metaphysics*.

As to morality, one could plead that all gregarious animals force certain modes of conformity on members of the herd or pack. Surely, these are continuous with hominid and then human demands of conformity for the good of the group. In an evolutionist perspective it seems evident that these demands will correspond to some degree with the real needs of the group, and that they will be interiorized, emerging in the sense of right and wrong implanted in its members. We find the same basic needs, which evolution assures will be met in somewhat different form in different species.

When we come to aesthetics, this can be seen just as a matter of brute reactions, not based on underlying objective standards, but explicable psychologically ("Music is auditory cheesecake"[3]).

To the extent, however, that this kind of reduction seems implausible, we will be readier to agree that the coming of language brings with it new goals and purposes; that language is not just a tool, offering more effective means to preexisting goals. Indeed, one could argue that it is not simply a technology either—even taking on board what Marshall McLuhan showed about the way new technologies transform us. Language is rather fundamental to all our technologies.

And so the second approach to the issue is to examine the nature of language itself, and to see whether or not it can be fully understood without supposing such unprecedented concerns. This is the approach that has been followed in the first chapters, and that I will continue throughout the rest of the book. The considerations of the previous paragraphs about the attractions (to some) of reductive explanation help explain the temptations to adopt a continuity perspective, and to see the interspecies differences as matters of degree, or of differing means to the same ends. The reductive account is meant to undercut, even refute, the phenomenology which tends to underscore the sui generis nature of linguistically informed modes of life.

This reductive continuity approach encourages the concentration on description, or alternatively on the coding of information as the main function of language. From this perspective, the step to language can be read mainly as an advance of technique, furthering the continuing ends of survival and prosperity by more effective means.

The attempts which I mentioned in Chapter 1 to present the learning of signing by chimps as a step on a continuous path, one form of which

---

3. Steven Pinker, *The Blank Slate: The Modern Denial of Human Nature* (New York: Viking Publishing, 2002), 534.

has led to full-fledged language in our species, partakes of this reductive continuist approach. In my discussion in that chapter, I tried to show that the nature of our linguistic capacity shows that to be very doubtful.

The chimps learned signs one by one, but words can't be acquired in this way. A word only makes sense within a whole language; just as our sense of what we can say is always bounded by our recurrent experience of what cannot (yet) be said; and our grasp on particular things and situations exists on a background of the larger whole of which these things and situations are segments. There is a triple holism here, which is quite absent in the signing capacity that chimpanzees master.

But even if one is comfortable with the continuity approach, and is willing to accept reductive accounts of our moral and aesthetic judgments, the great complexity and subtlety of our power to encode information in language cannot fail to impress. And there is, indeed, a philosophical temper which combines an inclination toward mechanistic reduction with an enthusiastic appreciation of this complexity and subtlety, a temper widely shared in analytic philosophy and cognitive science.

And indeed, the coding power is awesome. It contrasts strongly with another way that we humans can convey information, through mimetic gesture. This latter is holistic and iconic; whereas descriptive language is analytic and combinatorial.[4]

When we try to make sense of what goes on here, combination would appear to take place according to rules, which we might call grammatical and syntactical. And the grammars-syntaxes of all languages seem to share certain basic features, and can be analyzed in terms of subject and predicate, or reference and predication. But this structure admits of great complexity. Alongside such simple sentences as "John kissed Mary", we have more elaborate ones, like: "the furry dog, that John bought last week, hurried off, grabbed the stick between his jaws, then ran back and laid it at the feet of Mary". We can analyze this into noun phrases and verb phrases (NPs and VPs), which have to be seen as hierarchically arranged. The subject term, the dog, is identified through its features: furry and having been

---

4. Eighteenth-century accounts of the origin of language often supposed a dual source for our evolved capacity, in expressive cries on one hand, and in gesture on the other. And in fact, they are often combined in discourse, as we shall see later on. But interestingly, in the gestural languages that have been developed among people who are deaf and/or mute, the gestures themselves take the analytic-combinatory features that we find in standard human speech.

bought by John last week. The whole noun phrase embeds a verb phrase (that John bought last week) within it.

Sentences like these can then be combined in larger texts, such as stories, and for this purpose are linked in various kinds of anaphoric or cataphoric reference, through pronouns and other terms. For instance, the next sentence in a story starting with the long sentence above might read: "This dog was really remarkable", where the deictic term "this" makes the link.

Mastering all this, grammar in its fullest extension, and the creation of stories and other texts, takes a long time, usually well into the teen years.[5] And the question obviously arises: how do we do it? Analyzing the rules and modes of combination has been an important part of human knowledge since the great early grammars; Sanskrit and Greek provide origin points in the Indo-European world. On top of this, questions arise about this capacity itself: how did it arise in evolution? And how do successive generations of children acquire it? Chomsky's conjecture about the latter question is that features of these rules and modes are built into our heredity, so that the narrow range of evidence, in the (often corrupt and ungrammatical) speech of the adults surrounding us, clues us in to the grammar of our linguistic community.[6]

All this to say that, whatever one might think of these theories, there is an important intellectual agenda here that needs to be pursued: understanding the capacity which underlies rule-following in grammar, syntax, and semantic construction more generally. My HHH-inspired critique is not in any sense aimed at dismissing or downgrading this agenda. Quite the contrary. But what I will try to show can be summed up in two basic points:

First, that the functions of description and information-encoding, whose underpinnings this agenda tries to explore, are very far from exhausting

5. See the interesting work of John A. Lucy and Suzanne Gaskins, "Grammatical Categories and the Development of Classification Preferences: A Comparative Approach," in *Language Acquisition and Conceptual Development,* ed. S. Levinson and M. Bowerman (Cambridge: Cambridge University Press, 2001), 257–83.

6. Mark C. Baker in *The Atoms of Language: The Mind's Hidden Rules of Grammar* (New York: Basic Books, 2001) conjectures that the differences between the grammars of different human languages can be accounted for by a finite number of different "parameter" settings. Children are genetically programmed so that they need merely pick up which settings apply to their mother tongue in order to speak correctly. And there are other interesting conjectures: for instance, Denis Bouchard proposes that we might explain the development of Saussure's paralleling of distinctions of *significant* and *signifié* in neurological terms, through the development of "Offline Brain Systems"; see his *The Nature and Origin of Language* (Oxford: Oxford University Press, 2013), part 3.

the functions, uses, and potentialities of language. This will go hand in hand with attempts to show the features of linguistic awareness which defy the reductivist-continuity interpretation. These two endeavors amount to two facets of the same intellectual project, just as the reductivism and descriptivism they criticize constitute two facets of the inadequate view of human language and life which has exercised underserved power in our culture.

Second, I want to show that the linguistic functions which theories of semantic construction or innate grammar have mainly tried to explain, namely, the description of independent, self-standing objects,[7] cannot be exercised independently of the other functions identified in my first point. It is not as though we could exercise this descriptive power without any capacity to carry out these other functions—as we might imagine that we could have used our ordinary language to describe the world around us without ever having embarked on storytelling or novel writing. This would be a terribly impoverished world, but it appears possible. One can even imagine a rigidly puritan society in which any kind of fictional storytelling is forbidden. But the other capacities and functions I will outline in the following pages don't exist in this kind of side-by-side relation with our everyday descriptive powers; they are interwoven and inseparable from them.[8]

2

Let me start by embarking on the first point, what the HLC leaves out.

In the perspective of the descriptivist approach, the language capacity must include the ability to generate descriptive vocabulary, words which can be used to describe the realities we come across. But the HLC, and the theories which descend from it, can't even give an adequate account of this capacity. I shall try to show later that much of our vocabulary can't be

7. The contrast case to these descriptions would be those which try to convey our desires, feelings, motives, reactions, moods; and/or descriptions of objects in their significance for us. I will expand on this in Chapter 6. But descriptions as such also contrast with the performative dimension of discourse.

8. "Ordinary language, stripped to its bare descriptive skeleton, turns out to be only a part of a far larger and more variegated pattern of activity." Rowan Williams, *The Edge of Words: God and the Habits of Language* (London: Bloomsbury, 2014), chapter 1, section 1. I came across this very illuminating book very late in the process of completing my own. But I found considerable overlap with what I wanted to say, formulated in a quite different idiom. It is though we had been traversing the same terrain, but from different starting points.

generated in the way it supposes. This is because it has no place for (what I called in Chapter 1) the particular constitutive powers of language.

But besides conferring this capacity to create vocabulary, becoming linguistic animals alters our way of being in the world, and with each other. The information-coding view tends to see language as providing immensely useful *instruments* for defining and communicating knowledge about the world. But language creates a context for human life and action, including speech, which deserves attention in its own right. We relate to this context not only, or even primarily, as to an instrument which we can pick up or lay down. Rather it is the medium we are in; a feature of what we are. It opens for us other dimensions of existence, which we cannot ignore if we want to understand the nature of language and of our existence in language. It is these dimensions that are often overlooked when we focus on description, or coding information, as the central function of language.

In anticipation of the discussion in later chapters, I want now to enumerate briefly some features of linguistic existence, on one hand, and of the uses of language, on the other, which are too often sidelined. I will present five points: the first two concern ways in which language changes our world; and the remainder show how we expand our articulacy, and generate new vocabulary, in ways the HLC can't understand.

1

First of all, there is the feature that we discussed in Chapter 2: the relation of language to joint attention, or communion. The human capacity for this more intense and conscious mode of being together is a condition for the development of language, as we saw there; and it is also regularly renewed and sustained in linguistic exchange. This is one way in which the development of language transforms our way of existing as an animal species.

To be inducted into language is to be in a relation of potential communion with others. In principle, this could relate us to anybody and everybody; but in practice, we live in certain circles or communities: family, village, political society, religious or affinity group, and so on, which are the sites of recurrent, often regular, even close to constant or continuing, realization of communion. To possess language is to be, and to be aware that one is, in social space.

Social space matters. From the very beginning we seek communion, intimacy, love, and we never grow beyond this need, even though later a host of less intense, and less personally engaging relationships also arise in our lives. These relations have meaning for us, in the sense of significance in our lives. They matter in various ways, big or small.

But as language beings we also need to make sense of these relations: love, friendship, links with compatriots, brother- and sisterhoods, churches, parties, each with their demands and norms. We can only live in these relations, and carry out what they require, in some articulation: what it is to be a friend, lover, citizen, worshiper with this congregation, and so on. At first this articulation is given to us by our family and culture, but we may also change it (even radically as in conversion), or alter, refine, and clarify it, on our own initiative.

These articulations of human meanings can be called "interpretations", not because they emerge from personal acts of interpreting, because at first and for the most part they don't; but because they can be changed by such personal acts, and that is essential to their nature.

I talk here of "human meanings", and I will talk also of "metabiological meanings", terms which are closely related, and need some explanation here. The contrast class to human meanings could be described as "life meanings". These also have significance for us, but this is something we share with other animals. Like them it matters to us that we preserve our lives, that we find the means to live, food, shelter, and so on. But issues like defining the meaning of life, or living up to the demands of love, touch us alone.

Life meanings are modes of significance that things can have for an organism or agent who pursues certain goals or purposes which can be identified from outside even by beings who don't share these purposes. So we can attribute them to animals, or each other, independent of self-understanding. We only have to identify the animal's needs and the patterns of action—hunting prey, eating grass, building nests—by which they meet these needs. We can work out from these further life meanings, even in cases where the animal itself doesn't discriminate. We can work out, for instance, that a certain species needs some nutritional element in their diet, even though they themselves don't react selectively to it. Life meanings are defined by objectively recognizable patterns of need and action.

But the case is different with human or metabiological meanings. These concern goals, purposes, and discriminations of better or worse, which can't be defined in terms of objectively recognizable states or patterns. If what I seek is a meaningful life, or a profound sense of peace, or to be at one with the world, to be reconciled with things, to enjoy deep communion with my loved ones, and the like, what I'm after can't be captured in some objectively identifiable pattern. In order to see what's at stake here, one has to get inside the language of self-description, catch on to what a meaningful life is for me (or my culture in general), what I mean by a sense of peace, what profound communion requires.

We could put it this way: the language of human meanings doesn't translate into that of objectively identifiable states, those which can be grasped from outside without reference to the agent's self-understanding. There is a certain incommensurability here. The discriminations involved can't be expressed in external terms. Human meanings open perspectives on ourselves and our world which can't be simply aligned with life meanings.

And, of course, life meanings hold for humans too. They impinge on our lives, independently of how we understand them. I need some kind of mineral in my diet, and I don't yet know that. But nevertheless life and health are meanings which concern me, and which move me, and we can say that, in consequence, because of the facts of biology, "needing calcium" is a significance-attribution which applies to me.

But the aspiration to or need for love or friendship can only impinge on me, and motivate me to act, in some articulation. Outside of any articulation, I can't see what I need here, whereas in the calcium case, I know and must know that I want a healthy, vigorous life—and, indeed, I react to preserve my life even without thinking. And as a consequence, (an undistorted) self-understanding is a crucial condition of these human needs being met. They are, in that sense, metabiological.

True, you can see from outside that I need a certain kind of love, just as you can that I need calcium, but (if you leave aside the well-known health benefits of a happy relationship) this can only be based on your articulation/interpretation of human meanings.

Now of course, proponents of the enframing, or reductive-continuist, perspective on language and human evolution have trouble with human meanings. They can't translate them, but they can (try to) offer a reductive *explanation* of them. The different modes and qualities of sexual love can be ignored, and the externally identifiable pattern of "pair bonding"—where male and female remain together after mating and take care of offspring—can be defined as crucial. We can then offer an account in terms of natural selection of the prevalence of this pattern among humans: because human children are so helpless for so long, nothing else can ensure species survival. Similarly, morality can be explained as the reflex in us of the pattern of social cohesion and mutual help which has ensured human survival. The widely different understandings of what morality consists in, the different kinds of inspiration which sustain it, the diverse understandings of belonging, all can be ignored as epiphenomenal.

Once more a crucial issue turns on what one thinks of such reductive explanations. If one finds them unconvincing, then one will recognize that one of the crucial "uses" of language is to establish and maintain the various forms of human contact or relationship, for their own sake, from casual conversation over the back fence, through various forms of belonging and solidarity, reaching right through to the most intimate communion.

And another important use is to articulate these relationships, their meaning and demands. We need to find "names" for them in a sense. Does that sound familiar? Are we back in HLC territory, where we find names to describe things? But articulation here is a quite different matter than finding words for independent objects. This is because the words here help shape the meanings they can be used to describe. There is a constitutive dimension to their introduction, that the information-coding perspective in unaware of and can't cope with. I will expand on this in Chapter 6.

2

Another feature of linguistic consciousness is that it carries with it, at least as background, a sense of the whole, in the various dimensions I alluded to above. We sense that the words we now use in outer or inner speech are part of a larger linguistic capacity; that what we can now express has boundaries; and that the places and objects which we now focus on are part of a larger whole in space and time.

The world as we live it at any time is full of things and states which we can describe, matters that we can formulate; and at the boundary, there are others that we can't yet articulate, but might be invited to at any moment. And we sense that we could find a way of doing this; taking off from expressions which are already familiar, we could manage to formulate what has been (to us) up to now inexpressible. In the terms of Merleau-Ponty (that we cited above in Chapter 1, section 4): on the background of our already achieved "*parolee parlées*", we could generate new "*paroles parlantes*".[9]

---

9. See Maurice Merleau-Ponty, *La Phénoménologie de la Perception* (Paris: Gallimard, 1945), 229.

In Chapter 1 we looked at Herder's understanding of linguistic awareness. *Besonnenheit*[10] is a kind of focus on the object named. But this means
that the word we use comes out of a sense that this is the right word. This
implies two of the holisms mentioned in the previous paragraph: first,
the right word figures as such among many possible words, actual or to
be invented; so language as a whole has to preexist. And second, the
object named stands out from a context, a background; so there has to be
a sense of the whole situation, geographic, social, cosmic.

And so language involves a different way of being there, being where
you are; a there-and-not-elsewhere. There is a contrastive sense; of object
as against context, here as against whole background.

But within this kind of holistic awareness, there are different stances possible, various kinds of focus. Most of the time we are fixing on some particular object, with some particular issue in mind, and then the holisms
retreat into the background. I examine this particular object with the aim
of getting accurate knowledge of it, or an adequate explanation of how
it came to be, or a grasp of how I can use it as an instrument. Or I am no
longer fully aware of my surroundings, but am preoccupied with some
problematic meeting with the dean next week. Or I am dreaming of escape to the country.

But there is also a stance which might be thought of as unfocused; just
being here, with a sense of the whole background streaming in. I look at
this tree, and sense the sun, the whole wood, the distant horizon, my life
as in a stream of time, how this place calls up memories; and the meaning
of all this. I sense that my zone of focal awareness is surrounded by a corona of potentially articulable meanings, corridors that I might explore
through new formulations, true *"paroles parlantes"*.[11]

Just being there in this sense is the threshold from which we can step to
what Heidegger calls "dwelling". But he has a richer sense of what this involves than was captured by my description above. Heidegger's understanding of language draws heavily on the tradition of the HHH; and along
with this he inherits the Romantic idea that we are in some way fed,
strengthened, nourished by this wider context. This connection is realized

10. "reflection".
11. Evoked in the time consciousness of Virginia Woolf's *Mrs. Dalloway.* See the interesting
discussion of this work in Paul Ricoeur, *Temps et Récit,* vol. 2 (Paris: Seuil, 1984), 152–67. There are
also, of course, negative forms of this multiple solicitation by liminal meanings: for instance, when
fears or anxieties impinge on me and destroy my concentration.

by articulating all the meanings that the "thing" has for us; meanings which are inextricably linked to the wider context. Indeed, Heidegger sees this articulation of liminal meanings as a charge laid on us by language; it is part of our telos as language beings, which is why the repression of this liminal awareness in modern technological society is so damaging and destructive to ourselves and to our environment.[12]

This demand is captured in Heidegger's special use of the term 'thing'. The "thing" is not the objectified entity, which is the focus of scientific study or the search for possible instrumental use. Rather it is the locus of the full corona of liminal meanings, which it presents and invites us as language beings to explore.

The thing about a "thing" is that in being disclosed it codiscloses its place in the clearing. The later Heidegger introduces the notion of the "fourfold" [*Geviert*] to explain this: mortal and divine beings, earth and sky. Take a humble entity, like a jug. As it shows up in the world of a peasant, as yet unmobilized by modern technology, it is redolent of the human activities in which it plays a part, of the pouring of wine at the common table, for instance. The jug is a point at which this rich web of practices can be sensed, made visible in the very shape of the jug and its handle which offers itself for this use. So much for the human life which coshows up in this thing.

At the same time this form of life is based on, and interwoven with, strong goods, matters of intrinsic worth. These are matters which make a claim on us. They can be called "divine". So these too are codisclosed. Heidegger imagines this connection as arising from an actual ritual of

12. See my "Heidegger, Language, Ecology," in *Philosophical Arguments* (Cambridge, MA: Harvard University Press, 1995), 100–126. Heidegger's notion that the condition of being a linguistic animal lays a charge on us to articulate the liminal meanings finds (perhaps too enigmatic) expression in some of his well-known dicta, like: "For, strictly, it is language that speaks. Man first speaks when, and only when, he responds to language by listening to its appeal" [*Denn eigentlich spricht die Sprache. Der Mensch spricht erst und nur, insofern er der Sprache entspricht, indem er auf ihren Zuspruch hört*]; see Martin Heidegger, ". . . Poetically Man Dwells . . . ," in *Poetry, Language, Thought,* trans. Albert Hofstadter (New York: HarperCollins, 1971), 214; Heidegger, ". . . dichterisch wohnet der Mensch . . . ," in *Vorträge und Aufsätze,* vol. 2, ed. Friedrich-Wilhelm von Herrmann (Frankfurt am Main: Klostermann, 2000), 64. Or, "Mortals speak insofar as they listen" [*Die Sterblichen sprechen insofern sie hören*]. There is a "call" [*Ruf*] to which we respond, emanating from a "silence" [*Stille*]; see Martin Heidegger, "Language," in *Poetry, Language and Thought,* 206; Martin Heidegger, "Die Sprache," in *Unterwegs zur Sprache* (Pfullingen: Neske Verlag, 1959), 27–29. There is a filiation between Heidegger's understanding of language and David McNeill's notion that "to the speaker, gesture and speech are not only 'messages' or communications, but are a way of cognitively existing, of cognitively being, at the moment of speaking." McNeill, *Gesture and Thought* (Chicago: University of Chicago Press, 2005), 99. See also the very penetrating and interesting discussion of the later Heidegger in John Richardson, *Heidegger* (New York: Routledge, 2012).

pouring a libation from the jug. But I doubt if the Christian, Black Forest peasantry of Swabia (as against the ancient Greeks) actually did this kind of thing; and it is sufficient to point out that the human modes of conviviality that the jug codiscloses are shot through with religious and moral

meaning. Perhaps the pastor said grace, but even if he didn't, this life together has central meaning in the participants' lives.

And so on through the other two dimensions of the fourfold: earth and sky. All these are codisclosed in the "thing". Heidegger says that it "assembles" [*versammelt*] them and they "sojourn" [*verweilen*] in it.[13] When this happens, then the clearing itself can be said to be undistortively disclosed. (The "clearing" [*Die Lichtung*] is Heidegger's term for the fact that things show up at all.) The undistorted metadisclosure occurs through this fourfold-related manner of first-order showing up. Being among things in such a way that they show up thus is what Heidegger calls "dwelling". It involves our "taking care" of them.

> Staying with things, however, is not merely something attached to this fourfold preserving as a fifth something. On the contrary: staying with things is the only way in which the manifold staying within the fourfold is accomplished at any time in simple unity. Dwelling preserves the fourfold by bringing the presencing of the fourfold into things. But things themselves secure the fourfold *only when* they themselves *as* things are let be in their presencing. How is this done? In this way, that mortals nurse and nurture the things that grow, and specially construct things that do not grow.

> [*Der Aufenthalt bei den Dingen ist jedoch der genannten Vierfalt nicht als etwas Füntes nur angehängt, im Gegenteil: der Aufenthalt bei den Dingen ist die einzige Weise, wie sich der vielfältige Aufenthalt im Geviert jeweils einheitlich vollbringt. Das Wohnen schont das Geviert, indem es dessen Wesen in die Dinge bringt. Allein die Dinge selbst bergen das Geviert nur dann, wenn sie selber als Dinge in ihrem Wesen gelassen werden. Wie geschieht das? Dadurch, dass die Sterblichen*

---

13. Martin Heidegger, "The Thing," in *Poetry, Language, Thought*, 161–84; Heidegger, "Das Ding," in *Vorträge und Aufsätze*, 2:27–50.

die wachstümlichen Dinge hegen und pflegen, dass sie Dinge, die nicht wachsen, eigens errichten.][14]

The extensions of language that one needs to be fully aware of this, to be fully nourished, are poetic. So "poetically man dwells" [*dichterisch wohnet der Mensch*].[15]

So we might call the "unfocused" sense of just being there "protodwelling",[16] whereas the deeper exploration of the meanings enables "dwelling" in the full Heideggerian sense.

Now the different possible stances tend to repress or mask each other. For instance, the objectifying stance of modern epistemology, whereby language has to map independent objects, tends to mask dwelling, as does the technological stance which wants to mobilize things in the world as "standing reserve". Unhiddenness [*aletheia*] of one focus/stance involves "hiding" another.[17]

But the holistic predicament which invites to protodwelling is ineradicable. It is "originary" [*ursprünglich*]. Certain stances lead to the forgetting of protodwelling, and thus to mutilations of the human. And they can also lead to false theories of language, which ignore dwelling and its protocondition. But the original predicament is inescapable, because this linguistic consciousness is the condition of all these special stances and foci.

---

14. Martin Heidegger, "Building Dwelling Thinking," in *Poetry, Language, Thought*, 149; Heidegger, "Bauen Wohnen Denken," in *Vorträge und Aufsätze*, 2:25–26.

15. Heidegger was deeply indebted to the Romantic understanding of language, which he drew on and developed in his own way. See Mark Wrathall, *Heidegger and Unconcealment: Truth, Language, and History* (Cambridge: Cambridge University Press, 2011). This debt can be seen, among other places, in the important role he attributes to "poetry" [*Dichtung*]. There is a tradition of post-Romantic poetics, within which the articulation of liminal meanings, recurring in different ways, has a crucial place: for instance, in Baudelaire, Mallarmé, Rilke, and Celan. The importance of Hölderlin, and among twentieth-century poets Rilke, for Heidegger speaks for itself in this regard. I want to return to this tradition in a proposed companion study on post-Romantic poetics.

16. This state is also the antechamber from which one can practice "mindfulness".

17. Of course, singling out this way of being related to the whole "fourfold" [*Geviert*] is typically modern. In earlier times our embedding in society was in turn englobed in the cosmos and the divine. It is only since the Romantic period, and its take on the Enlightenment (I say "take" and not "reaction", because I see the two as in continuity), that the meanings in our relation to nature are explored outside of an already established theory of the cosmos.

This protodwelling can be seen not as a fact simply of "consciousness", our grasp of things, but as a way of being in the world, inhabiting it. Merleau-Ponty sees speech and gesture as "inhabited" by meaning; but the primary role of meaning is to make us "inhabit" the world.

3

Now the exploration of meaning that constitutes dwelling, alongside the articulation of our different modes of relationship, discussed in the previous point—all this is just one example of the whole field of articulation of human meaning, a crucial "use" of language of which the information-encoding approach cannot make sense. As I will argue in Chapter 6, the country of language includes other provinces beyond the description of independent objects which the HLC focuses on.

But our road map takes us farther afield than this. When we examine what is involved in articulating human meanings, we will see that this often draws on what I called in Chapter 1 "enacted" meaning. So understanding language and the creation of linguistic meaning takes us beyond the words to the whole sphere of the expressive-enactive, illustrated in Chapter 1 by our macho biker. Our horizons have to expand if we are really to understand language, and incorporate a wider range of symbolic forms. I'll expand on this in Part II.

4

Then there is discourse, the real-time activity of conversing with other people. This is, of course, already taken care of in the information-coding perspective. It is the point at which the code is put into practice, and information is encoded in speech. In Saussurean terms, it is the point where langue issues in parole, or in more contemporary mode, where linguistic competence comes out as performance.

But discourse is more than parole; real-life performance can't be accounted for by what is generally understood as linguistic competence.

Speech acts involve more than emitting the appropriate words. They also involve bodily action, stance, gesture, tone of voice, and the like.

Now in the light of our earlier discussion, these issues might be considered external to the strict remit of a theory of linguistic meaning. They can be hived off as above, the different illocutionary forces—statement, question, command—can be segregated from an account of the formation of the propositional content which is common to all three.

But will this really turn out to be possible? Has gesture, for instance, no role in determining the content of what is conveyed in discourse? Can it be totally disregarded? Even iconic gesture? We shall see reason to doubt this as the discussion proceeds.

5

And then there is another role for discourse. This concerns its constitutive force: the way human beings set up, sustain, and transform different social footings in linguistic exchange. Certain crucial human realities that we try to understand in language are created in discourse, and cannot simply be treated as extralinguistic. I shall discuss this at length in Chapter 7.

Here too, we will see that the development of our resources of speech depends on the creation of enacted meanings. And among these enactments, ritual has a crucial place, as I indicated in Chapter 2.

It will be clear from all this that language as speech can only exist in symbiosis with various forms of embodied action—gesture, enactment—as well as other symbolic forms, music, dance, poetry, and other modes of artistic expression. The "country" of language goes way beyond the "province" of information-encoding, important as this is.

3

I have been expanding on my first point, that there are other functions and dimensions of human language than the description of independent objects.

But my second thesis is also beginning to surface here, the claim that we cannot just hive off these other functions and leave description untouched. Some of these unbreakable connections are already surfacing in the last two points, about the importance of discourse.

For example, the original cases of formulating-encoding and communicating information occur in human speech. Both in the history of the species, and in each individual who grows up in human society, they occur before the more refined and "excarnate" methods in which writing and more formal and interlocutor-distant modes of communication (like academic lectures) are mastered. But one can argue, and I will later, that in the original conversational context, gesture, as a mode of holistic-iconic communication, plays an essential role (point 4). And that certain of our crucial social relations are created in discourse, and without these the very social contexts in which distant, excarnate communication (formal lectures, learned papers, and treatises) can exist would never arise, nor be sustained (point 5).

It will also turn out that all linguistically relevant creation of meaning cannot be understood on the Saussurean model, where *significant* can be distinguished from *signifié*.

Or so I will argue in subsequent chapters.

PART II

From Descriptive to Constitutive

4

The Hobbes-Locke-Condillac Theory

1

So let's take a step back, and look at what I have been calling the "HLC" theory. I mean the account of language which developed, among others, with certain paradigm thinkers of the seventeenth and eighteenth centuries. I want to foreground Hobbes, Locke, and Condillac. This is the theory which Herder challenged, in the form of a thesis of Condillac about the origin of language.

We can start with Hobbes. He argues in *Leviathan* that the power of speech was a great boon to human kind, because it is essential to society. "Without it, there had been amongst men, neither commonwealth, nor society, nor contract, nor peace, no more than amongst lions, bears of wolves."[1]

"The general use of speech, is to transfer our mental discourse, into verbal; or the train of thoughts, into a train of words."[2] This transfer serves two principal uses: to register thought, and to communicate.[3] In the first case, language serves as "notes", in the latter as "signs". Hobbes stands at the origin of the modern view of language as a mode of information coding. "Notes" encode thoughts. And then "signs" pass these encoded thoughts on to others.

---

1. Thomas Hobbes, *Leviathan,* ed. Michael Oakeshott (Oxford: Blackwell, 1989), 18.
2. Ibid.
3. Later Hobbes will add two other uses: we can speak in order to delight ourselves and others; and also words can be ornaments.

This second use is essential to our political life, which takes us beyond the condition of wolves, bears, and lions. But the first is also essential to us. It allows us to think much more effectively. Language allows us to think in universals, as we might say, using concepts and not just proper names. "The proper name bringeth to mind one thing only, universals recall any one of those many."[4] And Hobbes gives his famous example: a deaf-mute (lacking language) might be able to puzzle out for a given triangle that its angles amounted to 180 degrees. But he would have to recommence this arduous empirical study with each fresh triangle. Whereas speech enables us to establish in one operation the universal truth about triangles.

Speech thus allows us to reason really effectively. Hobbes sees reasoning as a species of reckoning. Take reckoning, for instance, in the context where you want to arrive at the grand total of entities of a certain class. This can much more expeditiously be achieved if you already have the things sorted into (already counted) subclasses. Speech makes this possible.

This notion of reasoning draws on the immense prestige of the resolutive-compositive method, in the wake of the new Galilean model of science. To understand reality is to break it down into its component parts, and then map how they combine. This was the method Hobbes himself used to make sense of the polity.[5] And this method was already becoming enshrined in the modern epistemology whose most influential figure was Descartes. This epistemology stressed that our knowledge of the world was built from particulate "ideas", or inner representations of outer reality. We combine them to produce our view of the world. Error arises, not in the particulate ideas but in the manner in which we combine them in thought. We need to do this carefully and methodically in order to arrive at truth. The key issue is the search for a method.

---

4. Hobbes, *Leviathan*, 19–20.

5. "Concerning my Method, I thought it not sufficient to use a plain and evident style in what I had to deliver, except I took my beginning from the very matter of civill government, and thence proceeded to its generation, and form, and the first beginning of justice; for every thing is best understood by its constitutive causes; for as in a watch, or some such small engine, the matter, figure, and motion of the wheeles, cannot well be known except it be taken in sunder, and viewed in parts; so to make a more curious search into the rights of States, and duties of Subjects, it is necessary, (I say not to take them in sunder, but yet that they be so considered as if they were dissolved (i.e.) that wee rightly understand what the quality of humane nature is, in what matters it is, in what not fit to make up a civill government, and how men must be agreed among themselves, that intend to grow up into a well-grounded State." Thomas Hobbes, *De Cive: Philosophicall Rudiments Concerning Government and Society,* ed. Howard Warrender (Oxford: Clarendon Press, 1983), 32.

Hobbes's notion of reason as reckoning takes its sense from this context. Reasoning is combining, and language helps us to do this expeditiously and on a grand scale. The great proviso is that we be clear about the meaning of our terms. Each must be carefully defined semantically, and then must retain the same meaning in all the larger reckonings in which it figures. Otherwise, if the original definitions are vague or uncertain, or if they are forgotten in further reasoning, we become entangled in our thoughts, "as a bird in lime twigs."[6] The big danger is that we take over, on the authority of tradition, impressive-sounding but ill-defined terms, and thus are led to absurdity. This is bad enough, but what is worse, sedition-mongers can use these arguments to upset the order on which our life and security depends. "Words are wise men's counters, but they are the money of fools, that value them by the authority of an Aristotle, a Cicero, or a Thomas."[7]

"To conclude, the light of human minds is perspicuous words, but by exact definitions first snuffed, and purged from ambiguity; reason is the pace; increase of science the way; and the benefit of mankind the end. And on the contrary, metaphors and senseless and ambiguous words, are like *ignes fatui*; and reasoning upon them is wandering among innumerable absurdities; and their end, contention and sedition, or contempt."[8]

In the context of the modern epistemology, Hobbes sees language as first designative; that is, words take their meaning from what they are used to designate. And he sees it secondly as instrumental. Clear designation, fixing unambiguously the meaning of each term, is the indispensable instrument of reasoning.

The use of a word, that is, a sound or mark to designate something, is purely arbitrary. There was an alternative tradition in the Renaissance, which drew on the Kabbalah, and also earlier notions of the creation as made up of "signs", which postulated a language attuned to reality, in which each term gave insight into the object it designated. This surfaces in the legend of an Adamic language, based on the chapter in Genesis where Adam gives names to the different animals.[9] The Bible seems to be saying that the names Adam gave to things were the right names. Perhaps this was because they were really suited to the animals named. I raise this here, because as I will

6. Hobbes, *Leviathan,* 21.
7. Ibid., 22.
8. Ibid., 29–30.
9. "And out of the ground the Lord God formed every beast of the field, and every foul of the air; and brought them to Adam to see what he would call them: and whatsoever Adam called every living creature, that was the name thereof" (Genesis 2:19).

discuss in the proposed companion study, these ideas returned in the Romantic period, in the epoch of Hamann and Herder, and form the background for important themes in post-Romantic poetics and thought.

But this whole set of ideas was utterly foreign to Hobbes and the other thinkers of the view I'm dubbing HLC. The word can only be introduced to designate an idea which has arisen in the mind. Its entire meaning is given in this designation. There cannot be some excess meaning contained in the name itself. This name is purely arbitrary.

In this respect, the HLC lines up with a dominant theme of modern linguistics, articulated by Saussure. The allocation of a particular signifier to a given "signified" is quite arbitrary, or as this is frequently expressed "unmotivated". This brings us back to a very old issue, raised by Plato in his dialogue *Cratylus,* where the eponymous character lays out before Socrates the counter-Saussurean thesis that words aren't arbitrary, that their very sounds indicate what they are used to describe. Socrates seems to go along with the argument, but then turns to demolish it. I want to return later to the complex of issues invoked here.

But for the moment we can see that Hobbes is firmly on the anti-Cratylist side. The whole enterprise of reasoning (= reckoning) would be subverted by this supposed excess of meaning implicit in the name. And for the same reason, metaphors must be banned. The metaphorical expression claims to bring out something in the "target" object by referring to it in terms drawn from the "source". Just what this extra insight amounts to is very difficult to say, and if one could say it clearly it would amount to translating the metaphor into literal speech. So this, along with other tropes, and also tricks of rhetoric, has to be scrupulously avoided if language is to serve reason. We will see how strong this resistance to tropes is in the whole tradition of thinking in which the HLC figures.

For his part, Locke takes over the basic theory of mind in nature that Hobbes assumed, and also of the demands on thought.

(1). The demands on thought are: self-scrutiny, and reconstruction according to defensible principles. This requires breaking our thinking down to its atoms, and seeing how they can be responsibly connected. In book 4 of the *Essay,*[10] Locke gives the principles of careful inductive connections; of what would later be called empiricism.

---

10. John Locke, *An Essay Concerning Human Understanding,* ed. P. H. Nidditch (Oxford: Clarendon Press, 1975). References to this work will be identified with three figures, referring respectively to Part, Chapter, and paragraph.

(2). The picture of the mind in nature has it being affected by the world through perception. Ideas "are produced in us . . . by the operation of insensible particles on our senses."[11] This makes dents on the mind: in the primary reception of data the understanding is purely passive.

Thought is the working over of an inert raw material. It is both the building and its materials. The mind is like a room, containing the materials we use for building.[12] Language is part of the construction machinery.

The issue is control. We need language to build a believable picture of the world. The danger is that we get carried away by our instrument. The need is for clarity, perspicuity, to have always in mind the grounding of the word in thought. Hence definitions are crucial. There is a certain ideal of the transparency of language, its unobtrusiveness; it should just let thought be properly overviewed.

Locke brings about a certain reification of the mind, which became a crucial part of his legacy to later ages. We can see here the insertion of his theory of language within the modern epistemology, and also the same double motive which powers both of these.

The demands on thought (1) require self-examination, the turn inward to a radical reflexivity. They demand self-responsible thought, where each person checks for him/herself. Following Descartes, this can best be achieved by breaking down the input into the basic data, prior to any interpretation. The "simple idea" serves this function of the basic epistemic building block. Let's call this the "T perspective".

But at the same time, the construal (2) of the mind in nature tends to accredit the same picture. This is a mechanistic account (M), as we saw, in which the mind is passive. But this account also points to a minimum unit of impingement on the mind by the "insensible globules". Bringing the T and M perspectives together naturally leads us to identify the atomic impression of M with the basic epistemic building block of T. Mechanistically, the mind is simply the recipient of the impingement, but this passivity is what ensures in the order of thought that the basic unit of knowledge is a quite uninterpreted datum. Causal passivity is the basis of an epistemic foundation, which is prior to any working of the mind and its power to combine.

This leads to the reification of the mind, and its contents, which finds expression in the metaphor of a construction using given materials.

11. Ibid., 2.8.13; see "globules" at 4.2.11.
12. Ibid., 2.2.2, and also 2.12.1.

Locke postulates the same two main uses of language as Hobbes did: "The registering of the consequences of our thoughts", and communication with others.[13] Locke starts right off talking about God's design of man "for a sociable creature" as the reason for language. The reflections above about the relation of language and thought touch mainly the registering function, which in fact extends to the important activity of making a picture of the world. But the picture of the relation of thought to language also shapes their concept of the communicative function. The doubly motivated atomistic analysis of thought $T + M$ tends to accredit Locke's basic picture of the mind as an inner room.[14] Thoughts occur inward. Communication is a matter of translating them into an outer medium.[15]

So thought and hence language is first of all monological. Languages are of individuals first, but they are common because they converge. When I speak of "first" here, I don't mean that my language preceded common speech. I mean that in principle each person has their own language; and that the phenomenon of a common speech can be analyzed into a convergence of individual languages. That's because speech exists where words are hooked up to thought; and this hookup has to occur in thought, which means within. This leads to a "Courier" theory of communication. The outward sound is like the courier service which delivers my thoughts into your mind.

Thus Locke says that words are the "marks . . . of the ideas of the speaker."[16] They can't be marks of anything else for the meaning connection is made by and in the mind. He speaks of words as "signs" of these ideas, and as "signifying" these ideas. But nevertheless we are often too precipitate, and "in our thoughts give them secret reference to two other things": first, to ideas in the minds of others, and then we "often suppose the words to stand also for the reality of things".[17]

He returns to this point, with the affirmation of a clear anti-Cratylist position.[18] Words have meaning "by a perfect arbitrary imposition."[19] This

---

13. Hobbes, *Leviathan,* 18–19.

14. He speaks of the brain as "the mind's presence room"; Locke, *Essay,* 2.3.1.

15. Ibid., 3.1.2.

16. Ibid., 3.2.2.

17. Ibid., 3.2.4–5.

18. Ibid., 3.2.8.

19. See also ibid., 3.2.1: a word is connected to an idea by "a voluntary imposition, whereby such a word is made arbitrarily the mark of such an idea."

is intimately connected to our liberty. There is an inner connection between the rejection of meaningful order, of an order of signs in the universe, on one hand, and the self-responsible thinking by which we build our representation of the world, on the other. To do this, we have to be masters of our own lexicon. Right thinking is linked to an ideal of liberty. A common language involves something analogous to a contract. "Every man hath so inviolable a liberty to make words stand for what ideas he pleases."[20]

We are always in danger of slipping away from this understanding of our freedom, which is also a responsibility. We speak like parrots;[21] and with long and familiar use, we "are apt to suppose a natural connexion" between words (and hence ideas) which really have none.[22] We have to fight against this bewitchment. The parallel to Locke's politics is evident. The imposture of a vocabulary unratified by my reason can lead to the imposture of tyrannical political rule unratified by my consent. Locke, like Hobbes, turns his anti-Cratylism to political purpose. Only the goals are diametrically opposed in these two thinkers. For Hobbes the really important "arbitrary impositions"—those governing the politico-legal sphere, as well as religious ritual—are attributed to the sovereign; for Locke they are in the gift of the individual.

In Part 3 of his *Essay,* Locke makes the same point as Hobbes about the generality of most terms, and the great utility that this has for our thought.

Locke thus embraces the main features of the designative-instrumental view. Condillac, writing in the eighteenth century, develops a more sophisticated version of this theory. But I will just mention here two of his additions or amendments. First, he thinks of language as enabling us to focus our attention. The "instituted signs" of language make us capable of doing this. They give the subject *"empire sur son imagination."*[23] Secondly and relatedly, he has a theory about how the development of language enriches our conceptual armory. Of course, for any given coinage, there must be an idea already there which can be given a name. But since a new word can fix our attention on its object, it will often enable us to mark certain distinctions between features of the object, previously confounded because

20. See references in ibid., 3.2.8, to Augustus; and to the liberty of Adam (3.6.51).
21. Ibid., 3.2.7.
22. Ibid., 3.2.8.
23. "dominion over his imagination"; Étienne Bonnot de Condillac, *Essai sur l'Origine des Connoissances Humaines* (Paris: Vrin, 2014), 1.2.4.45–46.

they are faint. These newly distinguished phenomena in turn are named, and our thought progresses.[24]

Seen this way, linguistic meaning appears a very down-to-earth, non-mysterious thing. The wonder we might experience that there is such a thing at all, that sounds can take on meaning—something we might experience, for instance, if we repeat a single word over and over again, and feel it losing its sense—this wonder, which may have been part of the motivation behind more ontically ambitious theories of language, dissipates. First, there is no meaning as such, there is just the meaning of sound X for subject(s) A, B, C, and so on. We take a firmly anti-Cratylist position; meanings are all arbitrary; they are set up by and for certain people. In Saussure's terms, they are all "unmotivated": nothing in this sign calls for it to have this rather than that meaning. All linguistic signs are "instituted" (Condillac's expression) at some point. They are human creations and can be altered by humans.

Second, as noted above, we can see a certain analogy to contract theories of political societies, which grew at the same time, and at the hands of some of the same authors. Instead of seeing the order of the polity as reflecting that of the cosmos, so that the king is not just a particular individual who has been thrust into an important role, but he is rather the contemporary embodiment of the King (following the theory of the King's Two Bodies[25]), we understand this order to have been decided on by individuals in historic time who contracted with each other to set it up, and could contract again to alter it. The order is demystified; and, in a somewhat analogous way, so are the meanings of the language we speak.

2

We can see the main features of the designative-instrumental view of language: its interweaving with the modern epistemology which comes down to us from Descartes and Locke; its tendency to reify the mind (grounded in the two facets of that epistemology: a foundationalist justification of thought, and a mechanist theory of perception); its voluntarism ("arbitrary imposition"); its two kinds of atomism: one kind applies to the objects of thought, ideas which need to be combined; the other to the subjects of

24. Ibid., 1.2.5–6.
25. See Ernst Hartwig Kantorowicz, *The King's Two Bodies: A Study in Mediaeval Political Theology* (Princeton, NJ: Princeton University Press, 1957).

thought: individuals; and finally its constitutional anti-Cratylism, which carries with it a phobia against tropes of all kinds.

But so what? Who's interested in this view which is plainly superseded in our time? We just have to review a theory like Locke's with the eye of a post-Fregean reader of philosophy to see it as quaint and unsophisticated to an almost unbelievable degree. Frege has made a profound transformation in our thought. Even if he didn't do this single-handed, his work has become associated with changes which have rendered much of the HLC obsolete.

This is undoubtedly true. But I will try to maintain that a great deal has carried over from the classical HLC into the mainstream of post-Fregean analytic philosophy—or at least a very broad stream of modern philosophy which claims Fregean ancestry. My claim is that this continuing legacy is in many respects deeply at variance with the truth. The crucial error, then and now, is closely related to the crucial error underlying modern epistemology itself.

The double motivation I identified earlier underlies this epistemology, and makes it look better than it is. On one hand, there is a methodology for ferreting out error, and building more reliable conclusions, which involves holding back on inferences, even canceling some that have been too hastily made, in order to identify the basic evidence. This is what underlay Descartes's rules for the direction of the mind. In a later work, the *Discours de la Méthode,* he advises us to divide up our problems "into as many parts as possible and as was required in order to better to resolve them" [*en autant de parcelles qu'ils se pourrait et qu'il seroit requis pour les mieux résoudre*].[26] This was the norm of thinking (T). To this was joined a causal story about how ideas come into the mind: M. The two together made the epistemology look unattackable.

The error was to infer from the value of this methodology in lots of cases to its universal applicability, and indeed, to infer that in one sense this is how the mind always worked, viz., building an overall picture from basic evidence, even though sometimes it did so hastily and without adequate attention. Hence the corrective value of the methodology. Whereas the real way the human mind-in-the-world functioned was very different, and in its ontogenetically earliest forms were quite irreducible to an atomist account. But we can learn in certain contexts that permit of it to apply this

26. René Descartes, *Discourse on Method and Meditations on First Philosophy,* trans. Donald A. Cress, 4th ed. (Indianapolis: Hackett, 1998), 11; Descartes, "Discours de la Méthode," part 2, in *Œuvres de Descartes,* ed. Charles Adam and Paul Tannery (Paris: Vrin, 1973).

method with very good effect. For example, in the court of law we try to force the witnesses to say what they saw, to peel off the layer of overhasty inference which may send the innocent man to jail. In other words, epistemological thinking takes an advanced and locally appropriate method as providing the key to how the mind always works, even though in practice our fallible minds often ignore the strictures of that method. Put another way, it involves reading this method into the very ontology of the mind.

I will claim that the HLC, in common with much post-Fregean philosophy, makes a similar error. It takes a late realization of disciplined human thought, reasoning in a regimented vocabulary of empirical descriptive terms and patterns of inference, for an indication of how language in general works, or at least descriptive language. It ontologizes an advanced method, and in this flies in the face of much which we have come to know about language and its ontogenesis in the human agent.

3

This is the justification for dragging all that old stuff up again. In order to see what survives of it, let us look at what Frege overturned.

First, (1) "validity" [*Geltung*]: you can't describe the relation between word and object just as another factual correlation or causal link. In order to do justice to it, you have to enrich your account with normative terms. The proper relation between 'chair' and chairs is something like: 'chair' is the correct term to describe chairs. You have to introduce a normative dimension to characterize speech. There is always some issue of getting it right or getting it wrong.

This is Frege's contribution to the battle against "psychologism", which others also waged at the time: for instance, Husserl, Russell, and others. These thinkers finally overthrew the reductive idea which Mill had espoused, that the laws of logic could be explained by the laws of psychology. That $2 + 2$ can't $= 5$ has nothing to do with some supposed psychological impossibility of thinking "$2 + 2 = 5$".[27] This puts paid to what I called the reification of thought by Locke.[28]

27. Mill held that logic "is not a science distinct from, and co-ordinate with Psychology. So far as it is a science at all, it is a part, or branch of Psychology." John Stuart Mill, *An Examination of Sir William Hamilton's Philosophy,* quoted in Hans Sluga, *Gottlob Frege* (London: Routledge and Kegan Paul, 1980), 26.

28. This is in fact another facet of the fundamental insight of Frege with which I began Chapter 1. "*Besonnenheit*" ("reflection" or "being in the linguistic dimension") means that our use

The second point (2) is really the first from another angle. Michael Dummett describes this Fregean contribution as the "extrusion" of thought from the mind.[29] Thinking, this normative activity, has to be seen as a game played among many players. The properties of a move in the game can be described independently of the particular event of this move being made by player X at time T. If I shoot the ball into the end zone, we will be called offside. This is quite independent of the features of the individual act. The coach will want to know why: was I distracted? Too worked up? And so on. But all these are irrelevant to the normative properties of the move. Similarly from proposition p you can infer q; and this is so quite independently of what a speaker might have had in mind when he uttered p. As Dummett puts it on another occasion: "the study of thought is to be sharply distinguished from the study of the psychological process of thinking."[30]

Obviously, these first two points are facets of the same idea. If you see thinking as a many-person language game (or group of such games), then you take it out of individual psychology into the public realm; and by the same token, you see it as governed by rules which cannot be reduced to psychological laws.

(3). Sense/reference: 'chair' rightly applies to chairs. It applies for a reason. You can articulate this, getting the "connotation" of the word. But 'furniture' also applies to chairs. It also applies for a reason, but the reason is not the same; there is a different connotation, but some of the same extension. This chair is a piece of furniture. So we have the same object here, and two words, with two meanings. You can't just define meaning in terms of the designatum, of the objects. You need a three-term relation. A word applies to something in virtue of its meaning. You can make a reference to something with it, but you make this through its sense. The sense is the "route" you take to get to it. You can get to the same object through more than one route. Saussure will talk of signifier/signified; or we can speak of a sign and its referent. The straight designative theory, where the meaning of the word = associated thing (or idea), that is, a simple two-place relation, becomes impossible.

---

of words responds to a sense that they are the "right words"; the utterance cannot just be causally explained as what the present stimulus triggers. An issue of "validity" [*Geltung*] arises.

29. Michael Dummett, *Origins of Analytic Philosophy* (Cambridge, MA: Harvard University Press, 1996), 129.

30. Michael Dummett, *Truth and Other Enigmas* (Cambridge, MA: Harvard University Press, 1978), 458.

To recap (1–3), a sense is not the same as an idea. A sense is not a thing, a bit of the world, even a bit of the psyche. It is a normative reality. A word may conjure up all sorts of things in your mind—the current, everyday language sense of 'connotation'—but these have nothing to do with its sense. This is something objective; in fact public, shared.

(4). Primacy of the sentence: language is essentially making judgments, or asking questions, giving commands. We can't understand it as simply combining words, because a judgment is a very particular way of combining, as is asking questions or giving commands. So we can't understand a language as consisting first of a lot of terms (concepts), and then of judgments; as though we could learn the first before the second. The old logic—concept, judgment, reasoning—classified things mistakenly. In fact judging is primary; concepts are isolated bits of judgment. A word only has a meaning (reference) in the context of a sentence. We see the important influence of Kant here.

(5). Reference/predication: the sentence is not just any old combination; it has a peculiar inner structure, with differentiated functions. We get something through a reference, and then we predicate something of it. A difference of role distinguishes concept and object; or function and argument, to use the Fregean terms; Frege deserts the old logical description of the proposition as S is P. The function/argument analysis allows for many-placed predicates.

(6). Sense/force: even a reference/predication combination is not yet an assertion. As a matter of fact, such a combination can be taken up into an assertion, but also into a question, or a command. So we have to distinguish the level of force.[31]

We can see in Locke's *Essay* that he could never come to grips with this problem, with what an act of assertion consisted in. In chapter 7, on "particles", he tries to come to grips with terms like 'is', in sentences like "the house is red". Each word means what it designates. We can grasp what "house" and "red" designate, but what about "is"? Certainly it doesn't describe an extra feature of the red house. So its meaning must be an action of the mind. But he still can't say what distinguishes an affirmative sentence from a simple list: "house, red", or even "house, act of the mind, red". Frege's points (4)–(6) take us definitively beyond this muddle.

31. I made reference to this in Chapter 3.

Alongside Frege's revolutionary work, there was a vast development in logic, and thus in the ways in which sentences can be related to each other, or derived from each other. Frege also contributed to this in a very significant way, most especially in his developing a logic of quantification. He helped show how the inner constitution of a sentence contributes to its logical relations to other sentences. What emerged from all this was a greater appreciation of the combinatorial nature of language, how out of a given set of elements, for example referring expressions and predicates, a wide range of different sentences can be formed, some of them never uttered, or even imagined before.

(7). This combinatorial understanding of language reminds us of Humboldt's famous saying that in language we make of finite means an infinite use.[32] As I argued above in Chapter 1, this has been too simply and reductively understood as the thesis that, with a finite vocabulary, an infinite number of sentences can be generated. Noam Chomsky took up this idea, enriching it with the notion of a recursive application of rules: he said that she said that they said, and so on.

I will return later to the wider (and deeper) meaning of Humboldt's dictum, but for the moment, we need just remark that for a whole host of reasons, twentieth-century thinkers had a much greater appreciation of the systematic character of a language, rather than seeing it simply as an assemblage of words. This included a sense of its combinatorial and hence productive nature; but it also included an interest in rules of inference, and hence in bodies of propositions linked by these, as also in more exact definitions of certain expressions, in terms of what they entail. Obviously Frege made a great contribution to this domain. But the more general change of climate toward a greater recognition of system and linkages and rules is harder to trace. It undoubtedly owes something to Humboldt, and his image of language as a web, but it also shows the influence of Saussure who dethroned the linkage word-thing in favor of the alignment of sound differences (signifiers) with distinctions among meanings (signifieds). This line of thinking was continued and developed through the Prague school,

---

32. "[Language] must therefore make infinite employment of finite means." Wilhelm von Humboldt, *On Language: The Diversity of Human Language-Structure and Its Influence on the Mental Development of Mankind*, trans. Peter Heath (Cambridge: Cambridge University Press, 1988), 91 [*Sie [language] muß daher von endlichen Mittel einen unendlichen Gebrauch machen*]; Humboldt, *Schriften zur Sprache* (Stuttgart: Raclam, 1973), 96.

through Troubetzkoy and Jakobson. And we should also add the contribution of Benveniste.

These latter developments are not specifically Fregean. As a matter of fact, they owe a lot to what I consider as the rival "HHH" theory. But they are part of the general climate of our time, and they have been incorporated into philosophical thinking, including that self-identified as "post-Fregean". The systematicity of linguistic coding has become an important explicandum for this philosophy, which in itself constitutes a very important advance in our thinking about language, as I argued in Chapter 3.

4

After all this revolutionary change, what remains of the thrust of the HLC? As a matter of fact, a significant amount. First, the post-Fregean successors of the HLC are still immersed in various ways in the modern epistemology which stems from Descartes. Second, they are actuated by some of the same epistemological goals, to define a form of thinking which will procure reliable knowledge, and for them the paradigm for this is modern natural science, although they also are willing to include bits of our everyday knowledge of the world which can meet their standards. Third, while in some ways they have escaped atomism, in others they have not, as I hope to show. Fourth, they remain staunchly anti-Cratylist, and tropophobe (or else they entertain a reductive account of tropes). And finally, all these are sustained by a Cartesian-type error, that of ontologizing what seems to them a good method (and is, indeed, for some purposes). That is, they take a late-achieved, regimented language of accurate description and inference as the key to language in general, and that in the teeth of the twentieth-century philosopher who most volubly and convincingly denounced this erection of one language game into the paradigm for all, Ludwig Wittgenstein.

Let's take the second trait first, the epistemological goals of much post-Frege analytic philosophy. How does language serve to acquire reliable knowledge, and how does it sometimes deviate from this path so as to create mere simulacra, statements that claim to be true but are actually confused, or empty, or merely apparent assertions? This was an obvious concern of the Vienna positivists, and powered their attempt to denounce and extirpate "metaphysics". But in less obvious and perhaps virulent forms it still survives. And this is in a direct line of descent from the thinkers of the

HLC. Their stress on clear and distinct definitions of simple ideas, which powered their anti-Cratylism, arose from their concern with the scientific reliability of the outlook which emerged in the combination of these ideas.

But there is now a second range of questions which has become crucial in the post-Fregean world. This concerns the origin and development of language, and hence of necessity touches on the evolution of humanity from out of the class of primates. This origin question arose in the eighteenth century, and Condillac famously responded to it with his account of the birth of language, which as we saw provoked Herder's response. Condillac's account was in the spirit of the whole HLC tradition, one which sees language as serving certain definite purposes, in Hobbes's version, "registering" our thoughts, and communicating them. These enable us to do much more effectively what prelinguistic hominids were presumably already doing, like getting to know their environment, and communicating and coordinating action with their fellows.

I called this in Chapter 1 an "enframing" account, because the new capacities which language enables fit within an already existing frame of ecological action. But with the rise of the HHH we see a quite different view. Herder's account of language origin in terms of *Besonnenheit*[33] postulates that language transforms our world. I am using 'world' in a Heidegger-derived sense to designate our surroundings in their significance for us. New meanings arise in the new space of questions which language opens. Human ecological action has to deal with a whole range of new questions, on top of those we share with other animals. The step to language involves far more than providing more effective means to the perennial ends of survival, prosperity, effective combination, avoidance of mutual destruction.

But these supposedly new ends and new meanings are hard to grasp in the no-nonsense terminology of instrumental efficacy that Hobbes and Locke offer us. They seem strange and "mysterious", hard to get a handle on, and threaten to involve us in moral and aesthetic issues where what should prevail are the canons of science.

Thus the streams that follow the HLC into our post-Fregean philosophical context want to represent linguistic meaning as something down-to-earth, and nonmysterious. What distinguishes us from animals is not some creative power, but rather the ability to describe things, to characterize

---

33. See note 28.

states of affairs; let's call this "depictive" power. This power can then be the basis of a number of other capacities; through depiction, we can accumulate knowledge of the world, that is, of ourselves and our surroundings. This can eventually take the form of 1) science, formally constituted bodies of established knowledge. And it can also be used in 2) deliberating what we should do. We can depict the state of affairs we want to realize, and then use our depictions of causal relations to determine how we can bring this about. Thirdly, knowledge and deliberation can be carried out not just by individuals, but collectively, because language enables us to 3) communicate and expand knowledge and deliberate together.

How then do we acquire language and its depictive power? In the HLC perspective, this seemed relatively simple. It sufficed that we come to attach certain words to certain objects. This, of course, will be an inner mental operation, since we are only aware of the objects surrounding us because they arouse ideas in the mind. But by attaching a word to an idea, I become capable of enjoying the fruits of the depictive power—universality and control, as just described—and by coming to agreement with others on our words, I can benefit from all the advantages of collective effort.

But the glaring inadequacies of the HLC were dealt with convincingly in what we might call the "Frege revolution", which has been the basis for much twentieth-century analytic philosophy. One crucial contribution of Frege, as we have seen, was to take the issue of meaning out of the realm of intramental psychology and into that of public, shared normativity. Frege helped put an end to "psychologism". But another of his crucial contributions was to make sentence meaning central. It was not something that could be derived from the meanings of individual words. On the contrary, "only in the context of a proposition [sentence] has a name meaning" [*nur im Zusammenhang eines Satzes hat ein Wort Bedeutung*].[34] Frege thus helped overcome the double atomism of the earlier theory, that of linguistic meanings, and that of the individual subject. Whether this overcoming was thoroughgoing enough, we will have to determine later.

In Frege's view, a sentence combines a subject expression with a predicate expression, usually to make an assertion. The subject expression picks out an object, and the predicate expression attributes a property to that object. On the basis of this insight, we can see that questions and com-

---

34. Ludwig Wittgenstein, *Tractus Logico-Philosophicus,* trans. C. K. Ogden (New York: Harcourt, Brace, 1922), 3.3.

mands also involve similar combinations of reference and attribution, although these are put to different ends than assertion. What is crucial in all these cases is the "propositional content", consisting of object referred to and attribution (let's call these "depictive combinations").

The Frege revolution showed how linguistic meaning could never be explained simply by focusing on the meanings of individual words, in the sense of the things these words were used to talk about. Rather what is crucial is the meaning of depictive combinations, and then the speech acts we accomplish by means of them, for instance, assertion, question-asking, order-giving. In other words, linguistic meaning has to be understood in the context of certain activities, of which the building of depictive combinations was seen as the most crucial, but which extended to other things "we do with words". Just how far this context of activities extends without which linguistic meaning as we know it is incomprehensible, and what actions it includes, remains one of the big issues of twentieth-century philosophy, which is still open today. Wittgenstein played an important role here, in arguing that the essential context reaches much farther than was recognized in the mainstream philosophical tradition. I shall return to that crucial issue shortly.

But meanwhile we can see how the original HLC ambition to give a "modest", mystery-free account of language, considered as consisting primarily in its depictive power, got a new lease on life, once it had undergone the Frege revolution. For Frege, in his efforts to give an account of mathematics, which would also serve for descriptive language, developed the resources of logic to a considerable degree; most notably in introducing quantification. The ambition to achieve a transparent and sober account of depictive power could be usefully redefined. Instead of seeing the meanings of given words or expressions as the objects they designate, we can define them as the role they are ready to play in depictive combinations. These can in turn be used to make different kinds of speech act, for instance assertion, question, order.

This classification of acts puts us already in the "pragmatic" dimension, as against that of pure semantic meaning. I mean by this the dimension in which language serves to get things done, and/or to alter our relations with our interlocutors. If I give you an order, I do something which might easily eventuate in your doing something for me; and in any case, I modify our relationship; because you now have either to do what I say or you risk creating some strain in our relationship (if I'm an irascible sergeant and you're a private, this might be a considerable understatement). A question arises, how far we need to go in this dimension in order to provide the essential context for the exercise of the depictive power of speech. For instance, I may utter the assertions: "the train is leaving in five minutes"; or "that bull looks as though he is about to charge"; while I and my interlocutors both understand these as speech acts of warning. I'm telling you in effect: "you'd better rush to get on board", or "for God's sake, get out of his way!"

A standard classification arose in the mid-twentieth century, thanks to the work of Austin and Searle, which distinguished between levels of speech acts: on one level, there is the locutionary act, what I actually attribute to what, or otherwise put, what depictive combination, I put forward; on a second level, is the illocutionary act, what move I am making in the exchange with my interlocutors; am I asserting something, asking a question?, and so on. On the third level is the perlocutionary act. When the Ministry of External Affairs informs the ambassador of Ablesonia that our government "takes a very serious view of the arrest of some of our citizens within their territory", this is an assertion about our attitudes, but it also trails a (vague) threat; and it is meant to produce a result (releasing or properly charging our unfortunate compatriots). This eventual release is the perlocutionary effect sought. How this classification works in detail is not exempt from controversy; and what levels of the act are relevant to depictive meaning involves the big issues about context which I want to come back to later.

But for the moment, let's look at another dimension of the Frege revolution which gave theories of depictive power a great new field of expansion. The resources of Fregean logic, including truth-functionality and quantification, make it possible to organize a host of possible sayables as derivations from more basic assertions. In this way, the products of our depictive power can be organized, one might say "regimented", in relation to more basic depictions. This defined what Robert Brandom refers to as "the classical program of semantic analysis". The characteristic attempt is to show "whether, and in what way, one can make sense of the meanings expressed by *one* kind of locution in terms of the meanings expressed by *another* kind of locution."[35] Brandom sees this concern as lying at the heart

35. Robert Brandom, *Between Saying and Doing: Towards an Analytic Pragmatism* (Oxford: Oxford University Press, 2008), 1.

of analytical philosophy: "I think of analytic philosophy as having at its center a concern with semantic relations between what I will call 'vocabularies'. Its characteristic form of question is whether, and in what way, one can make sense of the meanings expressed by *one* kind of locution in terms of the meanings expressed by *another* kind of locution."[36]

This opened a big field for the antimetaphysical drive of twentieth-century positivists and others who felt themselves to be the heirs of classical empiricism, and hence of the HLC. Brandom described what he calls "the classical project of philosophical analysis as having the task of exhibiting what is expressed semantically by one vocabulary (one sort of meaning) as the logical elaboration of what is expressed by another."[37]

Now traditionally, these projects were driven by metaphysical (sometimes expressed as antimetaphysical) suspicion. Certain supposed realities were illusory or fraudulent, those postulated by religions for instance; or goods or values, like those of ethics or aesthetics, that claimed an ontological grounding (as against those which were seen as subjectively projected). But sometimes the suspect entities were condemned as merely superfluous posits, without warrant in reality, such as the self (Hume), or natural necessity (again Hume), or "society" and other such terms for collectivities (methodological individualists [and also Margaret Thatcher]).

Brandom describes the two most widespread such projects of reduction, empiricism and naturalism.

What is distinctive of empiricism and naturalism, considered abstractly, is that they each see some one vocabulary (or vocabulary-kind) as uniquely privileged with respect to all other vocabularies. Empiricism takes its favored vocabulary (whether it be phenomenal, secondary-quality, or observational) to be *epistemologically* privileged relative to all the rest. In what I think of as its most sophisticated forms, the privilege is understood more fundamentally to be *semantic,* and only derivatively and consequentially epistemological. Naturalism takes its favored vocabulary (whether it be that of fundamental physics, the special sciences, or just descriptive) to be *ontologically* privileged relative to all the rest. In both cases, what motivates and gives

36. Ibid., 1.
37. Ibid., 31.

weight and significance to the question of whether, to what extent, and how a given target vocabulary can be logically or algorithmically elaborated from the favored base vocabulary is the philosophical argument for epistemologically, semantically, or ontologically privileging the base vocabulary. These are arguments to the effect that everything that can be known, or thought, every fact, must in principle be expressible in the base vocabulary in question. It is in this sense (epistemological, semantic, or ontological) a *universal* vocabulary. What it *cannot* express is fatally defective: unknowable, unintelligible, or unreal. One clear thing to mean by "metaphysics" is the making of claims of this sort about the universal expressive power of some vocabulary.[38]

The stigmatized entities could be shown to deserve exclusion, either by being shown to be unintelligible in relation to the base vocabulary (the objects mentioned in meaningless "metaphysical" statements), or else by our showing that everything useful which could be said in statements mentioning them could be said perfectly adequately in the terms of the base vocabulary (all statements about society translated into statements about individuals, all statements mentioning material objects translated into statements about sense data, and so on). These putative objects could thus be eliminated without loss.

But sometimes the object of relating base to target was the positive one of saving some suspect entities which might otherwise be relegated to outer darkness. Thus Hume's suspicion of natural necessity, something beyond the mere correlation he wanted to reduce it to, could be answered by showing that we can make perfect sense of it. This is a "saving" derivation that Kant claimed to accomplish; and Brandom does something analogous in this book.[39]

Another exercise which continued the basic thrust of the HLC consisted of attempts to characterize the kind of capacity which knowing a language consists of by means of an axiomatic theory. Donald Davidson and Michael Dummett are prominent philosophers in this field. The intuition behind this enterprise was articulated, among others, by Humboldt. Whoever knows a language presumably at any given moment commands a finite (if large) vocabulary; but they are capable of generating an indefinite

38. Ibid., 219.
39. Ibid., chapter 4.

number of sentences, including some never before pronounced. This un-limited productivity of language has been taken very seriously in the twen-tieth century. Chomsky invokes it as the background of his theory of syntactic forms, which are allegedly universal among human beings.[40]

Now these theories continue the thrust of the HLC once it is put through a Fregean turn. The meanings of words and part expressions are given now by the axiomatic semantic contribution they make to the sentences they are part of. But this contribution is assessed extensionally. That is, we are looking for their contribution to sentences defined by their truth condi-tions. There is no attempt to grasp the particular way in which a given lan-guage discloses the things it is used to describe. Thus I understand what you say when I come to have a correct theory which enables me to offer truth conditions for any sentence you utter. I need not be interested in any difference between our two languages in the ways in which they frame or disclose our worlds. It suffices that I can predict the truth conditions of your sentences in my own terms. The idea is that any difference in the sense of our expressions which manage to hit the same referent will come to light after repeated exposure to your language. If you refer to Venus as "the morning star", and I refer to it as "the evening star", the semantic differ-ences will be evident from other expressions where you speak about eve-ning and morning. What doesn't so come to light can be ignored.

Now this extensionalist semantics reedits the attempt of the HLC to de-fine meaning in terms of object designated, turning away from the issue of how language discloses the world. But the attempt has been transposed into a much more sophisticated key thanks to the Fregean revolution.

Another, more extreme, reflection of objectivist semantics is evident among those theorists who were interested in demonstrating that, for in-stance, chimpanzees can master "language" up to a certain level. They never considered that chimps' use of signs to request something, or to solve a problem where this achievement was rewarded, might be different in its nature from parallel human behavior. Language was understood in both cases as the use of signs to get what the agent wanted. The attempt was to teach chimps signs, one after the other, and build up to language unit by unit, hoping to reach a combinatorial stage where the animal can put together signs of the order: 'Kanzi', 'want', and 'banana' to express the request for a banana.

---

40. See Noam Chomsky, *Aspects of the Theory of Syntax* (Cambridge, MA: MIT Press, 1965).

The achievement of the apes (particularly bonobos) was sometimes very impressive, and undoubtedly shows a high intelligence, but the differences with human language were ignored. Any code which can be introduced one sign at a time has to be different from language as understood by Saussure, where what is crucial is differences and not individual linkages.

In all the different ways just enumerated, the basic focus of the HLC on language as objective depictive power continues among many analytic philosophers even after the Frege revolution.

5

The continuity of much post-Fregean thought with the HLC should be evident. The same concern for reliable knowledge, free of mystery, actuates both; as also the belief in a nonmysterious depictive power by a semantic theory which relates our verbal descriptions to objects which are evident to all in the world. This relation can either be understood as fixed for each word individually (HLC), or else as relating depictive combinations (propositional contents) to their truth conditions in the world (post-Fregean variant). Of course, in the latter case, mastering a language is not just memorizing vocabulary; it is knowing how to deploy a complex combinatorial system. This will include being able to make one-on-one connections: knowing that 'cat' is used to refer to that particular mammal, and that 'furry' is that sort of property. But it will go way beyond that, because we will have to make and understand rather different combinations: for example, "that cat is furry"; "is that cat furry?"; "if that cat is furry, then it can't be Aunt Mabel's"; and so on. The particular links might be thought of as the "axioms" of a combinatorial theory; and the "theorems" might take the form: ' "the cat is furry": is true if and only if the cat is furry.'

Now this combinatorial theory could be given two important philosophical applications, as we have seen. It can be used (a) in the way Brandom describes, for what one might call "hygienic" purposes, to show that everything we want to say can be said using a certain vocabulary, which from one or other normative standpoint (objectivist, scientific, nonreligious, morally neutral, etc.) is considered acceptable. This can be done with the aim of stigmatizing and altogether marginalizing the terms and assertions that don't fit the norm. Or it can be applied in a more relaxed way, to show, for instance, that the normatively inadequate assertions have their own legitimate, but quite different uses, which must be kept separate from the ones that our regimented theory allows. (Or it may be hard to judge which of these aims is operative; think of the Vienna positivists classing metaphysics as a species of "poetry".)

Or, assuming the success of the above enterprise, we can (b) try to work out a theory of meaning, in the sense made famous by Davidson. Or at least we might put forward the hypothesis that such a theory could be worked out. This theory would allegedly match or mirror the competence that a normal speaker of the language possesses. It would explain why, from the familiarity of certain axioms, such as the examples above concerning 'cat' and 'furry', the competent possessor of English could make and understand a whole range of different utterances in different circumstances, among them the sample utterances above.

A deeper issue, whose outcome rides on both these claims, is the explanatory one I raised at the beginning of the previous section: what is the place of language in human life? Does it just expand our means? Or does it also transform our ends? If the latter, how can we understand this transformation? Can an "enframing" account suffice to make sense of what language brings? This is the crucial range of issues raised by the HHH.

So what is wrong with these enterprises? With the "hygienic" one (a), in principle nothing. We indeed have (or at least hope we have) something like a regimented vocabulary, and rigorous modes of combination, in the case of natural science, which meet high standards of exact verification, and certainly eschew certain kinds of descriptions (e.g., those conveying moral and human meanings) which would compromise these standards. If the aim is to delineate a specialized vocabulary, this can certainly be both possible and highly useful in certain circumstances, as the example of specialized sciences shows. The whole issue reposes in how we view the areas that lie outside the regimented zone. If our aim is, like the Vienna positivists, to show that what lies outside cannot consist in real depictions, that assertions beyond the pale have no truth-value, then big questions arise.

Those who want to push back against such (to them) outrageous claims could either (i) try to show that some of the incriminated statements (metaphysical, or moral, or aesthetic) have perfectly good validity conditions, and thus are as "objective" as the acceptable assertions within the regimented system. Or (ii) they might agree that other uses are not depictive, but claim that language as it really is in nature is not restricted to the depictive function. Wittgenstein, particularly in his *Philosophical*

Investigations, is understood to have argued something of the sort. Our "mental cramps" come from assuming too quickly that statements of the same logical form must depict things of the same form. "I'm in pain" must be construed like "the cat is on the mat", as having the form "F(a)". We fail to see that the uses of language are much more various, and we get into a muddle when we fail to take account of this.

Or we might go farther, and claim not just that there are valid assertions which fail to meet the regimented norm (i); and not just that there are nondepictive uses of language which may misleadingly be classed as depictive (ii), but also go on to say (iii) that these two kinds of nonstandard uses are inseparable from the language capacity itself. That is, that the standard depictions wouldn't be possible for a being who didn't have the nonstandard uses (either extranormative depictions or nondepictions) in its repertoire.

Now I would like to make this maximal claim (iii). So I'm looking for a way in which the question can be framed. Brandom perhaps obliges in his recent book quoted above. Brandom is a moderate. He wants to discontinue the stigmatizing bent of the tradition. He claims that there is a point in attempting to relate base to target vocabularies, even if one is ready to abandon the hope of totally circumscribing in this operation the scope of the (permissibly) sayable. One can try to establish such linkages, because both success in some cases and failure in others will reveal something about our different vocabularies and their relations. We can have "Metaphysical discrimination without denigration."[41] But the successful cases are particularly important, because the relation between base and target can be made particularly definite and perspicuous.[42] And there is also another motive. "The Metaphysician aims to *construct* a *technical, artificial* vocabulary with that same expressive power [sc., in which "everything can be said"]. Why? The greater control that regimentation gives vocabularies whose basic semantics is stipulated—in some other vocabulary (no escaping the need for hermeneutic understanding)—and the rest of whose semantics is computed algorithmically."[43]

Now in spite of certain expressions of suspicion, reminiscent of a certain stigmatizing naturalism, in other works by Brandom (e.g., language not mysterious), I want to take him at his word, and enter some remarks

---

41. Brandom, *Saying and Doing,* 229.
42. Ibid., 213.
43. Ibid., 227.

in the spirit of a friendly amendment. These remarks will deal with the possible limitations of the pragmatist semantics he espouses; which limitations would be very revelatory about the nature of language and its place in human life.

Brandom introduces a very useful concept, which should provide the framework for this discussion: an "autonomous discursive practice (ADP), in the sense of a language game one could play though one played no other, or a set of discursive abilities one could have though one had no other specifically discursive abilities."[44] Brandom thinks that any practice worthy of the name would have to include the capacity to make assertions—and derivatively, ask questions and give commands. (He thinks that Wittgenstein's imagined language in para. 2 of the *Philosophical Investigations* doesn't qualify).

Now I don't want to challenge this restriction of an ADP; perhaps it is unimaginable that there could be one which didn't allow for assertions. But I want to pick up on the restrictive clause: a language game one could play *though one played no other*. What I want to highlight is whether we could have the assertion game with its commitments and entitlements without also exhibiting other linguistic or paralinguistic abilities. The question is: how self-sufficient can this game be?

This is one issue, which relates particularly to (a) (the "hygienic" project). There is another which challenges (b) (the theory of meaning project). It raises overlapping questions, but is differently framed. The overlap is clear, because a theory of meaning which really mapped the competence of a live speaker of any language would have to be able to derive all the depictions and nondepictive uses which are inseparable from this language competence. Now if some form of thesis (iii) is true, and the essential conditions for the normatively defined range of depictions include other uses, then a valid theory of meaning would have to be able to derive these uses. So one way to test whether a certain set of regimented normative uses is self-sufficient would be to see whether the corresponding theory of meaning could generate all the indispensable uses as well as the core ones.

How do you test this? This is indeed, a problem, because no one has yet generated a real live theory of meaning; all we have are general principles on which it might be developed. But we might reason with Davidson that, given a theory which really matched the competence of a speaker, and where

44. Ibid., 41.

this competence was expressed in terms of his/her recognizing extensional truth conditions for all utterances he/she could make or understand, then it ought to be possible for someone to pick up the language by "radical interpretation".

This concept, based on the Quinean notion of "radical translation", designates a process whereby I pick up the language of a speaker whose language is initially totally unknown to me, without the help of any "crib" or translation manual. Such learnings from scratch have occurred in human history, by explorers, missionaries, and refugees. But this doesn't prove that Davidson's notion of what learning involves is correct.

The notion that learning a language is learning how to generate extensional truth conditions for its depictive combinations continues the HLC bent of a "modest", nonmysterious notion of language meaning, based on pairing expressions with objective states of affairs. What this theory excludes as part of what you have to know/understand to speak a language includes at least two things: (A) a grasp of the Cratylist dimension, if any, of expressions of the language, that is, the way in which they portray the nature of their object; and (B) a grasp of whatever "thick" cultural meanings, concerning for instance, rites, social relations, collective actions, hierarchical relations, modes of purity and impurity, and so on (again, if any) turn out to be essential to grasp the expressions which pertain to these ranges. To the extent that understanding these is essential to grasping a given language (or some of its crucial uses), and perhaps is even essential to understanding what the truth conditions of certain depictive combinations are, it will not be true that understanding a language can be defined purely in terms of generating extensional truth conditions.

But it should be possible to see whether extras like (A) and (B) can be dispensed with, or whether learning them is a condition of knowing how to speak/understand a language. I will turn to this question first. Then I will double back to the Brandomian issue of the scope of an ADP which includes depiction. The answer to the theory of meaning question will help in this further enquiry, but there are also extra considerations which will have to be invoked here. The discussion of both of these questions will then, I hope, enable us to cast light on issue (C), concerning the place of language in human life.

5

The Figuring Dimension
of Language

1

I have been arguing that there is a continuity in theorizing about language between the early modern HLC and much mainstream analytical post-Fregean thinking. But this theorizing, from the beginning and still today, has a double thrust. On one hand, there is an attempt to explain how language arises, and how it works, what capacities are central to our language use. On the other, strong norms are proposed about legitimate use. Hobbes and Locke preach to us about the need for careful definitions, and the dangers of metaphors and tropes. And Robert Brandom has described the prophylactic purposes to which various "regimentations" have been put, stigmatizing various irresponsible, "metaphysical" pseudostatements. An explanatory-descriptive goal is pursued along with a normative goal.

Thus, on the normative side, we see two great imperious demands made by HLC thinkers: (1) each term of our language must be carefully introduced by a clear definition, and we must stick to this definition in all subsequent uses of the term (unless we explicitly revise it); and (2) we must stay away from metaphors and tropes in general in our reasoning with the terms so introduced.

But this advice seems to flow quite naturally from the descriptive theory. Ideas occur in the mind, either through the impingement of the world through perception, as Locke thought, or through the mind's closer scrutiny of existing ideas which may bring to light distinctions hitherto unnoticed (this was stressed by Condillac). We then attach words to some of these. This enables us to build a picture of the world through combination and inference, particularly through the efficacy of ideas designating classes of things. The two main points of this naming are that it permits such reasoning and combination, and that it makes possible communication with others (and hence also collaborative building of our world picture).

If that is what is going on, then obviously the two norms are justified. There is no point in switching in midreasoning the idea attached to a name (violating [1]). As to (2), using metaphors or tropes involves referring to A through B (or identifying A and B—I will expand on this point below), which clearly constitutes a violation of (1), and also renders inferences either false or at best uncertain (does what follows from B also follow from A?).

The explanatory account and the normative advice come close together here, since what violates the two commands constitutes such aberrant uses of language.

Or to take (2) from another angle, metaphorical expressions serve not only to designate their referents, but they also characterize them in a certain way. "The night folded around us like a mantle" tries to say something about what this going out into darkness was like. It portrays the experience, gives a semi-icon of it. I want to introduce the verb "figure", used transitively, for this kind of portrayal. Now the nature of language for the HLC is that words are connected to ideas "by a perfectly arbitrary imposition". A figuring, by contrast, is not arbitrary; we grasp it, and often approve it, because it fits. So there is something abnormal about the predicate attributed to "night" in the above expression. It smacks of those (to the HLC) aberrant theories, derived from the Kabbalah, or the theory of an Adamic language, where each word fitted its object.

So description and explanation, on one hand, and normative pronouncements on the other, come close together. You can violate the norms, but what comes from that is so abnormal, it doesn't deserve to count as proper language use. You can only manage to say something confused, perhaps contradictory, anyway devoid of truth-content (in the language of Vienna positivism, "metaphysical").

By contrast, the position I want to defend in this book splits these norms from the descriptive-explanatory account from which they emerged. I can see a point in the norms because there are uses of language which depend on them, and which have their point, even an important function in our culture. But they can't be applied to all information-bearing uses of language. Our language is wider and richer than the regimented, specialized forms.

Let's look at what these are. (1) and (2) define the norms of (a) everyday language when it is used to make careful and accurate descriptions; and in particular, descriptions which can the basis of reliable inferences. Take for instance a court of law: "Now Mr. Jones, please answer carefully; when you first saw the suspect, was he carrying a firearm? No mere suppositions or conjectures or embroidery please; what exactly did you see?"

To (a) the HLC added two more domains, which were in a sense continuous with everyday description: (b) science, which extends these prescriptions into specialized domains, requiring new modes of operation and specialized terms, often incorporating mathematics. Both Hobbes and Locke make clear the utility of such disciplined language use for scientific progress. And also (c) the domain of inferences, augmented and made more exact by logic.

We might call this a-b-c complex the "Vienna constellation", after the Vienna positivists who wanted to restrict altogether the realm of sensemaking (or at least empirical sensemaking) to these domains, excluding "metaphysics", which was either nonsense, or at best "poetry".

It is clear that much post-Fregean thought is looking for an account of language covering the same basic constellation, even though domains (b) and (c) have been immensely developed in relation to their eighteenth-century analogues. Frege greatly improved and enlarged the domain of inferences, and a good part of the post-Fregean treatment of language involves applying this extended logic.

The attempts of regimented languages which aim to see what can be derived from some basic vocabulary have in the end a normative thrust. The base language itself is thought to have unimpeachable empirical credentials, whether these be epistemological (e.g., sense data), or naturalistic (e.g., physics); and the derivations must be logically impeccable. These requirements ensure that at the very least (1) and (2) are obeyed. I say "at least", because in contemporary philosophy, ontological requirements may be imposed. This is evident with what Brandom calls "naturalism", which can take the form of physicalism: all acceptable sentences must be derivable from propositions of physical science, through one or other mode of reduction.

This puts an additional, very powerful limiting requirement on acceptable language, because the language of post-Galilean natural science is expressly shorn of any reference to teleology or intentionality, and its basic explanations can't be in terms of the meanings things have for us humans.

They must have recourse only to, in that stringent sense, "objective" factors. This indeed, has been a condition of the far-reaching success of the natural sciences in their own domains. But to apply these conditions to language in general involves an extra step.

Imposing such ontological requirements adds a new principle (3) to the two norms I identified above.

Very often, most of the time implicitly, another restriction is operative in such attempts at regimentation, also inspired by natural science: (4) the correct description of any phenomenon is that from the observer, third-person perspective, not from that of the first-person agent. This, as we shall see, turns out to be the source of fatal errors in the theory of language.

These four principles animate many of the normative constructions of post-Fregean philosophy which try to draw the boundaries of reliable empirical language. But this normative outlook has crucial affinities to the descriptive-explanatory theories which have been popular in the post-Fregean world.

For an example of these latter, take Donald Davidson's formula for a theory of meaning, which is meant to map for a given language, or even for a given person, the shape of their capacity to speak the language they speak. Davidson's conception of a theory of meaning is of a deductive system whereby the truth conditions for any acceptable empirical statement can be produced as theorems following from the axioms of the theory. These axioms offer the definitions of the referring expressions and predicates of the language. They do this by relating the terms in question to the features of the world they are used to describe.

Since the theory of meaning of any person is meant to map her capacity to produce and understand these statements, a crucial part of this capacity must consist in her following (of course at a subconscious level) these deductive inferences. Hence the effort invested in showing what is the real "logical form" of action sentences, of sentences with adverbial modifiers, of indirect discourse, and so on. Every sentence produced or understood must be equivalent to one with the logical form permitting its deduction from the supposed axioms, or else the theory is falsified.

The axioms themselves relate some arbitrary, "unmotivated" word or concatenation of such to some referent, referent type, or property; in this way paralleling the hookup of word and "idea" that Locke invoked. And what you have learnt in grasping the axioms is to generate the truth conditions for any sentence which the theory generates from them. This is an "extensionalist" theory. That is, we are not interested in understanding the meaning of expressions of the language in the sense of the way they figure the phenomena they describe (we ignore entirely the Cratylist dimension, if any). We are only interested in the way these expressions combine to define truth conditions, however they may be figured.

All of this ensures that (1) and (2) are followed throughout. The deductive system cannot but cleave to the axioms (definitions), and the Cratylist dimension is utterly ignored.

Thus, like the HLC, modern mainstream post-Fregean analytic philosophy generates accounts of language which have a close affinity to its normative programs, conceived as programs for generating acceptable language as such, rather than designed to pursue special and limited objectives. Since I see these programs in the second (more specialized) light, and not the first, I have to show that they offer a seriously distortive account of language as such. I believe we can identify two basic features of their account of language, two assumptions which hide its distortive nature.

I: Words are introduced to designate features which have already in one way or another come to our attention (or they are linked in axioms to elements from which the truth conditions of sentences they figure in can be defined; these elements having already come to our attention).

II: The Cratylist, or "figuring" dimension of language adds nothing to our empirical description of the world; or at least nothing really informative about the *world,* although figures may help to register our emotional reactions to *things,* or our subjective feelings about them.

In the following pages, I want to dismantle these two assumptions.

But first a few words about (I). This doesn't mean that our empirical language is not in the course of constant development, as new features of our world come to our attention. Nor does it exclude in my individual case that my ability to identify things named in the public language may lag far behind, so that I have to play catch-up to master these terms.

In one obvious type of case, the features are prominent in our experience, where we learn what the meaning is in English of sentences like "that cat is furry". The success of cases where people learn another language in conditions of "radical interpretation", that is, where there are no cribs or translation manuals, depends on the fact, explored by Eleanor Rosch and others, that human beings more or less universally tend to notice certain kinds of objects, and treat them as entities, and certain kinds of processes and actions, and treat them as immediately comprehensible predicates. One may be tempted to repeat Austin's quip about "medium-size dry goods", except that some prominent members of this class of universally recognized things are "wet", for instance, animals and other human beings, as well as their actions, like walking, running, climbing, eating, and so on. Rosch has even noticed that common-sense, prescientific identification of animals starts somewhere in the middle of a taxonomic scheme; that is, the first words people learn are for, for example, cat and dog, and not for, say, canine (including wolves and foxes) or spaniel; let alone classifications at a higher level, like mammal. This ensures communication about these basic entities and processes even across large gaps in culture.[1]

But in a lot of other cases, we may be incapable of recognizing the entities or processes that are central to the truth conditions of the utterances we hear. As I stand with my garage mechanic staring into the strange conformation of metal and wires under the hood of my car, and I hear him say something like: "the X is off center", I nod sagely, because I'm ashamed to admit as an adult male in this culture that I am hopelessly baffled, and I'm praying he doesn't ask me something that will show me up. And when any of us walks into a workshop with whose operations we are not really familiar, we suffer the same experience that I do in the garage. It's not just a matter of not being able to name the different machines and processes; it may not even be clear to us where one machine ends and another starts. The scene doesn't obviously segment for us into units, so that we might ask: what does that thing do?

How things segment for us can be very different, depending on our skills, know-how, habitual activities, and culture, even though we all agree in identifying cats and dogs, running and eating. So that we may be unable to identify the things and processes which are involved in the states of affairs which constitute the truth conditions of certain depictive combinations. We will only be able to by acquiring the skills, know-how, habitual activities, attitudes, or even the way these combine in a rather

1. E. Rosch, C. Mervis, W. Gray, D. Johnson, and P. Boyes-Braem, "Basic Objects in Natural Categories," *Cognitive Psychology* 8 (1976): 382–439.

different culture. On this level, understanding the language requires understanding lots of other things, ways of acting and ways of being.

But all this doesn't invalidate (I). Once I am initiated into the activity going on in this workshop, or have taken my basic course in car mechanics, I will identify what is being talked about, when the attendant says: "the carburetor is flooded", and what is being predicated of it. The HLC theory obviously assumes that this process of familiarization can and does take place. Clearly other entities begin to show up when we learn to deal with things in certain ways, analogous to the way that Condillac sees us making finer discriminations on the basis of a first, basic vocabulary of things and properties.

Nor does (I) suppose that the meaning of the term is forever fixed, once defined. Terms are introduced contrastively to name different parts or facets we have noticed. But it may turn out that this articulation needs to be revised in the light of further experience. We find, for example, that we can't distinguish just two forms here, but we need to discriminate three; so A and B have to be modified in definition to make room for C. By the same token, we are often aware even beforehand of the fragility of our terms, of their being "open-textured", or essentially contestable.

Of course, Hobbes and Locke did talk of sticking to our original definitions, but we should cut them a little slack, in order to get to the crucial issues for us today. We need to update them to take account of Saussure, just as contemporary philosophy has updated them to take in the findings of Frege. The HLC authors thought of language as a capacity we could build up one term at a time (cf. Condillac's "just so" story of the origin of language). Introducing a term meant tying some name to a particular phenomenon. But Saussure took account of the fact that terms get their meaning in contrast to others; "red" has the meaning it does because of its contrast to the other color terms that we use. It would be quite different if we didn't have "orange" for instance. So instead of understanding the linguistic code as a set of pairs linking word and thing, we have to see it as a relation between, say, differentially defined sounds (the signifiers) and differentially defined phenomena (the signifieds). "In language there are only differences without positive terms" [*Dans la langue, il n'y a que des différences, et pas de termes positifs*].[2] We carve out contrastive distinctions

---

2. Ferdinand de Saussure, *Course in General Linguistics*, trans. Wade Baskin (New York: Columbia University Press, 2011), 120; Saussure, *Cours de Linguistique Générale* (Paris: Patot, 1978), 166.

in the indefinite range of possible phonetic sounds, and line them up with contrastive distinctions in the phenomena we speak about.

So (I), thus updated, can take all these features in its stride. I want, however, to show that it has more radical defects. But in order to facilitate the exposition, I want first to deal with (II), the Cratylist question.

2

In general contemporary linguistic theories tend to treat language in Saussurean fashion, which justifies the updating we proposed above. Saussure also insisted on our defining the linguistic code through a synchronic take; the issues of historical development belong to a separate department of linguistic science. The code so understood can be seen as lining up a set of distinctions between sounds, and a set of distinctions between things. To know the language is to know how to report or understand reports in language through the use/grasp of these pairings; but these are in Saussure's term "unmotivated". Saussure situates himself firmly in the anti-Cratylist camp. Canines and felines in the world are matched in English by the "dog"/"cat" distinction; but elsewhere we will hear *"chien"*/*"chat"* or *"Hund"*/*"Katz"*.[3]

But this takes the spotlight off the creative uses of language, whereby we gain new powers of articulation. It might be thought that these are easy to cope with. If we take taxonomic examples, which we started on with dog/cat, we can imagine cases in which a new subspecies appears, a new kind of dog. Then we alter our existing list of subspecies, which are supposed to register the different sorts of dog. Or else, more alarmingly, mules appear, fudging horse/donkey; but we just add another slot, somewhere between a category and a subcategory. And so on.

Now this scenario perfectly matches (I); the object comes to our attention, then we name it. And it also obeys (II): the name coined will be arbitrary, or "unmotivated" in Saussure's sense. (Of course, only the new features of the object will bear an arbitrary name; if we have discovered a

---

3. Of course, Saussure didn't hold that languages always divided up the signifieds in the same way. European languages all have words for "dog" and "cat", but there are still differences among them, not to speak of languages more distantly related. I could say "I'm going to Toronto tomorrow" when I'm taking the train, but I'm using the same word I would use if I were planning to walk. I couldn't do this in, say, German or Polish.

new subspecies of dog, the first word in the name will have to be '*canis*'.)
In addition, the neologizing, the coining of the name, will be an explicit
upfront activity, proposed to and agreed by the scientific community.

But this is not the only scenario for the creation of new terms. There are
cases where we feel a sense that there's something new to be said. This may
be at first inchoate; we are groping for something, we know not quite what.
And then we coin a new expression which resolves this tension. We have
found the "right" word (see Chapter 1). Then this can be taken up by others,
sometimes immediately, and even without noticing the neologism, sometimes after consideration. They also see this as fitting, appropriate, the
"right" word; it becomes part of the language. Obvious examples are available in popular terms of recent coinage, like 'cool', 'uptight', 'off the wall'.

Principles (I) and (II) define their own notion of the "right" term. This
is the one already in the lexicon, the product of an earlier arbitrary naming.
Or else, following the scenario above, it is the product of a new naming
which alters or reorders the lexicon to make place for it. But the neolo-
gisms I'm talking about in the previous paragraph aren't right in this sense.
Rather they render the phenomenon accurately; they "fit", "portray", in
short "figure" it. There is no moment of explicit naming. They are offered,
and immediately understood, and become part of the language. Or if not
understood immediately, they are eventually grasped without further explanation, which is not the case with a new technical term or the name of
a new species. We can call such coinages "articulations"; they render us
articulate in a new way or a new domain.

Of course, not all terms which are immediately understood can be said
to "figure" their objects. This term seems to fit what we often call metaphors, but similes and analogies can bring about something of the same
kind, viz., figuring one phenomenon or domain A through another, B. But
there are new words which are immediately understood which don't function like metaphors, but rather like metonyms. Take our word 'bead', as
in a string of beads (prayer beads, worry beads). It appears that this comes
from an older English word meaning "to pray" ('bede'), and could have
been immediately understood because of the close connection of such
strings with the activity of praying.[4] Or think of the popular German word
for a cell phone, '*Handy*' (borrowed from English).

---

4. See Andrzej Pawelec, *Prepositional Network Models: A Hermeneutical Case Study* (Krakow:
Jagiellonian University Press, 2009), 66–67.

On one understanding of metaphor, it involves attributing to A some property or feature of B which is inappropriate to A. The term is "borrowed". It doesn't really "belong". But it brings out by "figuring" an aspect or feature of A that we couldn't articulate before. But there are new coinages which can be immediately understood which aren't really articulations in the above sense. That is, they don't add to our capacity of articulating features of our world, although they can give us a handy term to use to describe what would otherwise require complicated locutions.

Take the example of 'key'. This involves a simple extension through analogy: thus we speak of some document as offering a "key" to a given code. The analogy is plain. Just as my house key gives me access to my locked home, and my car key enables me to start my car, so this document gives me access to the message which is hidden in code. So we find a way of speaking of this new domain of codes and decoding (A) through the more familiar one of keys in locks giving access (B). In a first use, the word is obviously inappropriate (in the sense of lexically unsupported); keys belong in the domain of locks. But it barely produces a shock at its first introduction, and we rapidly become able to apply it to new domains without reflecting on the source.

And it doesn't really add to our articulacy. We had a way of talking about it before. I come across a document which I can't understand, because it's in code. And someone offers to give me a "schedule giving the meanings in English of all the signs of this code". This longer expression designates what we would now call a "key". We've been given a handy term, but we were perfectly capable before of describing what it names, only in a more clumsy locution.

And indeed, the standard updated HLC account can explain this kind of extension in its own terms, without recourse to the notion of metaphor. A given term is defined on its introduction to apply to objects which have a number of characteristics. Cat = small furry feline with XYZ properties. But because of the incompleteness and open-textured nature of the terms in our lexicon, we may be induced to revise it in the face of experience. So we can come across cases where some features apply, and not others, and we will be led to make a decision: new coinage, or extend the scope of the term. Here one of the features defining 'key' is its function of giving access, and we can choose to enlarge the extension of the term to include things sharing this function, although not other properties of what were originally called "keys" (small metal object, fitting into lock, etc.). Indeed, it is a fact that many of our terms for human artifacts are defined partly in terms of their functions, for example 'chair', 'table', and so on (this will later on figure in my argument). And this allows us to extend them outside of their original domain. Thus we speak of a "seat of government".

But there are other metaphorical attributions which do articulate something new. Let's take the example made famous by Max Black: "the chairman ploughed through the discussion".[5] Or I might say of a politician: "he plays his cards very close to his chest". Or we might describe the boss in a certain enterprise by saying: "he was an eagle among rabbits" (this doesn't have to be a metaphor; we could use a simile in this case to the same effect).

What is happening here? We are figuring one object or event through another, for example the chairman's action through that of a farmer ploughing his field, the politician's behavior through that of a poker player, the boss's way of treating his employees through the image of a predator bird. What does this accomplish?

In the first case, I might have said: "the chair was rushing us, he was ignoring our desire to discuss the issues more thoroughly", and the like. But the metaphorical attribution brings all this and more out in more vivid form. It brings out the determined, the ruthless insensitivity with which he drove (another metaphor) the meeting, by invoking the ploughman, who is (rightly in his case) intent merely on digging the furrow, sweeping all obstacles in his path.

How does the metaphor do this? It is crucial to this kind of attribution that there be something inappropriate in it—only in this case the inappropriateness is more striking than in speaking of a "key" for the code, which was simply wrong in lexical terms. Chairing a discussion is quite different from ploughing a field, political life is not ("literally"[6]) a poker game, the boss is not a large predator bird. One might even say, invoking the famous expression of Gilbert Ryle, such attributions often involve a "category mistake"[7] (e.g., taking a human for an animal). So there is something initially surprising about a new metaphor; we may not get it right away. Indeed, in some cases we may never get it. There is a tension

---

5. Max Black, *Models and Metaphors: Studies in Language and Philosophy* (Ithaca, NY: Cornell University Press, 1962), chapter 3.

6. One mustn't reify this expression, as though some meanings were "literal" as such, and others "metaphorical". The better term to use here would be 'lexical' or 'usual'. At any given moment, a metaphorical attribution violates or at least goes beyond the usual meaning; but this evolves over time, among other things through the force of "dead" metaphors. See Paul Ricoeur, *La Métaphore Vive* (Paris: Seuil, 1975), study 1, for the Greek word used by Aristotle.

7. Gilbert Ryle, *The Concept of Mind* (London: Hutchinson, 1949).

between target and source, between tenor and vehicle; we partially resolve the tension when we grasp the facet of the target (which I'm calling
A here) which is brought out by the source (B). The insight here arises in
the field of tension between A and B. The metaphor constitutes (what at
first sight is) an inappropriate figuring of A through B, which yields an
insight when one grasps an appropriateness of a new kind, viz., the insight about A that the tension with template B brings to light.

So we're dealing with something in the Cratylist (figuring) dimension of
language which makes a positive contribution to its information-bearing
function, thus negating principle (II) above. Or does it?

   The HLC tradition wants to say that tropes either confuse things, or if
they add something clear it is not information about the world; rather their
function is to evoke certain subjective feelings or reactions. So metaphors
in rhetoric can be seen as ornamental; they please us, and thus dispose us
favorably to what they apply to; or else they portray the object in a dark
light, and make us disapprove of it. And certainly approval/disapproval is
in play in the above examples. The initial inappropriateness of the attribution (its "category mistake") in at least the first two cases carries with it a
sense of morally or ethically inappropriate behavior. The single-minded de-
termination to prevail of the ploughman sits badly with the role of chair;
politics is a serious activity, meant to benefit the whole society, poker is a
mere pastime; if it has a further purpose, this is aimed at increasing my
wealth. The metaphors show the chair and the politician respectively in a
bad light, as unworthy of their calling. As for the eagle among rabbits, a
Nietzschean might see this as praise of the boss so described. But for most
people, this expression recruits no sympathy either for the subject (the eagle figure) or for his victims (the rabbits). But you get a sense of his ruthless and unfeeling behavior toward them, and of their timid acceptance of
domination or inferiority.

   But does this mean that the attributions add no information? Perhaps
the purely ornamental figures add none; but are ethical condemnations to
be classed as purely subjective reactions, as with "emotivist" theories of
ethics? This remains to be proved. And how can we ignore the way these
images bring to light a whole facet of the manner the agents in question
are operating, a feature of the "style" of their action? In regard to the
chairman attribution, I began to enumerate the features of his behavior
one might cite to show the image appropriate: he didn't listen, he pushed

the agenda relentlessly forward, and so on. But the image sums up these features and many more. It tells us something.

However, there is a downside here, which will deter anyone intent on framing only sentences which can figure in tight deductive relations. One obvious reason why metaphorical attributions are unsuited to this role resides in their very nature; they find their meaning in the tension between their two poles, A and B. Understanding them involves a winnowing process;[8] not everything pertaining to ploughing is brought to bear on the chair's behavior. If one wants to accept the inference from "X ploughed the field" to "X prepared the field for planting", then this is going to wreak havoc with our deductive system.

Another reason, closely related to this, is that there is usually a certain indeterminacy around what exactly is being asserted by a metaphorical attribution. Our mode of assessment of these may be subtly different from certain kinds of more "literal" assertions. We may not say, of for instance the eagle-among-rabbits attribution, that it is either simply true or false, but we praise such attributions in other terms, as offering insight into an important aspect of the A domain in question. Or we criticize them as "exaggerated": something, for instance, that friends of the chair might say when they hear the first attribution above. Our sense here is that this kind of issue doesn't permit of the same kind of unambiguous affirmation or negation as, for instance: "the cat is on the mat", or "the meter reads 5.3", or "that is a typical Siberian tiger".

Some theories of metaphor minimize its importance. Davidson holds that there is no such thing as metaphorical meaning. The meaning of a metaphorical utterance is simply determined by the literal meanings of the words it contains, just like any utterance.[9] Not surprisingly, this means that sentences used metaphorically are usually false. "This is not to deny that there is such a thing as metaphorical truth, only to deny it of sentences. Metaphor does lead us to notice what might not otherwise be noticed, and there is no reason, I suppose, not to say that these visions, thoughts or feelings inspired by the metaphor are true or false."[10]

8. See Ricoeur, *La Métaphore,* study 6, 258 and 373. Ricoeur speaks of the need to put the source image through a "screen" or "filter" in order to grasp its meaning.

9. Donald Davidson, "What Metaphors Mean," in *Inquiries into Truth and Interpretation* (Oxford: Oxford University Press, 1985), 245–64.

10. Ibid., 257.

"What distinguishes metaphor is not meaning but use."[11] The use a metaphor has, and can accomplish if we can grasp it, is to "make us notice aspects of things we did not notice before; . . . they bring surprising analogies and similarities to our attention; they do provide a kind of lens or lattice, as Black says, through which we view the relevant phenomena." But "since in most cases what the metaphor prompts or inspires is not entirely, or even at all, recognition of some truth or fact, the attempt to give literal expression to the content of the metaphor is simply misguided."[12]

Up to this last sentence, one might think that Davidson was simply following Black. There is no special metaphorical sense of "ploughing through" which applies to what the chair did to the discussion; or of "playing cards close to one's chest", applied to the politician. The force of the metaphor lies in the shocking, "categorically mistaken" attribution of these terms to chair and politico respectively. This can yield insights, make features of the situation come to light. This potential is trivialized in the talk of "aspects of things we did not notice before" which we are prompted to "notice", and especially when what we are prompted to is mostly not a recognition of "truth or fact". The idea seems to be that "aspects of things" are lying around, ready to be noticed, and metaphors trigger this noticing. There seems no recognition that they can create a perspective in which things show up that wouldn't otherwise.

But this seems to assume that (a) these aspects were already evident and readily discriminable before the metaphorical description (genetically, you didn't need B to get at A; it was already visible on the surface); and (b) that the list of what the metaphor makes us notice "is not finite in scope or propositional in nature".[13] This seems to be part of what makes the attempt at a literal paraphrase misguided in Davison's mind. Whereas what in fact makes this attempt supremely difficult is the close link between the metaphorical statement and the insight is generates. Metaphor, for Davidson, seems to reduce to another way of making people notice things; something that in certain contexts could also be effected by a lie.[14] Its specificity is lost.

In the light of this, what do we mean when we speak of a metaphor going "dead"? As we just argued, a new metaphor gets its meaning through the

11. Ibid., 259.
12. Ibid., 261, 263.
13. Ibid., 263.
14. Ibid., 258–59.

tension between target and source, A and B. But as the original insight sinks in, we become capable of operating with the target area directly. We pick up on features that justified the original surprising and shocking attribution. So we now banally speak of a politician playing his cards close to his chest; the way he withholds information, tries to hide his strategy, and so on, triggers this description directly, as it were, and allows the original source image of poker playing to recede into the background. We have a new "usual" expression, which people can use without reflection on where it comes from. This is stage one of a metaphor's "dying". Stage two comes when people have no idea any more of what the original source was. And I suppose one could add a stage three, where speakers are no longer even aware that the term arrived in their vocabulary through a metaphorical transfer.

We can recur to our 'key' case to see this process in an advanced stage. This is a very minimal metaphor (if we want to dignify it with this term, as against calling it a simple extension). It barely produces a shock at its first introduction, and we rapidly become able to apply it to new areas without reflecting on the source. This is phase one. Nowadays everybody sees why we speak of a "key" to a code, because we all know how important real, literal keys are. We have all lost our house key or car key. But let's imagine that in twenty years' time, "literal" keys will have disappeared. You get into your house, or start your car by pressing your fingers on a pad, or giving a command to a voice-recognition box. People might still go on using the term 'key' as what "unlocks" a code. People who had forgotten all about "literal" keys would have no trouble applying it. X says: "here's a key to military intelligence"; Y replies: "I'll try it. Whoopee, it works" (or "damn it's useless"). Historians of language would have to explain to people what the original keys were, and how they functioned, but no one would need to take History of Language 101 in order to use the expression correctly.[15]

We're in exactly this position with regard to familiar contemporary expressions. I'm not sure that I know what a "tenterhook" is, but I often use the expression "I'm on tenterhooks waiting for that exam (or election) result". I have read an account in Snaevarr[16] about the origin of the expression "a flash in the pan". I've already forgotten the details, but it concerns

---

15. I owe this example to Pawelec, *Network Models,* 78.

16. Stefan Snaevarr, *Metaphors, Narratives, Emotions: Their Interplay and Impact* (Amsterdam: Rodopi, 2009), chapter 3; I have learnt a great deal from this interesting book.

one of the mishaps which happened to early versions of the musket. But before I read this account, and after I forgot it, I could still say things like: "the (admittedly well-attended) opening meeting of my opponent's campaign has turned out to be just a flash in the pan". (And note that some of the rhetorical force of this expression still holds, because of the force of fire metaphors. My opponent may have promised in his opening speech to "set the Prairie on fire", and all this makes his present minimal impact look ridiculous.)

Phase three comes about when we are no longer aware of the metaphorical origin of a common term. I am reliably informed that the French word 'tête' comes from the Latin word 'testa', meaning "little pot"; and the same must be true for the Italian word for "head". But one needs an expert in etymology even to suspect this origin.

The process of a metaphor "dying" can be seen as a kind of "normalization" into ordinary prose description. It has often been remarked that ordinary empirical language tends to drop out of sight. It doesn't call attention to itself, but focuses on what is being talked about. In Michael Polanyi's terms, the focus of our attention is on what is being said, and the words drop to subsidiary status.[17] So we often remember very confidently what someone has told us, and relay it to others, but with the proviso: "these are not his exact terms". In a multilingual context we may even forget what language the conversation was in. Only the "message" survives. As Todorov puts it, "the discourse that simply makes thinking known to us is invisible and thereby nonexistent" [*Le discours qui nous fait simplement connaître la pensée est invisible et par là même inexistant*].[18]

The contrast is often made with emphatic modes of language, rhetorical flourishes, striking expressions, poetry, where the language precisely does call attention to itself, and is often firmly lodged in memory.[19] The process of normalization of a striking image, as it begins to be applied routinely to the target domain, gradually robs it of its salience and pushes it down toward the invisibility of ordinary descriptive speech.

So an important distinction arises in connection with these extensions of articulacy that open a hitherto unnoticed facet of A (a new domain) by

---

17. See Michael Polanyi, *Personal Knowledge: Towards a Post-Critical Philosophy* (London: Routledge, 1962), 57–59.

18. Tzvetan Todorov, *Littérature et Signification* (Paris: Larousse, 1967), 102.

19. For instance, Roman Jakobson's contrast between prose and poetry; see Ricoeur, *La Métaphore Vive* (Paris: Seuil, 1975), 186, 280–82.

casting it in terms of B (an already familiar domain). This move enables a new, otherwise unavailable articulation of A. But is this just a fact about the genesis of this way of articulating A, something which can be dispensed with once this way has caught on? Or is the bifocal nature of this articulation something that must continually remain alive, so that you don't fully get the point unless you're aware of the source domain (B) in its difference from A? In other terms, do all metaphors face normalization as an ineluctable fate?

There isn't a single answer to this question. In some cases, metaphors are heading for a heat death of their semantic source image. In others, this source is not essential, but can constantly remind ourselves of its existence (e.g., some of the cases of phase two; you can always become aware once again that an initial meeting after which the campaign stalls is not the same thing as a "literal" flash in the pan [whatever that was]). But there are cases where the source is continually at work, producing fresh applications. We'll come to these later.[20]

But even where the metaphor dies, leaving in its wake new routine, even lexicalized expressions, it has nevertheless left its mark. If I may use my own image here, its death has fertilized the field of routine expressions with which we describe our world. A totally anti-Cratylist position can't take account of this creative-inventive side of language, which involves figuring A through B. If we want to explore our actual language capacity, as against set the norms for some special regimented domains, we cannot ignore the Cratylist dimension.

So metaphor makes a dent in principle (II). But it might also be thought to break principle (I). This latter insists that the designate of newly coined terms must have already reached our notice. But is this true of the features which first appear to us in the tension of a metaphoric attribution? Certainly not if we follow the model of the new coinage in Linnean classification I cited in my first scenario of neologizing above, forced on us by an uncharted species. The phenomenon is there first, and demands to be

---

20. Bifocality seems very hard to eliminate in a metaphor like *homo homini lupus*. Man and wolf are being used here as types. (We could argue that this is unfair to wolves, because they don't so easily turn against and kill conspecifics as we do.) But part of the force of this utterance is the struggle between the two foci. Humans (A) are being understood through wolves (B)—or "wolves". But one of the points of the phrase is the clash between our, inevitably normative, notion of the human and the picture of the "wolf", ravening, bent on destroying and eating its prey, merciless, ruthless, a mere force of nature. (Hobbes should be arraigned by the Animal Liberation Front for gross calumny.)

named. Even where the phenomenon is still largely hidden, we can say that we recognize it as needing a name. For instance, we ask: what is the cause of this disease? We can't properly describe this, but we identify something there to be discovered.

But in the case of metaphoric attribution, the phenomenon swims into our ken along with the attribution. It comes to light in the tension between the two foci, A and B. The attribution makes it possible to intuit and then articulate for the first time what it discovers for us. There is a creative side to language, what I have called its constitutive side (or one facet of this side, as we shall see in the next chapters), which the HLC covers up, and the HHH has tried to articulate for us. It is what enables the creation of what Merleau-Ponty calls *"paroles parlantes"*.[21]

In the kind of creativity we're dealing with here, discovery and invention go together. The new attribution can be seen as a discovery, but we needed to place the object in this field of tension to bring this to light. Creative invention is crucial to the discovery here. We will see lots of cases of this, and I want to examine others in this chapter, before we go on to another, even more striking case of the creativity of language in the next chapters.[22]

3

In the preceding discussion, I have been dealing with one-off metaphorical attributions. We could call these punctual metaphors: particular descriptions which apply to a certain range of cases, particular events or activities which are figured through another event or activity (chairing a meeting through ploughing a field). But there can also be more pervasive systems in which one domain is figured through another.

I want to come in the next section to what we might call structural templates, where the structure of domain B is used to make sense of domain A in some systematic fashion (e.g., Lakoff and Johnson templates, like "Life Is a Journey"). We can perhaps call these metaphors, if we like. But what is really important is the way in which one domain can be illuminatingly

21. See Chapter 1, note 39.
22. The capacity for metaphor is not a product of sophistication. It is there among young children. As witness this remark by one of Elizabeth Anscombe's children, who had been too long sitting with his legs tucked under him: "Mummy, there's a fizzing in my foot" (personal communication). We also see it in the mimicry of young children: e.g., playing "dentist", with a pencil standing for the "drill".

figured in terms of another. The A through B structure applies here, although in a different form.

But in this section, I want to look at what underlies many such more systematic figurings, and that is our sense of what it is like to engage with different kinds of things in different sorts of situation. For the mainstream conception that descends from the HLC, our being able to recognize objects as exemplifying term X is our perceiving the canonical list of features that figure in the definition of X. But my basic hypothesis here is that our sense of X frequently goes beyond grasping such features. For a whole host of objects, including familiar things and situations in our world, our grasp of X also incorporates a sense of the ways in which we can engage with X, deal with X, and pursue our objectives in the presence of X.

We're in the realm here which I called above significances, or meanings, in the sense of meanings for us as active beings. So the child's sense of a tree is of something that can be climbed, that you can hide in, that can get in the way of a game of backyard hockey, and so on. There are two levels to such senses. One is what I have just described: ways we can engage with the object concerned. (This level of meanings is what Gibson was calling attention to with his term "affordances".)[23] The other is more urgent, it concerns ways we are drawn to or called on to engage with it. We describe the latter levels of meanings in terms such as 'attractive', 'repulsive', 'dangerous', and 'enticing'. These two levels are intimately related. We look out from the garden into the woods, and see it structured by the paths that one could take to pass through it; that is level one. But let's say that you have an urgent reason to get to the other side; or you find the forest enticing; you have a desire to lose yourself in the green and birdsong. Then these paths have meaning in stronger sense; they urge you forward. Or else, to take a case with the opposite weighting; you suspect that an enemy will come to get you through this wood; then the path is full of menace, and you want to get away from it.

Now our sense of an object is often partly constituted by such a penumbra of meanings, potential (level one) or actual (level two). And of course, that is why some such meaning is often built into the lexical definition of an object. Chairs are to sit in, that's how they can be engaged with, and how they invite us when we're tired. So this function is built

---

23. James J. Gibson, *The Senses Considered as Perceptual Systems* (London: Allen and Unwin, 1966).

into their definition (as "giving access" was with 'key'). We can see why this explicit reference to function is such a frequent occurrence in our language. But my point here is that such explicit mentions are simply the tip of a bigger iceberg, the penumbra of meanings which surrounds our grasp of familiar things.

We should assume that such a sense of meanings also exists in (at least higher) animals. The point here is their relevance for our grasp of language.

This penumbra of meanings can be seen as a kind of (at first implicit, unarticulated) understanding of our world. (This is close to how Heidegger uses the term.) This understanding is rooted in our bodily know-how, which enables us to make our way in and around our immediate surroundings, and deal with the objects that show up in it.

The human infant spends his first months learning how. He learns how to stand upright, to walk, to climb up on chairs and stairs, and (alas, later) to climb down, to get around, to grasp and examine and later play with toys, to run, eventually climb trees, and so on, into childhood. All this time, neuronal connections are being formed in the brain; some chains are atrophying, others are becoming firmer, the ones he needs to stabilize all these skills.

What we have here is know-how. He knows his way about in his living space: house, perhaps yard. He doesn't have the kind of grasp of this space that a map can give us, but he can get where he wants to. This know-how is analogous to that of higher animals, the family dog for instance, who will never learn language.

Applying our (adult) language, the language he will later learn, to his situation, we can say that the properties of things which stand out in his world are not the neutral terms which might figure in a scientific description, or an inventory of furniture. Rather what he picks out are what Gibson calls "affordances". This chair is climbable, and indeed, tempting to climb; that way, through the kitchen, is open into the garden; this space, in the cupboard is crawlable and mysteriously draws him. His world is filled with gerundive properties: this ring is to-be-put in the mouth, that ball is to-be-thrown on the floor (for the nth time!).

For both child and animal, as well as for us adults a good deal of the time, knowing our way around is a kind of understanding. No matter how much we learn to see the world in a way which abstracts from human meanings, as we do when we objectify things for scientific purposes, meanings are inescapable. Although we can step outside of this magic circle of agent-related meanings for certain selected domains and purposes, it is clear that we cannot live totally outside it. No matter what, we do have to get around in the world, find paths and get around obstacles. The range of human meanings or Gibsonian affordances will always shape our world. We need only think of distinctions like "up" and "down", or "within reach", "out of reach", which we could never imagine dispensing with, and which are intrinsically related to our way of being as bodily agents in the world. It is clear that up and down are not related to some "objective" standard, like away from or toward the ground. This latter may be sloping, and although these directions may be aligned with the center of the earth, this is not a benchmark available to human perception. Up and down make sense to us as embodied agents who need to learn to keep their balance in upright posture, and need to adopt a stance or gait that will maintain it.[24]

Meanings in this sense are primary and inescapable. And that is because the know-how that makes them figure in our world is in a certain sense in the body. The open way into the morning garden full of birdsong draws the child, pulls him into this path. He feels this in his dawning response as he starts to move. His world is full of lines of force. Take one of the feats of his first year, learning to stand up and keep his balance. He is drawn to rise, to try to stay upright, to begin walking, at first very uncertainly. To master this skill of keeping one's balance is to experience a kind of equilibrium in one's posture in relation to the world. There is a zone of comfort, of secure equilibrium, and surrounding it force vectors that might pull us out of balance. The zone of balance is a center point or axis where these different forces come to rest. Our experience of this is bodily; one might say that the body knows.

Merleau-Ponty speaks here of "motor intentionality". The first word conveys that the know-how lies in our ability to make our way around; the second emphasizes that this constitutes a way of grasping the world which surrounds us. This is not explicit knowledge of an independent object, but it nevertheless is "about" something; it is an understanding of our world.[25]

---

24. See Sam Todes, *Body and World* (Cambridge, MA: MIT Press, 2001), 264–65.

25. See Sean Dorrance Kelly, "Grasping at Straws: Motor Intentionality and the Cognitive Science of Skillful Action," in *Heidegger, Coping, and Cognitive Science: Essays in Honor of Hubert Dreyfus*, vol. 2, ed. Mark Wrathall and Jeff Malpas (Cambridge, MA: MIT Press, 2000), 161–77; the discussion in Merleau-Ponty's work is in *La Phénoménologie de la Perception* (Paris: Gallimard, 1945), part 1, chapter 3.

What does this know-how, which he begins to acquire in infancy, contribute to the child's mastery of language? How does our learning to speak draw on these bodily skills? Does it draw on them at all? This is a crucial dimension of language which has been explored in very insightful ways in the work of George Lakoff and Mark Johnson.[26]

Lakoff and Johnson speak of the sensorimotor schemata which underlie our basic skills. I prefer to use the term 'template' (which also figures in their work), and speak of the templates we draw from our motor intentionality. I want to emphasize the dimension of understanding implicit in these basic abilities of ours. Their hypothesis is that these basic abilities contribute, in the first place, to (1) the way we segment our phenomenal world, and recognize basic objects, actions, causal links, and ways of being affected by our world. And in the second place, (2) they provide templates by which we can structure and make sense of other more complex and abstract dimensions of our experience which arise later.

To illustrate the first point, the research of Eleanor Rosch and others, as I mentioned above, has identified what they call "basic level categories", the first level at which the things which surround us are recognized and the level at which they are most easily retained and recalled. These are in the middle range of what we will later establish as taxonomic hierarchies. Take animals, for instance. Children learn first, and adults afterward will most easily recognize, cats and tigers, or dogs and foxes, rather than the more general categories of felines and canines, or the more specialized species Siamese and terriers. The experimental results showing this are pretty stable across different cultures, although there are obvious variations due to different cultural and environmental experience. For instance, country people will often recognize the main genera of trees: oak, ash, maple, and so on; whereas city people may just see "trees". But in general, the preeminence of the middle range is evident across societies and cultures.[27]

I took animals as an example, but the same principle is evident in other domains. We learn to recognize chairs, tables, sinks, TVs, before we can operate with 'furniture', 'electronic media', or 'dining room chair' and 'coffee table'. We also learn basic actions: push, pull, hit, squeeze, swimming,

26. George Lakoff and Mark Johnson, *Metaphors We Live By* (Chicago: University of Chicago Press, 1980), and *Philosophy in the Flesh* (New York: Basic Books, 1999), 257. Also George Lakoff, *Women, Fire and Other Dangerous Things* (Chicago: University of Chicago Press, 1987); Mark Johnson, *The Body in the Mind* (Chicago: University of Chicago Press, 1987).

27. Rosch et al., "Basic Objects."

walking, grasping; and the kinds of causal relations between things which manifest the same kind of effects (one billiard ball hits another and pushes it into the basket).

The hypothesis is that these basic-level objects and actions or events are easy to recognize, partly because they exhibit certain definite kinds of part-whole gestalt (so that if someone says "imagine a chair", it's easy to do, but if they say "imagine furniture", your mind boggles), but partly also because of the kinds of interactions we have with them (petting the cat, sitting in the chair), and the functions they fill or purposes they serve in our lives.[28] In other words, these things stand out because of the way they mesh with our motor intentionality and our related gestalt perception of wholes and parts.

Before we get to more explicit templates, we can see this implicit understanding at work in the way we group certain meanings. A good example of these is provided by prepositional networks. Interesting studies have been made modeling such networks. This is because prepositions are used to invoke some constellation of things, within which we as agents can see ourselves as differentially placed (sometimes the constellation shows up only from the "egocentric" perspective, sometimes we are conceiving it from another point of view); or in relation to which we can engage in certain kinds of action.

The purpose of network models is to explain how a single preposition can cover rather different constellations, without our having any sense that we are operating with a polysemic term, even though analysis shows that there are important differences. Take 'over', as analyzed by Lakoff.[29] We can suppose that 'over' originally was used to describe something (a trajectory: TR) hovering or moving above a landmark (LM). The bird flies over my garden, the sword of Damocles hangs over my head. But then it can be extended: "lay the tablecloth over that table"; the TR now is not above in the normal sense, but covering the LM. And then an even farther extension: Ralph lives over the bridge, meaning not: Ralph lives in some structure that has been erected above the bridge; but rather: Ralph lives on the other side of the bridge. We can conjecture how this use could arise: you have to travel over the bridge to get to Ralph's place, so the expression "over the bridge" can through a metonymic extension come to designate a place on the other side of the bridge.

---

28. Lakoff and Johnson, *Flesh,* 27; Lakoff and Johnson, *Metaphors,* 162.
29. Lakoff, *Women,* 416–61.

These extensions are socially created. They happen because they are taken up and accepted generally. Of course, in any particular case, we might challenge the analysis into original and extended cases, but what seems undeniable is that the polysemy is held together as such (and not as a mere homophony—like 'bank' as both a river's edge, and a financial institution) by some sense of the connection.[30]

We can contrast this with our scenario above of alterations in a taxonomy to accommodate a new species, which is a paradigm operation of neologizing according to principles (I) and (II). The taxonomic cases looked simple, because we have a system with a fixed structure, where the issue can arise of adding slots, or splitting an existing slot into two, but where (a) the need to make some such change can be readily evident, in virtue of the principles of the taxonomy, and (b) the changes don't disturb the structure. But in the 'over' case, polysemy breeds outside of any preexisting structure, or what we might understand as an original set of criterial properties. Ralph living over the bridge has nothing to do with his being above or on some LM. The addition works because hearers can sense and accept the connection, the analogy, metonymy, or whatever.

Let's see the difference between the two scenarios. In the taxonomy one we discover a new object, and we devise a new name. And here another aspect of the Saussurean theory comes to light: this name is quite arbitrary, or as it is often put "unmotivated", as are signifiers in general; that is, it doesn't in any way reveal or indicate the nature of what is named.

But the 'over' scenario is different. There is not exactly a new "object" here. Presumably before the metonymic extension of 'over' people said things like "Ralph lives on the other side of the river". What we have here is rather a new way of articulating this situation, a new way of disclosing it (or "making it show up", to use Bert Dreyfus's rendering of Heidegger's "erschliessen"). The closest analogy in the taxonomy scenario is the invention of the principles of taxonomy themselves—although, of course, there is no comparison in the scale and significance between the history- and world-making contributions of Linnaeus and that of the anonymous coiner of 'over' in this new use.

But in another way the two cases are in stark contrast. The extension of meaning which gives us the new sense of "over the bridge" trades on our way of dealing with our world; in this case, it draws on the fact that the

30. See Pawelec, *Network Models,* chapter 2.

path to Ralph's place (for us on this side of the river) runs "over the bridge" in one of the earlier senses. But the Linnaean taxonomy was arrived at by our breaking away from the way things first present themselves. We can suppose that various folk taxonomies also draw on certain (to us) obvious differences in gestalt between familiar animals, or else on the role these creatures play in our lives as domestic animals, or as game, and so on. This role determines the way we deal with them, which means that what is at first salient for us is the "affordances" they offer us, to use Gibson's expression; that is, the ways in which they can serve or obstruct our purposes, and the various approaches to these ends which they allow, facilitate, or obstruct. It is this range of meanings which stand out for us.

Because these affordances are roughly the same for all humans, it is not surprising that these taxonomies are very similar from culture to culture. The same animals are picked out, and at the same level in the taxonomic hierarchy (e.g., 'dog' is more salient than 'mammal', or than 'terrier', as Lakoff and Johnson argue, following Rosch).[31]

But the step to modern scientific taxonomy involved a break with this kind of anthropocentrism; it required that we find another range of criterial properties for classification which steps outside of the range of their meaning for our purposes, and fasten on "objective" features which can allow for greater insight into how they function. How they reproduce becomes essential to the classification, and the differences in this domain are very often not evident on the surface. So whales can cease to be fish.

This is a crucial step, which shows that while our first off way of articulating things may be shaped by their significance for us in our dealings with them (as Ralph's living "over the bridge" was by the path we have to take to his place), we are not imprisoned in this approach, and the desire to know and understand reality better can take us beyond, leading us to step outside this way of centering on our own agency, to move from a "subjective" to an "objective" take on things.

We can see how this step outside of human meanings was involved in one of the shifts which was foundational for what we understand as modern science. I mean here the shift from an understanding of motion as requiring a constant application of force to continue, to the new inertial understanding, where force has the role of initiating movement, or in general of

---

31. Lakoff, *Women,* 46; Rosch et al., "Basic Objects."

changing velocity. The first outlook seemed obvious, and made sense to us, because we ourselves only move through constant effort, and similarly, we can only move other objects by continuing to push or pull them. The adoption of the inertial paradigm required that we step outside of this whole manner of understanding. It is no accident that a founding feature of this modern scientific tradition is that it eschews all classification of things in terms of human meanings.

Because the taxonomy scenario fits within this more experience-distant mode of understanding the world which has been central to modern science, we can see why the HLC tradition can easily be persuaded to see its mode of neologizing as paradigmatic, and can ignore other cases, like metaphor and experience-mediated polysemy, as in the case of 'over'.

But I am running ahead of my argument. I want to return later to metaphor and understanding something "through" something else. For the moment, let's return to the discussion of the 'over' scenario in its contrast to the taxonomic one. The contrast shows up in the absence of the two features attributed above to the taxonomic change. In the 'over' case, the new expression 'over the bridge' (really a new and distinct use of this expression) is not at all "arbitrary". On the contrary it immediately reveals what it is used to assert, and is immediately comprehensible; that is, the connection can be grasped even in its first use. It follows that there is no need for an explicit act of neologizing, introducing the new expression. As a consequence of this, polysemy of this sort can easily pass unnoticed. People don't have to notice that the term has been given an extended sense. The novelty can and often does remain quite unremarked (which is why it often takes linguists to point out and chart polysemy).

The various models which attempt to chart 'over' and similar cases all raise very difficult questions. Andrzej Pawelec discusses Lakoff's treatment of 'over', and similar attempts to chart a network for the Polish preposition 'za' (which partly overlaps in meaning with 'over').[32] Pawelec argues that Lakoff tries to conclude too much from these cases. We can see how some extensions are understandable in view of the way we engage with certain constellations of things as humans, but it is too much to claim that we are programmed by innate schemas to make exactly these connections. We need much wider study of different languages to see what universals are at work here.

32. Pawelec, *Network Models,* chapters 2–3.

Another point Pawelec makes is that it is very difficult to establish which are the basic uses of a term like 'over', and which are derived and have come later. There is often more than one way to reconstruct a prepositional network model. But the phenomenon which we can cast light on is the very fact that different constellations—for instance that invoked by "the plane is over the city", and that invoked by "Sam lives over the bridge"—are held together without even a sense of polysemy in the same preposition. The connections are rooted in our sense of how we can engage with the things concerned, and that is why there is no sense of strain in moving from one to another.

Pawelec notes a similar kind of unnoticed variation in criteria in the case of the length/width distinction analyzed by C. Vandeloise.[33] Vandeloise identifies different scenarios in which we identify length rather differently. Some truly linear entities (a piece of string) have length ascribed to them but no width; roads have length along the direction of travel, and the width is perpendicular to this. Mobile entities, like moving cars, have their length evaluated parallel to their direction of movement. While with immobile multidimensional entities (e.g., house or table), the assessment may depend on the vantage point of the observer. But in geometry, "the length/width of an entity is its greatest/smallest nonvertical extent". These differences are rarely consciously noted by speakers who feel they are using monosemic terms. We can understand this apparent monosemy if we take account of the "pragmatic bridges" between the different situations. The connection between the first and second cases (strings and cars) is made because both allow movement, of the eye or hand along a string, and of vehicles on a road. Even an oddly shaped tractor, very short from stem to stern, but taking up a lot of lateral space will be judged wide and short, whereas geometric shapes could not be seen that way. As we move outside our grasp of things in terms of meanings and affordances, the criteria shift. These contexts correspond to different ways of "questioning" reality,[34] and the different criteria for the same concept make sense to us in virtue of these shifts in our line of access.

So bodily understanding can cast light on unnoticed polysemy. But it may also be the source area of "metaphors" by which we understand the

---

33. C. Vandeloise, "Length, Width and Potential Passing," in *Topics in Cognitive Linguistics,* ed. B. Rudzka-Ostyn (Amsterdam: John Benjamins, 1988), 403–37; see Pawelec, *Network Models,* 136 and ff.

34. Pawelec, *Network Models,* 143.

world around us. It can be the B which casts light on certain of the phenomena we encounter (A). We can see how our sense of being agents maintaining balance can shape our perception of other things. Let's look again at this feat of a child's first year, learning to stand up and keep his balance. He is drawn to rise, to try to stay upright, to begin walking, at first very uncertainly. To master this skill of keeping one's balance is to experience a kind of equilibrium in one's posture in relation to the world. As I said earlier, this zone of balance is a center point or axis where different, potentially disruptive, forces come to rest.

Our experience of this is bodily; one might say, as I did above, that the body knows. This is the original bodily experience of balance. And this can enable us to experience balance in other things. For instance, in a painting. Indeed, it is often hard not to experience balance or its absence in some scenes. And we can carry the template farther, and speak of a balanced personality, of a mind which has lost its balance, of a balanced program, a balanced budget, and so on.[35]

4

But I want now to go beyond mere punctual metaphors and models for suppressed polysemy and look at what we might call structural templates.

Lakoff and Johnson argue that our motor abilities for dealing with things provide us templates which can allow us to structure and make sense of new domains beyond the basic level of our interactions with the objects and getting around in our spatial environment. These templates can combine to form cognitive models, scenarios, narratives, semantic frames that give their shape to more "abstract" domains of cultural and social interaction, or even to scientific or mathematical theories.

Examples of templates that arise in our basic-level spatial interactions are: (a) the "Container": a certain area contains some entities; these are "in", others are "out"; the entities can move into or out of the container—this template already contains implicitly what will be worked out later as the Boolean logic of classes;[36] and (b) the "Source-Path-Goal" template, drawn from our experience of going somewhere, moving from an origin point

35. See Mark Johnson's interesting discussion of balance in *Body*, chapter 4. For the whole question of bodily understanding, see Hubert Dreyfus and Charles Taylor, *Retrieving Realism* (Cambridge, MA: Harvard University Press, 2015), chapters 2–3.

36. Lakoff, *Women*, 456.

through intermediate terrain to a destination, and/or our experience of seeing an object on a trajectory moving from one point to another. This too has its own in-built spatial "logic": for example, if you have traveled from A to B, and then from B to C, you have traveled from A to C.[37]

Template (a) can then be used to structure a number of domains beyond the spatial. We speak of being "in love", or in some state, like depression, which we are anxious to get "out" of as quickly as possible. Template (b) is used to structure a whole host of activities. Basically any kind of minimally complex purposive enterprise can be modeled on the journey. My ambition is to be prime minister, and I "set out on the path" (joining a party, running for Parliament, gathering a following), but I "get stuck" on the road. I "lose my way" by getting involved in the wrong issues. Now I "don't know where to turn". But I hope you can help me "get back on track", so that I'm once more "making progress" toward my goal. Much of our language for purposive action reflects this template.

This creative application of templates is what Lakoff and Johnson call "metaphor". One can quarrel with this extension of the term from the more familiar range of figures known to rhetoric and literary criticism. But the analogy which motivates the extension is that we have once more here a grasp of A through B, although we are no longer dealing with one event (his chairing the meeting) figured through another (the farmer ploughing), but rather with a relation between whole domains, whereby one is structured through a template derived from another; for instance, understanding my bid for political power in spatial terms as a journey. We can borrow from the established language for analyzing metaphors, and describe one of these as the source, the other as the target. I draw the structure from the journey as source in order to make sense of my target, the enterprise of becoming prime minister.

But Lakoff and Johnson see "metaphor", in their sense, as a much more serious, indeed indispensable, contribution to our thought than do views which give literal speech the primacy. This primacy has been upheld by a very powerful philosophical tradition in our culture. Language is used to name things. Words are applied to things. The thing designated in each case is the literal meaning of the word. To talk of one thing by using a word meant to designate another can add color to one's discourse, may make for good rhetoric, but hardly can contribute to clarity. Indeed, some

37. Lakoff and Johnson, *Flesh*, 31–34.

have seen it as very dangerous. We saw this tropophobic view with Hobbes above, where he branded metaphors as ignes fatui; and "reasoning upon them is wandering amongst innumerable absurdities; and their end, contention and sedition, or contempt."[38] So even when we use tropes, the only meaning that counts is the literal meaning. Figures can suggest or insinuate something, but solid information is alone conveyed by the literal meaning.

Now against this, Lakoff and Johnson contend that metaphors in their sense (in my usage, templates) can give structure and shape to a domain. In some cases, it would seem that without recourse to the template we would find it difficult to talk about matters in the domain at all. In other cases, the template is dispensable; indeed, there may be several different metaphors for a given domain, and we may judge some better than others; but nevertheless, each template structures the domain very differently, and brings out features (or alleged features) which the others do not.

These structural templates illustrate even more clearly the inseparability of discovery and invention. In fact, Black has pointed out the analogy between such structural or sectoral metaphors, and models as they figure in science. For instance, Maxwell representing an electric field on the model of an imaginary incompressible fluid. The model here helps to articulate the domain in question. The issue is not whether there really is such a fluid, but the way the analogy enables us to make sense of the domain we are examining.[39]

As an example of the first kind of template, those which seem indispensable, think of certain orientational metaphors; say, around the dimension up/down: happy is UP, sad DOWN (my spirits rose, sank); health and life are UP (I fell back into a coma), good is UP, bad is DOWN (that was a low blow), more is UP (inflation has risen). First of all, these templates seem anything but arbitrary; it is hard to imagine reversing them, so that happy would be DOWN. But secondly, so many of the things we want to say, and the nuances we want to convey, as well as the integration of these

38. Thomas Hobbes, *Leviathan,* ed. Michael Oakeshott (Oxford: Blackwell, 1989), part 1, chapter 5; cited in Lakoff and Johnson, *Metaphors,* 190. Hobbes might be answering Lakoff and Johnson, focusing on some of the same examples. He finds "absurdity in the use of metaphors, tropes and other rhetorical figures, instead of words proper. For although it be lawful to say *the way goeth, or leadeth hither, or thither; the proverb says this or that,* whereas ways cannot go, nor proverbs speak; yet in reckoning, and seeking of truth, such speeches are not to be admitted" (part 1, chapter 5). Similar points are made by Locke.

39. Ricoeur, *La Métaphore,* study 7, 302–4; see also Black, *Models.*

with our body language (shoulders slumped when sad), would be unavailable without these mappings of "high" and "low" spirits on this spatial dimension.

Other examples of templates which it would be hard to imagine living without are those which structure our understanding of time. Time as something which flows, like a river; and we can either place ourselves on the bank, watching it flow by, or see ourselves as carried by the river itself, away from an unrecoverable past toward an unknown future. There seems to be an irresistible draw to spatialize time in one or another way, which can lead us to adopt philosophically questionable doctrines, but which provides models which enable us to talk about it: time flies, time moves inexorably, time undermines the most solid structures.

Another example of a template which greatly expands our articulacy in its target domain is the casting of a purposeful enterprise as a journey that I mentioned above. How would we substitute for all the talk of "straying from the path", "losing my way", or for talk of being "stuck", or "making progress" without recourse to this source?

Let's look now at a dispensable template that Lakoff and Johnson mention, the template: "Love Is a Journey". This may be hard to get away from in our culture, but it may not make the same sense in other cultures, and can be challenged at certain moments even by us. Lakoff and Johnson show how pervasive this metaphor is in our contemporary world: "our relationship is going nowhere", it's "at a dead end"; "honey, we're spinning our wheels", "we're at a crossroads"; "we're going in different directions".[40] This template is, of course, related to that which understands purposeful action as a journey; and then by extension, life as a journey (connected to the notion of "life plan"). The journey of love is one we take together, instead of apart; but alas, "we may have reached the end of the road".

These extensions of the journey template may make sense to us, but they don't necessarily resonate in other cultures. And even we can raise the issue whether what they reveal is more important than what they hide. One partner may protest: "why do you always talk about getting somewhere? Love is communion, a state of mutual connection, nourished by strong moments, but still persisting between these. Your constant

---

40. Lakoff and Johnson, *Flesh,* 123. Another striking example is the way in which Aymara speakers think of the past, not behind us as we do, but in front, while the future is in the space behind. (They resemble Benjamin's angel of destruction!) See David McNeill, *Gesture and Thought* (Chicago: University of Chicago Press, 2005), 46n.5.

restlessness is destroying our communion." Here two rival ways of making sense, of reading the significance of events in our life together, confront each other. The protesting partner is in a position somewhat analogous to a scientist who challenges a reigning paradigm, saying: if you stick with this paradigm, you'll never get to the crucial factors.

This example, and the analogy with the paradigm in science (which I invoked in connection with Black above), shows how important such templates can be. To lapse for a minute into Heideggerese, different templates "disclose" rather different things, a different shape of the terrain in question (as I too, lapse into metaphor). And what discloses some things can also hide others. But in some cases, with the "indispensable" templates above, we can only attain rather minimal and poor disclosure of a domain, if we don't have recourse to them.

What conventional metaphors and templates have in common is that they involve figuring one object or event, or whole domain, through another. What tropophobes like Hobbes would have us do, when we come to reasoning, is translate what we say with these figurations into "literal" speech, that is, speech which is purged of bifocality, which no longer involves reading one reality through another. Hobbes finds "absurdity in the use of metaphors, tropes and other rhetorical figures, instead of words proper. For although it be lawful to say *the way goeth, or leadeth hither, or thither; the proverb says this or that,* whereas ways cannot go, nor proverbs speak; yet in reckoning, and seeking of truth, such speeches are not to be admitted."[41]

But how do you translate an expression like "high spirits" into "literal" speech? "Good spirits"? "positive mood"? How to say "Time marches on"; "my campaign has ground to a halt"? You could cite a lot of the information that underlies that third judgment (we're not recruiting any more people, our supporters are discouraged, etc.), but that doesn't quite render the force of the lapidary judgment. As for the first case, "high spirits", there is all the thick embodied meaning residing in 'up', 'high', 'erect', as against 'down', 'low', 'slumped', which is lost in any rendering in other terms. But that's exactly my point, Hobbes might reply, followed in this by architects of the "regimented" systems of post-Fregean thought. Of course, you can't translate 'high spirits' by 'positive mood', or some such. Of course, there is an excess of (linguistic) meaning. But this has to do with what you mis-

41. Hobbes, *Leviathan,* part 1, chapter 5.

erable hermeneutical philosophers have been calling "human meanings", in this case the embodied sensibility of the speakers. You are dealing with the significance of this state of positive mood for the agents. But you can't reason with this kind of attribution. For one thing, these significances can vary from person to person; for another, any reading of one object through another can wreak havoc with the deductive system we are trying to erect. (I have to concede this point; indeed, I showed it above in discussing metaphors.)

Now some such exact system of inferences is clearly involved in Hobbes's notion of "reckoning". From his point of view, these human meanings are the stuff of rhetorical froth, not of the hard core of empirical meaning.

We can recognize here the influence of the ontological requirements on valid reasoning which have often been imposed on rigorous thinking under the authority of post-Galilean natural science, with its sidelining of human significance (requirement [3], in the list at the beginning of this chapter).

But whatever the validity of this restrictive notion of reasoning, and whatever the scope of the regimented modes of description which meet its requirement, we cannot deny that the way human language actually works, in the wild, as it were, involves disclosing things through metaphors and templates, in short bifocally.

This view of live metaphor or template as productive stands over against the primacy of the literal, and contests it on a number of crucial points. First, it makes the body central; many of the most basic metaphors are rooted in sensorimotor schemata. Second, connected with this, it makes significance, that is, the meanings things have for us, crucial. The source domains: containers, journeys, arise in our grasp of ourselves in the world as agents, where things being in or out matters, and where journeys fulfill purposes, get us to a goal. These three things: disclosive metaphors, the lived body, and the ineliminability of (human) meanings, go together.

By contrast, the primacy of the literal has no place for the lived body; body can enter its account only as the site of underlying unconscious mechanisms; and it has no place for meanings. I mentioned above that the philosophy underlying literalism has a long pedigree in our culture, but particularly powerful and virulent versions of it were invented in the twentieth century. They continued in some fashion the earlier mentalistic theories of meaning, like those of Hobbes and Locke, which construed meaning as a link between word and idea (or word and thing via the idea of the thing in the mind). But they wanted to do away with the "mind" as a substance altogether, and proposed to reconstruct an objectivist semantics linking language and world directly. Accepting the Fregean reconstruction of the Lockean theory, which understands the proposition as made up of a reference and a predication, we ascribe meanings to referring expressions by linking them to objects in the world, and to predicate expressions by linking them to properties. These linkages then allow us to assign a meaning to reference-predication combinations, that is, propositions, and this yields a completely "objectivist" or extensionalist semantics.

A truly objectivist semantics (which would go beyond what Davidson proposes) would anchor our language to the natural world as revealed by natural science, answering the centuries-old dream of a scientific language which really mapped the world as it truly is. The meaning of all sentences that had a meaning would be given in terms of their truth conditions in the world as mapped and classified in science.[42] But this couldn't take account of the way we structure and thus disclose certain target domains in the bifocal figuring of A through B.

There are remarkable Whorfian effects that have been documented, where different cultures structure similar target domains by very different sources. Where English and other similar languages identify spatial locations by using prepositions: the stone is under the table; the temple is on top of the mountain, Mixtec does the same job through a metaphorical projection of body parts. So the stone would be located by something equivalent to "the table's belly"; the temple by "the head of the mountain". "I am sitting on the branch of the tree" comes out something like "I am sitting on the tree's arm".[43]

And of course, all this time, we have to be aware that these literalist theories themselves depend on certain powerful received templates. Why do they think of our computation as going on in the brain, rather than the whole organism, or even the organism-interacting-with-the-environment?[44] The reason seems to be the power of the original Cartesian notion that thought is "inner", situated "in" the mind (the "Container" schema with a vengeance). When this construction is put through the materialistic transposition, the role of the "mind" is taken over by the "brain", which is equally an "inner" organ.

---

42. See Lakoff and Johnson, *Flesh*, chapter 8; Lakoff, *Women*, chapter 11.

43. Lakoff, *Women*, chapter 11.

44. Alva Noë, *Out of Our Heads: Why You Are Not Your Brain, and Other Lessons from the Biology of Consciousness* (New York: Hill and Wang, 2009). See also Dreyfus and Taylor, *Realism*, chapter 5.

And this brings us to a very important issue. Different structuring metaphors are like paradigms, as I asserted earlier. They can disclose certain things and hide others. We can be led seriously astray if we take certain of our templates as absolute, as revealing everything, or at least everything important.[45] This happens when we become obsessed with a certain template, and cannot see where it might mislead; indeed, fail to see it as a template, to which there might be alternatives. At this point, we are close to Wittgenstein's description of our predicament in modern philosophy. "A picture held us captive."[46] I think something like this is true of the tradition of modern epistemology since Descartes, which has enslaved not only Cartesian dualists, but also all those mechanistic reductivists who claim to have repudiated totally Cartesian dualism, including those who believe in objectivist semantics, and who sideline metaphor!

But captivity in distorting pictures is of relevance not only in (bad) philosophy; it also has social and political importance. Certain structuring metaphors have acquired ascendancy in our civilization, which if taken alone will blind us to what is inhuman and destructive in our behavior. Lakoff and Johnson cite the schema "Time Is a Resource": time is something to be used, managed, not "wasted", and employed to maximum effect.[47] Such an ontology of time, which comes down to us partly through an important theme of Puritan preaching,[48] has become central to our capitalist civilization which privileges instrument rationality. This schema can be extended into the structuring idea that "Time Is Money". Under the pressure of this dominant frame, even leisure time becomes a resource, to be used "to maximum effect" (to recover from labor, to attain maximum enjoyment, to prepare ourselves to work better after the holidays). There is

---

45. Unlike punctual metaphors, structural templates cannot go fully dead (reach phase two), that is, lose all sense of the original image. That is because the template can be a continuing source of new expressions. (In the "Love Is a Journey" template, someone could invent the new expression "we're spinning our wheels".) The original image is in this way still operative. But there is another way in which the template can be lost from view, if it becomes so obvious and taken for granted that it is not seen as one among many possible construals, as allowing for an alternative way of conceiving the domain. That is what it means to absolutize a template as in the case referred to in this paragraph, and stigmatized by Wittgenstein.

46. [*Ein Bild hielt uns gefangen*], Ludwig Wittgenstein, *Philosophical Investigations*, trans. G. E. M. Anscombe (Oxford: Blackwell, 1997), 1.115; Wittgenstein, *Philosophische Untersuchungen*, 1.115. Philosophy, Wittgenstein said, suffers from too one-sided a diet of examples.

47. Lakoff and Johnson, *Flesh*, 161 and ff.

48. See Max Weber, *Die Protestantische Ethik und der Geist des Kapitalismus* (Weinheim: Beltz Athenäum 2000), English translation: The *Protestant Ethic and the Spirit of Capitalism*, trans. Talcott Parsons (New York: Scribner, 1958).

a truth to all this, a truth which has come to be in our civilization; but what this frame can do is occlude other ways of relating to time, devalue them, make them disappear for many people. And this cramps and distorts our lives.[49]

In many cases of structuring metaphors, there is a clear asymmetry between source and target. We understand love as a journey, but not journeys by love. But this kind of understanding one domain through another can also sometimes be symmetrical. Think of kings and divinity. Here there seems to have been some mutual interpenetration: we understand God as King; but we have also in many cultures come to understand kingship as participating in the divine. "There's such a divinity that doth hedge a king."[50]

But another kind of bidirectionality applies to a lot of ordinary metaphors, where not only does the source make us look at the target differently, but the fact of the two being put in relationship also changes our sense of the source. Rowan Williams (to whom I owe this point) offers a couple of examples: "Weeping skies" cannot be a literal description, but the association of a rainy day with grief points up something about weeping by associating it with the weather as well as pointing up something about weather by recognizing its irresistible linkage with mood in our interpretation of it, our "humanizing of it as a phenomenon that casts light on ourselves." He makes a similar point about "money talks": we underline the power of money with this expression, but we also hint at the way "talking" in our society is implicated in power.[51]

5

I have been discussing in the above pages (punctual) metaphors, and (structural) templates. But there are other modes of expression in which we find the relation of A through B. There are articulations through what the Romantics called "symbol". This exhibits a more radical form of disclosure of

49. In the proposed companion study to this volume, I want to focus on the distortions of lived time wrought by the hegemony of objectified time in our civilization, as revealed through post-Romantic poetics, as we can see in Baudelaire, which Benjamin well recognized in this poet.

50. Shakespeare, *Hamlet*, act 4, sc. 5.

51. Rowan Williams, *The Edge of Words: God and the Habits of Language* (London: Bloomsbury, 2014), 500.

A through B. Structural templates, I have been arguing, disclose different aspects and features of their target domain, and in this way are analogous to scientific paradigms. The more radical case is where the A domain wouldn't be accessible to language at all without the terms of B; or else would only be accessible if it were understood very differently. The A domain only becomes open through an extended use, which we might think of as metaphorical, of the terms of B.

An example, which is perhaps universal, is the use of the language of up and down to describe character, which I touched on above. We see this in a term like 'upright', or 'a low form of life'. Of course, we can convey some of the force of the first attribution by saying: "he doesn't cheat, he doesn't steal, you can count on his word", and so on. But the precise force of 'upright', which is carried by the symbol of standing up, of being "unbending", can't be translated out. Nor can we imagine this image going "dead". The links between the spatial and the ethical here are partly mediated by the connections between pride, shame, and dignity, on one hand, and posture, gait, self-projection, on the other. It is hard to conceive a human life in which these connections didn't exist: that is, either in which pride and shame played no role, or in which posture was not a paradigm domain of expression for these matters. The man of pride stands upright, ready to face down the reproaches of his adversaries. This has something, though not everything, to do with the fact that 'upright' is a prominent term for morally righteous.

Maybe we could see this as an extreme case of a very useful template. But an example which goes beyond this is the use of the language of inner depth to describe subjective life. We speak of a deep question, a deep matter. We speak of depth psychology. Somebody says that "way deep down inside", he really loves her, or he believes in God, or he agrees with Nietzsche. In a final moment of struggle, someone "reaches deep down inside himself" to make a supreme effort.

"Deep" here contrasts with "superficial". The superficial is what doesn't engage us very "deeply". If I struggle to stay clear of this master metaphor, I can say it doesn't engage our whole being. Consistent with this image, the superficial is what may easily hide what lies beneath, in the depths of our being. If you're just living on the surface, you may never really be aware of what lies hidden there. You're not a very deep person; in fact, you're "shallow".

But of course, we didn't always talk in these terms. The distinction inside/outside applied to subjective life had a different sense in earlier times, as I have tried to show elsewhere.[52] Plato in *The Republic* seems to be proposing a distinction which we would be tempted to code with the contrast: superficial/deep. He talks about those who are lovers of "sights and sounds and beautiful spectacles,"[53] as against those who love wisdom, who yearn for the unchanging truth of things. The latter is what you long for with your whole being, when this being is in harmony with itself, the former is what engages just the desiring part of you, when it's at odds with your reason. This difference can't be got at with a surface/depth contrast; it's more a question of what engages just a part of you, as against the whole; or of what relates you to mere appearance as against the "really real".

So the language of inner depths isn't a universal human one (as that of "upright" and "bending" may well be). But my claim would be that it would be next to impossible for the kind of beings we have become in Western civilization to do without this language, in spite of the valiant efforts of Nietzsche and others.[54]

Another example would be the moral/religious languages of defilement, stain, or impurity to designate evil, wrongdoing, sin. As we look over the range of human cultures in history, we can see that these are not universal, any more than our modern sense of inner depth is. But they are very widespread, and moreover, some variant seems to crop up in the most unexpected places. They are by no means confined to older or more "primitive" forms of religion. Robespierre sought to purify the republic by eliminating its "corrupt" elements. Recent decades have seen much "ethnic cleansing". Peddlers of pornography are widely thought to refer to their wares as "dirty pictures". On top of this, it is by no means clear that the abandonment of this kind of language doesn't create the need for other master images of evil, like those of missing the mark [*hamartia*], becoming lost, being captive, alienation, and the like.[55] Nevertheless, it seems that one can construe one's moral life in such a way as to bypass this image. But for those who do

---

52. See Charles Taylor, *Sources of the Self* (Cambridge, MA: Harvard University Press, 1989).

53. See Plato, *The Republic*, 475d.

54. "Oh, those Greeks! They knew how to live: what is needed for that is to stop bravely at the surface, the fold, the skin; to worship appearance, to believe in shapes, tones, words—in the whole Olympus of appearance! Those Greeks were superficial—out of profundity!" Friedrich Nietzsche, *The Gay Science*, trans. Josefine Nauckhoff (Cambridge: Cambridge University Press, 2001), 8–9.

55. Paul Ricoeur, *Philosophie de la Volonté, Tome 2: Finitude to Culpabilité: La Symbolique du Mal* (Paris: Aubier, 1960).

conceive good and evil in these terms, the image is indispensable, even as depth seems to be for our psychic life.

We want to speak of "symbol" here, because on one hand, there is no simple identity between moral evil (the A domain), and ordinary (physical) dirt; while on the other, this understanding of moral wrong can only be articulated in terms of uncleanness. The symbol in this sense is unlike the allegory, which allows an independent description of its target domain. Symbols are the indispensable way of access to what they are about.[56]

Of course, for those deeply immersed in the cultures they define, these symbolic languages don't appear as such. The nonidentity of defilement and ordinary uncleanness may not show up; or the two kinds of cases, if they are distinguished at all, may appear unproblematically describable by the same term. Just as for us the step from deep waters to a deep person may seem quite obvious, just another kind of depth. And in certain cultures, a sense of defilement (say, when served food by someone of a lower caste) may be very strongly felt, inducing disgust, even nausea. This is particularly the case where the agents concerned are "porous", as against "buffered" selves.[57]

But at some stage in the culture's evolution the difference between dirt and moral defilement does come to light, and becomes problematic—as when Christ says in the New Testament: it is not what someone takes into himself, but what comes out of him, "that defileth a man."[58] Or else, we encounter another culture in which some of the same wrongs show up through another master image, and this shows the difference (analogous to the way looking at Plato above can detach us from our unthinking commitment to a language of depth). But as long as we're strongly (and deeply!) held by the culture, the very force of such symbolic attributions as "he has blood on his hands" serves to weld the two levels together.

The notion of symbol I have used here is the one we owe to the Romantics. How can the infinite be brought to the surface, to "appearance" [*Erscheinung*] asks A. W. Schlegel? "Only symbolically, in pictures and signs" [*Nur symbolisch, in Bildern und Zeichen*], he answers. Poetry is what

56. Ibid., 22–24.

57. See Charles Taylor, *A Secular Age* (Cambridge, MA: Harvard University Press, 2007), 35–43. A similar concept to the "porous self", that of a "dividual" (as against "individual"), has been explored by anthropologists. See Karl Smith, "From Dividual and Individual Selves to Porous Subjects," *Australian Journal of Anthropology* 23 (2012): 50–64.

58. Matthew 15:10–11.

achieves this: "Poetry . . . is nothing other than a perpetual symbolizing: either we seek an outer shell for something spiritual, or else we relate something external to an invisible inner reality" [*Dichten . . . ist nichts anderes als ein ewig Symbolisieren; wir suchen entweder für etwas Geistiges eine äussere Hülle oder wir beziehen ein Äusseres auf ein unsichtbares Inneres*].[59]

A symbol, I have been saying, is like a metaphor, it involves our acceding to A via B, for example, sin or moral defilement through ordinary, everyday soiling. But it is also unlike, say, my using the ploughman image to criticize the chairman's handling of yesterday's discussion. For one thing, we already have a language to describe the activity of chairing meetings, whereas we (or the people of the relevant culture) only have this language for the moral defilement which follows on wrongdoing by descrying and articulating an extra level of meaning analogous to but beyond ordinary soiling. Dirt is our route of access to this semantic domain. This is one reason why the analogy with metaphor often will not appear to those immersed in the language. Another reason is the role that issues of defilement may play in our lives. The terms were not coined to satisfy some impulse to disinterested description of the domain. Sin can be an urgent threat, cutting us off from God, or communion with others, or a full integrity of being (and this "integrity" provides another example where we articulate a moral property via a leap beyond the everyday distinction whole/broken). Symbols of wholeness (e.g., Plato's harmony of the soul, or communion with God and the saints) can play a crucial role in inspiring or empowering us to overcome brokenness; symbols of purity to cleanse defilement. Symbols can help bring to bear what I called in another work "moral sources".[60] I will return to this issue in Chapter 6.

In the light of these differences, we can think of symbols like defilement as sleeping metaphors, because at some point their enigmatic nature comes to light, even to those who find them meaningful. What exactly is sin or moral defilement? It evidently is not identical with ordinary soiling. But what exactly does it consist in? This question can be acutely raised by challenges to the going view like that of Christ in the New Testament just cited above. The enigma which attaches to all strong metaphors (what exactly in B applies to A? or what exactly in A makes B an appropriate mode

---

59. See Charles Taylor, "Celan and the Recovery of Language," in *Dilemmas and Connections: Selected Essays* (Cambridge, MA: Harvard University Press, 2011), 57; A. W. Schlegel, *Die Kunstlehre*, ed. Jacob Minor (Heilbronn: Henninger, 1884), 80–81.

60. Taylor, *Sources*.

of access?) comes to the surface. And we begin to engage in a new kind of discourse, which is described by Ricoeur in the famous chapter "The Symbol Gives Rise to Thought" ["Le Symbole Donne à Penser"].[61] We attempt to resolve the enigmas of the symbol in the language of philosophy, a task which we may never completely succeed in; or may only make headway in through a "mixed discourse" [*discours mixte*] which cannot completely be purged of symbols. Again, I want to leave further discussion of these issues to later chapters.

What I have been calling "symbols" here have some analogy to certain works of art: novels, poetry, music, dance, and so on. The first two of these constitute uses of language. Sometimes they can consist entirely of descriptive sentences—a realist novel for instance. But this work can communicate a sense of things (human life, fate, the passage of time) in a way which is irreducible to literal description. Such works involve, as I shall argue in Chapter 6, nonassertoric presentations. They don't describe what they disclose [*erschliessen*]. This gives us further reasons to question the sidelining of the Cratylist dimension.

6

I have been discussing punctual metaphors, different kinds of templates, and symbols, but there is also another way in which figuring, or the iconic, finds a place in ordinary discourse. The examples in the above sections have all concerned uses of language. But we should also take into account the role of iconic gesture. David McNeil and Adam Kendon[62] argue that iconic gestures not only frequently accompany speech, not only occur alongside the verbal descriptions which match them, but also play a role in our struggle to find the right verbal articulation.[63] Not only do gestures "figure" in the sense of this chapter, but this figuring may help us find the words which are adequate to our descriptive intentions. If this is so, then not only

61. Paul Ricoeur, *The Symbolism of Evil*, trans. Emerson Buchanan (New York: Harper and Row, 1967), 347; Ricoeur, *La Symbolique*, conclusion.

62. McNeil, *Gesture*; Adam Kendon, *Gesture: Visible Action as Utterance* (Cambridge: Cambridge University Press, 2004). Besides the iconic, McNeill also notes three other kinds of frequent gesture: deictic, metaphoric, and beat. An example of the last is when an utterance which is segmented into three points is accompanied (at the right moment) by my holding up first one, then two, then three fingers. See *Gesture*, 38–44.

63. See ibid., chapters 2–3.

is encoding information in the original speech context not such an excarnate activity as it appears when we consider writing and formal scientific communication, but we would have to recognize here an original kind of figuring which helps guide encoding, and this would make it much less surprising to see figuring cropping up in the discourse thus generated. This would also mean that the clear Saussurean distinction between langue and parole, and the derived contemporary distinction between competence and performance, is not all that sharp, because the know-how of gestural performance would be needed to complement a linguistic competence defined uniquely in terms of the grasp of rules. This is indeed what McNeill argues: our sense of a well-formed utterance tells us when we have reached our goal, rather than generating the successful result. "The dialectic [[between static code and dynamic expressive process]] is brought to a halt by the speaker's intuitive recognition of a linguistically well-formed utterance."[64]

7

So what do we think of the account of language that emerges from the post-Fregean transform of the HLC? We saw four features of this account at the beginning of the chapter. First the two basic ones:

I: its words are introduced to designate features which have already come to our attention; and

II: the Cratylist or "figuring" dimension adds nothing to our empirical description of the world, but serves only to register or evoke some positive or negative reactions.

To these may be added two other features which we often find in post-Fregean thinking:

III: there can often be ontological restrictions: descriptions should be compatible with physicalism, that is, the terms used should be ultimately reducible to those which figure in natural science; or

64. Ibid., 64.

alternatively, the terms used should meet some requirement of empirical observability.

Then

> IV: it is often assumed that the correct description of a phenomenon is that from the observer, third-person perspective, as against that from the agent's first-person perspective.

This account, either in its minimal (I and II), or maximal (I–IV) forms, nourishes two projects: the first is a normative one: develop a language in which an (ontologically or epistemologically) respectable account of the world, in propositions which are susceptible where necessary of logical regimentation, can be cast. The second is explanatory: develop an account of our language competence which can draw on our understanding of logical relations to show the meanings of different sentences as theorems of a certain number of axioms. This will take account of the systematic and potentially infinite capacity of our language to generate new such sentences.

It should be clear from the preceding argument that the explanatory project is a nonstarter. It requires our theory of meaning to neglect far too much: analogy, metaphor, as extensions of articulacy; templates, symbols, gestures, and the rest. Surely, these expand what we are trying to explain: language competence.

A theory of meaning, in the intended sense of an account of the competence which a speaker of language possesses, cannot simply consist in an account of how to derive truth conditions of depictive combinations from axioms defining arbitrary, "unmotivated" meanings. Some other competence is involved which enables the ordinary speaker to coin and understand original expressions, not derived from a regimented T-theory, which in Cratylist fashion figure or portray their objects. In other words, a rigorous combinatorial theory, based on core semantic definitions with "arbitrary" (unmotivated) terms, and augmented by logic, cannot derive these inventive uses, which depend on Cratylist insights. So this theory can't map the contours of the sayable, nor can it account completely for ordinary speakers' competence in any language. This type of theory of meaning thus fails, both because it cannot account for our learning linguistic meanings in certain domains: for example, social and cultural meanings (as we shall show in the next chapters); and because it can't cope with the inventivity of real human language across all domains (as we have just argued).

But you can eliminate all these powers, if you imagine a core of language games which concentrate on making and understanding assertions, within more or less fixed taxonomic frames, which can be relatively clearly and unambiguously determined to be true or false, even if one lacks the elements to do so now. This will mean that you steer away from rhetoric, and in general from (all but dead) metaphor (highly stigmatized in the tradition that lies behind this kind of theory); and of course, you will find issues concerning human meanings extremely iffy and unsettleable, particularly in regard to the often interminable interpretive disputes to which they give rise. And when one comes to nonassertoric presentations, these have to be deemed completely beyond the pale of the well-regimented language use that we will want to map.

This offers the basis for a normative project. And this has, of course, been in the background all along. The issue here is, how imperialist does this normative project want to be? That a language which meets the specifications of the previous paragraph, including requirements (I)–(IV), can be highly useful, even indispensable in certain contexts, such as natural science, has already been amply demonstrated. That everything else worth saying could be reduced to this language, including what we want to say about ethics, aesthetics, human character, history, politics, and so on, seems wildly implausible. The attempt to liberate a unified territory, based on the Vienna constellation, and grouping natural science, common sense and logical inference, must founder; ordinary common-sense speech is irremediably addicted to tropes, metaphors, symbols, and templates.

But one last claim could be made: a language based on requirements (I)–(IV) could be what Brandom calls an "autonomous discursive practice" (ADP), in the sense of a "language game one could play even if one played no other."[65] Would it be possible for us to drop all these other things: tropes, images, symbols, templates, and of course, gestures and literature, and just have this austere language of description and explanation? (I won't even ask the question whether this would be desirable.) This is a question about human beings; we are not asking whether some kinds of

65. See Chapter 4, note 44.

beings which could be imagined could meet these austere and limiting specifications.

It is one of my basic claims in this book that this kind of restricted language is a human impossibility. This is the basis of the third "holism" which I introduced at the beginning of Chapter 1: the impossibility of human language in the narrow sense outside the whole range of "symbolic forms". I'm not ready to argue the full case here, but a number of things have come to light in this chapter which make the outlook for this kind of restricted language less than good. If scientific inventivity draws on the same powers of analogy and metaphor, and seeing A through B, which we have noted in ordinary speech, then we would lose more than the capacity to make unfounded utterances by restricting ourselves through imposing (I)–(IV).

8

All the above shows that the Saussurean thesis of arbitrariness needs modification. It is often presented as an obvious "objective" fact about language, definitively relegating to an unscientific past various theories of linguistic motivation, whether they are of the sort explored in Plato's Cratylus, or the kind we see in Kabbalistic and Renaissance theories of the original language of Adam (e.g., when he named the animals), which purportedly had the excellent feature, since lost, that each term was attuned to and revealed the nature of its referent.

Now the Saussurean thesis will not be overthrown as applied to each word envisaged separately. Plainly, what 'dog' says could and is equally well rendered by '*chien*' or '*Hund*'.[66] But it can be misleading when applied to moves within language that involve combinations and relations of words. We will see this later on in regard to certain texts (e.g., narratives). But we can see it here in coinages which involve extensions of meaning. Frege, it

66. One might even argue that the nonmotivation of meaning at the level of the word is an essential feature of language as an analytical-combinatorial mode of information coding. Some words may appear "motivated", words like 'coocoo', 'quiver', 'slink', 'babble' (see John Lyons, *Semantics*, vol. 1 [Cambridge: Cambridge University Press], 104 for a number of interesting examples). But even where this might provide part of the motivation for selecting the word, this cannot suffice to define the meaning. "Coocoo" is used as a name to refer to a kind of bird (or perhaps its call—or even both). But in either case it functions as a noun (or two). "Babble" is a kind of action, hence a verb. All this has to be understood before these sounds can function as words. The terms of language are essentially unmotivated, as Saussure said.

can be claimed, once and for all showed the inadequacy of trying to understand linguistic meaning starting simply from the meanings of individual words. "Only in the context of a proposition [sentence] has a name meaning" [*Nur im Zusammenhang eines Satzes hat ein Wort Bedeutung*].[67] He gave the telling case for this thesis, that of the declarative sentence, or assertion, which had to be seen as a combination of reference and predication. It would be remarkable if this were the only "context" [*Zusammenhang*] in which this principle held.

Behind this readiness to extend the context principle, which I am here noticing and endorsing, lies the influence of a tradition in the study of language, which I have referred to as the "HHH" outlook, invoking Hamann, Herder, and Humboldt, but also including other influential figures, such as Merleau-Ponty. The concern of this tradition has always been to understand how language opens up new ways of articulating our grasp of reality. This can be examined either through an attempt to define what new kind of awareness comes with language, and/or through a grasp of the different kinds of articulation which can arise through the development of language. From this point of view, the very idea of articulating the relation of species in a Linnaean taxonomy would figure as one such significant creation of a new form.

Seen in this light, it will appear that anti-Cratylism has limits. Because new ways of articulating can arise as transformations of old ways, and just because of this, the new articulation can be immediately understandable, experienced as totally "natural", not arbitrary at all.

Now Brandom is no old-style positivist. He has learned a lot from Wittgenstein (as have we all), and is willing to accept that the regimented system of objectivist semantics may not be able to embrace all of the sayable. He nevertheless sees a point in the enterprise, in order to reveal something about those vocabularies which do connect, and those which don't. But it may be that the "unaccessible" areas of normal speech are much bigger than he suspects.

Of course, we owe to Wittgenstein this challenge to such tightly organized semantic systems. He attributes what he sees as the diseased rage to systematicity to an inability to recognize the great plurality of uses of language. The outer form may make it look as though we were making Fre-

---

67. Ludwig Wittgenstein, *Tractus Logico-Philosophicus*, trans. C. K. Ogden (New York: Harcourt, Brace, 1922), 3.3.

gean assertions about standard objects, but this misleads. We may not be making assertions at all. Or the way these assertions work may be quite different from the Fregean norm. Brandom is impressed by Wittgenstein's arguments, but doesn't agree that we have to give up any systematic account of language.[68] But maybe the principal issue concerns what we would count as "systematic". If we take as our model Brandom's regimented semantic connections, then systematicity may be impossible even if we enlarge our connectives to include his "pragmatically mediated semantic relations".[69] But on a looser model, an illuminating understanding of language as a whole may yet be possible.

In fact, Hans Julius Schneider reads Wittgenstein as offering such an account, in which something analogous to the metaphorical extensions we have been discussing takes place. Wittgenstein seems to be arguing against a certain kind of projection in our understanding of language. We understand a sentence like, for instance, (1) "he has an idea", on analogy with (2) "he has a dog"; and so we postulate an object, analogous to the dog, only in some way "inner", a mental content. Now the notion that there must be a particular kind of inner mental content [*seelischer Vorgang*] whenever someone has an idea, as there indeed is an external (canine) object when someone has a dog, is indeed, a mistake. But the mistake is not that sentences of this form require this kind of object, so that when we come up with a statement like (1) on the basis of (2) we are committed to finding such as object.

Rather what is happening here is something like a metaphorical projection. We have already mastered sentences like (2), where we talk about owning standard objects, and then we coin something like (1) applying it to this new case which bears a similarity to the original one, but is nevertheless different. We are doing something which has analogies to what Lakoff and Johnson have suggested, when we speak of our bank account increasing by saying it has "gone up". Of course, the bank account is not in any sense in a new spatial position above where it was before. But some natural sense of analogy enables us to speak of the change as in these terms, and be immediately understood. This gives us a new way of talking about increase and decrease of fortune. The projection makes this new language

---

68. Robert Brandom, *Between Saying and Doing: Towards an Analytic Pragmatism* (Oxford: Oxford University Press, 2008), 4–7.

69. Ibid., chapter 1.

possible. "For a projection through which a secondary meaning is constituted, it is instead . . . typical that it creates for the first time a possible
articulation: the 'figurative expression' is used to open up an area of discourse that otherwise, without the projective step, would not be available"
[*Fur eine Projektion, durch die eine sekundäre Bedeutung konstituiert wird,
ist es . . . typisch, daß sie eine Artikulationsmöglichkeit allererst schafft: Der
'bildende Ausdruck' wird dazu benutzt, einen Bereich sprachlichen Handelns
zu erschließen, der ohne ihn, ohne den Schritt der Projektion, nicht zur Ver-
fügung stünde*].[70] The error here is not that of the ordinary speaker, but
rather that of the philosopher reflecting on this. His blindness is that he
accepts an objectivism of meaning, where words always pick out objects of
the same kind; he can't see where metaphor is at work. So he thinks
either that there must be some inner object for (1) to be true; or else he
thinks that the "logical form" of (1) distorts the "real form", and that we
must find some other way of saying what we mean here. The similarity of
Schneider's thesis to the ideas I've been defending here should be evident;
and this is not coincidental, because he is one of my key sources for the
thesis I'm developing. He documents another site of the creativity of language, where the form of one kind of sentence in one domain can offer a
template for the articulation of sentences in a quite different domain.

On this reading of Wittgenstein, he is not simply a negator of all attempts at systematicity. On the contrary, he sees how different uses are
linked. But these links involve projective steps of a metaphorical type (understanding A through B); and these are not in the repertory of analytic
philosophers seeking the kind of semantic relations which Brandom
examines.

70. H. J. Schneider, *Wittgenstein's Later Theory of Meaning: Imagination and Calculation*, trans.
Timothy Doyle and Daniel Smyth (West Sussex: Wiley Blackwell, 2014), 86–87; H. J. Schneider,
Phantasie und Kalkül: Über die Polarität von Handlung und Struktur in der Sprache (Frankfurt am
Main: Suhrkamp, 1999), 335.

6

Constitution 1

The Articulation of Meaning

1

In Chapter 5 I discussed how what I called "figuring" can extend the reach of our descriptive powers. The time has now come to take on the issue of semantic innovation in general.

We must take seriously Humboldt's often repeated point, which I invoked in Chapter 1, that possessing a language is to be continuously involved in trying to extend its powers of articulation. In other words, we always sense that there are things we cannot properly say, but we would like to express. There is always a "feeling that there is something which the language does not directly contain, but which the [mind/soul], spurred on by language, must supply; and the [drive], in turn, to couple everything felt by the soul with a sound" [*Gefühl, daß es etwas gibt, das die Sprache nicht unmittelbar enthält, sondern der Geist, von ihr angeregt, ergänzen muß, und den Trieb, wiederum alles, was die Seele empfindet, mit dem Laut zu verknüpfen*].[1] This endless striving to increase articulacy is the real point behind the famous Humboldt saying about using finite means to infinite ends. The "finite means" here doesn't refer to an existing stock of words, as the Chomskian interpretation seems to assume; rather it is the finite stock

---

1. Wilhelm von Humboldt, *On Language: The Diversity of Human Language-Structure and Its Influence on the Mental Development of Mankind*, trans. Peter Heath (Cambridge: Cambridge University Press, 1988), 157; Humboldt, *Schriften zur Sprache*, ed. Michael Bühler (Stuttgart: Reklam 1995), 146.

of sounds at our disposal, with which we can find expression for an unlimited range of phenomena.[2]

Some readers may find Humboldt's image of a perpetual and urgent striving to greater articulacy somewhat overdrawn (though I don't share this reaction), but what can't be denied is that we sometimes have just this experience; and it is not only poets, novelists, and artists who feel this, although it is the very stuff of their existence, but also just about everyone at some point in their lives. We may want to describe a landscape, or the expression on someone's face, or the sense we had of what moved someone to act as they did. But perhaps the place where we can feel this most urgently is when we try to understand our own feelings and motives.

The difficulty in this kind of case will often involve resistance, an unwillingness to admit to certain feelings or reactions, but it may also come from lacking the words, the distinctions, the nuances to get at our feelings.

What Humboldt is on to here is the experience of wanting to say what we cannot yet satisfactorily express. We can't say what is missing here; we will only be able to do this after a successful articulation. The HLC model, of coining a word for an idea which is in the mind (or some object we observe), frequently doesn't apply to this situation. Nor does the demand that the expression we use should apply "by a perfectly arbitrary imposition"; rather we need to find a formula which figures the phenomenon we are trying to disclose, be this through metaphor, or analogy, or creative extension of existing terms, or whatever.

The "right word" here discloses, brings the phenomenon properly into view for the first time. Discovery and invention are two sides of the same coin; we devise an expression which allows what we are striving to encompass to appear. This is a crucial facet of our language capability, which I will call "articulation".

Now this works out differently in different cases. One area in which we struggle with inarticulacy is when we're asked to give an account of a complex event, which was perhaps at first confusing. "Please tell the court, Mr. Jones, exactly what you saw on this occasion." You strive to put the events in order, see the connections, and relate the different threads to each other. "First X entered, he was carrying a gun, but just loosely, not pointing it; then Y turned . . ."

2. *Scriften*, 96.

Telling a complex story like this is something we master well after learning to speak, as the work of John Lucy has shown.[3] Children only master this art of putting complex, many-person stories into form, using pronouns, sometime in their teens.

We experience this need to put things into form in other contexts as well. For instance, we enter an unfamiliar laboratory, and we can't quite figure out where one of the objects stops and another starts, or how things are connected. Or someone with absolutely no knowledge and experience of chess looks at a chess game, and tries to understand the different permitted moves. Compare these situations to the way we experience them after we know our way about. In these cases, we usually learn how to navigate these scenes along with learning the words for the key features, like the different instruments in the laboratory, or the different moves in chess and their consequences.

Our capacities in this area can be described as our ability to encode information, in the sense described in Chapter 3.

But there is a more sophisticated analogue to this kind of situation, where we feel a need to (re)order; let's say we have an anomaly-producing paradigm, and we strive to imagine a new one. This we sometimes do by moving from one comprehensible-in-ordinary-life model to another: for example, see things not as little corpuscles impacting on each other, but as existing in a tensile milieu, or a field of force.

These different situations form together one kind of predicament where we can struggle for articulacy, to impose a certain form. The challenge arises from a field of objects which we only imperfectly understand. This is the domain of language which the HLC has always been concentrated on, both in its original and its post-Fregean forms, as we saw in Chapter 4. But the challenges are different if we look at another set of domains, those of our feelings or what I have been calling "meanings".

These often overlap, feelings incorporate some attribution of meaning to the situation: "it frightened me" entails: "it seemed menacing". Feelings usually relate to states of affairs, in their meaning for us. I am speaking here of meanings in the sense of the significance that things have for us; this covers at its widest stretch any way that things, or states of affairs, or what they portend, can be nonindifferent for the agent, or

---

3. John A. Lucy and Suzanne Gaskins, "Grammatical Categories and the Development of Classification Preferences: A Comparative Approach," in *Language Acquisition and Conceptual Development,* ed. S. Levinson and M. Bowerman (Cambridge: Cambridge University Press, 2001).

an agent. So to describe a "human meaning" is to describe a way in which something, say, impedes one of our purposes, or furthers it; to describe an obstacle, or a facilitator. But since any thing can bear many descriptions, we might better speak of descriptions of things in meaning terms. The tiger roaming the woods, or the virus working in some organism, can be described by the zoologist for themselves, as it were; but the tiger in the woods behind my house, who has tasted human flesh and is now hungry; the virus which has just entered my organism— these have crucial relevance for me. Under this aspect they are meanings for me.[4]

But this kind of meaning touches only one level of relevance. Tiger and virus are meanings for me qua biological organism. We can also talk of the meanings of things which are instrumental. This path is handy for me to get to work; that new building is an obstacle in my way, forcing me to make a long detour. The good weather will allow us to plant our crops; but the excessive rain later may damage them beyond repair.

But there are also situations which are favorable or unfavorable, pleasant or unpleasant, which make us happy or sad, where we are not dealing with instruments to some distinct purpose. Nor do these situations touch us simply as biological organisms, though that is often relevant too. Here we begin to zero in on an area where we often need articulation. I shall return to this shortly.

Now in a whole range of everyday cases, meaning and feeling go together; meanings are felt. Someone's action can make us cross or angry: or make us glad or grateful; can wound us, or soothe us, even make us feel better. You cross me, and I'm mad, hopping mad; a friend dies and I'm sad, really bereaved. The feeling here is the response to what has happened, to the state of affairs which is its intentional object.

But some of the things we call feelings don't fit this model: tickles, itches, pain, nausea. These feelings don't have intentional objects which occasion them. The pain just *is* the intentional object, and it too has a meaning. It is terrible, and must stop. But with anger and gratitude, there is this structure, where the feeling projects some description of the intentional object. This is why it makes sense to try to argue someone out of his anger: no

---

4. I have discussed some of the issues in the following paragraphs in "Self-Interpreting Animals" in *Philosophical Papers 1: Human Agency and Language* (Cambridge: Cambridge University Press, 1985), 45–76.

offense meant, I didn't know, and the like; but not out of being tickled or nauseous, or out of toothache.[5]

We might say that the feeling/emotion, in the standard case where the occasion is an intentional object, is a way of being aware of the object, through affect.

This is the standard case, but there are "rogue" cases, such as when I'm angry and don't know quite why. The whole atmosphere here is making me feel uncomfortable, and I want to lash out, but I can't quite identify what's doing it. Maybe you're all making me feel inferior, but I don't know whether you're really trying to do this, or it's just me overreacting. Still, there is an intentional object here, viz., my feeling uncomfortable in *this company*. But there can be a more extreme case: say I haven't even identified this; I just feel unstructured anger. Or I can be sad, and not find any reason.

That's a deviation in one direction, but in another direction you get lots of cases where you identify the meaning, but don't have any affect. The chairman says to the board, "I'm afraid we're in for a rough time in the markets", but his teeth aren't chattering, and his spine isn't tingling; it's just a way of noting the (apprehended) meaning of the current economic situation.

But what is particularly interesting here are the meanings that couldn't exist for us without the affect, that is, without (in the normal case) our experiencing the affect, or (where we're dealing with others) our coming to grasp what is it to experience it. These are what I called in Chapter 3 the "human" or "metabiological" meanings.[6] To repeat some of the examples mentioned in that discussion, these meanings arise for us when we seek to find meaning in our lives, when we strive for a certain communion with loved ones, when we seek moral rightness or ethical virtue, or some condition of serene equilibrium in our lives.

My claim here is firstly, that knowing that a certain meaning of this range is at stake in a certain situation is something of which we have, and

---

5. The view of feelings that I am presenting here has much in common with the understanding of the emotions which Martha Nussbaum developed in the superb discussion in her *Upheavals of Thought: The Intelligence of Emotions* (Cambridge: Cambridge University Press, 2001), especially chapter 1, where she defends "a modified version of the ancient Greek Stoic view, according to which emotions are forms of evaluative judgment that ascribe to certain things and persons outside a person's own control great importance for the person's own flourishing" (22).

6. In the meaning of Chapter 3, metabiological meanings can only impinge on us through some self-articulation, and the needs or aspirations they involve can only be met through (the right) self-understanding.

can continue to have, an immediate sense, what we might call an "intuition"; and secondly, that this intuition is not without affect. It is a felt intuition. This doesn't mean that every time we refer to this meaning, the
affect is present. To take an example from our moral convictions, it isn't
the case that every time we say "murder is wrong" or "human beings have
a right to life" we feel something; these remarks can occur in a routine description of currently accepted principles. But at high points where we
focus again on the intuition: somebody is proposing to murder, or challenging that this is a moral norm; or we are asked to say what is wrong
here, the feeling once more becomes salient; and this happens as well as
when we admire people who refrain from participating in mass murder at
great cost to themselves; and in other like cases.

This is not true of other cases where we also speak of intuitions which
can be repeatedly experienced, but quite affectlessly, like those of gram-
maticality; I know immediately that "colorless green ideas sleep furiously"
is nonsense, without its mattering to me in the least. Or I can intuitively
identify the right way to respond to a situation according to conventional
etiquette, even though this leaves me cold.

We can see why this is so in the light of the earlier discussion. Just because
these human meanings can't be identified with any objectively recognizable pattern, they can only impinge on us under some description which
invokes them, which can make them palpable. Hence the link to affect.

The contrast is with biological or "life meanings", or with merely instrumental meanings. We may have an immediate intuition that some plant
is poisonous, or that the stock market crash will affect our portfolio, but
this can be replaced by a reasoned account of how this is so; and in either
case can be grasped without affect.

I can learn how a virus is dangerous (a paradigmatic meaning term) for
me by learning the biology, whatever feelings it awakens in me (maybe I'm
in an aseptic environment, or I don't care whether I live or die). I can learn
how the recession is going to impact on my investments, but I had already
decided to renounce all property and go and live as a hermit in the wilderness. In parallel fashion I may learn just as a fact about the world that
members of another culture resent being addressed directly and frontally.
I guide myself accordingly, but I feel nothing here. These are not my
meanings.

But I couldn't understand what pride is, or what it is to see certain deeds
as admirable, or what it is to see the world as meaningless, or what people

mean by "integrity", or a full life, without a sense of the feeling, uplifting or devastating, which these features inspire.

But don't we often contrast reason to feeling in these judgments of what is worthwhile, or admirable, or morally binding? We say things like: "I know this is the right thing to do, but the idea of doing it repels me." Our feelings don't align with what we recognize as good or right. Now we can't understand these cases as simply pitting "reason" against "feeling". We couldn't have the sense that something was right or worthy unless we knew what it was to recognize something as right or worthy, and this recognition cannot be dispassionate. It may be that having recognized acts of a certain description (helping someone in need) as right, we come across a case which seems to fall under this description where we recoil. This may be because the case raises issues we hadn't considered, and we are confused. For instance, let's say I am a doctor who subscribes to and strongly feels the binding nature of the Hippocratic oath; I am called in to attend a patient who is on the brink of dying. Suddenly, I recognize him as the gruesome dictator who is undertaking genocide; with him gone, thousands will be saved. Of course, in this case, reason wouldn't unambiguously dictate that I go on abiding by my oath. But let's say that what makes me recoil is no higher cause, but just that this man is my personal enemy. Here it does seem that "feeling" is rebelling against "reason". But if "reason" weren't grounded here on some felt sense of right, if the "right" thing was just read off some code which had been handed to me, then it wouldn't be moral reason which was guiding me.

What this means is that there is no *dispassionate* access to these meanings; that in the first-person case, for them to be meanings for me, values that I recognize and which move me, I have to experience the felt intuition of them. And to remain meanings for me, I have to be able to renew this experience. If they later "go dead" on me, I may feel the loss, I may struggle to recover them, but they are no longer meanings that I effectively recognize.

And in the second- or third-person case, there is no dispassionate *understanding* of what is at stake in these meanings. Understanding them is grasping their point, the point they have for those who live by them. But I as outsider can only grasp this point, if I have some sense of what it is like to experience it, to feel it, to have the appropriate felt intuition.

The case where I need to grasp meanings I don't share is important, because these are often peculiar to certain cultures, or even to subgroups within a culture. This may not be immediately obvious. I mentioned above pride, and we can include its nemesis, shame. This clearly fits our description of the metabiological. To be proud (or ashamed) of some act I have committed is to feel something, the particular kind of lift (or cringe) of satisfaction (or shrinking away) that belongs to this dimension of experience.

And, of course, pride/shame are human universals, like anger or jealousy or envy. You can't grow up without learning words for these reactions, and for the situations which trigger them—although these latter certainly vary from culture to culture. The proper objects of pride and shame are not the same everywhere, but the reactions occur everywhere. That these words enter our vocabulary is unproblematic enough. Our parents, or other caregivers, in the framework of joint attention, see our reactions, for example of fear and anger, and teach us these terms; and also the corresponding situation-meaning terms: menacing, provoking. Indeed, as we argued in Chapter 2, these caregivers help us to identify our goals and aversions, help to give an emotional shape to our experience, without which we might flounder in unfocused rage, or else depression.

But now the reservation I made in the above paragraph is worth underlining. Pride and shame seem to be human universals, but what triggers them in one civilization or culture can be very different from what arouses them in another. And even within cultures, there may be profound differences. I am proud of my prowess as a successful bank robber, while you despise people who think that this is a worthy achievement. If I am a relative of yours, you're ashamed of me. This points to an important feature of these nonbiological, noninstrumental meanings, which we are calling "metabiological": they impinge on us not singly, as it were, but in interconnected skeins. Pride and shame refer us to activities or achievements which are thought worthy or unworthy, and these to moral or aesthetic distinctions, or classifications of character, which underpin these judgments. Even when we're dealing with ubiquitous meanings, how they figure in our lives will be determined by other meanings which are culture-specific.

These skeins are, as it were, constellations of meanings which are defined in terms of each other. Pride and shame are given their sense by what are defined as objects of credit or discredit in the culture. But the dependence may also go in the other direction; we may reconceptualize pride and shame so as to exclude certain objects from their field; for instance with the acceptance of a view which rules out involuntary features as relevant objects for either; we can only be proud or ashamed of features which we have brought about ourselves.

And the skein stretches wider: pride/shame exists in our culture in a field where it contrasts with the alternative guilt/innocence. This is not so everywhere, and the relation between these two dimensions of judgment varies greatly from culture to culture, and even, to a lesser degree, between individuals.

But let's take as example a human meaning which is clearly not ubiquitous, which only occurs in our time: what people in our contemporary civilization call "meaningfulness". I mean the sense that such and such an activity (discovering a cure for cancer, becoming a millionaire through devising and selling a new useful device, founding a hospital or school) would give (or has given) our life real meaning. There are certain societies in which this whole issue wouldn't arise, for instance a society where the vocations of men and women, or certain classes of men and women, are clearly fixed. Men are to be warriors. Your life may be a failure: you lack the skills of a fighter, or you are a coward. But this is another kind of (catastrophic) failure, not a lack of meaning. The issue of significance in life can only arise where such rigid attribution of vocations no longer exists.

Now we in contemporary society may indeed be puzzled why someone puts a given activity in this category (say, winning at tiddlywinks), but the puzzle only exists for us because we know what it is to feel something as meaningful, and can't see how this feeling relates to that activity. But there is no understanding of what meaningfulness is without a sense of how it feels, the sense that it makes our life worthwhile, that it gives solidity and substance to our biography.

The same goes for our sense that some action is admirable, is morally noble, that such and such a virtue renders its possessor ethically superior, and so on. The recognition of this kind of superiority, and of the virtues and properties which confer it, has to be felt by those who subscribe to the outlook concerned; and it is this feeling which puzzled outsiders are challenged to struggle to understand. Understanding here is grasping the point, the nature of the concern for a meaningful life, the shape of a life which imposes itself as admirable, noble, and the like. But you can't grasp the point without some sense of what it is to experience it.

This close relation of moral insight and affect can inspire epistemological worries: if our access to these meanings is through feeling, how can we know that they are really valid? The danger of a virus can be shown scientifically, but how can the admirability of some deed be demonstrated to those who doubt it? I may point out to you what it cost the agent to accomplish it, or what great consequences flowed from it. But this will only convince you if you share my admiration for this effort, or these results. Now I don't think that our mode of access to these meanings makes it impossible to offer criticism and correction to any putative attribution of them; on the contrary, and I will return to this issue shortly below.[7] But it is clear that this will not proceed as it does in the case of the dangerous virus.[8]

And we can understand that this deviation from the empirical-scientific mode of proceeding has inspired certain modern forms of rationalism to seek (what they see as) a firmer foundation for ethics, for instance in utility calculation, or appeals to universality. I will return to this in section 3.

There are whole ranges of terms which designate metabiological meanings in the above sense. There are words for qualities of life or ways of living it: like 'meaningful', but also 'dashing' or 'pedestrian', 'with integrity' or 'opportunistically'. In this range belong various virtue terms: 'generosity', 'human understanding', 'sensitivity', 'loyalty', 'devotion to truth'. Some of these also define motives, like charity, compassion; and often motives enter into the definition of virtues.

Then there are terms for our stances to things: 'cool', 'engaged', 'enthusiastic', 'standoffish'. There are ways in which we experience our lives: serene, troubled, confused, empty; as charged with meaning, or flat and empty; or there is the experience called "acedia", or melancholy, which Baudelaire called "spleen". These latter overlap with what we call "moods".

There are the ways we segment the field of motives: love/lust, love/like, the different kinds of friendship that Aristotle distinguishes.

And there are a range of aesthetic terms, which we apply to landscapes or works of art: 'balanced', 'troubled', 'arousing', and so on.

---

7. I have discussed what critique and correction involves in "Explanation and Practical Reason" in *Philosophical Arguments* (Cambridge, MA: Harvard University Press, 1995), chapter 3.

8. Obviously, in these cases we can find the vocabulary we need to describe the meanings in the way that HLC theory postulates: we learn something about the processes in the world, like the ravages caused by a virus, or the operation of the markets and their effects on our bank accounts, and find the words we need by fixing agreed descriptions to these phenomena.

This list is very incomplete; it is just meant to give a sense of the impressive place of the metabiological in our vocabulary and our lives.

Where does our vocabulary for these metabiological meanings come from? Some of them are obviously ubiquitous, and often strongly felt in ordinary life, as we saw above with anger, envy, jealousy, pride, and so on.

But how do we, either individually or as a culture, go beyond these obvious, basic cases, and find more refined and subtle terms for how we feel: 'uneasy', 'troubled', 'serene', 'alienated'? How do we learn to describe our world as full of meaning, or flattened, deprived of meaning?

Unlike the basic cases, these feelings/meanings arise in certain cultures and not others, and they are connected through skeins of meaning to a whole host of other discriminations which belong to this culture: its virtues, values, morals, sense of beauty, sense of fullness, its understandings of shame, and (where this is important) guilt.

These cultures often change as a consequence of original perceptions of meaning on the part of individuals or small groups. See the rise of terms like 'sincere'. How does this innovation occur? This kind of novel creation is very unlike the case where we notice a new phenomenon and affix a name to it. We are rather creating new terms for a domain which as yet lacks words.

2

With this in mind, let's look at the issue of how novel meanings can be described or formulated. How do cultures develop, change, and diversify? There seems to be a problem here because, on one hand, the new term is meant to name a meaning which is only accessible through affect, through our feeling it, while on the other, without the word—or some other mode of expression for it; I return to this below—the meaning in its full articulated form cannot be felt. All that we experience initially is an unstructured sense that something important needs to be brought to light.

This demonstrates how linguistic innovation in this area takes us outside the paradigms of the HLC. This saw new terms arising through our finding a word for an idea which has already occurred to us. This can be because we encounter some object, say, a new flower; or we can exercise scientific imagination, and hypothesize, as the ancient Epicureans did, that the objects around us were made up of tiny, indivisible constituents, which we will call "atoms". These new objects become part of our world through invention.

This model of neologizing makes sense when it comes to the description of independent objects. These objects are independent in the sense of being self-standing: their existence and nature is independent of our proffered descriptions; on the contrary, these are proffered in an attempt to portray these objects correctly.[9]

So a word is introduced to designate a new reality which presents itself; or which we invent to explain what is before us. Our predications are made with the aim of stating how things are with the phenomena. With the progress of knowledge, terms will often be redefined in order to portray the reality correctly (for instance 'atom').

But things are different with human meanings. To grasp a new meaning is to discover a new way of feeling, of experiencing our world. This cannot precede the expression, as the concept of a "tiny, indivisible constituent" preceded "atom". It can only enter my world through (enacted or descriptive) expression. Take the case of the 'meaningful'—predicated of a life—mentioned above. It is clear to start with that the term couldn't be introduced in the first place without a rich skein of other meanings, implicit judgments of the significance or weight of certain activities, perceptions of triviality, notions of a "career", and the like. But this is not the crucial point here; something analogous can be said of the theoretical terms we use to describe self-standing objects. The important difference is that articulating the issue with the term 'meaningful' inflects our sense of meaning in a new direction, one which accepts the plurality of possibilities open to each person, which abandons the old ideas about predestined vocations, and which opens a new way of discriminating better or worse life courses, along with the corresponding felt intuitions. This shape of experienced meaning doesn't precede the articulation, but comes about through and with it.

The constitutive power of language operates here in a different way, one might say at a different level, than it does in our description of indepen-

9. Clearly, in speaking of "independent" objects, I am taking on board a "realist" view of truth in our descriptions of the world around us, and, by extension, in natural science. For a more detailed argument in support of this position, see Hubert Dreyfus and Charles Taylor, *Retrieving Realism* (Cambridge, MA: Harvard University Press, 2015). Of course, exactly what in the world of independent realities can confirm a given proposition or theory depends on the proposition or theory, in the sense that these define the shape of the "facts" which ratify (or fail to ratify) them. But this involves a rather different "semantic logic" from that implicit in the definition of human meanings; see below.

dent objects. There it is our powers of description in general which provide the background on which we innovate and coin new terms. We are dealing here with the general constitutive power of language (Chapter 1, section 7). Here, in the realm of metabiological meanings, expression opens new and unsuspected realms. The new enacted and/or verbal expressions open up new ways of being in the world. We are in the domain of cultural innovation. We are concerned here with a particular constitutive force of certain expressions.

The blindness of the HLC to this mode of constitution is of a piece with its tendency to favor the description of independent objects above everything else.

The Humboldtian aspiration to articulacy operates differently in this realm of meanings than it does with the description of independent objects. With objects, we may have to struggle to find a form which makes sense of the way they fit together, perhaps inventing a new paradigm in order to do so; with meanings, we struggle to find expressions which give them a defined form, which then gives them a new bearing in our lives.

Many of the meanings in our lives come to exist for us when we mark distinctions heretofore unnoticed in our life experience. Take joy, for example; one of the things we come to distinguish, along with happiness, a sense of well-being, and serenity, out of what was earlier experienced as an undifferentiated positive condition. Or we can take the separating out of indignation from an originally undifferentiated anger; or of remorse from a general dissatisfaction at the consequences of our action.

Prior to the articulation, the as yet unnamed import may be felt in a diffuse, unfocused way, a pressure that we can't yet respond to. After articulation, it becomes part of the explicit shape of meaning for us. As a result it is felt differently; our experience is changed; it has a more direct bearing on our lives.

Articulated meanings may draw us more powerfully, but they may also repel us more decisively, as when young people become clear that they don't want to follow the way of life that their society proposes for them now that they grasp what it involves. Articulation here alters the shape of what matters to us. It changes us. When I make the shift into a framework of authenticity and see an activity I was previously inexplicably drawn to as constituting "the meaning" of my life, its new salience strengthens its hold on me. But when I come to understand my painful, paralyzing state of confusion as acedia, or melancholy, or "spleen", I am already living it differently. I have taken the first step out of paralysis; my situation already has a shape for me, as we can see in Baudelaire's "spleen" poems.[10]

The new articulated descriptions allow the world to impinge on us, to move us, in new ways. That is why we call them "constitutive". In the terms of Chapter 1, this articulation operates primarily in the existential, rather than the accessive, dimension.

But this kind of articulation requires words. There is no analogue here of our wordlessly noticing a difference between objects which lie before us in our perceptual field. We come to grasp joy, or remorse, as a new kind or quality of feeling with its own properties. But this grasping of a difference based on criterial features is of the essence of linguistic "reflection" [*Besonnenheit*] in Herderian terms. Joy emerges from a vaguely felt difference into a recognizably distinct experience when we find the words. Someone uses the term in a context of joint experience where its special nature stands out; they enact joy, as it were. Or we read about such an experience in a novel, or, more rarely, in a treatise. And similarly for remorse or indignation. The words here, the new terms and the descriptions, carry the constitutive force.

Metabiological meaning terms that we embrace articulate a deeply felt import, and as such they are never just "arbitrary impositions"; they express the import. In the case of terms which come down to us from our ancestral culture, they are learnt from caregivers in emotionally saturated contexts, so that they forever resonate with the meanings. The simple words 'sad' and 'happy' retain their resonance throughout our lives. In the case of new coinages, there is frequently some metaphorical force, some "figuring" in the sense of Chapter 5—as we see in the biting of remorse, for instance.

The contrast between the two orders of description can perhaps be seen in this way. When we are trying to describe the world, hitting on a model, like our Epicurean or Lucretian atomism, may bring order to our initially confused perceptions. The model brings (at least seeming) clarity to the world, but it doesn't make it different. What its introduction alters is our initial state of confusion, transforming it to clarity.

When I see that the issue which really concerns me is meaningfulness, or integrity, or being generous and giving, I also bring clarity into an initial confusion. But what I am clear about is not something other, independent of my clarified vision; what I have clarified is my sense of what

---

10. I will examine this in the proposed companion study.

really matters, and a clarified sense is an altered sense. When I come for the first time to feel that one of the things which matters crucially to me is following my own path, finding my own way of being human (in other words, when I embrace an ethic of authenticity), I change the shape of what matters to me. I might feel (and people frequently do) that I have been feeling this all along, and just now am recognizing it, but this recognition gives a new force and clarity to this meaning. It is not like discovering the name of the odd breed of dog my neighbor walks every morning. The discovery has motivational force.

It is this kind of articulacy, which changes its object—which is in other words, constitutive—that we are trying to understand. In this sense, what we are naming and clarifying is not really an *independent* object, in the meaning of the (HLC) act, that is, self-standing.

This is not to say that we cannot search for an underlying explanation of someone's feelings or experience which is as yet unknown to the agent herself. We all do this and psychotherapy couldn't proceed without it. In this there seems an obvious analogy with our explaining rising heat through increasing kinetic energy of molecules. But the disanalogy comes when the patient herself grasps this explanation. Then the phenomenon we sought to explain itself alters, that is, her life experience and her capacity to deal with her situation.

Imagine someone who suffered earlier in life a profoundly disturbing, even traumatic, experience. As a result, whenever he finds himself in a situation reminiscent of the earlier one, he (without conscious intent) does everything he can to flee it, and as a consequence frustrates his own goals (say, sustaining a love relationship). If therapy can bring this underlying mechanism to consciousness, and as a result the patient can come to dismantle the panic reaction, his life experience is transformed, and he can now do things he couldn't before.

We can express this distinction, between describing independent objects and introducing new constitutive expressions that alter the field of meanings, by bringing out the different semantic logics involved. There are two here, or perhaps three.

The first is (1) the familiar one from the HLC: we come across a new phenomenon, say a new species of rodent, and we coin a term for it. Let's call this the "designative" logic. The second is (2) the "constitutive" logic where introducing the new term reorders or reshapes the field of phenomena it helps describe. Crudely put, in (1) the phenomenon comes first, then the term; in (2) it is the reverse, or more accurately the new term and the reality it describes are coeval.

But we can identify a third logic (3), in those situations where we project an underlying mechanism to explain the phenomena described by logic (1), such as atoms, or fields of force and the like. Here the term and the reality it purports to describe are coeval, in the sense that they enter our world by the same act (unlike the new species of rodent, which we then name), but the verification of these mechanisms depends on their success in explaining phenomena named under logic (1). They figure in underlying theoretical accounts; whereas in (2) new terms reorder the primary phenomena of experience.

Verifying entities of level (3), along with those of (1), follows the logic of a correspondence theory of truth: find an account which corresponds to an independent reality. Not so, the terms of semantic logic (2).[11]

But the discussion cannot end here. I have just said that new terms in (2) reorder the phenomena of experience, the meanings we feel. But surely these experienced feelings refer beyond themselves to orders of reality which we could be getting wrong. On one hand, we use certain terms of this range to describe ourselves and others, as for instance finding deep meaning in artistic creation, or suffering deep melancholy. But I could be deceiving myself here: I am really excited by the money and fame I am getting out of my semiscandalous works; or you may be deceiving me by pretending to some deep condition of melancholy where you are really a disappointed suitor. There are, we might say, factual issues here.

On another level, certain crucial metabiological meanings raise another kind of issue of rightness. I'm speaking of those involved in what I have called "strong evaluation",[12] be they moral, or aesthetic, or whatever. This exists where what is valued comes across to us as not depending on our desires or decisions, or on whether or not we grasp it; rather the valued reality comes across as such that our not appreciating it, far from under-

---

11. It should be clear that the difference between these three logics doesn't lie in the fact that in some the person trying to articulate her thought is more *active* and *creative* than in others. One might get this impression if one remained with the standard notion of naming in the HLC: one just appends a word to a preexisting idea. But we have seen in Chapter 5 that even describing phenomena that appear before us (logic 1) has a creative dimension in which we "figure" them; and it goes without saying that the positing of underlying mechanisms (logic 3) is also a creative activity (with some connections and analogies to figuring as I mentioned in Chapter 5). The big differences lie in the kinds of creativity, and in their manner of ratification.

12. See my "What Is Human Agency?" in *Philosophical Papers 1*, 15–44.

mining its value, would on the contrary reflect negatively on our ability to perceive it. This kind of valuation obviously holds with our perception of what is right or good, or worthy or admirable, in whatever sphere, whether we're dealing with the true, the good, the beautiful, or judgments of expertise in some specific domain. The issues here are often described as "normative".[13]

This might seem to reestablish the analogy between the two semantic logics. Both our perception of the things around us and, as we might put it, our perception of value make claims about the way things are in some sense independent of us, claims which could turn out wrong. But in fact a crucial difference remains.

I mentioned above that in both cases the introduction of a new term may bring clarity. In the case I alluded to earlier, when we enter an unfamiliar factory or workshop, we may not be able to distinguish one machine from another until someone shows us how the different mechanisms work, and then the scene segments itself. This is analogous to the case where acquiring new terms clarifies our feelings, as jealousy, or remorse. But the difference is that in the first case we have a brace of different ways of examining the things in the workshop: we can move around among them, examine them from different perspectives, try to move them around, make them work, and so on. Being told about the machines can facilitate our exploration but isn't a condition of its possibility.

This seems analogous to the way we might explore a field of moral deeds to determine which response would really show courage, which would amount to real generosity, and the like. But this kind of examination requires a sense of what values are at stake here, and this is not possible without the felt intuition which makes us privy to the issues involved. When we grasp a new vocabulary (e.g., of joy, serenity, remorse, generosity), and hence alter the shape of the issues we recognize, we become capable of explorations we couldn't make before.

There is, indeed, an analogy with theoretical innovation, or paradigm shifts, in empirical science, which in fact open us to new questions. But the disanalogy is that the "paradigm shifts" in the realm of meanings come through the change in felt intuitions which the words bring about in us,

13. The point that I made in the previous section, that our awareness of human meanings is not dispassionate, that we are dealing here with felt intuitions, will be mainly developed in the following pages in connection with our normative insights. But we should not forget that the insights by which we correct our self-descriptions also impact on our feelings. When I realize that my "remorse" was phony, and really I was concerned about looking bad, I cannot but feel somewhat ashamed (negative), and perhaps also have a sense of liberation from illusion (positive).

not through a changed understanding of how things work which may be dispassionately contemplated. (Of course, scientific discovery is often accompanied by a passionate sense of the beauty or order of the universe, but the resulting theories may be shared by people who lack this sense altogether.)

In the realm of meaning, the felt intuition is our gate of entry into the field we want to explore, even while our exploration may change the shape of the field, and hence of our further explorations. Our acquiring new meaning terms is what opens these gates, and that is what makes these terms in a special way constitutive.[14]

This means that we should clarify the different distinctions we might invoke by talking of dependence or independence. There are in fact three. (1) The first concerns what I have been calling "self-standing" objects, which would exist even if we didn't; I mean us as knowing subjects experiencing meanings. It is such self-standing objects that our natural sciences study, including (at least a good part of) biology.

The second distinction concerns our metabiological meanings. These are part of the range of dependent things in sense (1) (they wouldn't exist if we didn't exist). But they, unlike other meanings (painful, pleasurable, itchy, and nauseating) are dependent in another sense (2), that they can only exist for us through linguistic or other forms of expression. They are not independent of our modes of giving expression to them, be this through words or enactment, or works of art.

But as we have seen this by no means signifies that issues of truth don't arise in relation to these meanings. So while dependent in senses (1) and (2), there is a third sense (3) in which they are independent, in that our experience of them can be faulty and inadequate and need correction.

There are in fact, as I mentioned above, two dimensions in which our language for meanings has to be responsible to reality that we don't control. One (the "factual") concerns the adequacy of our descriptions, of self and others, and our situations, and following this requirement can call into question the adequacy of our present vocabulary. The second dimension

14. The fact that we need to have a sense of the issues involved before making evaluative judgments, along with the fact that this sense comes through felt intuitions, is what lies behind the much talked about alleged split between "facts" and "values". From a description of things shorn of human meanings you cannot deduce any attributions of value. This is, of course, true. But the conclusion that facts and values lie in different realms requires the additional assumption that moral or value statements aren't really "factual"; and this begs all the crucial questions in this domain.

("the normative") concerns the validity of what we value, of the norms, goods, virtues we want to seek.

So there is this third sense of independence, where the demand for undistorted, not-too-self-indulgent self-description, on one hand, and the claim to strong value, that is, value independent of our recognition, on the other, lays a burden on us to get things right. One or other facet of this burden is unavoidable in this domain of our metabiological meanings, and sometimes both impinge. And correspondingly, with these meanings, we have the sense that we can be wrong, that we can easily fail to get it, and often do.

There is first of all the sense that we often have that some of our meanings are enigmatic, that the words we use for them express them, but leave much unsaid. We sense that they need further clarification, and thus that we might end up understanding them very differently than we do today. And beyond this, we are aware that we are capable of failing through confusion, or inexperience; through too great an attachment to our own comfort (seeing what really matters would make big demands on us). Or we can't get it because what really matters would reflect badly on our image—in the light of what's really important our present performance doesn't look good. Or perhaps the reality reflects badly on some aspect of our cherished identity—our nation, for instance. We can easily fail to get things right, through pride and/or prejudice.

Or perhaps we are frightened; we can't get close to a certain range of questions without triggering panic connected to some earlier traumatic experience, as with our patient above.

But whatever the possible reasons they arise often enough to give us a sense that we have more to learn, that we need to see things more clearly, or that we have got the hierarchy of values wrong. To recur to my earlier example, where I am proud of my success as a bank robber, your being ashamed of me may begin to work on me, to the point that I come to see that there are other really important things in life which my career of crime undermines. The field of value I recognize and live in becomes realigned. Or the discovery may take the form of my clarifying some confusion; as I now see things it was notoriety, being much talked about, or being much admired in certain circles, which I confounded with living a really valuable or admirable life.

If I can call up a simile drawn from free-standing objects, the skein of my interrelated meanings can come across as a landscape, partly hidden by fog, where some features hide others, and others again are too distant to be made out exactly. This "landscape" implies a double call on us: first, to live up to this sense of what is important; and second, to get it more clearly in focus. This involves changing ourselves in these two dimensions. And we sense that these two transformations are connected; part of the fruit of getting better is seeing better, and vice versa.

Now our way of making sense of the "landscape", as it appears to us, may include a theoretical account, which makes reference to "free-standing" realities. Some may understand the human psyche as the site of powerful and primitive desires, which come from deep in our human, even animal past, and which are precariously controlled by the codes of civilization. This can be offered both as an explanation of our desires and aspirations, but they also offer images through which we read these desires. Think of the impact of Stravinsky's *Le Sacre du Printemps*,[15] both positively and negatively, on early twentieth-century understandings of human life. Or we can read our desires through an evolutionary-causal account, of the patterns of behavior which were selected for in the prehistory of the human race. Or, in a completely different register, we may see our aspirations to the good as called out in us by God, or following Plato, by the Idea of the Good. Or we may think of ourselves as reenacting an order of things, a right and noble order, which comes to us from our ancestors.

All these are etiological accounts; they offer explanations for our felt intuitions; they each present a causal background which supposedly underlies them. In this way they make sense of them, and so render them plausible to those who accept these explanations. But they by no means offer a merely dispassionate explanation. They color the meanings, help shape the felt intuitions. The sense that certain commandments were revealed by a loving God, or that some of our impulses come from deep in our psyche, which was formed in a distant past, or that this way of life reenacts an order hallowed by time; all these form part of the felt intuitions which move us in each of these cases.

And in whatever vocabulary we couch it, accepting one of these explanations can actually bring about changes in our sense of felt meaning, in our metabiological "landscape", through naming it differently, through adopting new descriptions. These will often be proceeded by an inchoate, troubled sense that something needs to be articulated here—the sense that

---

15. *The Rite of Spring.*

Humboldt describes in the passage at the beginning of this chapter; but the change is consummated by our new articulation.

This, of course, parallels our ability to describe and explain free-standing reality more coherently thanks to the articulation of a new paradigm, only in this domain of meanings the change of description effects a change in (one level of) the reality, viz., the pattern of meanings we live by, the "landscape" as we live it and feel it. The words help determine the claims we want to make about value, even if they don't decide their validity. This is what it means to say that our articulations in this domain are constitutive.

To put the contrast in another way, in this domain to have access to meanings is to experience, to feel them (they are dependent in sense [1]). But the words we use to talk about them don't come after the experience (for this is dependent in sense [2]), as they can with pains, tickles, and other sensations (which are only dependent in sense [1]). Rather the words help shape the feelings, and hence our access to the domain.

But to return to a question which arose earlier, if there are issues about right or wrong, or at least better or worse perception of meaning, but if on the other hand, we are not engaged in mapping an independent, free-standing reality here, how can we ever judge that we are getting it righter, that we are improving our grip on moral, or aesthetic reality? This is the conundrum that has led many to see our "values" as ultimately "subjective", as just "projected" on to a reality that in itself is neutral, devoid of meaning.

But I claimed above (end of section 1) that it is possible to speak of correcting our views in this domain, of making a passage from a less to a more reliable "take" on the things which matter to us. How can we do that?

We can perhaps distinguish two paths: one might be called "external", the other "internal", or alternatively "indirect" and "direct". The first is opened for us by the etiological stories we tell. These make reference to self-standing realities, like God, or evolution, or our deeper instincts, or our ancestors' lives, to recur to the examples above. And in each case, a challenge can be offered. Our faith in God might be shaken, in a whole host of ways, independent of the way in which faith in Him shapes our felt intuitions; or we might come to see that the evolution of humanity didn't happen in the way we previously believed; or that the continuity we supposed in our deep motivation from our animal background doesn't really hold; or else that our ancestors were engaged in some very questionable activities: rape, plunder, genocide.

All these challenges may undermine our sense of what is really to be valued, may weaken and make more hesitant our felt intuitions. They have a negative impact, sowing doubt, but stopping short of offering a positive alternative that we can intuitively embrace. To see how we can move forward to another, more adequate positive view, we have to explore the "internal" or "direct" road. We tread this road when we, for instance, arrive at what we feel is a better position through, say, (1) resolving some confusion, or (2) giving weight to certain considerations which we had managed to hold at bay, but now can no longer refuse, or (3) experiencing another facet of the activity we valued which forces us to alter our take on it.

Thus, (1) I may come to see that what I felt as moral remorse for some action was more a sense of my looking bad, more actuated by the wound to my ego, than by a sense of moral lapse; two grounds for this reaction which were confused and overlapping may be separated out, with the result that one falls away, and our assessment of the original response is altered.

Or (2) I was so enamored of my new success that I wasn't really taking in the impact it had on my family, or my friends, or other people in general. Once I come to take this into account, the success begins to look very questionable.

Or (3) I throw myself into a movement which I am convinced is essential to sustaining democracy, but then I come to see this way of mobilizing has drawbacks; say, it is very hard on certain people; or perhaps it turns out to be easily recuperable by sinister élites.

All these revisions are distinct from the case where, keeping a certain goal constant, we revise our original action because it fails as an adequate means to this end, and pass to other measures designed to encompass it. Because unlike this shift in instruments, these transitions inflect our perception of value, and thus our felt intuitions. This is obvious in case (1), where we separate out two distinct reasons to regret a past action. But it also applies to the other two cases, where our success looks and feels different now that we see what is involved; it now looks narrow and tawdry (case 2); or where our sense that some movement incarnates the intrinsic satisfaction of democracy and collective self-realization is fractured when we see its shadow side or intrinsic futility (case 3).

I am speaking of this path of change as "internal", because the confidence that we are making headway comes from the transition itself. We sense that we are getting a better grip on reality when we overcome some confusion (1), or come to take a wider or more comprehensive view on things (2 and 3). The confidence is based, first and foremost, on our sense of the transition as an error-reducing one, rather than on our comparison of two takes, before and after, with some independent, self-standing reality, although we may afterward be able to reconstruct the move in that form.

Another example of such reasoning through transitions is (4) where we come to see, perhaps through some process of gradual growth, that some relationship, some activity is really important to us, or important generally to human beings. We are confident that this is a positive change because we sense this as a change in insight as well as a shift in what we sense as important. Getting better and seeing more have gone together.

The confidence that we have a better grip comes through the transition. This is analogous, and indeed connected, with the case where on, say, picking up a hammer, we shift our hold on it until we feel that our grip is secure. Knowing that this is a better hold is inseparable from having *achieved* this firmer grip. Or again, wanting to make a secure judgment whether grandma's new portrait is hung straight, we move around so as to get the best view of the situation. We know this is the best vantage point because we have put ourselves there.

Our movements forward in this perception of metabiological meanings, a domain as we saw of felt intuitions, often have this form, of reasoning through the transitions we have brought about.[16] And whether we go this route or the "external" one, our new insight has to be ratified by a felt intuition before it becomes our new conviction. Whatever objections arise on the "indirect" route, and however much they shake us, only this ratification can bring us to a new strong evaluation.

My sketch of the two routes here is provisional; both the "direct" and the "indirect" ones are richer and more varied, and less easy to separate, than I have described here.[17] In particular, the indirect route has more resources than I have canvassed here. I will return to this in the next section.

We can now see more fully the shape of the constitutive power of language in this area of human meanings and the felt intuitions we have of them.

---

16. I have developed this point further in "Explanation and Practical Reason."

17. Among the recourses of the "direct" examination of our felt intuitions is the identification of seeming contradictions between them, and the attempt to resolve them. This is what Rawls called the search for "reflective equilibrium". See John Rawls, *A Theory of Justice* (Cambridge, MA: Harvard University Press, 1971).

First, this domain is only opened for us through the articulations of inter-linked skeins of meaning; and second, new insights which reshape the skein are only clinched through new articulations.

The HLC model of neologizing: first a phenomenon appears, then we give it a name, may seem to work for what I called above the human universals: pride, anger, sadness, joy. Mother sees the kid react, and says: "don't be proud" (or perhaps "you should be proud"), and the kid knows this is the term for that feeling, just as he learned that 'dog' and 'cat' named those animals. Put this way, meaning-naming looks the same as designating animals or furniture. But this ignores the immense impact of the parents' naming of emotions for the shaping of these emotions, which I discussed in Chapter 2.

And it also ignores the way in which these universal meanings operate within skeins or "landscapes" which differ across cultures, and also across times as these cultures evolve and change.

Pride and anger can't just be *named*, like toothache. Or at least, their naming is charged with expressive resonance, as I indicated above. But we can see that they have a special status among meanings which can give them this appearance. There are certain basic dimensions of meaning for which we learn words very early: desire and aversion (want, don't want, like, hate), pleasure and pain, discomfort; gladness, sadness, anger, joy, jealousy, pride, shame, and the like. Without these there is not yet such a thing as the shape that meanings have for us and which we can avow. Further development introduces complexity, richness, nuance; it marks distinctions which alter the shape of meanings, like my sense above that remorse is not the same as my feeling bad because I look bad, or my distinguishing indignation from ordinary anger. We develop a rich vocabulary of reasons and occasions for pride, anger, and the rest.

And thus these basic words become part of the broader skein of meaning of adult life. These words are foundational to the shape of meanings for us, rather than reordering this shape. But this makes them even more clearly constitutive.

3

We can illustrate some of the above points, as well as adding other dimensions to the discussion, if we focus on one prominent area of metabiological meanings, which we call the ethical or moral.

In contemporary philosophy, these are often distinguished from each other, and the moral is hived off as a self-sufficient domain. Morality is what tells us how to act, what our obligations are to each other. According to many contemporary philosophers, these injunctions can and should be generated ideally from a single source, or a single basic criterion, though there is much argument about what this criterion should be, opinions dividing between two great schools: those who follow a utilitarian approach versus those who in one way or another are inspired by Kant. Where Kant demanded that the maxim of one's action should be universalized, contemporary forms of this theory ask us to act on a norm that all those affected by the action can accept (Habermas);[18] or act on a justification that others can accept, provided they accept the principle that justifications be universal (Scanlon).[19]

This connected skein of obligatory action principles which is often called "morality" is contrasted to "ethics" which purports to define the shape of the good life, and which is often expressed in terms of those aspects or components of the good life which we call "virtues".

The thesis that morality is self-sufficient amounts to the view that its principles of obligatory action can be defined independently of any particular view of the good life. But this thesis seems false. Morality in the political sphere involves respect for others' rights, for instance liberty. But what is involved in respecting your liberty? Does adopting a law prescribing seatbelts in cars infringe our liberty in any meaningful sense? Certainly not in the sense that forbidding expression of political opinions, or the exercise of religion does. In fact, interpreting the scope of the liberty to be respected requires us to take account of what is really important in human life, which is a key to ethics, that is, to any conception of the good life.[20]

Or again, certain of the principles generated by "morality" can't be properly carried through without drawing on certain virtues. Thus we are all enjoined today to treat our fellow citizens with respect, and our governments must treat us all with equal respect. But you can't treat everyone with respect unless you possess certain virtues, for instance a sensitive understanding of cultural differences, and a certain generous outreach. Of

18. Jürgen Habermas, *Between Facts and Norms: Contributions to a Discourse Theory of Law and Democracy* (Cambridge, MA: MIT Press, 1992).

19. T. M. Scanlon, "The Structure of Contractualism," in *What We Owe to Each Other* (Cambridge, MA: Harvard University Press, 1998), 189–247.

20. There are also other issues here. For instance, morality as obligatory action cannot account for the goodness of supererogation, going the extra mile.

course, there are certain things that morality enjoins which don't require this kind of understanding, for example refraining from murder. But it would be a highly impoverished moral code which only included such purely external observance, where the "spirit" in which one acts is irrelevant. Morality can't consist simply in forbidding or enjoining such objectively identifiable patterns of action.

And in fact, it can't rely simply on rules or principles of whatever sort. Human beings, and their needs and situations, are too diverse; we cannot define how we ought to treat them exclusively in terms of codes. At some point what the code prescribes will bear too heavily, even inhumanly, on some people, as when justice needs to be tempered with mercy, or some principle of equal treatment needs to take account of special needs, so that a valid general rule requires that we make reasonable accommodation.

And there are also situations in which new and (by most of us) unforeseen needs are articulated. Good examples in the last half century can be seen in the demands formulated by feminist movements, by homosexuals, by disabled people. Without a certain openness and sensibility, people are often at first unable to recognize the human needs involved in these demands, and feel the force of the claims made. We are all limited in this regard, more capable of picking up on needs of some kinds rather than others. And this means that the widest possible capacity to see the human reality of others, to let them get through to us, is a virtue essential to morality.

This means: not to let our own way of grasping and evaluating people and their situations, in which we are inevitably deeply invested, screen out the human reality of the other, and blind us to it. This capacity overlaps with the "negative capability" of which Keats speaks, but it also draws on the resources of benevolence in us, of philanthropy in the fullest sense of this word.

So, short of the utopian moment when all present and future human needs have been recognized in some supercode, morality can't be insulated from ethics. They are interwoven. Moreover, the relation is even closer than I have outlined here. Take the principles which are at the apex of what we consider morality today. These include universalism, which stipulates that all human beings, and not just the members of our group, or gang, or nation, can make moral claims on us; and humanitarianism, obliging us to come to the aid of human beings in need wherever they are, or whatever race, religion, nationality they belong to; and equality, which forbids discrimination on the basis of sex, race, religion, and a host of other such differences.

We are all aware that we humans didn't start our career on earth recognizing these principles. On the contrary early human societies were tightly knit around their own needs and survival, which they sought to fulfill often in rivalry with other groups. Often their name for themselves was simply their word for "human being", and their name for others sometimes implicitly denied full possession of human properties, like language (e.g., "barbarian", "*niemcy*"). We have come through a long, drawn-out process, which includes the Axial revolutions, the great world religions, philosophical developments like Stoicism and the eighteenth-century European Enlightenment(s), and in more recent centuries, the great campaigns against slavery, colonial conquest and exploitation, imperial rule, to this recognition, at least in theory, of universalism.

Nor can this process be explained by a slow, gradual expansion of the range of human sympathy. There has been some of that, but the greatest advances involved a sharp discontinuity, an awareness that we are called to go beyond the usual, comfortable limits of our solidarity. The Stoic idea of the world as a cosmopolis, the line from the "Ode to Joy": "All men become brothers" [*Alle Menschen warden Brüder*], the biblical phrase: "In Christ is neither Jew nor Greek"; all enshrine the idea that we must break out of the limits of the polis, of blood brotherhood, of linguistic or cultural identity, into a broader solidarity.

And this breakout is accompanied by a certain exhilaration; we are uplifted by the sense that we are realizing our true vocation as human beings, hitherto obscured by narrow horizons and unfounded conflicts.

In short, our sense is that in answering this call, we are acceding to a higher, fuller, truer form of human life, as individuals, as societies, as humanity in general. But then the highest principles of morality define also an ethical ideal, a view of the good life. On this level, the boundary between the two falls away.

And the majority of our contemporaries do share a sense that this way of living is higher, and that the story of how we came to recognize these principles is one of progress, however mitigated by what we have lost on the way, and by the fact that the progress is largely in aspiration only, since our practice has not only lagged behind, but has become in some respects even more horrifying.

Why has this fusion at the apex of ethics and morality been so much ignored; why is it so hard to recognize in modern Western philosophy? This comes in part because of the profound suspicion under which the ethical traditions of the ancients have fallen in modern (post-seventeenth century) culture, particularly in the wake of the scientific revolution. Plato and Aristotle offer us visions of a higher, more properly human way of life, but what could this mean in the light of the new post-Galilean science of nature? One of the crucial features of the new science, in relation to its Aristotelian predecessor, was that it eschewed any talk of higher and lower levels of being, and concentrated on real, efficient-causal relations. Moreover, the ancients claimed to show us what was higher through reason, the faculty which could grasp the true nature of things, and hence of humanity. But the new dispensation had no place for this kind of reason. The metaphysics of materialism excludes this possibility. I will call this the "materialist exclusion". One of the most trenchant restatements of this in our day is John Mackie's "argument from queerness". "If there were objective values, then they would be qualities or relations of a very strange sort, utterly different from anything else in the universe. Correspondingly, if we were aware of them, it would have to be by a very special faculty of moral perception or intuition, utterly different from our ordinary ways of knowing everything else."[21]

And so our admiring attachment to this, or any other ethical ideal has to be reinterpreted in distorting ways. One is "sentimentalism", a tradition running up from Hutcheson, through Hume and Adam Smith, and still taken up in various forms in our day.[22] This stance starts from a reaction against the idea that "reason" can deliver an ethical insight, much less move us to action. Samuel Clarke held that there are certain "eternal and unalterable relations in the nature of things themselves . . . [so that] actions agreeable to these relations are morally good, and that the contrary actions are morally evil."[23] This could be made sense of in the light of some Pla-

---

21. J. L. Mackie, *Ethics: Inventing Right and Wrong* (New York: Penguin, 1977), 38.

22. See Rachel Cohon, *Hume's Morality: Feeling and Fabrication* (Oxford: Oxford University Press, 2008); Joseph Duke Filonowicz, *Fellow-Feeling and the Moral Life* (Cambridge: Cambridge University Press, 2008); Shaun Nichols, *Sentimental Rules: On the Natural Foundations of Moral Judgment* (Oxford: Oxford University Press, 2004); Michael Slote, *Moral Sentimentalism* (Oxford: Oxford University Press, 2010); also another interesting position inspired by Hume: Simon Blackburn, *Ruling Passions: A Theory of Practical Reasoning* (Oxford: Clarendon Press, 1998).

23. Quoted in Filonowicz, *Fellow-Feeling*, 158.

tonic or Aristotelian theory of the Form of the human, but for many in the eighteenth century it made sense no more. What was needed to explain morality was a motive force; and Hutcheson postulated to fill this gap a "moral sense", which enabled us to discern moral good and bad, just as ordinary sense allows us to see colors, and which at the same time motivated us to love and seek the good and eschew the bad.

Leaving aside the problems connected with this concept of "moral sense", the crucial move, taken up by Hume, was to explain moral discernment and action by an attraction, built into our nature largely through the force of sympathy, for traits of character, like "benevolence", which issue in actions which redound to the benefit of others, and by a repulsion for the contrary traits and actions.

Now the view I've been presenting here has some affinities to Hume's. Because like him, I believe that our perception of, say moral virtues, or morally admirable ends, cannot be dispassionate, that our intuitions here are felt intuitions. But the difference here is crucial. The inclinations that Hume and other "sentimentalists" ascribe to us are brute reactions. They are triggered by certain features of character or action, but not in any sense motivated by insight into the *value* of these features. This in spite of the fact that our emotional reactions are described by Hume as "approbation" or "disapproval", which would seem to carry some implication that the features are worthy or unworthy of this approval.[24]

Whereas what I am saying is that an essential part of our motivation when we act is such an insight into the goodness or badness of the action. This insight may be only minimally spelt out. The protest at some horrendous proposal may consist of nothing but the interjection: "but that's murder!" But the point is that something more can and sometimes has to be said about what's wrong here, and about the goodness of the way of life in which this kind of action is excluded or minimized. Reason enters into our thinking in this situation, and not just to determine causal relations, as Hume thought, but also hermeneutically, to explicate the original insight.

Take two cases, where we can see that Hume's thesis of the motivational inertness of merely causal reasoning seems to fit:

---

24. Of course, Hume does allow for our making such judgments of worth, but they concern simply facts about, for example, whether the act concerned was really done out of a benevolent motive, or facts about what causes what; facts which by themselves would be motivationally inert.

Case 1: You show me a cushion which is soft and pliable, really has give. Suddenly I see that this would make my car seat more comfortable. Here the Humean analysis really works. Comfort is something I desire, and this desire turns an originally inert fact about the cushion into the springboard for action. But the desire for comfort is just a surd; you can't argue people out of it, saying that isn't really comfort—even though you might say: focus on higher things, and you won't worry about comfort.

Case 2: You are explaining to me the principle of the lever, complete with the history, Archimedes, and so on. This may fascinate me intellectually, but it is motivationally inert until I see that I can remove a large rock in the middle of my garden. But why do I want to do that? To put a big table in the center; why that? To gather friends and family, in beautiful surroundings; but why that? Because then the current of love flows; we achieve a kind of communion. My desire for this is not just a surd. We can see this in two ways.

First, a wiser person can say: you're right to seek communion, but this can be much deepened and enriched if you are able to be more open with your children, share your thoughts, and so on. This is not just a causal route to the original goal as originally conceived; we are transforming the goal, claiming that this is a better, a fuller version of what we originally aimed for. The increased communication is an intrinsic feature of the newly conceived communion. This is, in other words, reconceived.

Then I receive a second piece of advice: this is more important than you thought; make more room for it in your life. This can combine with the first. Often we come to this kind of reassessment in the course of life (even without advice from others); the felt intuition dawns. We're not dealing with surds.

Is Hume's position ultimately sustainable? Is it even coherent? We recognize benevolence as a virtue. Hume's account of this is that we respond to this trait of character, and to the acts it generates with a positive stance of approbation. So much, so agreed. But is this response just a surd, a de facto feature of our emotional makeup, or is it something more, viz., an insight into a (putative) moral good?

What's the difference? Well, a favorable reaction is just a reaction, whereas an insight can admit of, maybe even calls for, expansion, development, clarification. Moreover, an insight into moral goodness shows us something we can admire, something we are drawn to bring about in our own lives, whereas a reaction may quite lack these features.

We can clarify this with a contrast case. Let's say we know someone who is jolly, always telling jokes, cheers us up whenever he is around. He undoubtedly elicits a positive reaction. We like him, we warm to him, we value his company, but there may be no admiration, no sense that we must do likewise, and no insight here that calls for further exploration. He makes us laugh, period.[25]

Whereas with benevolence we may ask: what does it really consist in? Are there fuller and more striking forms, beyond the less demanding ones? How does it fit into the good life? Does it conflict with other virtues, or desirable outcomes, and how to deal with such conflicts?

And there is more than one answer on offer for each of these questions. One direction of development (which appeals to me) is to say: yes, there are higher forms. Benevolence becomes greater, and more admirable, if one can detach oneself from various modes of self-absorption; for instance from the motive of looking good; or that of feeling good or superior, because of the contrast with other, stingier people, to the point where you come to enjoy, to be invested in, their remaining stingy. There are clear cases where we have a powerful motive to overcome this kind of schadenfreude, when we're dealing with someone we love, and we want above all to help them out of their self-narrowing predicament. A fuller form of benevolence would be where we could come to react this way with anyone, not only close loved ones.

This is one way the insight might develop. But there are others. Someone might think that this heroic, even "agape-istic" mode of benevolence is asking too much of the fragile, self-bound creatures we are; that this striving after an impossible perfection can only lead to self-mutilation, and perhaps to an even nastier form of felt superiority. Such a person would recommend that we be satisfied with the less disinterested benevolence of *l'homme moyen sensuel*,[26] and eschew the search for higher perfection, repudiating the "monkish virtues".

A third position would take this suspicion of self-abnegation even farther, would see agape as a cover for a twisted will to power, motivated ultimately by hatred and revenge.

---

25. Hume mentions a case of this kind to illustrate the contagiousness of moods. See his *Enquiry Concerning the Principles of Morals,* Section IX, paragraph 203. See David Hume, *Enquiries,* ed. I. A. Selby-Bigge (Oxford: Clarendon Press, 1902).

26. The average sensuous person.

I am not proposing to resolve this issue here, just to illustrate how an insight into the goodness of benevolence opens calls for further development, and in the process opens up potential controversies, illustrated here by the contrast between a horizon of greater selflessness, a Humean, and then a Nietzschean position. Issues of this kind are at the heart of our enquiries and disputes about ethics, as I will argue below. In particular, these different views on what we might call the "emotional economy" of proposed virtues, and hence our views on possible or impossible human ethical transformations, play a central role in these disputes.

But all this leads up to the question: is the favorable reaction to benevolence, which Hume rightly points to, a simple reaction, or a felt insight (which may later have to be modified, as the enquiry/dispute proceeds). What was Hume getting at? What could he have been getting at? It would appear that his official view about his own theory saw approbation as a simple reaction. To admit insight would be to open the door to reason— admittedly a hermeneutical reasoning, not one of knockdown arguments or revelations of the undeniable. On the other side, it is clear that approbation wasn't a knee-jerk reaction. We have to recognize some act as one of benevolence before we approve it, and that may demand enquiry into the agent's intention in acting (did he have an ulterior motive?), as well as causal reasoning (if the act manifestly did harm, and this was obvious to the agent, could he have been benevolent?). But the reasoning Hume admits concerns only contingent efficient causation, whereas developing a moral insight leads rather to a change, even transformation of the goal sought.

So Hume must have been conceiving approbation as a reaction. But could this be possible? That is, could there be a favorable reaction (in this case to benevolent acts and people), which is the basis for our moral/ethical views, but is nevertheless not the expression of a (putative) moral insight, but a simple reaction? Can anyone even imagine the phenomenology of a response of this kind, which is similar to our feelings for the amusing companion, but which at the same time launches us into the dimension of moral approbation and disapprobation?

And consider what Hume actually does in his theory of morals. He ends up making an important revision in certain traditional moral views, and splits benevolence from the "monkish virtues" of self-abnegation, so that they are to be placed on opposite sides in a new morality of utility and humanity. (This, in spite of the fact that St. Francis could be considered a knight of agape-istic benevolence, if we allow an anachronistic evocation of Kierkegaard.) This is deriving an "ought" from an "is", with a vengeance (not that Hume disapproved of this derivation).

And consider also how those who embrace Hume's metaethics generally approve heartily of this substantive ethics, with its suspicion of self-denial, and of religion. Whether this endorsement is right or wrong, something seems fishy in the derivation.

A similar problem, and slippage, arises from Hume's invocation of sympathy. Hume—and many sentimentalists—treat sympathy as a surd. But in ethical life as it actually is lived, sympathy is not just a background causal condition which makes morality possible; it exists in different forms and variants, and can call for cultivation.

Take Iris Murdoch's case of the mother-in-law who learns to see her daughter-in-law in a new light, a more charitable light, one which allows them to have a less tense human relation, one more open to the flow of sympathy.[27]

Or take a situation that parents may confront, and often do. You care for your child, but the motivation is mixed and many-layered. One layer is pride in the child, either pride in yourself for producing such a child, or the sense that child is fulfilling your dream. But you may need to get relatively free from this in order really to see the child, what she wants, seeks, needs. You have to focus beyond yourself; set aside your deep investment in the child to let her appear. There is sympathy of a kind here, but not simply as the de facto basis of love; it asks to be realized.

This is analogous to and closely linked to the expansion above of the good of benevolence; we need really to see other people beyond our self-absorbed projections, to develop the virtue of open sensitivity that I described earlier. But we have shifted registers: from sympathy as a surd, a de facto explanatory factor of human ethics, to sympathy as a virtue we ought to cultivate.

In attempting to render the moral "kosher" in terms of modern philosophy, sentimentalism subtly but crucially denatures the phenomena.[28]

---

27. Iris Murdoch, *The Sovereignty of the Good* (London: Routledge and Kegan Paul, 1970), 17.

28. In fact, many of the modern expositions of sentimentalist views read as much like attempts to propound new ethical ideals as they do analyses or explanations of human morality. *Ce sont des plaidoyers qui s'ignorent.* See, for example Slote, *Moral Sentimentalism,* a very convincing defense of care ethics.

And attempts are regularly made to refute sentimentalism from a rationalist perspective. Obviously, if you derive morality from de facto desire,
you lose sight of why it is binding. Suppose I don't share the sympathy-
powered reactions which Hume and others attribute to me. Am I then
beyond the reach of morality, and unable to feel its force?

The felt need is to find a way of proving that we are bound to morality.
And so we get the Kant-influenced attempts by Habermas, Korsgaard, and
others to show that we are logically bound to, for instance, accept universalism, on pain of self-contradiction; performative (Habermas) or straight
logical (Korsgaard).[29]

But this also denatures the phenomena. Apart from the fact that the arguments don't seem to work, and that egoistic behavior, however condem-
nable, doesn't seem self-contradictory, what is compelling about morality
is denatured by rationalism as well. What draws us to follow moral pre-
cepts is not that we avoid contradiction, but the intrinsic appeal of a higher
way of being. Once more, as with sentimentalists, a powerful sense of the
force of this appeal shines through the writings of rationalists, but they
cannot give an adequate account of it. They invent arguments against the
background of powerful universalist intuitions. From within these intuitions, it does indeed appear that you need a good reason to exclude anyone,

29. I have perhaps forced Korsgaard's argument here into an alien mold. The basic idea is that
humans have autonomy, which means they can make principled, not random choices; this means
choices out of their "practical identity"; this is "a description under which you value yourself, a description under which you find your life worth living and your actions to be worth undertaking."
Christine Korsgaard, *The Sources of Normativity* (Cambridge: Cambridge University Press, 1996),
3.3.1. Practical identities are thus crucial to humans. As a human you have to value the capacity to
choose which they make possible. But that means you have to value them in others as well. Enlightenment morality falls out of this understanding of autonomy. "We are autonomous beings; we
choose to endorse certain ends and not others. What guides our choices is our practical identity.
But this capacity to guide yourself is one you have as a human being. So you must value humanity
in you, and this means humanity in like beings" (ibid., 3.4.9). The issue is: what is the form of the
"must" here. At one level it sounds logical: if you don't value humanity, you contradict yourself; to
which the answer might be: so what? But we could also read it: once you see the value of human
agency, how it manifests a dignity above all other beings, you cannot but respect it. This would
bring the argument back to its Kantian source, of the dignity [*Würde*] of rational agency. As an analytic philosopher, Korsgaard seems to be operating in the first register; but as a human being, she is
plainly somewhere in the second. But even this would leave the value of a Kingdom of Ends underdescribed. Scanlon, in *What We Owe* and *Being Realistic about Reasons* (Oxford: Oxford University Press, 2014), wants to avoid this kind of appeal to the constraints of noncontradiction. But his
own "contractualist" account of moral right and wrong seems exclusively focused on morality in the
narrow sense, and on argument in terms of "principles". I found much to agree with, however, in
the appeal to reflective equilibrium, and that we always start reflecting in medias res, being already
actuated by (what seem to us) valid reasons.

and that such reasons are impossible to find. But being told you are contradicting yourself could never generate the intuition. There are no knockdown arguments which can accomplish this. Reason in this domain must be hermeneutical.

But the feeling persists that there is something wrong, incomprehensible, which goes against everything we know, in the ethical appeal to a higher way of life. Modern science shows that in nature there is no higher and lower. The mechanistic exclusion remains powerful.

How is this shown? Well, in natural science these categories have no place. Very well, but we're not dealing with inanimate nature, in abstraction from human beings. Obviously without humans there can be no ethics, which concerns the good life for humans. But what if humans themselves can only be explained in terms of post-Galilean natural science? Here we have come to the assumption, often accepted without argument, which underlies this unease with ethics. And this assumption is very questionable.

But still, the question persists: what sense can you make of the higher? Do you just mean that people are happier? But then what does that have to do with a morality which binds? Yes, the supposition that some life is higher does go along with the idea that there is a deep satisfaction connected to living this way. But this can't just be expressed by saying "happier", as though this satisfaction was just like any satisfaction of desire, only there is quantitatively more of it. Rather the notion is that the satisfaction is deeper, carries more weight. We're beginning to recur to the same kind of metaphor: higher, deeper, and more weighty. But that doesn't mean that we're moving in a circle. Because we all know what it means to say that the satisfaction we derive from fulfilling our vocation, or seeing our children grow up, or contributing to the peace and welfare of humanity, is deeper and more weighty than others. Of course the assumption here is that we are fulfilling a crucial human potentiality that otherwise would be neglected and unanswered. With the word 'potentiality', we are obviously nearing Plato-Aristotle territory, but the rationale doesn't have to be their notion of Form. Indeed, the rationales offered are many, in the variety of etiological stories which people invoke to explain and/or justify their ethical views.

But perhaps our deepest ethical commitments will always carry with them some element of enigma, even after the most convincing hermeneutical attempts, and the best etiological story. We may have to remain without a satisfactory account of what 'higher' means. But it is better to rest, at least provisionally in enigma, than to invent accounts which meet our metalevel requirements, while distorting and covering over the central phenomena.

The above, perhaps too lengthy, argument is meant to show that morality can't be insulated from ethics. The two form a package that can't be analyzed into self-contained modules. If we call this Ethics in the broad sense, then it includes other elements as well. It involves some understanding of the possible forms of human motivation which can power, or impede, ethical action, an account of what I called above the "motivational economy" of the good.

What are the impediments? An answer often given: simply egoism. But the obstacles can be more varied. The causes of noncompliance with even a minimal universal morality are hard to count. Karl Barth spoke of "indolence" or "inertia" [*Trägheit*],[30] but there are many other modes and facets of failure (or what Francis Spufford calls "HPtFtU"):[31] narrowness of vision, incomprehension of the other, sliding into xenophobia (a collective egoism, perhaps), enmiring oneself in one's own troubles, sinking into resentment at the trials we suffer, and so on. Then there is the projection of evil onto others, in order to feel good; the defense of identity by rejecting/ excluding nonconformers, particularly those that upset us; lashing out at those who trigger our inner conflicts. An ethical outlook without some idea of its impediments in this sense is very incomplete. Believing that a code is the essence of the ethical often facilitates falling into one of the traps just described.

But our sense of the motivations also includes factors on the positive side. What is it that moves us to do good? Here the answers vary widely. There is Christian agape, Buddhist *karuna,* Humean sympathy, the respect for the moral law that Kant identified, or our sense of our own dignity as human beings, and what this requires. But whatever the answer, it is usually the case that we are far from being exclusively or single-mindedly motivated by this higher impulse. Any Ethic will project a direction of potential transformation that will make us (more) capable of encompassing the good, and of doing what is right.[32]

30. Karl Barth, *Church Dogmatics: Volume II, Part 1: The Doctrine of God*, trans. Rev. T. H. L. Parker et al. (Edinburgh: T&T Clark, 1957), 173–75.

31. Francis Spufford, *Unapologetic: Why, despite Everything, Christianity Can Still Make Surprising Emotional Sense* (London: Faber and Faber, 2012).

32. Of course, some people may have less elevated ethical aspirations, and/or may see themselves as closer to realizing these, whatever they are. But they will necessarily also be aware that others fall

These projected transformations also vary greatly. Some are much more far-reaching than others. Some religious outlooks put the bar very high: Christian sainthood, Buddhist awakening; and we have also seen atheist outlooks whose adherents projected transformations which most others thought unrealistic, like Marx's communism.

And this brings us to the question of how to bring about the transformation, however conceived. This raises the issue of what I have called "moral sources".[33] What can strengthen our commitment or élan to the good or right? What are the things, the recognition of which, or the contemplation of which, or the contact with which, can infuse this strength in us?

Every Ethic proposes some answer to this. For Plato, it was contemplating the Idea of the Good. In the Abrahamic religious traditions, it was approaching the God of Abraham through prayer and the practice of the Law, or devotion to Jesus; or in other traditions, the answer might be bhakti, devotion to Siva or Krishna; or meditation on the Fourfold Noble Truths; for Kant the contemplation of the self-given law of reason inspires awe [*Achtung*] in us; or we find ourselves inspired by the principle itself of universal human solidarity.

But strength and dedication can also be mediated to us by exceptionally good and/or right-acting people: some saint, or hero, or exceptional political leader (e.g., Nelson Mandela), who has risen above the temptation of personal ambition, or resentment, or desire for revenge, who is, on the contrary, really moved by the common good. Thinking of such people, being with them, can infuse strength in this way.

In a similar way, being in contact with nature, with the force of life we sense in it; reflecting on the good in human nature, on the continuing force of love in human life; returning to great works of art, music, literature, both in their intrinsic depth and force, and in what they say about the human spirit—all these can be powerful forces.

An issue arises in relation to all these sources. How do they strengthen us? Is it just that they trigger some highly positive reaction in us? Or do they really impart force? For believers, in relation to the religious sources just mentioned, clearly the latter is felt to be the case. But what is it with the inspirations from Nature and Art? When I am moved by Nature, is

---

short, and will have some views about what obstacles make others fail, and what motivations helped them to succeed. Indeed, they can sometimes be tiresome in explaining this to you.

33. See Charles Taylor, *Sources of the Self* (Cambridge, MA: Harvard University Press, 1989).

that just a fact about me (or less subjectively, about most human beings)? Or is there some force running through Nature which I am tapping into, opening myself to? When I am moved by Beethoven's Ninth Symphony, clearly the force that I feel is that of the human spirit which is responsible for its creation. The case in this sense is analogous to my being inspired by a great human being, by Mandela for instance. But does something else stand behind this human achievement, as the words in the fourth movement of the Ninth Symphony suggest?

And in the case of Nature and the specifically religious sources, the issue of subjective reaction versus objective force will inevitably be raised.

The point is that we frequently have a sense, in recognizing these sources, of which it is. The Christian believer has the felt intuition that her own power to love comes from being loved by God,[34] rather than from her reaction to the idea of God; or her sense may be that perhaps now it is only the idea, but that it could be more in a further stage of spiritual development. And when Wordsworth spoke of "A motion and a spirit, that impels / All thinking things, all objects of all thought, / And rolls through all things,"[35] he was clearly pointing to something he sensed outside himself.

And there are forms of art, common in the post-Romantic age, which strive to produce what one could call "epiphanies" which seem to point us to such external sources (more of this below). But this is often ontically very indefinite. Not to speak of the fact that this sense of an independent reality will often be accompanied by the doubt which is inseparable from faith.

So the package of Ethics incorporates morality, ethics, motivational impediments, sources. These in turn pose questions of their subjective versus transpersonal origin, which opens issues about what I called in the previous section the etiological story the Ethic implies or supposes. Obviously, the Ethical package and the etiological story overlap and complement each other. They form a broader and more complete package.

What is it to be convinced of one such package? At base and unsubstitutably, it is to have the felt intuition, even when one has done the maximum one can to control for confusion, blindness, inability to face certain realities, and the like. This is often talked about as the "experience" which grounds our conviction.

---

34. See 1 John 4:10, 19.

35. William Wordsworth, "Tintern Abbey," in *William Wordsworth: The Pedlar, Tintern Abbey, the Two Part Prelude* (Cambridge: Cambridge University Press, 1985), lines 100–102.

But something else deserves this title much more: this is the experience of striving to become better, or to come closer to the source. Because in this attempt, however feeble it might be, all these facets mentioned above come into play dynamically. How to strengthen the hold of the sources on us? Perhaps like Aristotle you will see the constant practice of virtue as the way to approach your goal; perhaps you will think rather of neutralizing your weaknesses, by avoiding certain situations. But you will in all likelihood be drawn to take other steps.

Perhaps meditation, perhaps imitating certain models; or by prayer if our understanding is theistic, or else by the practice of works of charity, or frequenting the sacraments, or spiritual exercises of certain sorts; Buddhists may practice certain forms of meditation or other exercises to detach themselves from the illusion of self. Our sense of the positive forces and the negative impediments is formed and constantly refined in this kind of active engagement with them. This is at the heart of the experience that confirms or disconfirms our initial Ethical sense.

There is a structure which is constant here, through all the variations in Ethical outlook: we experience a call, be it from our own nature, or from our noumenal self, or from the nature of reality, or from God; we respond to this in trying to live better, and/or in trying to overcome our limitations and blindness, and/or in striving to come closer to God and to be able to say fully, "Thy will be done"; or whatever; and this response then either produces a counterresponse: we become better; or we detach ourselves more from self; or we come closer to God; or else this counter fails to materialize. This is the structure of the interactive experience which confirms/disconfirms our initial Ethical commitments. It is the quality of this experience which in particular convinces or fails to convince us whence the call comes, from ourselves, nature, or beyond both of these.[36]

Are the transformations we have staked our lives on really possible? Or do they mask some illusion, as Nietzsche suggests when he grounds agape in ressentiment? Or are we blocking out a call to a more valid transformation, through insensitivity, self-absorption, or the inability to see people as they really are?

---

36. Perhaps the description in these paragraphs gives a too earnest a view of our ethical lives, which can't be generalized. Surely, some people are basically quite satisfied with themselves. Undoubtedly. But these people will also have some idea of what makes it possible for them to be so good, or successful, or effective, or whatever they admire—features that other less fortunate or endowed people lack. And they will certainly be concerned with not slipping from the heights attained, and sliding, say, into mediocrity.

We might surmise that this structure of call and response is present throughout human history; that one of its earliest manifestations is in ritual that aims to reconnect us to the gods, or to the order in the cosmos. One of the vectors of change in history, whose later developments are often described as "secularization", brings about an "immanentization": for certain people, both call and counterresponse are no longer considered "transcendent" in one or other sense; they no longer emanate from beyond nature, or beyond the human. These immanent forms add to the gamut of human possibilities, rather than replacing the "transcendent" forms that preceded them. But this addition changes our whole conception of the structure and its possible forms.

This is at the heart of the "direct" or "internal", or the "experiential" confirmation of our sense of Ethical meanings, and the static felt intuition of rightness is just one facet, one might say one precipitate, of it. But our Ethical intuitions can also be checked in another, also "internal" way. We may ask whether some of our intuitions are consistent with others, equally strongly held. And this may lead us to change some of our convictions, in search of what John Rawls calls "reflective equilibrium".[37]

And beyond these, there are also "indirect" modes of confirmation or refutation. The package of morals, ethics, motivations and impediments, and its etiological story offers a palette of possible motivations, and their potential transformations; and the question must arise: how well does this palette make sense, not just of our own experience, including any (perhaps small-scale) change we may sense in ourselves; but further, how much sense does it make of the ongoing narrative of human life as we see it around us, and in history? The issue is one of hermeneutics: can the sense we can make of things be challenged by a rival hermeneutic which can account for these matters, for instance varieties of action and feeling, and distinctions between them, that we cannot? No matter how anchored our felt sense of things may be in our elected package, a successful challenge of this kind will show it to be inadequate. This corresponds to what I called at the end of the previous section the "external" or "indirect" route.

I used the word 'hermeneutic' in the previous paragraph, and also earlier in the discussion of this section. This perhaps needs more elaboration. In the sense used here, it draws on the resonances of the traditional science/

---

37. Rawls, *Theory of Justice*.

art called hermeneutics, which was concerned with the interpretation of texts, and particularly of the Bible. The goal was to make the best possible sense of the text.

But this is now being applied in contemporary philosophy, and here by myself, to human action. Why this extension? Because explaining human action, or reactions, responses, attitudes, involves not only identifying their causes; it also requires that we make sense of these actions and responses. Making sense means making the actions/responses understandable, but in a particular sense of "understanding", which we might call "human understanding".[38]

Thus we often say things like: (1) "I can't understand him. He seems to be sabotaging, undermining his most cherished goal." Or (2) "that reaction seems totally over the top, uncalled for"; or (3) "he seems to be deliberately provoking opposition"; or (4) "why did she put her demand in those terms, which almost guaranteed refusal?" In all these cases, the actor is (provisionally) opaque to us; we cannot understand him or her.

We explain properly, we make sense of the action/response, when we add to, or complexify, the range of meanings or motivations actually operating here. We have to enrich our comprehension of the landscapes of meaning that these agents act within. Only we might use a different image here, and talk of a constellation of motives.

So to (1), we identify perhaps in the actor a will to failure. At some level, in some part of him, he's afraid to succeed; he can't handle success. To (2), we note that his interlocutor used words which seemed anodyne, but which triggered off powerful reactions in the actor, which puzzled us at first but which are understandable in the light of his history. The words used "pushed his buttons". To (3), we bring coherence when we identify another kind of will to failure than that operative in (1): he really wants at some level to continue the struggle, to keep the quarrel going; this battle vivifies him, he feeds on it. To (4), we come to see that these terms are

---

38. I am obviously invoking the tradition of "empathetic understanding" [*Verstehen*] invoked for human sciences since Wilhelm Dilthey. Max Weber makes the case for the indispensability of "*Verstehen*" to any explanation of events and social structures in history. See his discussion of "historical individuals" in "'Objectivity' in Social Science," in *The Methodology of the Social Sciences*, trans. and ed. Edward Shils and Henry Finch (Glencoe: Free Press, 1949), 70 and ff. Hence Weber's requirement on any sociological explanation, that it be not only "causally adequate", but also "adequate as to meaning" [*sinnhaft adäquat*]. See point 7 in the opening chapter "Basic Sociological Terms" in *Economy and Society: An Outline of Interpretive Sociology*, ed. Guenther Roth and Claus Wittich (Berkeley: University of California Press, 1978), 11–12.

essential to her identity, to her sense of integrity; so she had to couch her demand in religious terms, even addressing fierce, dogmatic secularists.

A hermeneutical account is one which strives to make (human) sense of agent and action, and a hermeneutical argument tries to show that one account does so better than a rival one. It was recognized early on that this required a kind of circular argument. The aim, in the original context of Bible interpretation, was often to make a particular passage clear which was uncertain or enigmatic. But the reading offered of this passage or verse had to make sense within the presumed overall meaning of the entire chapter, and ultimately, of the whole book of the Bible. One could thus use the sense of the whole to make sense of the part. But a question can always be raised; do we understand fully the meaning of the whole? Perhaps the meaning we see in this verse ought to call into question the idea we have of the whole, and lead to a reinterpretation. It is possible to argue in both directions, and hermeneutics involves a kind of circle, where one has to balance potential arguments in either direction against each other.

There is a circle here, but it is not a vicious one. It doesn't involve the notorious "circular argument", where one assumes the conclusion among the premises. On the contrary, the attempt is to bring the arguments in both directions into an equilibrium in which one makes maximum sense of the text.

Heidegger, and after him Gadamer and Ricoeur,[39] pointed out that something like the hermeneutical circle obtains in our attempts to understand what I'm calling here "human meanings". The "texts" here can be events, passages in the life of individuals or societies, or human history; or we can start from individual experiences: feelings, actions, decisions, and try to determine their meaning. Whatever meaning we attribute to the part has to make sense within the whole, whose meaning it also helps determine. The individual decision stands in this relation to the whole segment of my life in which it falls; the revolutionary turning point to the whole period in the history of society which it inflected; my momentary emotional response to the whole pattern of my feelings.

I believe that the notion of a hermeneutical circle can be generalized to understand how we operate with the skeins of interdependent meanings

---

39. Martin Heidegger, *Being and Time*, trans. John Macquarrie and Edward Robinson (New York: Harper and Row, 1962); H.-G. Gadamer, *Truth and Method*, trans. Joel Weinsheimer and Donald G. Marshall (London: Continuum, 2004); Paul Ricoeur, *Du texte à l'action* (Paris: Éditions du Seuil, 1986).

which are central to our human self-understanding, like that of pride versus shame, in contrast to guilt versus innocence, as well as their proper objects, which I mentioned in the first section; or the moral landscapes linking norms, virtues, and positive and negative motivations, which I have been describing in this one. Because here too, any change in one term disturbs the skein, and would have to be ratified by changes in others. Equilibrium can be restored either by making the ratification, or by refusing the original change.

There are examples in the above discussion of arguments in both directions. I argued, for instance, that our approbation of benevolence had to be seen as a putative insight into good, rather than as a brute reaction, because of how this experience opens into a whole chain of hermeneutical reasoning. The argument here runs from the potentiality of the part to generate a certain kind of whole. But there are also arguments in the opposite direction: Nietzsche is too firmly convinced that the appeal for mercy cannot but emanate from the slave's will to power for him to accept its face validity. Equilibrium comes when one has a plausible account on both levels together; or to put it as a double negative, when there is no palpable distortion at either level. And hermeneutical *argument* usually consists in pointing out something which a rival view distorts or cannot account for.

So to return to the Ethical "packages" discussed above, the moral/ethical-motivational distinctions incorporated in any one such involve expectations of how these alternatives will play out in human life around us and in history. The hermeneutical issue concerns whether and to what extent these expectations are met; or, otherwise put, whether they really capture the rich texture of this life and history, or rather make us unable to pick up on certain key features or nuances of them.

In the four cases above, the constellation of motives operating had to be expanded beyond what seemed on the face of it to be the goals of the action, in order to make sense of it. And arguments can arise about the capacity in general of a certain constellation of motives, sometimes linked to an ethical outlook or a more general philosophical anthropology, to make sense of human action. Arguments have been put forward, for instance, that proponents of rational choice theory can't explain much political action, including how people vote. And we can see how the rival views about ethical motivation I invoked above between Christians, Humeans, and

Nietzscheans positively invite attempts by one or the other to show that its rivals cannot make sense of certain pervasive actions, feelings, and aspirations which are visible in human life.

Similar arguments break out between different schools of historical interpretation. François Furet criticized the school of *marxisant* historians of the French Revolution on the grounds that their explanation of the Terror in terms of the external and internal military emergency couldn't account for the obsessive Robespierrian discourse of corruption and purity. For Furet, this phenomenon remained unexplained within the terms of mainstream republican historiography.[40]

To take another example, supposing that I am about to act generously, but I am challenged. The challenge is not to the particular act: my opponent is not saying: "Generosity in general is good, but in these circumstances, disastrous consequences will follow." Rather generosity itself is being challenged as a virtue.

To which I or others can reply: we point out role models, people we all admire who are generous; or we argue that generosity helps generate and sustain friendly, harmonious, trusting relationships, as against hostile, distant, distrustful and conflictual ones. In other words, it fits with and helps constitute a better order. Maybe we are living in a Christian or Buddhist society, so that both role models and reigning understandings of good order support this virtue.

But my challenger reads Ayn Rand. She shows this act in a quite new light: abandonment of my chance for greatness by sacrificing my means of achievement to help rather despicable, clinging parasites. An alternative ethic is proposed, that of great, self-starting and self-reliant achievers, in short, *Übermenschen*.

The conflict of interpretations is far-reaching, including radically different readings of the ordinary, non élite human being. But that is what makes it amenable to hermeneutical debate. Is that really a believable account of what makes humans tick?

These are the kinds of issue which are at stake between different packages, and they can play a role in convincing us to change, or refine, or reaffirm the package that our felt intuitions incline us to. Hermeneutical arguments

40. François Furet, *Interpreting the French Revolution* (Cambridge: Cambridge University Press, 1981).

of this kind can help arbitrate between different ethical outlooks, by testing the motivational constellations that each supposes. These issues about what makes sense of human life in general, along with argument about the respective etiological stories, constitute what I've been calling the "indirect" mode of support or refutation of our ethical views; while the attempt to make sense of our own ethical experience of struggle, which is at the heart of the "direct" examination of our intuitions, is itself a hermeneutical exercise. Both together help determine our outlook. New convincing intuitions can only come through the direct route, but arguments of the indirect kind, about sensemaking in general, can raise challenges that we have to meet.

And this interplay of our felt intuitions, our own potential inner confusions and selective awareness, and our hermeneutical acuity occurs against a background where uncertainty and doubt cannot but obtrude. For one thing, the meanings that our language opens us to, that inner landscape, remains to some degree always enigmatic, demanding further clarification. For another, the blindnesses that figure as impediments recognized by our own package—for example, the tendency to project our own evil outward onto others—cannot but suggest doubts about our own acuity. To what extent do we fall prey to other forms of the same thing?

To return to the issue between Hume and the rationalists of his epoch: Hume is right in seeing that our moral convictions originate in felt intuitions; but wrong in thinking that these intuitions are immune to reason. And the reasoning is not merely of the instrumental kind, whose role in determining our judgments Hume acknowledges. But nor is it the determining of "the eternal and unalterable relations in the nature of things" which Clarke invoked. Rather the intuitions offer insights, and the reasoning around these is hermeneutical.[41]

In the preceding paragraphs, I have been mainly talking of ethical reasoning between positions which are very far apart, where Christians or universalist liberals may confront Nietzscheans or followers of Ayn Rand. But although radical conversions do occur between such extremes, a much more common form of ethical change is less dramatic. It is better described as moral or ethical growth, coming to see more what the basic position we accept requires or involves.

41. See my "Reason, Faith, and Meaning" in *Faith and Philosophy* 28, no. 1 (2011): 5–18.

This kind of growth in insight often goes along with a growing capacity to act on our ethical convictions. Getting better and seeing better often go together, as I mentioned at the end of the previous section. This is best illustrated by seeing how it works out for a particular range of ethical views. Let me take the range which incorporates the hegemonic moral principles in our contemporary society, which enshrine universal human rights and the obligation to give humanitarian aid to all those in need, whether this outlook is powered by a Kantian or utilitarian philosophy, or by Christian agape or Buddhist ahimsa.

I argued earlier in this section that this kind of morality requires certain virtues, including sensibility that is capable of understanding others and generous outreach toward them. This is obvious when we move beyond our familiar circles and find ourselves in a multicultural society, or when we support humanitarian action in far-distant countries. But it is also needed in more homogeneous societies because many differences may easily escape the notice of people in positions of relative power, as contemporary feminism has repeatedly brought to our attention in recent decades. Without this ability to see difference—Keats's "negative capability"—the best moral rules (in principle) will often be applied in ways which thwart, block, or offend many people.

This kind of openness is essential if the accepted moral code is not to harden into something inflexible and even inhumane, as so often happens. We can think of the insensitivity to the needs and reactions of women in many male circles even today; of the rigid application of secularism [laïcité] in contemporary France (which we almost imitated in Quebec); of the flagrant underestimation among many senior clergy of the damage caused by abuse of minors. Even remarkable spiritual leaders can have their blind spots, as we see with John Paul II's treatment of the movement around liberation theology and base communities.

Practicing this virtue of openness leads to further insight into what the morality requires, and the improved morality opens the way to further insight. New issues open up, and new ways of dealing with them must be sought. Recognizing difference opens our eyes to certain dilemmas, hidden under previously projected uniformities. Religious practice among recent immigrants may take different forms than members of the host society have traditionally recognized; this requires new definitions of what we have called the "free exercise" of religion. These changes may incommode many members of the host society.

Or in a society which is emerging from a dictatorial régime, the full demands of retributive justice against the perpetrators of human rights violations under the old dispensation may be hard to combine with the need to make a fresh start which will enlist the support of all parties. This in turn points us toward a new frontier of ethical inventiveness: how can we create new forms of reconciliation and mutual trust which will allow us to navigate the dilemma between justice for past wrongs, on one hand, and creating a new basis for solidarity and social cohesion, on the other? This is the difficult issue which the South African Truth and Reconciliation Commission tried to resolve, and which many other countries have faced.

We can see from this example what growth in ethical insight can involve, and also how far-reaching it can be. Openness to difference, mandated by the universalist aspirations of our moral code, can lead to a modification of the code, making it more flexible and humane. This in turn can bring to light certain moral dilemmas; and these in turn may draw us on to project political changes that can help us resolve or at least navigate these dilemmas, by creating the basis of greater mutual trust and solidarity. Throughout we will have been following the thread of what the basic principle of our code requires in order to be integrally realized.[42]

4

But now if we return to our question of how cultures change and new meanings arise, we can see that verbal articulation is only part of the story. In this domain, the constitutive power of language operates as well on the level of enactment (as I glancingly mentioned in section 2 above). Thus in Chapter 1, I portrayed the biker as introducing a new meaning into our world, for which he has not yet found a word (but for which we might choose the term 'macho'). The bodily expression here is constitutive in a more obvious and direct way. The whole process of a new meaning entering and spreading in our world involves both enactment and articulation. The youth start talking about acting "cool" and "laid back", and they also behave this way. Many elders are puzzled and perhaps also repelled. But

---

42. I have discussed this kind of moral/ethical progression at greater length in "The Perils of Moralism" in *Dilemmas and Connections* (Cambridge, MA: Harvard University Press, 2011), chapter 15; and in Charles Taylor, *A Secular Age* (Cambridge, MA: Harvard University Press, 2007), 703–10.

after a while everyone comes to recognize and at least partly understand the new meaning—even if many still disapprove and want to resist.

Enactment is crucial here, but we should see that such articulation also shapes the meanings we live in its own way, and so is distinct from the kinds of articulations we devise to get a better grip on independent objects. I will discuss another facet of the constitutive power of enactment in Chapter 7, where will examine how footings are created and sustained.

Enactment can't do the same job as verbal articulation, because it operates, as it were, at a less articulate level. A newly enacted meaning (like our "macho" biker above) takes its place in our skein of meanings—our "landscape" to use the metaphor introduced earlier—while also altering the landscape. But it calls for verbal articulation if we want to understand better what it involves. We can speak here of a ladder of articulative expressions. The purely enacted are at the bottom. They can be grasped more fully when we can give them a name, and identify certain criterial features. But this step can also leave them in some way enigmatic. And so we are forced to go further, and to offer the kind of fuller account that I mentioned in the previous section: we show the place of this meaning in the larger skein or "landscape"; we may offer some story of how this arose in our world, explaining this in terms of cultural, political, historical developments (an etiological account); we may clarify further the role it plays in our lives, and in relation to other meanings; we may give some account of why we feel this and others do not; and we may argue that the palette of motivations it supposes gives a better account of our lives and history.

So the three rungs of the ladder are: enactment, verbal articulation of a name and crucial features, and a fuller account of its role in our lives. Think, for instance, of Bourdieu's account of how young people in Kabylie learn respect for their elders.[43] It starts with the inculcation of certain habitus; the young learn to bow, not to look the elder right in the eye; they learn to enact respect (rung 1). But then the different things you do to show respect, bowing, deferring, and the like are gathered together under some term or terms, like 'respect' (rung 2). This gathering may be done in ordinary explanatory prose, for example in a definition of respect, or a code of how to manifest it. But it can also be done through story, dance, and portrayal of exemplary figures, which are in the realm of symbol.

43. Pierre Bourdieu, *Sociologie de l'Algérie* (Paris: Presses Universitaires de France, 1958).

And at a further level, the young may be given a more developed idea of why elders deserve respect, of what they do for the community, of how important they are, and of the valuable relations that the respect of youth preserves, and which would be jeopardized by insolence or indifference (rung 3).

Now our ordinary grasp of a meaning draws on all three rungs. We couldn't just substitute a verbal account at rung 2 (say, a code) or rung 3 (a rationale for the code) and leave behind our embodied understanding of what it is to enact the meaning. We originally learn what love, respect, consideration, generosity, and the like are through bodily gestures and action: holding, caressing, attending and listening to, and so on. Our grasp of the gestures, for example of love, evolves, but our understanding of love remains anchored in them.

That is why, as I argued above (section 3), carrying out a code, for instance treating people with respect, requires certain virtues, for example of sensitivity to others' needs and aspirations, generosity, openness. To have these virtues is to have internalized the "gestures" of respect, as part of one's spontaneous response.

I'd like to make a parenthetical remark here: the existence of rung 1, enactment, shows that all meaning creation relevant to language doesn't have the sign structure, the structure of representation, where one can distinguish sign and object, *significant* and *signifié*. The behavior of our biker doesn't *signify* machismo (if that's the word we choose here), it *is* machismo. Of course, once the pattern becomes recognizable, I can pick up on a kind of swagger that alerts me that the guy I have to deal with here is macho. But for the biker himself this kind of split between sign and signified isn't possible. I made this point in perhaps too cursory fashion in Chapter 3. This is part of what I meant.

So rung 1 is often inescapable, but things may remain there; or stop at rung 2. And in many cases there is no separate stage at which we are just at rung 1; rungs 1 and 2 may operate together to introduce a new meaning; or one may be introduced simply by verbal articulation. But the ladder image helps show how these levels relate to each other when they are all present. The relation is hermeneutical, that is, the higher rungs interpret and clarify the lower, in a way analogous to the older hermeneutics which clarified texts.

Paul Ricoeur has done much to explore this relationship. His account really starts with the concluding chapter of his *Finitude et Culpabilité*,[44] titled "The Symbol Gives Rise to Thought" ["Le Symbole Donne à Penser"]. The symbols and mythology of early accounts of evil, like sin as a kind of stain [*souillure*], are enigmatic; they call for an account in "thought", that is, in philosophically responsible terms. They call for this, but their content is never totally and exhaustively rendered in these terms. Our understanding of these issues can never be fused into a single language.

Later Ricoeur makes a similar point, which I might render in terms of the discussion in this chapter. Our language of meanings, expressed in terms whose semantic logic is constitutive, always calls for further explanation. And much of this, like the "fuller accounts" of rung 3, also deploys terms with the more philosophically familiar "designative" semantic logic. To offer an etiological story, for instance, of the historical conditions of a certain meaning entering our world, we have to talk of political, economic, cultural developments, which now figure in our social science or historiography as independent objects. What we have here is a "*discours mixte*",[45] with terms drawn from both semantic logics, and this type of account resists reduction to a homogeneous language deploying only designative terms.

But this kind of reduction remains a goal for many thinkers. It is even the defining goal of a certain kind of "materialism", which is deeply influenced by the paradigmatic accounts of post-Galilean natural science and which eschews reference to human meanings altogether, let alone metabiological ones.

It is not that Ricoeur thinks that meaning terms can never be eliminated. He recognizes the importance of what he calls "hermeneutics of suspicion", of which Marx, Nietzsche, and Freud have produced famous and paradigmatic examples. Not all hermeneutics discover a meaning which one can affirm. It is just that he doubts that we will ever succeed in entirely eliminating meaning terms with a constitutive semantic logic. Even after Marx and Nietzsche have succeeded in discrediting older metaphysical notions of hierarchy, for instance, we find ourselves drawing on new notions of democratic equality, which cannot be cashed out in purely designative terms, but rely crucially on modes of self-understanding

---

44. Paul Ricoeur, *Philosophie de la Volonté, Tome 2: Finitude to Culpabilité: La Symbolique du Mal* (Paris: Aubier, 1960), conclusion.

45. "mixed discourse"; Paul Ricoeur, *Réflexion Faite* (Paris: Éditions Esprit, 1995), 36.

and social imaginaries. And the plurality of semantic logics entails also a plurality of logics of verification, as we saw above. (More on this in Chapter 7.)

In speaking of a ladder of articulacy, and of relations of interpretation between the three rungs, I by no means want to imply that we are always engaged in active interpretation, assembling higher rungs through a hermeneutic of the lower. On the contrary, we are inducted from our earliest upbringing into global accounts which are already there. These global accounts consist of webs of practices which we are enjoined to enact, articulated in skeins or "landscapes" of meanings, which in turn are justified by fuller accounts of their genesis and reasons. The working out of fresh interpretations and explanatory accounts becomes necessary when we introduce new meanings; and this work also becomes necessary when tensions arise in the established global accounts.

We experience these frequently today because of large-scale religious and ethical changes. For instance, earlier global accounts in which a moral code was seen as immediately given in the text of the Bible have been shaken and discredited for many people, while remaining strong for others. Those who can't go on in the old way are forced to reorder their ethical and spiritual understanding, either abandoning their religion or adopting a quite new way of living it. Or again, certain features of the traditional sexual morality—the condemnation of homosexual relations for instance—have fallen afoul of the contemporary ethic of nondiscrimination, which has been lent greater urgency by the growth of an ethic of authenticity. Tensions of this kind force us to innovate and to forge new outlooks. But for many people through history and even today, it has remained possible and even mandatory to remain within the house of meanings built for them by their forbears.

5

But let's return to the discussion of how new meanings are introduced and vocabularies formed: we see a younger generation introducing a new punctual meaning (chilling out in the backyard, that's cool, man). Or a reformer can launch a new global one: What did Athenians make of Socrates's claim: the unexamined life isn't worth living? (One can imagine one of the jurors muttering: What the hell is this unexamined life stuff? I'm voting for condemnation.) What we may need is something more than a description.

And in this case, we have Socrates; this life is what interprets the phrase. This life was enacted before Socrates gave it a name. This is a case in which innovation of meaning comes through enactment.

And this is far from an isolated case. We could also cite other great ethical or religious innovators: Christ, the Buddha. But we shouldn't confine our attention to the "highest" cases. The style of living designated by the word 'dandy' was introduced by Beau Brummel in the early nineteenth century, and later commented on and made famous by Baudelaire. There is a large domain of invented styles of life which we might be tempted to call "quasi-ethical"; for their practitioners they represent features of the good life, but we looking at them—and even the practitioners themselves—may not want to claim the title 'ethical'. Dandyism, we might want to say, is rather an "aesthetic" ideal; except that Nietzsche has taught us how porous, uncertain, and problematic this boundary between the ethical and the aesthetic is.

We might see the way of life in which 'cool' is a word of approbation as falling in this same quasi-ethical penumbra.

But how do we find the words to clarify a new meaning, in some cases, even before we enact it? How is it that people sometimes understand us, even without benefit of enactment? How do we articulate, that is, expand, the domain of the sayable?

Some of the examples I offered in Chapter 5 in an attempt to show the inadequacies of the Davidsonian theory of meaning, based on deriving theorems from axioms, can also give us a sense of what is at stake here. What expands the sayable can't be derived from axioms predating this expansion.

Let's look at some of these examples: a metaphor commits an obvious category mistake: the chairman ploughed through the discussion. The tension between these two noncombinable images: the chair presiding, the farmer ploughing, triggers the moment of insight, where you see the chair's behavior in a new light.

Something similar happens with the introduction of a new word, like 'cool' in contemporary English. Think of moving out of the sun into the cool of the shade, think of taking a long, cool drink there; there is a serene enjoyment, beyond agitation, going with the flow of things. Then someone applies the term to the music we're hearing. Or someone else applies it to a proposal that we go downtown to a certain bar. At first, we may not see the point. But then you see the proposal: this music, that visit to the bar, can be enjoyed in the same easy movement, beyond agitation, going with the flow. There's a proposal to feel like this about lots of things which are often not enjoyed, or enjoyed in a quite different, more frantic spirit.

Even more extraordinary is what we called in Chapter 5 after Schlegel, the "symbol". Take the example of moral impurity; we see sin, or being involved in the wrong, as a kind of state. And we articulate this state as a kind of uncleanness, impurity. In Schlegel's terms, we are using something external or visible to make something internal and invisible show up.

How does it come about? One way of getting at this is to ask, how do parents induct children into this language. Presumably the child already knows about getting dirty, washing hands before supper, being bawled out for spilling ketchup on his shirt, and the like. But now we have one of those very human distinctions, which wouldn't be possible without language: moral purity/impurity. How does the child pick up on it? Well, presumably, there's another kind of urgency, seriousness, this-is-absolutely-unacceptable tone in the parents' voice and demeanor. This is a special, different kind of uncleanness, rather like the music was a special, new kind of "cool", in the earlier example. You catch on.

And presumably something of the same kind happens when the prophet (if that's where it came from) introduces this notion of sin. Or the reformer transposes our notion of purity (like Jesus in the New Testament[46]). You catch on.

The condition for this catching on is that one is already in the linguistic dimension; linguistic in the wider sense that includes body language, tone of voice, urgency of communication, the whole mood which surrounds the exchange. This creates a force field which prevents you just remaining with ordinary dirt as the issue; another example of the first holism I mentioned in Chapter 1. Each new word supposes the whole of language. But in this case, it is not just our whole power of describing objects; it is our whole linguistic capacity, including its enactive dimension. There is a tension in the exchange, just conceptually between ploughman and chairman in the

46. "He called the people to him and said, 'Listen, and understand. What goes into the mouth does not make a man unclean: it is what comes out of the mouth that makes him unclean'" (Matthew 15:10–11).

metaphor, more pragmatically urgent in learning impurity between horrified reaction and just ordinary dirt, and this points to the new sayable; it opens the space that the new term can fill.

Something of this kind is going on when we manage to articulate what we might call the overall space of caring which we see as normative for us, when we define the basic alternatives we face in life. We confer on distinctions, familiar from elsewhere, a new sense which clarifies crucial meanings. Take the moral term 'integrity'. I have integrity when my words and my actions cohere, when I pursue what is really important without suffering deviation or distraction from irrelevant issues or contrary desires. The word 'integrity' resonates with me, because it bespeaks wholeness, unity; it overcomes dispersal, contradiction, self-stultification. With integrity, I am whole, united, not broken or dispersed.

We all understand this opposition: whole/broken, from a host of objects in our world. Through it we open out a new way of experiencing, that is, of understanding and feeling our lives. The contrast: whole: broken, reshapes how we feel the promise kept through adversity, or the bribe taken in violation of trust. The wholeness of the first act radiates strength, self-affirmation; the brokenness of the second spreads dismay, inner division.

As dirt did to sin, so the fate of everyday objects opens a path to this realm of strongly valued meaning. Or we might say, we use it as a stepping-stone to access and live in this realm.

We can see that different kinds of wholeness, unity, nondivision have served this purpose of mapping the shape of caring in a number of influential ways in our ethical traditions. Borrowing from music, Plato offers a contrast between inner harmony of the parts of the soul, and the discord of strife between reason and desire. The post-Romantic aspiration to heal the split between reason and feeling, or between duty and desire, which returned so strongly during the 1960s, with the call in 1968 for "opening up" [décloisonnement], overcoming the division between work and play, between workers and students, offers another example.

But this is not to say that all moral mappings privilege unity over division. One can experience life through the ideal of a glorification of the pure will, able to chasten desire; or the strong will, triumphing over the lower self. Or one can judge the Platonic drive for unity as a menace to the inherent diversity of human aspirations, and take a stance for "polytheism".

My aim here is not to endorse one of these readings, but rather to show what articulacy in this domain involves.

These uses of Schlegel's "symbol" illustrate one important way in which verbal articulation expresses the import it names, as we saw above in section 2. There is a metaphor-like relation of "figuring" between dirt and sin, nonfracture and integrity. We accede to A (sin) through B (dirt).

Let's take another way that we can find a path from outer to inner, from everyday reality to the space of meanings. We can understand emotions through bodily organs. Take the heart: it can bespeak a love interest: you have my heart; but also compassion: have a heart, the sacred heart of Jesus. And also courage: stout hearts, hearts of oak. How does this bodily "situation" of emotion happen?

The first-level answer seems to be that you feel the seat of these emotions to be the heart. "It warms my heart to hear that"; or "my heart is all aflutter, now that I hear her voice"; or "she broke my heart"; or "my heart bleeds" (as does the sacred heart).

But then we reflect: this seems "natural", but it actually varies between cultures. The Greeks seem to have decided things in what they called their "*phrenes*" (and we aren't entirely sure what that meant). Courage can also be in the gut; and for that matter, the gut is also the seat of compassion in the Bible.

And then there is also a process of unseating, of dissolving seated "mental states" into the empty box of the "mind"; which is what Descartes does.

How does seating/unseating occur? Seating comes about because we learn to live them and feel them like this. Learning to name the emotions can't be separated from learning to express them. You can't learn love without caresses; can't learn respect without bowing; can't learn piety without praying.

In the context in which we learn, that of emotion-charged communion, "experience and expression" [*erleben und ausdrücken*] are inseparably interwoven. Because in this between space of "joint attention" the child learns from the parent the distinct names, and expressions of the emotions. Emotions get definite contours, and are not just unstructured disturbances, agitations. We give the kids the words to describe what they're living, at the same time as we communicate ways of living and expressing these emotions. In this process of defining, naming, we learn to feel bodily states as having their emotional meaning.

What is learnt here is a constellation: of disturbances and feelings (including bodily), of goal, and name. It is terrible to be without this sorting; or where the sorting we have doesn't fit. There is a terrible sense of desperate need, but we have no idea for what. Children are rescued from this by caregivers, but it can recur later with new experiences, especially at puberty (see Chapter 1). Baudelaire gives an arresting portrayal of an analogous condition in his "spleen" poems: the paralysis of acedia without a recognizable cause. And then his poems themselves bring it to articulacy, and begin our (also his) liberation. I intend to return to this in the proposed companion study.

There is a heart-beating of love, a heart-beating of fear. A certain warmth is attached to love as the heart warming. A certain pain as the heart bleeding, even though not literally. A certain dearth or death of love as the heart breaking.

Love, compassion are learnt as incarnate in this way, through this organ and the feeling we locate there. But we can excarnate these emotions. This can come in critical examination, like in Augustinian self-distrust: do I really love her? Would I die for her? Am I really compassionate? Or do I just like the self-image? We mistrust our incarnate reactions. We ask questions: am I disposed to sacrifice myself?

What's going on here, in these "seatings"? A modality of Schlegel's phenomenon of the "symbol". We are striving to say something new, something "inner"; we create the words through already existing words which get used to say something new. So 'spirit' = breath, but goes beyond that. Another striking example is the one we just discussed: the notion of moral or spiritual impurity, pollution. We move beyond just physical dirt to reach a new meaning.[47]

We know that spirit is not the same as Spirit, that dirt is not the same as impurity. We are tempted to talk of "literal" and "figurative" dirt. But that makes metaphor the key to the relation, and that is not necessarily so. It isn't so at the beginning. The relation is more complex. We invoke and get to, disclose, have access to, sin and impurity through dirt, but we may conceive the relation as sin being a deeper and more cosmically significant case of the same thing.

But the important role of the symbol comes from the fact that we only get access to A through some B, as when we get our primary access to love

---

47. Ricoeur, *La Symbolique*.

and compassion through the heart; the heart as the lived seat of these emotions.

And like love and the heart, we can bring about a degree of excarnation. Critical moves begin to do this. So the Gospel says: not what a human eats, what goes in to a human, is what makes her/him impure, but what comes out of him/her.[48] When you express your hatred, you become impure. This doesn't lead to total excarnation, but begins to weaken the force of original access.

In the end, you get to more complete excarnation where a notion like purity of heart gives way to that of a single-minded will to obey the law.

There are two important points here: (a) the emotions, or spiritual states, in Schlegel's terms the "*Geistiges*", or the "*Inneres*", don't simply remain identical while we just have access through a different route; analogous to the referent remaining the same through different Fregean "meanings" [*Sinne*]: Morning Star and Evening Star. No, because we live it differently, conceive it differently in its "symbolic" as against its "detached" forms. Compassion without the gut isn't the same thing.

And (b) the question can arise of which is the truer form: does excarnation make us lose touch with what is really important? Compassion as "*splagnizesthai*" in the New Testament is a gut reaction, not a pure will in the Kantian sense. In which of these does the human most completely reveal God?

We could add issue (c): can we ever fully excarnate our emotions and intuitions of spirit and our separation from it (sin)? Answer from Christian standpoint: "no". We need the various languages of inwardness. Strong emotions can't be detached from the body.

So there is a kind of reciprocal relation here. We learn to distinguish the emotions by the way we feel them in our bodies, and communicate them through our bodies. But we also learn to identify our bodily feelings and their "seats" through the language of the emotions. This process of mutual definition yields the corporal geography of the emotions, which have their "seats" in certain "organs". These bodily verbal interchanges end up opening a field of the sayable and giving shape to it.

48. See note 38 above.

6

We've been talking about two ways of innovating, of coming to express or grasp a new meaning. One is through enactment, embodiment; and the other is through a description, like a metaphor or bodily "seating" which allows us to make a leap.

But how about a third form, the work of art, something which is neither expressive projection nor description? In a sense, the work of art was even more central to the development of Romantic expressivism (and hence to the HHH) than what I have been calling projection, or enactment. We can see this in the conception of the symbol, as opposed to the allegory, which played an important role in the aesthetic of the Romantic period, and indeed since. As described, for instance, by Goethe, the symbol was a paradigm of what I have been calling constitutive expression.

A work of art which was "allegorical" presented us with some insight or truth which we could also have access to more directly. An allegory of virtue and vice as two animals, say, will tell us something which could also be formulated in propositions about virtue and vice. By contrast a work of art had the value of a symbol when it manifested something which could not be thus "translated". It opens access to meanings which cannot be made available any other way. Each truly great work is in this way sui generis. It is untranslatable. I'll return to this shortly.

The work of art as symbol was perhaps the paradigm on which the early constitutive theories of language were built. In its very definition, there is an assertion of the plurality of expressive forms, in the notion that it is untranslatable into prose. From this standpoint, the human expressive-constitutive power—or alternatively, the linguistic dimension—has to be seen as a complex and many-layered thing, in which the higher modes are embedded in the lower ones.

Our earlier discussion (in Chapter 1, section 7) identified two modes of constitutive expression, by which new meanings could enter our world: one is the enactive (or the bodily-expressive) and the other includes forms of description or modeling which regestalt experience. This binary is often simply conceived as between enaction and description, it being understood that we have already distinguished the kind of description which attributes properties to things out there, from the kind of self-description which rearticulates, and hence changes, our experience. In terms of the discussion in Chapter 1, these correspond to rungs 1 and 2 on the ladder of articulacy.

But the "symbol" in this sense we're using here doesn't fit easily into the binary so understood.

We might put it this way: enacting doesn't represent anything. The biker is not portraying how macho young males act; he is too busy being a macho young male. And similarly with the child who has learnt to bow to his elders. When we get to the inner rebel, who begins to parody respect in an ironic way; then portrayal enters the picture, but by then things are already beginning to go wrong.

By contrast, we might say that the point of description is to represent, to say how things are with some matter.

But now this simple contrast, between enacting and description, is complicated by a third possibility. The work of art exemplifies a way of "representing" which is not description.

To take another example, look at mimicry, or mime (which can, of course, be itself a work of art, as with Marcel Marceau). Think of a young child reenacting a spanking she has received, by spanking her doll. This is her way of coming to terms with the experience, learning to make her peace with it. Here the representative dimension of the act is essential. A crucial feature of the Herderian view of language as "reflective" which we saw above, is that each word or gesture is proffered from out of a sense that it is the "right" one. The word I'm using is the right way to characterize what I'm describing; the biker's swagger is what fits the style he's enacting. When we get to the child spanking the doll, we can certainly discern an enactive dimension: she's trying to expressively reenact this upsetting experience in order to come to terms with it. But it is also clear that this can only be done through gestures which are right as a representation of the original action. The "right gesture" has both representative and enactive facets.[49]

But mimicry is not assertion. It's not clear from any act of miming what is being asserted; for this we need a pregiven context. I might be saying: this is how not to do things. Here there is a contrast with descriptive language, where there is generally a clear assertion sign with a defined scope. With mimicry, there can be assertive force which comes from the conversational context ("this is how he looked"); or from the ritual context, but this is external to the medium.

In other words, mimicry portrays without asserting.

---

49. See Merlin Donald, *Origins of the Modern Mind* (Cambridge, MA: Harvard University Press, 1991), 174 and 184.

This means that there can be articulating-constitutive expression which brings something new into our world, some new possibility, by portraying rather than enacting it, but which is not assertive description either.

Thus, I can bring in a new way of understanding my world by new scientific language, or by a new nuance of critical description. I can bring about a new way of being in the world by enacting a novel style of action, say, a new way of being unperturbed, unflappable, in a culture of exaggerated self-dramatization; or like Beau Brummel, mentioned in the previous section, I innovate the new persona of the "dandy". But something different from both of these happens in this middle possibility, opened by what I'm calling portrayal.

This is what we see exemplified in certain works of art. I will here look at this from the standpoint of the spectator/hearer/reader, rather than the creator. Thus I may get a sense of a certain kind of longing for the loved one through seeing *Swan Lake*; here through dance and music, both together. I might get an alternative such sense by hearing troubadours—who themselves, of course, straddled the boundary between enactment and portrayal, but what I get reading the poetry is a portrayal. One or other of these (to me) new possibilities allows me to begin to make sense of my confused feelings, thus shaping them in a certain way. I am offered a new way of articulating the meanings things have for me, analogous to what I might derive from some classification of the passions. But in this latter case, reading Epictetus, for example, what I have is a set of assertions: these are the types of emotions humans experience; whereas watching *Swan Lake,* I am given a portrayal without assertion.

Or again for me, Chopin's *Fantaisie-Impromptu* in C sharp minor articulates a certain as yet indefinable longing; it draws me into it, and makes it part of my world. I dare say I am not alone in seeing this in the music, and that this was not foreign to the inspiration Chopin had in composing it. A human possibility is articulated and disclosed here, but nothing at all is asserted.[50]

And then, I get a sense of a possible response to life and fate through Beethoven's String Quartet No. 15; in particular, the meaning of things which comes through the profound meditative stance in the slow move-

---

50. Roger Scruton speaks of "a peculiar 'reference without predication' that touches the heart, but numbs the tongue"; see his *The Aesthetics of Music* (Oxford: Clarendon Press, 1997), 132. This phrase is quoted by Alexander Bowie in his excellent and densely argued *Music, Philosophy, and Modernity* (Cambridge: Cambridge University Press, 2007), 70.

ment. Examples could be multiplied. Think of Rembrandt: the sense of life and the experience of life accumulated in the face of an older man.

But this can also be done through story, or a novel. For instance, we can come to sense a new spiritual stance in, for example, Fyodor Dostoevsky's, *The Devils*: Shatov comes to the insight that "we are all to blame"; this slogan directly echoes while opposing the objectified stance of scientistic liberals: that "no one is to blame"; but it also denies what these liberals share with the reactionaries, their sense of their own rightness, that all evil comes from their opponents.

There are assertions here. The (fictional) story consists of assertions. But the new spiritual stance comes partly/largely through portrayal. There is a kind of metaphysical-moral assertion here: "we are all to blame", but you don't get what all this is about unless you get inside the spiritual stance which is largely portrayed, not described.

Sometimes there are more robust attempts to give some description of the stance, or of the sense of the world it implies—as with Zossima's autobiographical sections in *The Brothers Karamazov*. But this never exhausts what the novel portrays. Generally criticism struggles to articulate the portrayed through description. And there is a fruitful dialectic between portrayal and description, carried through art and criticism.

Description and portrayal can therefore be interwoven, as in the novel; but also in troubadour song, as I mentioned above.

Then there are the new portrayals of inwardness in the twentieth century, which come across in the way the world shows up for the writer, and potentially for us all; these we see in Proust, Rilke, Beckett.

What I'm calling portrayal can be an alternative way of offering new models to understand human life, alternative, that is, to description, as I mentioned in Chapter 1, section 7. Portrayal can be another route to regestalting. So we can return to a binary picture of two tracks on which new human meanings can be defined: enactment and regestalting; only now we distinguish two modes of this latter: those involving description in the normal sense, and those which deploy portrayals.

Description, portrayal, enactment. These are three dimensions of constitutive expression. They are not necessarily clearly separated—as they are, for instance, in taking an inventory; miming an action; and the biker's swagger.

And some human institutions merge two or more. Thus ritual is a kind of enactive portrayal. The range of such portrayals in works of art is very varied. In some cases, for instance, representational painting, or the novel, the work consists of representations. In the latter case, it is full of assertions, about a fictional world. In many paintings, an assertion is clearly implied; in historical painting, for instance, or religious painting, or portraits. But there nevertheless can be a dimension of portrayal which goes beyond assertion. And this is often what we value.

I take an example from Roger Scruton's discussion in *The Aesthetics of Music*: he speaks of the dancers in Poussin's *Adoration of the Golden Calf.* The meaning of the painting lies not simply in what is represented. "I do not see only these dancing figures, and the scene in which they participate. I see their foolishness and frivolity: I sense the danger and attraction of idolatry, which invites me to cancel all responsibility for my life and soul, and join in the collective dance."[51] This commentary is implicit in the way these figures are portrayed, in their seeming tipsiness and foolish abandon. In a sense it too is represented, but only for those who can read it in their demeanor. Because of our capacity to read human expression, at least in this culture, we are capable of drawing out this moral lesson about our world, the ease with which we can be drawn to a fatal fascination with idols.

Now in a sense, one might say that this is what Poussin wants to assert. We are meant to read this as a truth about the human condition. But there is still a distance between this painting and an assertion in language. None of the attempts to formulate the moral here, neither Scruton's nor my gloss on his, nor anyone else's, are actually asserted by the work. Assertions by commentators, like Scruton's, have to be read in the painting. They are in this sense implicit. But it is not at all like what may be implicit in descriptions, that is, the assertions which can be drawn out as entailments from other assertions. Our reading is expressively rather than logically implicit.

That is why there will often be differences and uncertainties about what we read in a work of art. Take Bernini's famous statue of Saint Teresa, where her heart is pierced by a dart. Many have read in this a quasi-sexual ecstasy, which has scandalized some, while others have seen the profound insight, already implicit in the Song of Songs, that devotion

51. Scruton, *Aesthetics of Music*, 227.

to God has strong and deep affinities to sexual desire. How exactly to formulate what we see here will go on being debated. What exactly is being portrayed?

And indeed, even in the less controversial case of the Poussin painting, the translation into verbal assertions can never be either exact or exhaustive. There is always more in the work than we can say, as well as zones of uncertainty that we can't resolve. This is what underlies the thesis I mentioned in the previous section, recurrent since the Romantic period, of the untranslatability of the work of art. One point of origin of this lies in Kant's *Third Critique,* in the claim that aesthetic ideas can never be fully rendered by discursive concepts; from there it was taken up by the German Romantics, and repeated by Schopenhauer and others in the nineteenth century. It recurs in the aesthetics of Croce, which centers on a distinction between representation and expression. A work of art expresses an "intuition", an "immediate and preconceptual apprehension of the world", whose content can never be adequately rendered by assertions. And Croce's distinction in turn was taken up by Collingwood.[52]

Our ability to read painting and sculpture in this way obviously builds on our capacity to read human expression in life. But it also goes beyond this. Our feel for matter can also play a role. The sense of the massive and the solid in Rodin's sculptures imparts another dimension to the gestures they display. They incarnate their history and the drama they are enacting in a particularly powerful way.

But the relation to human expression allows us to see how a work of art can portray a new insight. It isn't confined to the illustration of already formulated notions about human life or the human condition, or the mimicking of already enacted expressions. This is analogous to the way in which a new gesture or way of holding myself can help inaugurate a new way of being in the world, as with the quasi-machismo of the biker, or the new stance of the "cool" and "laid-back". We can grasp what this is about, because we are not confined to a fixed vocabulary of gestures, as with the naval flag code, for instance; rather we read the human stance in the gesture and attitude, and thus can respond to novel forms.

In a similar way, novel insights occur in works of art. We might argue that the very particular take on idolatry in Poussin's painting, in all its nuance, finds expression here for the first time.

52. Ibid., 346.

So figurative painting contains both representations which can be considered as tantamount to assertions, but also something more; an insight about human life can be portrayed as well. And these are not separable elements. The insight is implicit in the representation.

Something similar is evident in the novel. This not only represents, but does so through descriptive assertions. But at the same time, what the novelist tells us about the demeanor of his characters, as well as (sometimes) of their thoughts, gives us an insight into their nature, and perhaps beyond this into the shape of the human condition. The case of Dostoevsky's *Devils,* cited above, as well as his *Brothers Karamazov,* illustrates this.

It is somewhat more mysterious how music as well can offer the kind of insight into human life and fate which we are able to find in painting and literature. Some people are even inclined to deny this of music altogether. What induces people to take this stance is the obvious fact that music can't represent the world the way that either figurative painting or prose description can. Once you eliminate the representation of people, or events, or landscape, where can the implicit insight lodge?

And yet others (including myself) go on experiencing music as a locus or source of this kind of insight. This was clear from my description of Chopin's *Fantaisie-Impromptu,* and of the slow movement of Beethoven's String Quartet No. 15. Is this just a matter of free association, where it all depends on the psyche of the listener?

This might appear to be the message of Anthony Burgess's *Clockwork Orange.* The young protagonist of this novel, when listening to the symphonies of Dvořak and Beethoven, finds his mind filled with fantasies of violence which immensely excite him, and even incite him to violent action. He is condemned to undergo behavioral conditioning in order to render him harmless to society, a change which also dumbs him down. Is the idea here that what music arouses in us is purely a matter of idiosyncratic association? Or is the author pointing to a disturbing fact about us humans, that our affinity for strength and order lies uncomfortably close to our excitement at inflicting pain and destruction? (Just as sexual desire lies close to devotion to God.)

The second reading is the only one which makes sense to me. We all are familiar with music that reminds us of something. "Ah yes, that tune. I can't help recalling the summer of 1935, which we spent at the seashore; it was all the rage then." But music can express something, and this is a quite different phenomenon. A sad tune can remind us of a happy time, and vice versa; or a trivial tune of a profound experience. But the issue is what we can feel *in* the music. And my sense is that there can be a nonarbitrary answer to this question, one that doesn't depend on purely contingent associations.

I want to borrow from the interesting discussion in Scruton's book.[53] I think it helps to understand how music can have meaning in this sense, even though quite devoid of representation, if we move through an intermediate case, lyric poetry. In this form, the representational element can shrink to the absolute minimum level; we hear a voice, as it were, beseeching his beloved, or expressing his sorrow at the loss of her love. The crux of the "representation" is the expression of feeling by the implied author, although there may also be some description of the beloved. And yet there may be a profound understanding of the nature of love, of loss, of transiency, implicitly portrayed not asserted, in the poem, as in a sonnet by Petrarch, or by Shakespeare.

Lyric poetry is often personal expression; indeed, some might see this as the paradigm of the lyric. And it is often expression of feeling. But my state of feeling is never simply a fact about me. My feelings: love, hate, fear, hope, have "intentional objects"; that is, things to which it is appropriate to react to with the feeling in question. For instance, hope relates to a happy but uncertain outcome; fear to an impending danger. (Of course, these objects may at times be merely imagined.) So to describe my feelings adequately must also be to describe how I see the world. That's why a love poem can implicitly convey my sense of the nature of love, and of transiency, and perhaps also of the relation of love to transiency. (This take on the world which I respond to with feeling is what Croce called an "intuition".[54])

Perhaps this is a good place to start to understand how music also can have meaning by expressing a subject's feeling and/or take on the world. As with the poetry, there is a gamut of possibilities here. One can dwell more on the feeling; or one can convey through one's response in feeling a sense, often deep and complex, of one's take on the world. What is excluded here is the kind of thing one can (in principle) do in descriptive prose; that is, set out one's take on the world quite dispassionately, hiding as much as possible the response the world so understood evokes in you. Neither lyric poetry nor music can be dispassionate or deadpan in this way.

53. Ibid.
54. See Benedetto Croce, *Aesthetic: As Science of Expression and General Linguistic,* trans. Douglas Ainslie (New York: Noonday, 1922), chapters 1 and 2.

But how much does this help? One can indeed understand how poetry, written in language, can express feelings, and a take-on-things through feeling. Words offer a fine and varied semantic palette. But can music? True, we have a sense that certain tunes are jolly, others are sad, others are solemn. Perhaps some of these judgments are relative to a musical tradition, but within this they seem quite solid and nonarbitrary. But even so, this offers only a rather crude and restricted semantic palette. How does music acquire a richer "semantics"?

One answer is to point to the close interweaving of poetry and music in our history. Indeed, in some cultures they are inseparable. Bards sang the great deeds of heroes. They were singing poets. Music accompanied by words can acquire a certain semantic direction. We understand it through the contextualization provided by the words. This is what we see in opera, in cantatas, in liturgical music.

Does that mean that certain melodies or musical forms acquire a finer semantic nuance through mere association? It can't be this simple, because there is always a question of finding fitting music for the words. Some music just is wrong for a given libretto. This doesn't mean that it always has to reinforce the words. In opera, the music can be making a commentary on the action, expressing something different, even taking an ironic stance to it. Thus in *The Marriage of Figaro,* Bartolo's opening aria, "La Vendetta," sings the joys of exacting revenge. The music expresses serene and forceful triumph. If you just listened to the music on the radio with no idea of the action, you might think that some high principles were being enunciated. The gap between the two constitutes an ironic commentary on the base and egoistic anticipations of Bartolo. At the same time, I sense a third level here: the music is also a promise that the hope for a nobler world is not obliterated by the machinations of these clownish and grasping figures; this promise will be vindicated with the Count's aria "Perdona" in the fourth act. So the relationship is very complex, but the music is right.

Nevertheless some "semanticization" of musical forms does take place through the operatic and liturgical traditions. That is, certain musical forms: melodies, harmonies, rhythms, become expressive of finely nuanced meanings. But something analogous occurs in any artistic tradition. In literature too, great works echo through the writings of later authors, who draw on the resonances which the writings of, say, Shakespeare and Milton, have already laid down. Any literary tradition has a dense intertextuality. And the same is true of music (and, of course, painting).

But this isn't the whole story in our culture, because music also breaks free from the contexts which helped "semanticize" it. In the era of Beethoven and after, there is a striving for "absolute" music, that is, one which doesn't rely on story, or program, or accompanying words, or social context (like liturgy, praise for kings, or whatever).[55] Arguably, this has allowed composers to say further and deeper things. But the puzzle might be: in breaking out of the existing "semanticization", why hasn't it undermined their ability to say anything at all?

One part of the answer which Scruton develops is to point to the inner force field of tonal music; where certain moves call for certain kinds of answer, say, a move away from the tonic requires a return to it; and certain dissonances call for resolution. In a symphonic piece, "we hear anticipation and closure, development and variation, tension and release, and a process which lasts through these things, guiding and guided by them. In great masterworks this process does not have the character of succession only; it is like an argument, an exploration, which concludes as a narrative concludes, at the point beyond which it cannot go without detracting from its meaning."[56] So the structural features of Western tonal music as it has developed give it an inner shape and structure, which demands that we experience it as a process which is not simply random, but goes somewhere; and like an argument or story, it stops when it gets there.

Now this constrains our possible understandings of meaning; but by itself it remains on a formal level. The hearer grasps movement, development, senses tension and resolution, feels the music building to a climax. But when more definite thoughts and feelings and intuitions are called up in us, some sense of what is building, what the struggle is about, what the resolution consists in, does this just depend on each one of us, on our own inclinations and questions and outlook? That seems to be what's happening with the young man in *A Clockwork Orange*; he senses the building and eruption of force in the climax, but what this evokes in him is a scene of violence. This is very different from mere association; that tune recalls for me the summer of 19–, because of the accident of contiguity; whereas what

55. Downing Thomas, in his *Music and the Origins of Language* (Cambridge: Cambridge University Press, 1995), 6–7, argues that this supposed birth of "absolute music" was much exaggerated. The notion of a "musical language" preceded the Romantic era. But one might nevertheless argue that music, outside the traditional settings (liturgy opera, etc.), opened the way to new expressive possibilities.

56. Scruton, *Aesthetics of Music*, 233.

Burgess's fictional listener is hearing *is,* that is, has the sense of, forceful climax; but he goes on to read into this schema the gruesome acts which fascinate him.

Music, even "absolute" music, *says* something; in the sense not of assertion but of portraying through expression. But if we stayed with the conclusion of the last paragraph, the saying would be very minimal. The listener would grasp the form of a story, or argument, or struggle and its resolution, but would herself fill in what tale was being told, or conclusion argued, or struggle resolved. This would leave us no idea of how, say, a symphony might present us with a profound and nuanced view of the human predicament, of the kind we find in Poussin's painting, or Dostoevsky's novels, or at the heights of lyric poetry.

Scruton argues for something more than this in the following passage:

Consider Beethoven's Ninth Symphony. The plain, awesome statement of those opening bars leads to an extraordinary musical argument, in which every kind of tragic, defiant, and titanic emotion is shown to have been lying dormant in the initial gesture. There follows a frenzied dance, full of wit and paradox, in which the music recklessly disregards what is has discovered; from thence we proceed to a sublime meditation, full of longing in double variation form. The three movements leave a memory of contrasted dances, in which the listener's sympathy is led through the possibilities of an heroic solitude. Suddenly we hear a musical negation: the chord of D minor with an added minor sixth and major seventh, commanding a full stop to the dream of isolation. The lines of a recitative then emerge: phrases which take their meaning from the accent of human speech, and which effortlessly lead to the melody of the "Ode to Joy". This triumphant affirmation of community is not the cheap trick that it might have been: for it has received the stamp of musical inevitability. We are made to rehearse, in our extended sympathies, a particular movement of the soul. We return from private struggle to public comfort, and we feel this return as natural, inevitable. We sense that it is possible, after all, to explore the depths of human isolation, and still re-emerge in communion with our fellow men.[57]

57. Ibid., 359.

We can see that Scruton has built on the transitions of the music, the sense that it contains of conflict and its resolution, the sense of the inevitability of the transitions, to find in this work a profound vision of human life. Can we dismiss this as something just arbitrarily read into the work, on a par with the young hero of *A Clockwork Orange* and his fantasies of violence? (Of course, even in this case we wouldn't have simple association; the dramatic structure of the music itself matches, even if it does not uniquely designate, his dreams of murder and mayhem.) But I don't think that the vision Scruton sees in the Ninth Symphony is in similar fashion just one among many possible readings of its dramatic form. Of course, his interpretation is partly anchored in the choral movement, where the words give us an unambiguous sense of what is being celebrated. But that the first movement is a site of titanic struggle, that the third is one of longing and purification, seems to me undeniable. It is not just that the music seems to be resolving a felt conflict, but that this conflict is one that can find resolution is the triumphant affirmation of brotherhood.

The very nature of this kind of vision couched in a personal expression forbids any exact and final resolution of detailed differences of interpretation, as we saw with the Bernini statue. One may want to formulate the insight somewhat differently, but it seems to me that Scruton's account is in its general thrust correct. That is, it is both the case that Beethoven in writing the Ninth was struggling with an insight somewhat of this order; and that a hearing informed by other Beethoven works and works of the time will find this insight in the work.

But this work is perhaps exceptional. There are many works that fall between the two extremes: a merely formal structure, where we have to supply the content, on one hand, and a definite vision of the human predicament on the other. The powerful sense of order building itself as it drives forward, which we sense in some of Bach's orchestral music, exhilarates because it shows such an order underlying our messy and approximate reality, something that we might eventually come to full contact with. There is a promise here, but of a very indefinite kind. The promise lies in the fact that here, it would appear, someone has been able to descry and render this order.

In other cases, music can delight because it takes us into a region of human experience which we never suspected, but which is deeply moving. I mentioned the *Fantaisie-Impromptu* of Chopin earlier. I spoke of a sense of longing I feel in this piece. More precisely, it is like nostalgia for a lost paradise, but one I never knew existed before hearing this music. Certain passages of Brahms point to forms of beauty in the world that I would never have expected. I and any one could go on adding examples. Perhaps these are just proving to the reader that I have a penchant for reading my own preoccupations and fantasies into what I hear. But even if this were the case, it remains true that the kind of experience involved is of hearing something *expressed*. And the delight is inseparable from the accompanying thought that these hitherto unsuspected regions of experience are there, accessible; the magic casements open onto *something*. Some vision is imparted.

In other words, the experience here is clearly distinct from mere association, on one side (this reminds me of the summer of 19–), and from a simple infusion of energy and optimism on the other. Music can also affect us in the latter way, as when a lively tune distracts us from depressing thoughts and sets us dancing. But when music changes your mood (and of course when drugs do this for you), you move from anxious rehearsing of the dangers threatening you to a buoyant sense of optimism about the course of things. But in either case, what the optimism fixes on, its intentional object, as it were (which can be very indefinite: "I just *know* that things will turn out OK"), is not expressed in the music (or the drugs, of course). The experience is quite different from being delighted, even exhilarated, by what the music *says*. This can surprise us, even change us— even though it may be very hard to say how and why.[58]

I have been talking about music, but this phenomenon: being exhilarated by a new dimension of experience, even where you have trouble saying what and why, is also encountered in poetry and painting. I am very drawn by Gérard de Nerval's "El Desdichado," even though I don't really understand it, and regularly forget all the classical allusions, even after I have looked them up many times. It works on me in a way which is very analogous to music. But undoubtedly the magic works only because (in some simple, straightforward sense) I understand the words.

58. Bowie, *Music, Philosophy, and Modernity,* argues for a position rather similar to mine, that philosophy has something to learn from music, and that there is such a thing as "getting it right" in music, as there is in language. But the case is argued with a wealth of detail, and with a fine sense of how our understanding of what music can "say" has evolved in the last centuries along with the rise of Western modernity, and Romantic responses to it.

The fact remains that music, once taken on its own, seems to break away from all representation, but it nevertheless can portray meaning, can give us a sense of life which we would not have had otherwise. This is what has made it special among the arts. This is why Schopenhauer singled it out as a direct "reflection" [*Abbild*] of the Will, because it doesn't rely, as do literature and painting, on assertions or assertion-type representations as the basis for its implicit vision. The "untranslatability" (into assertions) of art, which can already be claimed for painting and literature, as we saw above, is thus true in a more radical sense for music.

The fact is that music, in ways we find hard to understand and going farther than lyric poetry, communicates its vision through a response at once expressive of subjective feeling, and also through this expression, revelatory of the state of things. "The great triumphs of music, it seems to me, involve this synthesis, whereby a musical structure, moving according to its own logic, compels our feelings to move along with it, and so leads us to rehearse a feeling at which we would not otherwise arrive."[59]

An important fact about the "symbol" or work of art in its own domain, that of "portrayal", is that, like enactive expression and descriptive neologism in their respective domains, it can introduce us to new thoughts and meanings that we might never have encountered otherwise. It represents its own kind of constitutive "right expression". As Scruton puts it, "We encounter works of art as perfected icons of our felt potential, and appropriate them in order to bring form, lucidity, and self-knowledge to our inner life. The human psyche is transformed by art, but only because art provides us with expressive gestures towards which our emotions lean in their search for sympathy—gestures which we seize, when we encounter them, with a sense of being carried at last to a destination that we could not reach alone, as when a poem offers us the words of love or grief which we cannot find in ourselves. Art realizes what is otherwise inchoate, unformed and incommunicable."[60] Art in all its forms has this extraordinary capacity, by giving expression to a feeling/vision which we have never (consciously and explicitly) had, to carry us to a new and unsuspected realm. But music, just because it has moved free from representation, and has put the greatest distance between itself and the prose assertion, possesses this capacity to a striking degree.

59. Scruton, *Aesthetics of Music*, 359.
60. Ibid., 352.

But the flip side of this is a certain ontic indefiniteness. So it is with music which captures something which is off the normal charts of standard emotions and their objects. So to recur to examples above, Bach, or Handel give us a wonderful sense of an order in things; one which exalts us and rejoices us. But it is less than totally clear what exactly this order consists in. Chopin's *Fantaisie-Impromptu* captures a deep and overwhelming longing; but for what? Perhaps we have not yet conceived of this object before hearing this expression of longing, and even now, cannot find the words for it.

The potential ontic indefiniteness may remain unrealized, or at least unnoticed. It can be that the whole context yields a definite interpretation: for instance, this music occurs in an opera, and there is a plot which tells you what is happening; or it is part of a liturgy, and we know that this is addressed to God, and to his Providence. But music can cut free from this: it can be "absolute" music.

There are no assertions, and yet part of the joy in music comes from the implicit affirmation. That order which Bach and Handel reveal we sense as really being there, and this is the reason for joy. The object of longing is real, and hence the joy in the sadness. Things have meanings we didn't suspect before. Dostoevsky's vision of the roots of violence and rebellion may also surprise us with a new and exhilarating vision, but we aren't tempted to speak here of ontic indefiniteness.

How can we understand the implicit affirmation in works of art, and our response to it? It's analogous to what happens when we see someone react to certain important events: they are perhaps overjoyed, or saddened. The nature of this person and his/her expression is such that it can carry deep conviction: not only of sincerity, that this is really how they feel, but also of their having insight. We believe the wise starets, because he formulates the insight in such a convincing manner. This is ideally distinguishable from the content of the assertions he formulates. But this same force of the manner can attach to responses on his/her part which are not assertions: the way he stands back and reacts with joy or sorrow. Our conviction is that he has grasped the meaning of this object, whatever it be. This same force of conviction can attach to music; even as it can attach to the meaning of things which is expressed in a novel, through but perhaps not in the assertions the novel contains. Hence our response of joy to the portrayals of order in Bach. The joy comes from the conviction that this vision has touched something real.

But the implicit portrayals of literature and painting, while they lie beyond assertions, nevertheless take off from them. Only music of the traditional arts seems to have cut loose from them altogether. And this radicality has been given a new value in the post-Romantic age. So that Pater could assert that "all art aspires to the condition of music."[61] With the development of nonfigurative painting, one of the traditional arts seemed to be responding to his call. And some modernist poetry can be understood in the same way.

Thus, in one dimension of their being, portrayals offer another example, along with enactment, of meaning creation which can't be understood simply on the model of sign and signified. A novel, a traditional painting, does represent something, but the full meaning of the work can't be accounted for in this way. Of course, this nonrepresentational "excess" is often most obvious in music. For me, the longing that Chopin's *Fantaisie-Impromptu* opens for me inhabits the music, is consubstantial with it. And much nonrepresentational painting prompts a similar response in the viewer.

I open a short coda to this section in order to introduce another issue. Earlier, in section 3, I discussed the issue of moral sources: the realities contemplation of which, or contact with which, strengthens our commitment to or élan toward the good. And the question inevitably arose: do they, for instance, contemplating God, or Nature, strengthen us because of some reaction these thoughts provoke in us? Or are we receiving a force which comes from beyond us? Which reading, the subjective or the objective, is the right one? We often have a strong sense of which it is, even though the skeptic may recognize that this doesn't constitute a final proof.

Now we frequently find in powerful works of art what we might call epiphanies of sources. The epiphanies of art increase/intensify our attraction to, commitment to, admiration of, longing for, the realities they disclose. The current runs in both directions: the artist constructs the symbol which allows disclosure, but the reality also changes us, revivifies something is us, just as contact with nature revitalizes us. Such epiphanies

---

61. Walter Pater, "The School of Giorgione," in *The Renaissance: Studies in Art and Poetry,* ed. A Philips (Oxford: Oxford University Press, 1986), 86. For an account of this special position that music has attained since the Romantic period, reflected in Pater's famous phrase, see the insightful discussion in Lydia Goehr, *The Imaginary Museum of Musical Works* (Oxford: Oxford University Press, 1992). I will also try to cast light on this in the proposed companion study.

frequently strengthen our sense that the objective reading is the right one, that the force comes to us from "outside", in the sense that it is beyond our powers to produce it.

I shall return to discuss this further in the proposed companion study to this work.

7

With this last discussion, we can see how the issue of the scope of language, of the forms which we have to explain in order to understand human language, has been once more extended and radicalized.

In Chapter 1 I mentioned, outside of the attribution of properties, three other ranges of meanings which are opened to us by language: the properly human emotions (or metabiological meanings), certain relations, and strong value. But each of these is carried on the three levels of expressive form that have crystallized out of the discussion in the book so far: the projective or enactive, the symbolic (in works of art), and the descriptive. We express our emotions, and establish our relations, and body forth our values, in our body language, style, and rhetoric; but we can also articulate all of these in poetry, novels, dance, music; and we can also bring all of them to descriptive articulation, where we not only name the feelings, relations, values, but also describe and argue about them. These line up in close parallel with the three rungs in the ladder of articulacy, which I introduced in section 4 above. The difference is that the giving of names and criterial properties to these meanings is included in the second rung in this chapter, as well as the artistic and "symbolic" rendering of their nature. But there are no hard and fast boundaries here. The names of meanings often have a quasi-metaphorical, or "symbolic" element in Schlegel's sense (sin as staining, integrity, inner harmony, remorse, etc.) The crucial difference between rungs 2 and 3 is that in the latter we attempt to give a reasoned, more or less systematic, "philosophical" account of the place of these meanings in our lives, as also of their validity or invalidity. We elaborate what I called above an "etiological story" of how these meanings come to be for us, and we may also argue that the version we accept is correct.

We could think of these three levels, or "rungs" as we described them earlier, as ranked in this way: each successive articulation allows us to take a freer stance to, and hence get a clearer articulation of, the meanings involved. What we live unreflectingly on the level of enactment, can be set out before us as something we can enjoy and contemplate in a work of art, and then made an object of description and possible analysis in prose. The superiority of the descriptive lies in its enabling clearly defined assertions; and along with this, and not possible without it, is the ability to operate on the metalevel, to make assertions about our first-order claims, and the language in which they are couched. Of course, sonatas, poems, or novels can refer to other works, and part of their effect often comes from these quotations, but this is not the same thing as making assertions about these other works. (Naturally, some character in a novel can make such an assertion, and it can even be that we take this rightly to reflect the author's view; but qua portrayal, the work makes no defined assertion.)

Of course, this ranking can also be reversed. It is possible to hold that certain meanings cannot be adequately captured at a freer, more analytical level. This has certainly been claimed against prose analysis on behalf of articulation in "symbol", as the above discussion intimated. And following my earlier discussion about political equality and that to be presented in Chapter 7, I will claim that certain key terms of political and moral theory cannot be fully specified without reference to the bodily-enactive level of their meaning. But whatever our views of their potential scope, these three levels offer different kinds of articulation, progressively favoring a free stance to and clarity about the meanings concerned.

This multilayered picture of the semantic dimension underlines afresh how our descriptions stand in a field of other articulations. Our macho biker above doesn't have a word for what he values. He lives it in projecting it, and he relates to a certain kind of hard rock that presents it in "symbol"; but he hasn't yet tried to describe it, say what's good about it, and he is no position to argue for it against critics. We think of him as maximally unreflecting, and yet he lives in a world of articulated meaning. Provided we take the word 'language' in a broad sense, englobing all expressive forms, his world is as linguistically constituted as that of the philosopher. That is just to say that he lives in a human world. In its most unreflecting, just-lived-in, underdescribed, *zuhanden*[62] form, this world is full of linguistic mediation, even taking 'language' in a narrow sense. Descriptive language doesn't erupt in a world of pure animal purposes. This is important to bear

---

62. "ready-to-hand".

in mind, both to understand the preobjective world, and to grasp the conditions in which descriptive language operates.

The relation between the three rungs of the ladder is quasi-hermeneutical. Indeed rung 3 offers a hermeneutic of our expressions at the symbolic level (2); and these frequently are attempts to explicate enacted meanings; which in turn act out what may originally have been an obscure sense of a higher or more satisfying way of being. For Socrates, the Buddha, as also Beau Brummel, and the prophets of cool, there is a first stage in which they find a way of giving expression in their lives of something they at first dimly sense as a better way of living (which constitutes, as it were, rung 0). This enactment (rung 1) is then given verbal or symbolic expression (rung 2); which at the final stage is the basis of a fuller account of the nature, origins, advantages of this way of life (rung 3).

The relation of the higher level to the lower is one of expression, trying to render something in a clearer medium. But it can also be seen as of the nature of an interpretation. Hence the term 'quasi-hermeneutic'.

Now unless the hermeneutic at rung 3 is totally transparent; or unless it is a hermeneutic of suspicion that succeeds in showing there is nothing there to be understood, there will have to be further recourse to the lower rungs. The accounts at rung 3 will never be self-sufficient; one will always need to refer back to the second rung, and often to the original exemplary enactments at rung 1. In the field of Ethics, exemplars are frequently ineliminable.

We can now see more clearly the difference between the two semantic logics identified above, the "designative" and the "constitutive". The first aims to find the terms to characterize a self-standing, independent reality: "in itself" as it were, that is, in abstraction from how it figures in the field of human meanings. We explore the external world by generating descriptions which can be clearly verified by checking them against independent, self-standing realities. Sometimes the description of everyday objects is generated by observing them; sometimes it is generated by sophisticated and complex theories about underlying mechanisms, which precipitate out verifiable descriptions, like "the meter reads 5".

With the second, we explore the world of meanings (which is not simply an "inner" world) by probing it through constitutive enactments and expressions-articulations, which then pan out or fail to convince, and are then sometimes replaced by other probes, which seem better, but remain perpetually vulnerable to such supersession. This second zone is the site of attempts to define the shape of significance. Its expressions, be they enactments or verbal articulations, in symbol or in philosophical prose, all aim to sketch some contour or facet of this overall shape of meaning, in the hope, never integrally fulfilled, of an ultimate ratification in felt intuition. This involves making sense of our struggle to realize these meanings, and/ or hermeneutical reasoning about human life more generally.

The struggle to realize our ethical outlook can lead to the kind of growth in ethical-moral insight which I described at the end of section 3, where the attempt to apply a code can lead to its modification, and then the perception of new issues and dilemmas, which prompts projects to resolve these.

This struggle is potentially endless; it cannot reach a firm and assured closure. This is because of a feature which is implicit in the above description, which we might call the duality of points of reference. (Sometimes this can grow to a plurality—in any case, a non-unicity). For instance, we need periodically to look again at our paradigm enactors of our ethical ideals (our exemplars) in order to redefine them more perspicuously; or else our expressed ideal (say, universal humanitarianism, following the example at the end of section 3) may turn out to require forms of enactment (in this case, generous openness to difference) we didn't originally anticipate.

Or our intuitions about the good, or about the right terms for self-description, may arise out of new, strong experiences. These new insights will in turn alter the shape of our future experiences, as we saw in section 2. But it may also be that future-marking experiences may cast a new light on our earlier formulations, requiring changes.

And so we are sent back and forth, between different points of reference, and this potentially without end. Closure here would require that the possibility of new unsettling experiences, or of newly discovered implications of our existing accepted terms, could be ruled out—not to mention the possibility that we might discover or devise a new and better interpretive schema. Because the impossibility of closure is closely tied to the hermeneutical nature of thinking in this area.

And so the aim of the exercise, and the nature of validation—characterizing the universe as it really is, and defining adequately the shape of significance—remain distinct in the zones defined by these two semantic logics, even if there is some overlap on rung 3 where we try to get clear on the place of our human meanings in the universe, in evolution, and in history.

An attachment to the HLC, and its assumption that the designative semantic logic applies everywhere, can easily lead us to misread the relation
between the first two rungs. Our propensity to enact meanings can be seen
as brute facts about us, on all fours with our tendency to react to certain
life meanings or instrumental meanings, as when we shy away from danger,
or are attracted to food when hungry, and the like. We would thus ignore
completely what I have called the "metabiological" meanings, as we do
when we study animals. This would mean that we pay no heed to what I
have called the "hermeneutical" dimension of enactment, the underlying
attempt to articulate, and be true to a certain sense of rightness.

It would follow that we could place the second rung, the naming and
description of enactment, on all fours with the naming of any other natural
phenomenon, and hence as partaking of the designative logic: first a phenomenon appears, then we give it a name. We saw above (end of section
2) that we can be tempted to understand our words for our basic reactions—
pride, anger, desire, aversion, and the like—on this model.

But this move ignores altogether the development of the interconnected
skein of meanings with its nuanced distinctions and its identification of
the occasions and reasons underlying our basic reactions. This domain
is the site of a quite different logic, where the attempt to articulate meaning
through enactment and/or description seeks ratification through felt intuition and the sense it makes of our lives. It has the structure of call-response,
followed by a counterresponse that ratifies or undermines our take, which
we identified at the end of section 3 in the particular case of our Ethical
commitments.

The developing skein of meanings in any culture proceeds through the
play of definition and ratification. And the ratification occurs on more than
one level. At our origin we are all inducted into preexisting skeins of
meaning. These shift through the change which inevitably occurs when
any generation takes up the culture of its forbearers—even when the new
cohort sees itself as faithfully reproducing what has been handed down to
it. They change again when the attempt to realize our moral code triggers
further ethical insight. And they also change because new articulations are
made by ethical reformers, or protagonists of a new style. These can be ratified or rejected on two levels. On the individual level, which we have
mainly been dealing with in the above discussion, agents may ultimately
be convinced or not to adopt the new outlook or style. But there is also
the question of cultural ratification, whether the new proposed Ethic or

manner of being becomes part of the established culture into which future cohorts will be inducted.

This whole play in point-counterpoint, the emitting of words and enactments and the deciding of their ultimate fate, can't be seen as just brute, factual reactions. Issues of rightness, appropriateness, and/or correct self- and other-ascription are at stake.

This is why our attempts to give an account of our enacted and named meanings on rung 3 takes the form of what Ricoeur calls a "*discours mixte*", where both semantic logics are in play. (In fact, all three logics enumerated above in section 1 come together here.) If a hermeneutic of suspicion could succeed in discrediting all metabiological meanings, or at least show them to be irrelevant to explain our social and political action; or if our basic reactions alone sufficed for this purpose, then this mixed discourse would be unnecessary. But as things stand, in our historical or sociological study of a given population we aren't just trying to see whether our descriptions match a free-standing external reality, following a designative semantic logic; we also need to grasp the meanings this population lives (or lived) by, meanings which they defined according to a constitutive semantic logic. We have to be able to grasp something of the way they operated within this logic, or we will fail in our descriptive/explanatory purpose. A fresh reading of these meanings may easily generate another historical or sociological account, which needs to be tested for the sense it makes of the target population's behavior. This requirement essentially defines the hermeneutical approach to human science.

Perhaps it might help to recap here the intrinsic connections between human meanings and hermeneutical thinking, in contrast to life meanings and instrumental ones. We could sum this up in four points:

First, (A) these meanings, for instance Ethical stances, start off in human culture as inarticulate intimations; and these have to be given some shape, some interpretation. They receive this sometimes first in modes of enactment, sometimes first in some sort of verbal definition, and sometimes also in portrayals, rituals, works of art; but eventually all three are involved in defining and clarifying them.

The second basic feature (B) these meanings share is that they are interpreted and articulated differently by different people, and eventually also cultures. This gives rise to questioning, sometimes disputes; and often mutual incomprehension and sometimes distrust between people, and even more between cultures.

Third, (C) these meanings are defined not singly and separately, but in skeins or constellations, where the meanings of individual terms are defined in terms of each other (see section 1). They are analogous to visual or aural gestalts, where a change in one part of the picture, or one note, alters the whole visual effect, or the melody.

This is what gives rise to the various forms of holism: like the hermeneutical circle, which we saw above at the end of section 3. In the original case of biblical interpretation, the meaning of some puzzling sentence is internally related to the meaning of the whole chapter, and cannot be fixed independently. Applied to our attempts to understand our lives, or some slice of history, this means that we can only make sense of various incidents, or episodes, in their relation to the whole life, or period.

But we encounter other holisms as well. In our ethical outlook, the good life is defined in contrast to other less valuable, or even bad or contemptible, ways of living. And the ethical ideal is bound up with some notion of the motives which favor it and those which impede it; while the description of a virtue is meant to make sense of the virtue as we enact it, and reciprocally, the currently accepted enactment is supposed to realize the excellence the virtue describes.

We have to move back and forth, between part and whole, between the meaning we give to one incident and that we attribute to a whole life, or a larger slice of history; between our ethical commitments and the motivations we praise or condemn, encourage or frown on; between the virtues we subscribe to and the practices that are meant to realize them; in each case, trying to realize or restore coherence. Issues of this kind are at stake, for instance, in many reform movements, which strive to return to basics, or to restore an original purity of ethical or religious commitment.

This necessary holism of interpretation helps to bring about change in our understandings, the more so in that these constellations of interdefined parts are always being expanded with the addition of new elements: new events in our lives, new experiences, new insights, fresh challenges from others. And in some cases these changes can pull us even farther apart from other people, parties, and cultures.

Progress in definition can indeed be made by moving back and forth within these constellations: from part to whole and back in the hermeneutical circle; or between the registers, that of enactment on one side, and that of verbal articulation of principles, on the other, within our ethical outlooks, and so on. All this in an attempt to bring these different phases into alignment with each other. But we never manage to release individual meanings from these constellations, so as to give one of them a definitive interpretation, which needs no further correction.

Now fourth, (D) we can see what distinguishes human meanings from what I called above life meanings (or biological meanings). These too are related to wholes; what will preserve my life, what will bring me health, nourish me sufficiently, all these define the needs of a single organism. But in the case of these life meanings, natural science can in principle break any single one out of the whole, and determine objectively and for everyone what it involves. They, unlike human meanings, can be identified with objectively describable states, which can be grasped from outside without reference to the agent's self-understanding.[63]

Take, for instance, the case of a "life-threatening disease". There may be disagreement about this, but the scientific criteria are quite determinate. Doctors may argue about whether any given illness deserves this name, but the factors which will decide the matter are not in dispute. Or let's take another case, where merely instrumental meanings are at stake. We are military commanders, at loggerheads about the strategy which will bring victory; here too the criteria are fixed and recognized by both of us.

But in the case of human meanings, differences of interpretation, along with the holism of understanding, make this agreement on criteria impossible. To take an example from earlier in the discussion: Nietzscheans oppose their aspiration toward a "superhuman" form of life to Christian charity. But there is no way to commensurate these as means to a common goal. There is not even agreement on what these alternatives mean: a Christian will not accept the notion that charity is an alternative expression of the will to power, largely fueled by resentment; and nor will she share the uniquely positive view of the goal of rising above the human, all-too-human. Here a gulf opens between the two kinds of meaning.

All this is involved in the claim I've been making about the essentially hermeneutical understanding of human meanings. These meanings cannot escape the circles which help determine their significance; and these circles are always changing. Hence they defy final and decisive definition.

We can thus understand why "scientific" attempts to avoid the hermeneutical involve simple and reductive theories of human motivation, like

---

63. See also Chapter 3, section 1.

"materialist" theories which stress economic motivations, meeting life needs; or those which posit power as a basic goal; or else prestige or pride (starting with Hobbes). In the last case, seeking prestige is understood as a simple "natural" reaction, which doesn't need to be understood in terms of the skein of meanings that define its occasions and reasons. These approaches stand or fall with their basic reductive assumptions.[64]

We can also see how the difference in domains of meaning relates to the differences in semantic logic. So "naming" plays a different role in the two domains, and hence in the logics appropriate to them. Take 'cool'. We could think that this "names" a certain way of being/acting, the way that 'dog' names certain canines. But in fact what is "named" here is a (supposedly) valuable or admirable way of being. And this doesn't preexist in nature, like canines do. It has to be invented, explored through being acted out, whether this process precedes or goes along with the coinage of the word. But just being invented doesn't confer validity on it as a valuable or admirable way of being. We might say, it's a reading of the valuable which can pan out or not.

This counterpoint of proposal and ratification has its analogue in the designative logic, as we see in the way in which the structure: puzzling phenomenon, theoretical explanation, then either support or refutation, is played out in natural science; but the way this works out is very different in the two cases.

Throughout the discussion in this chapter, in contrasting semantic logics, I have been trying to distinguish different ways in which we generate and validate new terms; in other words different ways in which the Humboldtian drive to bring new thoughts and experiences to expression can operate. I mean these to be taken as ideal types; there is no claim that the three enumerated above (section 1) exhaust the possibilities. Moreover, they can operate together. I mentioned above that the first (1), the "designative" logic, often functions in tandem with the third (3), where we postulate underlying mechanisms to account for the phenomena that we pick out in terms generated by (1). In our attempts at scientific explanation, terms generated by (1) and (3) figure together in the attempt to devise true and valid explanations of empirical phenomena.

By contrast, the second "constitutive" logic functions throughout in a quasi-hermeneutical way. Even the first attempts to act out some new

64. See also Chapter 4, section 2.

meaning follow an inarticulate sense of what is fitting or right, or good. Then the meanings thus enacted call for verbal articulation, and we mount the rungs of the ladder. Validation of these interpretations comes from a sense of a clarification of felt intuition on one hand, and from our greater ability to make sense of our lives in terms of the gamut of motivations they deploy on the other. But then this constitutive logic (2) operates in tandem with the other two in the "*discours mixte*" of rung 3.

In both large composite domains, that of (1) and (3) on one hand, in which we seek explanation of independent reality; and that of (2) involving enactment and verbal articulation up to the "*discours mixte*" on the other, we have a similar cycle of invention followed by (in)validation. But the two cycles operate very differently, and aim for distinct results.

But we are not dealing here with human constants throughout history. First, we have to see that this distinction of semantic logics has become much more recognizable owing to developments which have occurred in the last few centuries. On one hand, it certainly builds on and reflects post-Galilean science, which aims to describe and explain an independent reality in terms purged of human meanings. If we return to earlier periods in which the things which surrounded us humans—animals and landscapes—were totems, or sites of spirits and forces, the two logics were hard to distinguish, and remained unnoticed.

In fact, the distinction has become evident through the tighter definition of the "designative" logic by the HLC. This theory has a strong normative thrust, as we have seen: one should operate with clear and unvarying definitions of one's elementary terms, avoid tropes, and so on. The underlying normativity here is that of the modern epistemology of clear and distinct ideas and their combination, which in turn was deeply influenced by the paradigms of post-Galilean natural science. This theory was then refined by the reflections on language and logic of the last two centuries. Once this model has been tightened up, it becomes clear that there are contrast cases (e.g., human meanings) which it doesn't fit, phenomena which are not simply given as are the states of affairs through which we validate our scientific theories. In Chapter 7 we will see other ranges of such phenomena (e.g., footings), where the terms we use follow a constitutive semantic logic.

At the same time, a certain trend to anthropocentrism has also helped to make this distinction more visible. I referred a few paragraphs ago to the discussion in section 3 of the experience of struggle to realize our Ethical aspirations. We found a common structure in all such attempts:

we experience a call, to which we respond, and which brings about a counterresponse. In earlier periods the call was generally understood as emanating from outside or beyond us humans, or even beyond the cosmos (to use a common terminology, it was seen as "transcendent"). But now there are variants in which this call is "immanentized"; for instance, the call of conscience is seen as coming from ourselves. The more "transcendent" forms focus us on some reality outside ourselves, so that in both our knowledge of the cosmos and our grasp of the Highest, we are trying to conform to something exterior, and this masks the difference in semantic logic. The subtle distinctions between different kinds of independence, which we discussed in section 2, are not visible. Nowadays, immanentized versions of Ethical aspiration have certainly not replaced the more transcendental forms, far from it; but their presence in our contemporary world presents these aspirations in a new light.

Secondly, and of more lasting importance, the fact that the shape of meaning is first sketched through our enactments and interpretation, and then ratified or not in felt intuition, has opened the way for significant cultural difference. The development of the skein has taken place in each culture on the basis of endogenous initiatives. People in different cultures have explored the human potential for meaning definition in distinct directions that cannot be simply synthesized and may never wholly converge.

Now once we understand the constitutive semantic logic, we can see that verbal language cannot be understood if we try to grasp it in isolation of the whole range of symbolic forms. We could imagine a pure language modeled on that of post-Galilean science, which some philosophers have been dreaming of since the days of the Vienna circle; language purged of human meanings. But this could never be the whole of any human language. We could never get to the point of devising it and speaking it, if we weren't capable of developing the common meanings and goals which underlie it, as well as everything else we live by. But the languages which articulate human meaning (including enactment) constitute a series of attempts to express and make sense of the meanings which animate our lives, which attempts can never come to final closure in a totally adequate form, needing no further articulation. They will always draw on enactment and symbols. Without these, even the meanings of science—its point, its struggles, its glories—would remain beyond our ken.

8

The basic thesis of this book is that language can only be understood if we understand its constitutive role in human life. And in pursuance of this goal, I have tried to explain this constitutive force of language in terms of the "linguistic dimension", where the uses of either words or symbols, or expressive actions, is guided by a sense of rightness, which cannot be made simply a function of success in some (nonlinguistic) task. Language is the domain of right and wrong moves, but there is an ineliminable circularity here, in that the rightness or wrongness in question demands to be itself defined in terms of language. We are in the domain of intrinsic rightness.

Or otherwise put, we are in the domain of linguistic awareness, the "reflective" [*besonnen*] awareness that Herder rightly saw as inseparable from language. But we have to emphasize again that linguistic awareness is not limited to that facet of the semantic dimension, where the designative logic prevails; in other words, to that set of language games where we are concerned with accurate description of independent objects. This is a facet of language that has all too often crowded the stage and monopolized the attention of theorists of language.

Language is also used to create, alter, and break connections between people. This is indeed, ontogenetically its "primordial" use, as we shall see in Chapter 7.

And language can also open new spaces of human meanings: through introducing new terms, and/or through expression-enactment. This chapter, starting out from the Humboldtian concern with how we open new fields of articulacy, and focusing particularly on how we come to recognize and bring to expression new domains of human meaning, has shown how rich and varied the means are by which we accomplish this: not just acting them out, but also metaphor, the quasi-metaphor of the symbol, works of art in their ever-renewed forms.

But language so understood, and engaged in all these tasks, very rapidly leads us to take it in a broad sense, that of the whole range of "symbolic forms". And in this broader context—where we are no longer dealing just with words, but also with gestures, symbols, and works of art—it becomes even clearer that there is more than one form of intrinsic rightness. We have identified three, or four. There are (1) two kinds of descriptive rightness, (a) the standard kind of attributing properties, and (b) the self-articulative kind, which clarifies and transforms the space of human meanings; there is (2) enacted rightness; and there is (3) the rightness, the greater or lesser power and depth, of portrayals.

But we can also classify these powers differently, in terms of the kinds or fields of reality they open us to. This chapter has been dealing with the domain of human metabiological meanings, and it turns out that opening this domain involves enaction and self-articulative description as well as portrayals. Working in tandem, these three powers allow this field to exist for us, a field which has its own kind of independent reality, not that of self-standing objects, but that of strong value. This field can then be explored through innovations in these three forms of constitutive expression.

Looked at more closely, we can note the close relation between portrayals and enactment. Portrayals are often of enactments (e.g., novels). Or else they express what it is to live certain meanings. The productive back-and-forth between enactment and articulation mirrors the productive exchange between artworks and critical commentary on them.

Looking back to Chapter 4: at the end of HLC, we were describing the attempts in post-Fregean philosophy to validate a "modest", mystery-free understanding of language, one in which learning a language would be equivalent to learning to generate extensional truth conditions for its various depictive combinations. I remarked there that such a language would have to exclude (A) the Cratylist dimension, if any, of its expressions, and (B) whatever thick cultural meanings you'd need to grasp in order to understand terms designating social relations, hierarchies, modes of purity and impurity, and so on. The next chapter, Chapter 5, on "Figuring", showed that (A) cannot be ignored; and the present chapter has shown the same for (B). Moreover, we have seen that these dimensions of language are not only outside the remit of the "modest", mystery-free form, but that this latter (which I recognize as a valid and useful specialized language, indispensable for modern science) could never be set up and running without the background activity of the creation and definition of meanings, which this chapter has been describing. A child can't be inducted into language without also being inducted into (some) human meanings, enacted and named, in relations of intense communion (Chapter 2). By contrast, the disciplined languages of objective description suitable for science are comparatively late achievements of human culture, acquired in maturation, and never mastered by everyone. How this acquisition comes about, the teacher-student interactions in which it is inculcated, along with the underlying ethic of responsible thinking, these are questions which the "modest" theory essentially shuns (and must shun, because it lacks the terms). In the light of all this, it is clear that the "regimented", scientific zone can only be a suburb of the vast, sprawling city of language, and could never be the metropolis itself. This essentially validates the second basic contention laid out in Chapter 3.[65]

What this whole discussion suggests is that the phenomenon which needs to be carved out for explanation is the whole range of expressive-constitutive forms and that we are unlikely to understand descriptive language unless we can place it in a broader theory of such forms, which must hence be our prior target.

So constitutive theories must go for the full range of expressive modes (what Cassirer called the "symbolic forms"[66]). We will return to this question later. But first we need to explore another facet of the constitutive power of language.

65. I have tried to establish this point, taking a somewhat different route, in my "Language Not Mysterious?" in *Dilemmas and Connections,* chapter 3.

66. Ernst Cassirer, *The Philosophy of Symbolic Forms* (New Haven, CT: Yale University Press, 1953).

7

Constitution 2

The Creative Force of Discourse

1

In Chapter 6 we dealt with the constitutive force of certain descriptions. In this chapter I want to treat the constitutive, indeed, the "creative" power of discourse.[1] And this reminds us of how we can "do things with words", and the work on performativity of Austin and Searle.[2] But explicit performatives of the kind that this work focuses on, with examples like "I pronounce you man and wife" (said by the priest/mayor/registrar), and "I christen this ship the *Queen Mary*", make up only one manifestation of a broader field of the creativity of discourse. I prefer to start with the distinction Émile Benveniste makes between "*langue*" and "*discours*".[3] This sounds like Saussure's distinction between "*langue*" and "*parole*", but is in fact rather different. Saussure is distinguishing the (more or less) stable code [*langue*], with the use made of it on a particular occasion of utterance. It is closely related to the competence/performance distinction of much recent linguistics.[4] Benveniste in speaking of "*discours*" is interested in what we set up, bring about, or "create" when we speak.

1. I have greatly benefitted from discussions with Benjamin Lee in writing this chapter.
2. J. L. Austin, *How To Do Things with Words* (Cambridge, MA: Harvard University Press, 1975); John R. Searle, *Speech Acts: An Essay in the Philosophy of Language* (Cambridge: Cambridge University Press, 1969).
3. Émile Benveniste, *Problèmes de Linguistique Générale,* vol. 1 (Paris: Gallimard, 1966), chapters 18 and 19.
4. See David McNeill, *Gesture and Thought* (Chicago: University of Chicago Press, 2005), chapter 3.

When I open a conversation with you, even a trivial one, initiated by "have you read any good books lately?", or "nice weather we're having", what we set up is a focus of joint attention in the sense explored in Chapter 2, where what we are talking about is "mutually manifest", that is, it is not just for me, and for you, but for *us* undivided. We interlocutors (and there can be more than two) form a circle, in which those within are recognized as persons ("I" and "you", the first and second persons), and the humans or things that we are talking about are invoked indiscriminately in the "third person", which is not in this act of speaking explicitly accorded the status of person, since the same grammatical form can range over humans, animals, and dead matter.[5]

The speech event sets up a circle of communicators in a particular situation, which becomes the reference point for a host of deictic terms, which take their meaning from it: 'here', 'there', 'now', 'then', 'yesterday', 'tomorrow', and so on. In relation to this event is also what gives our use of tenses their concrete force: present, perfect, aorist, future, and so on. The verbs we use can even situate ourselves, or the historical events we talk about, more finely, through aspect. We can situate ourselves at the close or consummation of a certain process (perfect tense: "I am come"), or in the middle of it (progressive form: "I am coming").

This referential centrality of the speech event is inescapable; not that we can't devise on occasion special forms which get around this centrality and allow us to enunciate "timeless" truths, like "rabbits eat lettuce", or a statement of the inverse square law. We can also formulate what Benveniste calls "historical narration" [*récits historiques*], which make no implicit reference to the event of their enunciation.[6] But we cannot live our lives without invoking this referential centrality, or even learn language in the first place, and hence get to the point where we can invent such special forms.

2

So the speech event, or conversational exchange sets up a circle of communication, of joint attention. But its "creativity" goes far beyond this inaugural force. In the way we exchange, talk to one another, treat one another, we establish and then continue or alter the terms of our relationship,

---

5. Benveniste, *Problèmes de Linguistique,* 230–31.
6. Ibid., 241.

what we might call the "footing"[7] on which we stand to each other. We do this through our rhetoric, our tone of voice, the kind of remark I permit myself and you don't challenge, and on through an infinity of nuances.

Let's say we are friends, but I am older than you. I can respond to this by treating you as an ingénue, offering avuncular advice on frequent occasions, sometimes intervening in a bossy fashion, dismissing peremptorily some of your ideas, and so on. You for your part don't challenge this; you may even like it. The upshot is that what I call a certain "footing" gets set up, call it an uncle-nephew footing, in which we each have certain expectations of the other, in which certain moves are normal and expected, and others are surprising, even shocking, and in which certain obligations are implied on each of our parts, and the like.

We are at the heart of what is often called the "pragmatics" of speech. Establishing a footing by enacting it, challenging a footing by enacting an alternative, this is what contributes to shape what we expect from each other, (in part) what we sense we owe to each other, what follows from different moves we might make.

But much of this enacting and shaping may take place off our semantic map. I benefitted in my above example from the fact that we recognize and have named the "avuncular" style. But surely something like this existed before the word was coined, and exists today in milieus where it is not current. But in this and many other cases, we have found a name, and can talk about what goes on here. This is an important step in what Michael Silverstein calls "metapragmatics". Just as we can have metasemantic rules, like "a bachelor is an unmarried man", which describe and guide our semantic practice, so we can have metapragmatic terms which describe, express, and shape the pragmatics of our speech situation.[8]

Another example of a metapragmatic description is "promise". We can all recognize situations in which the footing I am on with you, or the footing which anyone is on with anyone else in our society, makes it such that when I say to you: "I'll be there tomorrow", I commit myself. Saying this constitutes a promise, but we could well imagine a world in which this

7. This term is borrowed from Erving Goffman, *Forms of Talk* (Philadelphia: University of Philadelphia Press, 1981), 124–59. See also the interesting discussion in Asif Agha, *Language and Social Relations* (Cambridge: Cambridge University Press, 2007), 177–78.

8. Michael Silverstein, "Metapragmatic Discourse and Metapragmatic Function," in *Reflexive Language: Reported Speech and Metapragmatics,* ed. John A. Lucy (Cambridge: Cambridge University Press, 1993), 33–58.

term has yet to be invented, but a sense of shock or violation ensues when I don't turn up, and everyone knows that I didn't have a valid reason.

If our world evolves so that lots of people imitate my deplorable behavior, and then say afterward: "I thought yesterday that I could make it, but it turns out I couldn't", thus interpreting their original statement more as a prediction than as a commitment, we then may feel that we may have to ask people who say "I'll be there": "is that a prediction or a promise?" The word is now used to shape the pragmatics of discourse.

The next step, where a lot begins to hang on these pragmatics, is codification, something which is often connected to legal definitions. When the slick seducer says: "will you marry me?", and the woman answers "yes", there is no point his arguing later on that he just wanted to see how she was disposed, that the question was a mere request for information. He can be sued for breach of promise.

Codification involves defining certain statuses and the expectations which arise from them, and setting clear criteria for who accedes to these statuses. Marriage is one such clearly defined status which carries with it certain privileges and obligations. And there thus have to be and generally are clear criteria for who is in and who is out. These used to include an explicit ceremony, which in turn had to include certain operative formulae, such as "I pronounce you husband and wife", said by a qualified official (priest, mayor, registrar). Now with the number of unmarried couples, the privileges and obligations accrue to people who have been living together for a certain period of time. But there are still clear criteria. And a similar codification applies to the marriage of gay couples.

The original discussion of performatives centered on such highly codified contexts. The chair says: "I declare this session closed", and it thereby is closed. I can no longer raise the point I was going to. The supposed puzzle arose originally from the fact that what looks like an indicative sentence describing an action should have this crucial effect in the real world. It might seem (although on closer examination this can be questioned) quite parallel to the statement by the chef on the TV lesson in cooking: "Now I'm putting the whole dish in the oven to cook for twenty minutes at three hundred degrees". This is just explanatory self-description. Whereas the chair is exercising this power he has to close the session in making the declaration. This is in the simple first-person present indicative, and not in the progressive form that the chef uses. And this kind of performative is often prefaced by "in virtue of the powers invested in me by . . .", and accompanied by "hereby".

Performatives of this kind don't need, of course, to be expressed in first-person form. "Passengers are advised that there may be unforeseen delays in service" (1). "Trespassers are warned that they may be prosecuted" (2). And even the implicit form can operate as a warning: "Trespassers will be prosecuted" (3). The power of these ritually operative formulae depends on their being an established order, such as I described above, with statuses and powers which can be conferred or taken away. In the case of (1) above, it may be that the airline's liability to pursuit by disgruntled passengers who have missed a million-dollar deal through a delayed flight will be lessened; and that is the reason why the airline gives the warning. Again, the police officer says: "I advise you that anything you say may be used in evidence against you" (4). And this makes a legal difference. What you blurt out, and wouldn't have if he said (4) sooner, may not be admissible evidence.

Or in a somewhat different case, the police chief, before he gives the order to throw tear gas at the unruly demonstrators, reads the Riot Act. This too alters the legal situation.

Austin's later theory allows for a three-term distinction, not simply the contrast between "constatives" and "performatives". As I mentioned in Chapter 4, he distinguished the "locutionary" act, from the "illucitionary" act, and these from the "perlocutionary" effect.

"The bull is loose in the field!" (5) has the illocutionary force of a warning, and its intended perlocutionary effect is that the hearer take evasive action. But the illocutionary force can be made explicit: "I'm warning you, the bull is loose!" (6). This distinction goes some way to meet Benveniste's objection to accepting the implicit form as a performative. "An utterance is performative in that it *dominates* the act performed because Ego pronounces a formula containing a verb in the first person of the present: 'I *declare* the meeting adjourned'" [*Un énoncé est performatif en ce qu'il* dénomme *l'acte performé, du fait qu'Ego prononce une formule contenant le verbe à la première personne du présent: 'Je déclare la séance close'*].[9] But what this discussion doesn't take account of is the distinction between performatives with operative ritual effect, and mere explicitations of illocutionary ef-

9. Émile Benveniste, *Problems of General Linguistics,* trans. Mary Elizabeth Meek (Coral Gables: Miami University Press, 1971), 237; Benveniste, *Problèmes de Linguistique,* 274.

fects. "I'm warning you, the bull is loose!" (6) is a mere explicitation; "I declare this session closed" (7) (said by the chair) really closes the session.

(But illoctionary disambiguation may be used to reveal the real legal situation. Take the following scenario: the captain and the lieutenant are on friendly terms; they often joke together and discuss critically their superior officers. One day the captain gives the lieutenant instructions. This latter then offers advice alluding to the disadvantages of this course of action. The captain replies curtly, "Lieutenant, that's an order".)

3

Let's return to the earlier example of our "avuncular" relation, which originally came to exist without benefit of this description. What I wanted to bring out with this case was the original power of (bi- or multilateral) discourse to create and sustain footings. If and when these become codified, the mutual obligations they entail clearly defined, the conditions of entry and exit from the footing set out explicitly, then it can come about that certain acts of discourse have clearly defined effects: "I pronounce you man and wife" creates this footing of married couple for the pair who stand before the officiant; or "I divorce you", said three times by the man to his wife, dissolves this footing for certain forms of Muslim law. But such formal performatives operate in a world in which at the same time (uncodified or precodified) footings are being created, sustained, and transformed by and in discourse itself. I want to come back to this in section 5 below, where I will examine the transformations wrought by discourse in our footings and relations.

But my "avuncular" story above illustrates the constitutive power of discourse, the second of the two major types of particular constitution. And of course, the whole story illustrates both types working together. First we set up this particular kind of unequal relationship (second type), then we make it articulate, find a word for it, make it exist for us *as* this kind of relationship—reflectively, in Herder's sense (and this illustrates the first type).

But of course, such newly created footings always exist in a broader social space, made up not only of a multiplicity of already codified footings, but also by some common understanding of the wider social order. And this is also subject to shaping, or reshaping, through enactment. Any footing, once it is established, involves certain expectations which the partners should meet. The "avuncular" relationship supposed that I should be willing to offer you advice, that I should respond to your expressed uncertainty, not with a brusque change of subject, but with a concerned examination of your predicament. It supposes a certain politeness and deference in you.

Footings have or acquire a certain etiquette, or ethos. They involve what Asif Agha, following Silverstein, calls an "interactional text".[10] This in turn involves the definition of a certain social typology, identifying what kinds of actors can play the different roles in a given footing. The master-servant relationship in any given society supposes a sharply differentiated social typology, defining who appropriately can fill which role. In a highly egalitarian society, where anyone might be employed for some defined task by anyone else, this footing would no longer exist. There usually evolves, around different social types, certain understandings of identity, and frequently stereotypes.

Along with this, and interwoven with it, we have what Agha describes as differences of "register". In different contexts, and with different people, we talk very differently. Consider the kind of speech we use in very formal contexts, like a deliberative assembly, as against our "unbuttoned" trading of jokes in the pub afterward. Consider the "high" vocabulary which the classical age thought proper for literature, versus the speech of ordinary life. Nicolas Boileau-Despréaux thought that a low and common word, like 'vache', had no place in a literary work; one should write 'génisse'.[11] Or we could think of "high" registers in another sense: how we should talk when addressing social superiors, versus how we talk among us plebeians. Differences of discourse register are recognized and conformed to in all linguistic communities, although they may not yet be named, and their norms codified: "polite" versus "informal", or "literary", "scientific", "religious"; or "regular" speech versus "slang".[12]

This is the phenomenon Mikhail Bakhtin recognized with the term 'heteroglossia', and it underlay the practice he called "voicing", as when I suddenly begin to talk in register which is not mine, which may be inappropriate for me; I break, say into upper-class English, or begin to speak

---

10. Agha, *Language and Social Relations,* 25. See also Silverstein, "Metapragmatic Discourse."

11. Nicolas Boileau Despreaux, "Reflexion IX," *Oeuvres de Nicolas Boileau Despreaux: Avec des Eclaircissemens Historiques, Donnes par Lui-Meme* (Amsterdam: David Mortier, 1718), 111.

12. Agha, *Language and Social Relations,* chapter 3.

with a Texan drawl; the parody works, and makes my point, by echoing this other way of speaking and way of being.

Now all of these—footings, their norms and etiquette, the social typologies and interactional texts they suppose, the registers our language makes available—have potentially fluid boundaries. These must be constantly renewed in practice, that is, they need to be reenacted; but are often in fact subtly changed. Of course, naming and codifying them introduces a certain rigidity. The rules for where and to whom you must use "high" speech in a hierarchical society are not only sharp, but also can carry harsh sanctions for those who violate them. But even these can sometimes be quietly undermined, or even openly rebelled against. Think of the recent shift to more familiar modes of address in many Western societies. In my childhood in Quebec, we addressed our parents as "*vous*". This has become unthinkable today.

4

Let's look again from another standpoint at the wider social order in which our footings, typologies, and registers exist. In our modern societies we distinguish different fields of activity, which we sometimes refer to as "worlds" of involvement: the fields of politics, of commerce and industry, of art, science, education, the world of theater, of the media, and so on. These fields exert different degrees of authoritative control over our lives—most inescapably, the political, but for most people also the commercial-industrial, in which they have to find a job or some way of generating income. The control they exert falls differentially on some people rather than others; and this can be determined by some rule: for instance, women can't apply for certain jobs, or run for certain offices. The power generated for some people in any given field can be overshadowed or reinforced or mitigated by that of another sphere (the political in the shadow of ecclesiastical power, or kept on a short leash by economic power). Certain ways of life, and the footings which arise within them, will be shaped by canonical forms or "scripts" or "interactional texts": how one must behave as a politician, captain of industry, housewife, jobseeker, or how one must behave within the footings of husband-wife, boss-employee, shopminder-customer, politician-elector, and so on.

These common understandings will be formalized or codified to various degrees. Certain institutions operate by fixed rules, at their hardest and most inflexible in the legal system. But others may be looser, cast in ill-defined stereotypes, or canonical images.[13] Lying behind all of these will be structural patterns, largely unrecognized by most people, such as the causal mechanisms in the economic system.

This wider social order can feel as though it is written in the nature of things, may be experienced as hard and inflexible ("social facts" [*les faits sociaux*], as Durkheim put it, should be seen as "things" [*des choses*][14]). But in fact, as we have just argued, it only goes on existing because it is reproduced constantly by people who act more or less according to the scripts prescribed. And of course, it is never reproduced perfectly because no canonical way of behaving is ever totally acted out as "scripted" in the common understanding of any epoch, which common understanding is never totally agreed, spawning at any moment multiple versions. Things drift, and change becomes evident when we look back in retrospect years later. And sometimes there is resistance; people want to change the script, as we saw in the previous section. (I want to return to this issue of how societies change below in section 5.)

But by and large, the social order will usually reproduce itself, more or less. How does this happen? And in particular, how does it happen in a social world in which boundaries are always vulnerable to drift?

Here I want to refer back to the discussion of Pierre Bourdieu's work in Chapter 1, section 6.[15] We generally reproduce the society in which we are brought up because we have been trained in certain "habituses", which are not at all stereotyped reactions, but flexible modes of improvisation.[16] A habitus is "basically the embodied sensibility which makes possible structured improvisation."[17] To take on a habitus is to embody certain social meanings. To recur to the example of Chapter 1, young people in a given society learn how to express their respect for their elders, in

13. Of course, talk here of "texts" and "scripts" is metaphorical. The actors are in some sense aware of what is required of them, but not in the express, consciously formulated register which a term like 'script' usually implies. We are in the domain of what I have described elsewhere as "social imaginaries". See my *Modern Social Imaginaries* (Durham, NC: Duke University Press, 2004), chapter 2.

14. "The first and most basic rule is *to consider social facts as things.*" Emile Durkheim, *The Rules of Sociological Method,* trans. W. D. Halls (New York: Free Press, 1982), 60.

15. I have drawn very heavily on the excellent discussion in Craig Calhoun's "Pierre Bourdieu" in *The Blackwell Companion to Major Social Theorists,* ed. George Ritzer and Jeffrey Stepnisky (Oxford: Wiley-Blackwell, 2000).

16. Ibid., 14.

17. Ibid., 32.

bowing, looking at the ground, speaking in the right tone of voice, and so on. They don't learn certain concrete movements, but how to embody/ express a certain attitude.

Society will reproduce itself when the meanings and values of our habitus match those of our institutions, hierarchies, understandings of who or what is superior and inferior, and so forth. Both habitus and institutions sustain what Bourdieu calls the "doxa" of a society. By this he means, in Calhoun's terms, "the taken-for-granted, preconscious understandings of the world and our place in it that shape our more conscious awarenesses. Doxa is more basic than 'orthodoxy', or beliefs that we maintain to be correct in the awareness that others may have different views. Orthodoxy is an enforced straightness of belief, like following the teachings of organized religion. Doxa is felt reality, what we take not as beyond challenge but before any possible challenge."[18] Calhoun quotes Bourdieu's claim that "the operations of selecting and shaping new entrants [to any field] (rites of passage, examinations, etc.) are such as to obtain from them that undisputed, pre-reflexive, naïve, native compliance with the fundamental presuppositions of the field which is the very definition of doxa."[19]

But of course, our compliance never depends, at least in a modern society, solely on habitus-induced doxa. The rules of our institutions, the canonical forms and scripts of various roles and footings, are also spelled out and justified. And to recur to the discussion of the last section of Chapter 6, besides habitus and explicit rules, there are always other media in which society presents itself and its basic values: exemplary stories, a certain reading of our history, and/or our founding fathers and their deeds, fictional portrayals. And beyond all these there are commemorative moments: our national day (Fourth of July, Saint-Jean-Baptiste Day), or memorial services to our fallen compatriots of the wars, or to other people who have died or suffered for our cherished values.

All these together feed into what I have called elsewhere the "social imaginary" of a given society.[20] This includes an articulation of the doxa, but may also incorporate various critical stances toward this.

18. Ibid., 29–30.

19. Ibid., 29, from Pierre Bourdieu, *The Logic of Practice* (Stanford: Stanford University Press, 1980), 68.

20. See my *Modern Social Imaginaries*. In many societies, the shared social imaginary may be differently inflected among different classes, or milieu. For instance, in many contemporary societies, the common understanding that we live in a democracy may be accompanied by different notions of what this means, between left and right, respectively; or between cultural minorities, on

Now the invocation above of commemorative moments brings us back to rituals, and to another dimension of how we "do things with words" (as well as with ritual acts).

5

And this in turn connects to the importance of ritual in the development of language, which I discussed in Chapter 2. In that chapter, I invoked Roy Rappaport's theory of the origin of ritual in human history. It originally related to the universe as an overarching order, which we might call the "cosmos" (drawing on the etymological connections of the Greek word with notions of order in the normative sense). He cites the *Ma'at* of the Egyptians, the *Rta* of the Vedic world. This cosmos includes ourselves, but also the gods or spirits, whatever higher beings are recognized. The order can suffer damage, deviations, and departures from its true nature. It is normative, but not integrally realized. We humans are responsible for some of these deviations, but we can also contribute to repairing them. And our principal means of repair is through ritual.

Repairing the order may be focused primarily on restoring our relation to this order, for instance on making peace with the gods, or recovering their amity, which is the aim of much early sacrifice. Much early ritual is "restorative".

I think there is a lot of truth in this picture of the early human predicament. But how are we to understand the persistence of ritual even in an age which (at least officially and publicly) shares none of that sense of a normative cosmos or of the role of higher beings in our lives? Or at least where the place of God in life and society is no longer something universally agreed?

Perhaps we can start with what I've been calling ritual efficacy of performatives in highly codified orders of statuses, such as those which bring about marriages, or close sessions of the council. This will, of course, not take us all the way, but they are a good place to start. Where is the analogy with what Rappaport and others talk about in connection with earlier societies?

---

one hand, and the majority, on the other. What figure as elements of doxa for one group may be objects of sharp criticism among others. One must exercise caution in talking about "the" doxa of whole societies (and even sometimes, whole fields).

Well, the acts completed by these performatives will not usually amount to repair of the orders in question (in these examples, marriage, and the preservation of good deliberative order), but they are meant to conform to them, and they certainly take these orders as normative. One or other of us may think that our established institution of marriage is bad, and our deliberative culture is too cramped and restrictive, but the general understanding of people who operate within these orders is that they are good.

So there is a parallel (affirming the orders) and a nonparallel (not being concerned with repair on this score). Let's look at a second feature: rituals often have "punch lines", or crucial parts which are stereotyped.[21] As Rappaport puts it, "the performers of rituals do not specify all the acts and utterances constituting their own performance. They follow, more or less punctiliously, orders established or taken to have been established, by others."[22] This matches the stereotypy of typical performatives, like "I pronounce you husband and wife", and "I declare this session closed".

But there is a disanalogy on this level too. I'm not quite sure how to put this, but we might say that in earlier ritual there is more uncertainty, more "play" between ritual and sought-after result than in the highly codified modern examples.

There are certainly a number of things which can make a marriage ceremony misfire, "infelicities" as Austin calls them. One of the parties is already married; the officiant isn't competent to perform the ceremony (not a priest, or the mayor, or a registrar, or a ship's captain). But once you've ruled out these possible lapses, the operation is pretty surefire.

But in the rituals of earlier societies, and those that still resemble them today, such surefire results are harder to encounter. This is partly because

---

21. It has often been remarked that these crucial formulae, which often consist of both words and actions, often have an iconic nature; they figure what they want to bring forth. There is perhaps an interesting connection with Melvin Konner's *The Evolution of Childhood: Relationships, Emotion, Mind* (Cambridge, MA: Harvard University Press, 2010), where he speaks of animal ritualization, as when a wolf in snarling produces a reduced icon of the action of attacking and biting, which can serve to communicate to another that they risk triggering such an attack. Perhaps there is an important continuity in deep evolution which underlies this similarity.

22. Roy Rappaport, *Ritual and Religion in the Making of Humanity* (Cambridge: Cambridge University Press, 1999), 32. Stanley Tambiah, however, points out that too much stereotypy and predictability can in the long run empty the ritual of meaning, and that there has to be a revival by charismatic leaders who recast the practice in fresh terms. See his *Culture, Thought and Social Action: An Anthropological Perspective* (Cambridge, MA: Harvard University Press 1985), 165–66.

the end result sought is harder to define and pin down than in the case of a valid wedding, or a session which has been terminated. Repairing the order of things, getting back on good terms with the gods, cannot be automatically ensured by (what looks like) a ritual of exemplary correctness. Take the Romans' relation to their gods. The crucial ritual of contact was the sacrifice with associated feast. The animal was killed, the "noble" entrails (heart, liver, etc.) were offered to the god (burned on his/her altar), and then the red meat was consumed by the assembled company. Certain defects could invalidate the whole operation (e.g., if the noble entrails were deformed, or missing). But even in the absence of these, success was nevertheless not ensured.[23] That's because the ultimate goal was one which couldn't be pinned down by a finite list of jointly sufficient ritual conditions. It was defined as the "*pax deorum*", the "peace of the Gods" by which was meant the normal condition of peaceful coexistence between gods and men, and the consequent goodwill of the gods.

There could be no strict equivalent to the contemporary case where a competent official says the "I pronounce you . . ." formula before two willing and unmarried participants. There might be much detail on what a ritual needs as preconditions, but not the uncertainty that it would be received, would be ultimately successful.

Ed Lipuma has observed something similar to the Roman case among the Maring in New Guinea (incidentally, the same people among whom Rappaport did much of his work). There is often uncertainty after the rituals of marriage alliances have been conducted whether they have really come off, whether the necessary preconditions were really met, and even what to an external observer may appear as a certain shifting of the goalposts to ensure that they are felt to have been. The rules may be subtly bent, accompanied by the assurance that they are what they have always been. So that what is held to be an unchanging tradition in fact evolves over time.[24]

But this kind of constitutional uncertainty and "play" can be seen in other important rituals of early society. Take the crucial alliance-forming

23. Jörg Rüpke, *Religion of the Romans* (Cambridge: Polity Press, 2007), 140–45.

24. Ed Lipuma, "Ritual and Performativity: A Melanesian Example," in *Exchange and Sacrifice*, ed. P. J. Stewart and A. Strathern (Durham, NC: Carolina Academic Press, 2008). For the background literature on this, and particularly backward performativity, see Ed Lipuma, "Ritual in Financial Life," in *Derivatives and the Wealth of Societies*, ed. Benjamin Lee and Randy Martin (Chicago: Chicago University Press, forthcoming), 80 and 130.

rituals of gift exchange, studied by Marcel Mauss,[25] and many others. There are certainly moves which can be seen as valid or invalid in this whole practice. For instance, Bourdieu points out that the timing of a reverse gift is of the essence. If someone gives you something, and you hasten to give him something back, you are insulting him, advertising that you don't want to be beholden to him. If on the contrary, you delay too long, you are taken to be saying that he's not very important to you, that he can be neglected. You need to be able to make nice judgments of the temporal interval, a sense of kairos, of the right time to replicate. And of course that right time will depend on a whole host of things: your past relation with him, your respective places in the hierarchy of society, and so on.[26]

But then rituals with similar features take place today. Take a ceremony of commemoration: say a country's national day (Fourth of July, Saint-Jean-Baptiste Day), or one where we remember our dead, fallen in the wars. Can we say that these have goals? Of course, a cynic could see them as having an external goal: the élites who stage them want them to stoke up patriotic feeling, so that the population will be more dedicated to what they define as the national purpose. This is a strategic goal, as when an employer throws a party for his workers to make them more cheerful and well-disposed to him. We can even operate in this way strategically with ourselves, as when we decide to relax and take a drink before we face some awkward and difficult question.

But my question concerns internal goals, ones the participants themselves seek in the ceremony. I think we can often find these. What actuates the participants in a Fourth of July ceremony may frequently be the desire to recover the vivid sense of solidarity, of sharing a worthwhile national goal, which tends to get frittered away in the day-to-day grind, and the frequent irritations, conflicts, and resentments of ordinary (and political) life. But like the Roman *pax deorum* this is something which cannot be guaranteed by even the best-conducted ceremony.

The desired outcome is not simply a side effect, like what the employer seeks out of the staff party. It is rather a genuine common goal, but one can never specify a list of jointly sufficient conditions.

So the modern world has analogues to the traditional ritual's combination of stereotyped formulae (except that we allow ourselves much more

25. Marcel Mauss, *The Gift: Forms and Functions of Exchange in Archaic Societies,* trans. Ian Cunnison (London: Routledge, 1990).
26. Bourdieu, *Logic of Practice,* 105–6.

improvisation in our national days) on one hand, and uncertain outcomes on the other. On this second level of comparison, where we contrasted stereotyped formulae which approach the status of near-sufficient conditions (the marriage ceremony) to rituals which can never attain this degree of certainty, the modern world seems to have examples on both sides.

But then when we recur to our first level of comparison, where we contrasted early rituals of repair of a normative order with those which merely conform to this order, we can see that our modern examples of uncertain outcome are also cases where something like repair is at stake; or at least the recovery of a condition of solidarity and joint dedication which is thought to lie at the origin of our society, but which we have slipped from since. It belongs perhaps to the very nature of rituals of repair that their outcomes can never be certain. But in any case, they appear to be a perennial feature of human life.

Lipuma speaks of the assurance of the success of rituals among the Maring, which involves unrecognized alteration of what were thought to be the conditions of such success, as "backward performativity". But backward performativity of another kind, which could be called "bootstrapping", is also a feature of the modern world.

I mentioned in Chapter 2 the example of the foundation of the United States with its federal constitution. This paradox has often been remarked upon. In the text of the Constitution, this is presented as the act of a collective subject, "the people of the United States". But this subject didn't preexist the adoption of the Constitution; it was the creation of this document. What preexisted the Constitution was the peoples of the different colonies, now states, which had been political entities for some time, and which had created the weak and unsatisfactory entity through the Articles of Confederation, which the federal state was meant to replace.

The operation was carried out within the horizon of modern social contract theory, which saw a people as being formed by a uniting of individuals, and then this people choosing a constitution. The bootstrapping maneuver consisted in presenting the Constitution as though it emanated from an existing people, and then making up the gap retrospectively through the ratification of the states and the consequent functioning of the new institutions. An order was not restored but a new one was created, through the power of performative utterance.

Both kinds of backward performativity raise an issue which I mooted in Chapter 2. Ritual often aims to restore or repair a larger order. But can this be separated from the function of defining order in the first place? As the earliest human societies struggled toward an understanding of the larger order in which they were set (and this sense of the larger order seems inseparable from human language), and if their only means to achieve this was a tandem of myth and ritual, then evolving ritual would be an essential part of their path toward this understanding. The evolving ritual of restoring order, or connecting to order, would be one facet of their progress toward defining this order (myth being the other), whether we see this as discovery or projection. What we see with the Maring on Lipuma's account, and what we noticed with the establishing of the U.S. Constitution, would be the continuation of a venerable, millennia-old human tradition.

What emerges from this discussion is that the gap between older societies based on notions of metaphysical or religious orders, and modern "secular" societies is not as great as we sometimes claim. We have our own "restorative" rituals in which we reaffirm order. This order, even for the most "secular" moderns, is founded on certain values or goods: in our contemporary cases, for the most part, these include human rights and democracy as a mode of government. Even those who want to eschew any metaphysical or religious "grounding" of these see them as somehow unrepudiable, as holding in the nature of things—perhaps in human nature, or even less sempiternally, in what civilized human beings have become (and thus we always had it in us to become).

So that for us ceremonies of repair are moments of rededication, and thus a return of allegiance to the order we recognize as normative. This is a feature of our lives which it is hard to imagine escaping.

But then, to return to the issue above, how we reproduce our social orders, we will have to include rituals of repair, along with the inculcation of habitus and doxa, as well as the handing down of explicit rules and canonical forms. And we have not even begun to talk of other rituals of repair, such as those involved in truth and reconciliation, and the overcoming of historic wounds and divisions.[27] With all this we are deeply in the domain of the constitutive efficacy of discourse, at a much deeper and more

---

27. We might also think of the role that festivals played in the period of the French Revolution. See Mona Ozouf, *Les Fêtes Révolutionnaires: 1789–1799* (Paris: Gallimard, 1988).

important level than that of the routine codified performatives which have
seized the philosophical limelight.

6

Our discussion of the creative power of discourse led to our raising the issue
of performative speech, and that in turn led to our discussion of the making
and remaking of orders through codification, or ritual and the associated
myth. But is there an informal analogue to this creative power, whereby
the discourse of social exchange, without reference to a cosmic order, or
without drawing on an already established code, could itself forge new relations and norms, and/or alter old ones? I think there is, and I want to go
on to illustrate this in the present section.

Let's return to an earlier phase of the argument, before the digression
about performatives and ritual. At the beginning of section 2, I was explaining how a footing between two people can be set up through the kind
of exchange which they come habitually to sustain between them. I gave
the example of the avuncular older person imposing a certain style of interaction which the younger partner, grudgingly or willingly, acquiesces to.
This was an example of a footing between two individuals in the private
sphere. But a similar process of creation through exchange can establish
new kinds of footing in the public sphere, linking whole categories of
persons, and hence can alter the social order. Unlike in the private sphere,
however, where, as I remarked earlier, the footing established may have no
recognized name (as my uncle-nephew style footing would have remained
semantically unremarked in a society which had not yet coined the term
"avuncular"), the process in the public sphere generally leads to an enriched
and altered metapragmatic vocabulary, involving the introduction of new
terms, or new, unprecedented meanings of familiar terms.

I will illustrate this with an example I invoked in an earlier paper. The
context of the argument in that article was a critique of Davidson's theory
of meaning,[28] but the example can serve a broader purpose. The example
in question was equality as a norm of the Greek polis, as expressed in such
terms as '*isêgoria*' and '*isonomia*',[29] and in such expressions as the Spartan

---

28. See my "Theories of Meaning" in *Human Agency and Language* (Cambridge: Cambridge
University Press, 1985).

29. '*isonomia*' can be roughly translated, using terms of our modern context, "equality of right",
and '*isêgoria*' as "equal freedom of speech".

'*homoioi*' for citizens. The last term refers us to likeness, similarity (as with "homogeneous"). Likeness and equality were basic tropes for this relationship.

My original conceit, in the context of a reflection on what it means to learn another language, was to imagine a Persian foreigner in Athens trying to understand what these cherished terms of discourse in the Greek polis mean; he might be thinking: I know what it means to be of like height, or color or strength or valor, but what is this Athenian nonsense about equal citizenship?

Here what I want to consider is how such a set of norms and relationships could emerge in the aftermath of the overthrow of kings (as also in Rome). We might think of an analogy: the sudden crystallization of a powerful sense of dignity denied among the young people in Egypt's Tahrir Square in 2011. But dignity is already a value which has been much articulated in the modern world, and respect for dignity is claimed as a realized value in certain societies. But in the Greek case, this wasn't so. How does equal citizenship arise unprecedented?

It has to emerge in a series of rhetorical moves, where people object that, for instance, their (equal) right to speak is being repressed; or that some prominent figure is putting himself above the rest of us. This comes with new terms, or older ones in new meanings (like 'tyrant' which earlier had a neutral or even positive sense). In the course of this, words like '*isêgoria*' emerge. They articulate new expectations and norms. In this case, the demand involved the equal capacity of citizens to contribute to public discussion. The point is that the articulation comes along with these expectations and norms, not after them. Citizens come to find certain established restrictions on speech, in favor of kings, or tyrants, or a narrow group of nobles, irksome and objectionable. They object, protest, and demand to be heard. The new norms arise out of this protest; they become internalized, and they find the appropriate new coinages in the conflictual exchange. We articulate the new norms, give them their names. The new words we coin in the process of articulation define and give shape to what we are demanding. That is what we mean in talking about "constitution" here.

And as I argued earlier, in this process, the two types of constitution are operating together. The new footings set up in discourse acquire a name. This articulation contributes to shape its object. Only in this case the agency is not an individual thinker, perhaps operating in a mode of quiet reflection;

rather it emerges out of a deliberating community, in often conflictual exchange. The creativity here essentially belongs to discourse.

I've been talking here about new articulations of norms and goals which arise from the inside, as it were, among those who demand them. There is also a quite different phenomenon, where uninvolved observers notice trends and give them a name post hoc, as with the reaction in the United Kingdom in 2011 to the rioting/looting of young people. But even this retrospective naming from outside is not without effect. It alters the way we live with this new phenomenon.

Now the force of the constitutive is evident in the way that ideals like equality are negotiated and renegotiated, and, in the course of this, transformed. In relation to the Greeks and Romans, modern Europeans were like the young people in Tahrir Square. Especially the Roman republic stood as an ideal of citizenship; for instance, for late mediaeval Italian cities, or during the American and French Revolutions. But a lot of work was still to be done. Citizen equality had to be given concrete meaning. To use a famous Kantian metaphor, it had to "schematized" in modern conditions. And this schematization has continued, with the result that the ideal is always being transformed.

Because the ancients didn't have our understanding of it. It was far from being a universal ideal. Slaves, women, were excluded; and, for certain patricians, so ought the plebs to be, because they couldn't live up to the ideal of active citizenship. (And even in the first years of the American Republic, certain Federalists assumed that political office was for the well off and wise.)

Think of how equality takes on new meaning. For instance, today gay marriage is demanded as a right in the name of nondiscrimination (which is another avatar of equality). Think of how this came about. The first key move was made about a half century ago as part of the sexual revolution. This was not just a demand to allow a less restrictive sexual code; it also in some ways changed the subject. The sexual revolution came along with the turn to an ethic of authenticity. So homosexuals had a right to "come out" without penalty, not just on the older grounds of avoiding gratuitous suffering (which motivated, e.g., André Gide's coming out in the 1920s), but more on the grounds that sexual orientation should be considered as an "identity", and as such deserved equal respect. This shift in the understanding of equality grows with the spread of an ethic of authenticity, with its accompanying notion of "identity" (now used in a new sense).

But this word doesn't come after the change; it helps to bring about the change.

The illusion that this is not the case, that the value was always there in our lives even before the word, comes from the analogue in this informal area to Lipuma's "backward performativity" in the ritual domain (section 5 above), and the "misrecognition" which he invokes in his paper on the Maring.[30] We persuade ourselves that equality *always* meant this, and that the minority who controlled things were just being hypocritical (in relation to their slaves, or their wives, or their workers, etc.) But this confuses two issues: (a) are things better when equality is defined this way? (to which I would want to reply, in respect of the changes since 1800, with a resounding "yes"); and (b) is that really what a norm like *isonomia* meant to those Greeks (but they were just hypocritically denying it to the majority), or what equality meant to the framers in Philadelphia? And here the answer will often be "no". Not always, sometimes there was a real difference of view, as with slavery in 1787, and some prominent figures, like Jefferson, were conflicted (although it's probably wrong to say that "equality" was the issue; more it was a question of who were bearers of the rights defined in the Declaration of Independence).

Now (a) is a moral-political issue on which we may want to take a categorical stand; but (b) is a historico-ethnographic question which requires a nuanced answer.[31]

7

I want to claim that a complex of key human phenomena, norms, footings, institutions, social orders, political structures and the offices that figure in them are constituted and transformed in discourse, often in rhetorical speech acts which purport to refer to established values, or invoke existing structures, but which in fact bootstrap. There is a gamut of such constitutive relations; at one end of the spectrum, we have the formal orders,

---

30. See note 24 above.

31. Asif Agha also gives examples of contemporary moves toward equality brought about in discursive interaction, like the hierarchic distinctions in mode of address between formal and intimate (exemplified by the "*tu*"/"*vous*" distinction in French, when addressing a single person, though in some languages the more formal mode uses the third person). In many European societies, the asymmetry in mode of address between superiors and inferiors, or parents and children, has been eroded, not through any formal decision, but in the process of interchange itself. See Agha, *Language and Social Relations*, chapter 3, especially 172–74.

social, legal, or cosmic; and here is where explicit ritual, and performatives, are situated. At other points on the spectrum, we find the zone where new norms, values, footings are being informally created and transformed.

An outsider to this context of transformation can treat the values and institutions as "already there". This would be the position of an historian in Outer Mongolia, whose family were herders, and who is now studying ancient Greek history at the University of Ulan Bator. (The family, say, lived in such a remote district that they weren't even touched by the Marxism of the Soviet régime.) The institutions, norms, and rhetoric of ancient Athens come across as new discoveries, already catalogued with canonical names, just as the animals of Africa do in geography class. It all seems to fit the HLC model of an insulated semantic dimension. But if ever our young student wants to become a real historian, or ethnographer, she had better come to see the distinction between the two cases. The animals were indeed already there before their names were ever uttered, but the language we have to describe the political life of Athens is the precipitate of the constitutive discourse in which this life came to be. And we don't really grasp this language unless we have an ethnographer's thick description of what this discourse was like, through its different phases and vicissitudes, struggles and resolutions, definitions and redefinitions.

And this brings us back to the earlier paper in which I invoked this example, in the course of a critique of Davidson's theory of meaning. The basic thesis of this latter argument is that I understand another group's language when I can give the truth conditions of any of their utterances in my own language. I don't have to understand how they "figure" the world, to use the term I coined in Chapter 5.

Now this is usually going to work for the objects we all recognize in the world around us: animals, people, basic actions, furniture, foodstuffs, and so on. But this will not work for the terms which help constitute our social and political lives (such as precisely in the Greek case, 'isonomia', 'isêgoria'). That defined the predicament of my poor Persian observer. He could understand what 'equal' meant in judgments of equal height, equal strength, equal skill driving chariots, perhaps even equal birth. But to understand 'isêgoria' he would have to have insight into polis life, its norms and ideals. And of course, he could acquire this. He would only have to do what good ethnographers do, and give himself a six-month (at least) field trip in Attica.

But unlike with talk about animals where you have already to be able to recognize dogs in order to learn the Greek word '*kuon*', you can't expect that he might grasp Greek political mores independent of coming to see how these key Greek terms work. Learning to find your way around the institutions, and learning how to use these words are not two separable stages like learning to recognize the fauna in Greece, and then learning what the Greeks call the different animals. On the political level, learning the language and learning to make sense of their political life cannot be separated. And that precisely because of the constitutive force of the language (i.e., discourse) in this domain.[32]

The new way of politics which made equality a central value arose against a background which included earlier forms of (kingly or élite) rule, and a traditional ethos (of the warrior and leader), and modified them both. Neither these background forms, nor the direction of modification, can be understood without reference to their key normative terms.

Our Persian can't give Davidsonian T-sentences in which phrases in Persian on the right side translate Greek sentences on the left, because the necessary Persian words don't (yet) exist. When he goes back and publishes his monograph in Susa on the weird life of Athenians, he'll have to do what ethnographers often do: give the term in Greek, and then make an attempt to surround it with imaginative, often neologizing, explanation, so that his readers get a grasp of what makes Hellenes tick. If this kind of contact goes on long enough Persian will be enriched to the point where simple translations are available (although this may be a treacherous process, leading us to believe that we understand things which still elude us).

8

And this brings us back to the main theme of the four chapters in this second part: how the HLC, even enriched and transformed by the work of Frege and others, still can't do justice to the constitutive force of language and its powers of figuration. It continues to espouse principles I and II enunciated at the beginning of Chapter 5 (I = words are introduced to

---

32. As Albrecht Wellmer puts it, "A Davidsonian interpreter remains forever in the housing of his own language" [*Ein Davidsonscher Interpret bleibt für immer im Gehäuse seiner eigenen Sprache*]; "Davidsonian interpreters cannot learn anything new in linguistic communication" [*Davidsonsche Interpreten können in der sprachlichen Kommunikation nichts Neues lernen*], *Sprachphilosophie: Eine Vorlesung*, ed. Thomas Hoffmann, Juliana Rebentisch, and Ruth Sonderegger (Frankfurt: Suhrkamp Taschenbuch Wissenschaft, 2004), 185 and 190.

designate features which have already come to our attention; II = the Cratylist, or figuring, dimension of language adds nothing to our empirical
description of the world). This makes it a good formula for devising a spe-
cialist language in which to carry on scientific work, or to couch certain
dispassionate, neutral descriptions of reality, which have their uses. But this
restriction makes it unable to capture human language as it exists in nature, or to yield an adequate account of what the human language capacity
consists in.

Once more, this privileging of sober, responsible description of independent objects at the expense of everything else in human language blinds
us to its true nature. What we have seen in this discussion of the range
of meanings I have called "footings" bears strong analogies to what we
discovered about the genesis of new human meanings in Chapter 6. As
was frequently seen to be the case with ethical, or quasi-ethical, standards, new footings enter our world through enactment; they arise between agents through often conflictual interaction. In some cases they
come about without benefit of metapragmatic description (like my example of my avuncular relation avant la lettre); but frequently the struggle
itself essentially involves newly coined words, norms, or ritual acts, as well
as new descriptions of historical exemplars, which are invoked on one side
or the other.

So like the case of the Socratic ethic of the examined life, or the cool
style of life, there is an intermingling of exemplary enactment, on one hand,
and verbal articulation, both of norms and of valued actions, goals or virtues, on the other. These are reciprocally related such that exemplars are
explained by articulations, which in turn have to be understood in the light
of exemplars.

And to this will often be added, as a third "rung", discourses of explanation and justification, explaining how these new footings arose, and what
is right (or wrong) with them.

So when we try to understand how new terms can arise in this vocabulary of footings, we find something analogous to what we saw with ethical
meanings; at the origin are attempts to realize what may be only dimly
felt as valuable ways of being. These may either involve from the beginning ways of talking, vocabularies of description and invocation, or come
later to generate these. This whole complex of deeds and words seeks ratification. This latter is complex in each case, but also different in the two
cases, the ethical and that of footings.

For the human meanings discussed in Chapter 6, two kinds of truth claims were implicit: that our descriptions of ourselves and others in terms of these meanings were correct, that is, devoid of error and illusion, and also that the norms and goods concerned were valid. Ratifying these meanings involves satisfying ourselves on both these scores.

With footings, this second kind of validation is also sought; in fighting to establish them, we make a claim to their rightness. But what is also involved in the struggle is the goal of establishing them de facto as the operative footings in our society or our world. This is what I called in Chapter 6 "cultural ratification". Here perhaps we should speak less of ratification than of realization.

But the general lesson for the major theme of this book is the same. When it comes to the language of footings, as was the case with meanings, the designative semantic logic misleads us, and a constitutive logic is at work. New terms don't arise simply because independently existing phenomena come to our notice and are named. They are generated out of enactment and the discourse of norms and exemplars which arises out of this enactment. Of course, once the footings exist we may encounter them as outside observers, as was the case with our Persian visitor to Athens, or our Mongolian scholar of the ancient Greek world. And of course, we are all in this position when we ponder the lessons of history, and engage in explanatory and justificatory discourse on the third, highest rung.

But this doesn't mean that we can just relocate these phenomena in the designative semantic logic. In fact we can't properly understand these footings or meanings if we treat them as though they preexisted there in nature, and weren't generated out of meaningful enactment, individual and social. To get them is to get their point, which involves understanding how they arise and endure or change. Otherwise put, to understand these phenomena, we have to understand the meaning they have for the agents concerned, the significance the footings, ethical values, and other human meanings have for them. But these are only understandable against the background of the practices from which they arise, and the words and images by which they interpret these. To treat their action as we do other parts of self-standing nature is to gravely misunderstand them.

To put the point another way, an account in social science or history of a given period in the history of a society can be faulted if one can show that the author has an inadequate or oversimplified view of the meanings their actions had for the agents; or, to make the point in another way, of the agents' motivations. We saw an example of a dispute of this kind around the critique that François Furet leveled at the Marxist-inspired historiography of the French Revolution. On the basis of their respective readings of the motives and meanings at play, they offered very different accounts of these crucial events, especially of the Terror of 1792–1794. They couldn't both be right.

This basic point applies to both kinds of constitution. But an important feature has emerged in this chapter which is particular to constitution-in-discourse. A use of language which plays an important role here is ritual. This links us back to the discussion in Chapter 2, where we saw that the language for the whole larger order in which humans and their societies live evolves through rituals of reconnection or "restoration". We can argue that such rituals survive even into an age where the earlier understanding of a cosmic or transcendent moral order ceases to be part of our shared understanding. They have a continuing role within the "immanent frame".[33]

So discourse constitutes not only footings, through enacting and reenacting them; it also through ritual shapes, and restores while reshaping, the larger human orders in which we live.

We can reiterate here two lessons that we drew at the end Chapter 6. First, this alternation of creation and ratification of meanings, which we see in slightly different form in the domain of footings, is the basis for the continuing generation of cultural differences.

And once more we recognize that understanding the language, even of ordinary prose speech, involves seeing it in the context of meaningful enactment, and the whole range of symbolic forms. Specialized pared-down languages, stripped of human meaning, may be ideal for certain important purposes, but these austere modes cannot provide the model for human speech in general. That is one of the main messages of this book.

33. See Charles Taylor, *A Secular Age* (Cambridge, MA: Harvard University Press, 2007), chapter 15.

PART III

Further Applications

8

How Narrative Makes Meaning

1

There is another facet of the creative or constitutive power of language which deserves examination. But this requires that we enlarge the scope of our enquiry, and look at units of discourse bigger than the sentence. Frege and others have taught us that crucial features of linguistic meaning only come into view when we go beyond an examination of the meaning of words, and consider meaning at the level of the whole declarative sentence. But perhaps another increase in understanding can be attained if we go beyond this to consider what larger texts can show us about language and its powers.

The example I want to look at here is the story—the telling of people and events and their complex relations, bound as they are inside a narrative. I want to defend the idea that stories give us an understanding of life, people, and what happens to them which is peculiar (i.e., distinct from what other forms, like works of science and philosophy, can give us), and also unsubstitutable (i.e., what they show us can't be translated without remainder into other media).

What can we communicate about people and life in a story? A story often consists in a diachronic account of how some state or condition (usually the terminal phase) came to be. This can illuminate things in various ways. It often gives us an idea of "how things came to be", in the sense of explaining why, or giving causes. It can also offer insight into what this terminal phase is like: we can perhaps now appreciate more its fragility or permanence, or its value or drawbacks, and the like. The story can also give us a more vivid sense of the alternative course not taken, and so how chancy, either lucky or unlucky, the outcome was. And it can also open out alternatives in a wider sense; it can lay out a gamut of different ways of being human, different paths or characters which interact in the story, and thus offer insights about human life in general. We can think of the simplest case like the list of characters and actions in folktales (as laid out, e.g., in a study like that of Vladimir Propp[1]): hero, false hero, victim; departure on quest, return from quest, and so on; or of the "grammar" exhibited in collections of stories, like *The Decameron* of Boccaccio.[2] These can be templates through which people can understand their lives. And of course, the stories we tell ourselves now, both fictional and historical, are many orders of magnitude more nuanced and sophisticated than these fables.

Now everybody would probably grant my first assertion above, that narrative constitutes *a* way of offering insight into causes, characters, values, alternative ways of being, and the like. But many would baulk at the second affirmation, that this form is unsubstitutable. Of course it may be in some cases, but the thesis here is to the effect that valid insight in the above matters can be given in a story which cannot be transposed to the medium of science, atemporal generalization, and the like.

2

Let's take first the case of the causal explanation of the terminal event that a story can convey. Here our thesis runs up against one of the powerful epistemological theses which descends from Hume, through Viennese positivism to much contemporary (analytic) philosophical thought. The attribution which emerges from a story would be of a singular causal chain. The terminal state follows from the preceding chain of events as understandable, believable, and even convincing. But one of the dogmas of Hume is that there is no such thing as a singular causal chain simpliciter. One can only say that A causes B if one can subsume this succession under a lawlike generalization linking events-like-A with events-like-B as invariably following from one another. So the causal attribution which seems to emerge from the story is either an unsupported suggestion, a hunch, or a

1. See Vladimir Propp, *Morphology of the Folktale*, trans. Laurence Scott (Bloomington, IN: American Folklore Society, 1968).
2. Tzvetan Todorov, *La Grammaire du Décaméron* (The Hague: Mouton, 1969).

link insinuated by rhetoric; or it takes its validity from an assertion in non-narrative form.

But this dogma is patently untrue. We make all sorts of singular attributions. An agent generally knows what he/she does just in doing it. I know I shot the puck into the net from the blue line; this kind of knowledge is usually inseparable from the action itself. Moreover, in virtue of our ability to "read" other people in their intentions and actions,[3] I can know Wayne Gretzky shot the puck into the net from the blue line (because I saw it). And going outside human action, I saw that the cupboard in falling over shattered Aunt Mabel's Ming vase.

Of course, our ability to make such singular attributions is often fed by experience, often of similar events; just as our ability to control our action, and know that we control it, will depend on lots of training experience, as when we learn to lift the puck off the ice toward the (unprotected) upper corner of the net. So we learn to discern more finely what causes what in the realm of human action, as well as in the interaction of physical objects without needing, or even in certain cases being able, to formulate general laws covering identical occurrences.

But the reply might be: OK, we don't do this, but wouldn't we be on more solid ground if we did base our singular attributions on general laws linking identical elements? No, I would like to say, and this isn't even always possible. These laws tell us about relationships between types of occurrence. But what we explain through a story is often a singular event. Sometimes certain known or discoverable generalizations may be involved in accounting for this event, but the account remains a singular attribution.

One of the reasons for this is that the story account may have to bring together a number of different factors, where the operation of each one *may* be illuminated by laws but the causal explanation involves combining them in some way. Take an accident on the highway; a car slides off the road. Now it was January, and there had recently been freezing rain; besides it was dark and there was fog; besides the road was badly graded: the turn should have been better banked. On top of that, the driver was a young (male) novice (I follow here the bias of insurance companies against young males). And yes, also he had several drinks at the party. Plainly all these

---

3. See Michael Tomasello, *The Cultural Origins of Human Cognition* (Cambridge, MA: Harvard University Press, 1999), chapter 3.

concurred in the accident, or at least are candidates for the role of part cause.

Now some of these are based on the record of like cases. Insurance companies have actuarial tables to motivate their dim view of young males. (But these yield only statistical generalizations, not real laws; maybe our young man was very cautious, unlike most of his age cohort.) But for many of them, we have a sense from experience of their relevance, but this may not be based on counting like cases. Generalizations like fog reduces visibility and ice makes roads slippery certainly enter here, but these are often picked up from a single experience.

But the causal attribution may include mention of all of them, that they all together produced the accident. Or we might claim that some of these didn't really matter, only some, or even one did. The difference between these two attributions depends on some imagined counterfactuals. Imagine a factor absent, and judge whether this would have obviated the accident. If it would have, then this is part of the cause. It was a necessary condition. If it wouldn't have, then the burden falls on the other candidates. This is the kind of reasoning which could eventuate in the selection of a shorter list of factors, even at the limit only one. It is the kind of thing that a commission of enquiry would engage in (supposing that this accident had sufficient public significance to justify such a thing).

How would one make such counterfactual judgments? Certainly scientific generalizations might help in certain cases. Some knowledge of how much alcohol there was in the blood of the driver might serve to eliminate the drinks as a cause. But even here, people react differently to liquor in the way it affects their reaction. In the end, we have to make an all-in judgment. Experience may help in this, but not simply by yielding relevant laws. We're in the realm of probable judgment, as with judges in the judicial process, rather than with scientists.

So one thing about stories which tell us how a particular event or outcome arose is that they typically involve a great many factors, some to do with causal relations in the physical world, others with human action. And even where some of these can be illuminated by causal laws, we need an overall judgment. And this, as multifactored as it may be, is a singular causal attribution. *This* accident was caused by night, or fog, or daredevil driving, or slowed reaction time (drink); right through the whole list. And often many factors are familiar to us not simply through causal laws governing their operation.

Another feature of such singular attributions, which R. G. Collingwood pointed out,[4] is that we often select not just through judging which were necessary conditions; we also winnow it further and zero in on the necessary conditions which were under the control of some agent. The agent might be the driver here. He couldn't help the night, fog, ice, bad grading of the road, but he certainly shouldn't have been driving so fast, and under the influence to boot. The judgment serves to underpin a moral assessment. Or if lots of people ended up in the ditch, we might point the finger at the Department of Highways, which insists on designing its roads so badly. This is a moral/political winnowing, where we're interested in what human action could (or could not) have changed the outcome.

We're dealing with a story here where human action plays a minimal part, where human interaction and motivation don't come into it. But what really interests us in this discussion is how stories tell us about the human condition, including the list of things I mentioned above: causes, characters, values, alternative ways of being. But even here in this example of the accident which minimally involves human action, values, and so on (certainly with no human interaction), we have a crucial feature of stories, that they bring together a heterogeneous bundle of factors: different kinds of events and states, and causal links. And in the human case, this is so in spades. A story, whether fictional or historical, will also involve human motivations, actions, interactions, differences of character, longer-term conditions, things good and bad that happen to people—in short, the vicissitudes of fortune, mutual sympathy, antipathy, and a whole gamut of attitudes to others. And more.

A history which tries to explain, say, the outbreak of the First World War, or the French Revolution, or the condition of contemporary Western democracy, will draw together all of the above, with particular emphasis on long-term conditions, economic and demographic trends, cultural differences, *mentalités*, which will have to be integrated with the shorter-term events, and interactions and mutual attitudes among the actors involved in the change.[5] It will be, as in the accident case, a singular attribution;

---

4. R. G. Collingwood, *Idea of History* (Oxford: Oxford University Press, 1993), 178.

5. Paul Ricoeur, in his magisterial *Temps et Récit*, deals with another attempt to sideline narrative, which originates not in Humean epistemology, but in the insights of the Annales School of historians, who wanted to get beyond the froth of superficial change which is given pride of place in "*l'histoire événementielle*", and get to the basic long-term structures which really explain what happens, in their view. Theirs was a history of "*la longue durée*". Ricoeur shows both the inestimable contribution that they made to historiography, and also their insensitivity to the limits of their ap-

and the story will certainly involve a number of more particular singular attributions. Did the (rather irresponsible) assurances given by the Kaiser to the Austrian government constitute a necessary condition for the (very harsh) ultimatum sent to Serbia? Did the flight to Varennes constitute a necessary condition of the radicalization of the French Revolution in August 1792?

At this level of historical explanation, we have seen another fallout of the misguided Humean epistemology, in the popularity of the "covering law" model of historical explanation. This was put forward by philosophers very influenced by Vienna positivists.[6] The idea being basically an application of the Humean view cited above: singular causal attributions cannot be made unbacked by general laws from which this particular causal attribution can be derived.

But this claim falls afoul of the same, or similar, considerations which I invoked in the accident case. First of all, there is the fact of heterogeneity, the great variety of factors, events, states, and so on involved in a story showing how a particular event or state arises; a heterogeneity which is even greater in the case of an historical account than of the enquiry into the road mishap.

But secondly, when we call to mind the know-how that we draw on to make sense of a story about human beings, we can see that the resources are even richer than we dispose of to understand what causes what in the world around us. We cannot at any moment after infancy be without a rich sense of what motivates people, of what is important and unimportant to them, of the differences which people exhibit in this regard, of the different kinds of characters, which show themselves in different modes of response, of the different possibilities of response, of life plan, of aspirations, and so on. To which we must add our sense of the different contexts in which people operate—intimate, familial, political, ecclesiastical, governmental—which grows and develops with our maturity.

---

proach. Even long-term structures undergo change, rise, and eventually may disappear; in a broader sense, these changes have to be seen as "events" (Ricoeur speaks of "*quasi-événements*"). And we can't deploy them effectively in explaining what happens unless we relate their operation to that of the agents actually operative in history, the human beings who propose, undertake, and resist change. See *Temps et Récit,* vol. 1 (Paris: Seuil, 1983), part 2, chapter 1.

6. "Historical explanation, too, aims at showing that the event in question was not 'a matter of chance,' but was to be expected in view of certain antecedent or simultaneous conditions. The expectation referred to is not prophecy or divination, but rational scientific anticipation which rests on the assumption of general laws." C. G. Hempel, "The Function of General Laws in History," *Journal of Philosophy* 39, no. 2 (1942): 39.

Our reception of the singular attribution in a historical text draws on all this understanding, either in commanding our immediate assent (or perhaps rejection), or in guiding the counterfactual thinking by which we test them (were the Austrians really misled by the Kaiser? Does the outbreak of August 1792 not arise from longer-term trends in the revolutionary movement which made the flight to Varennes more of a handy pretext than a cause?)

But how much can this understanding be backed up by general causal laws? At some particular points in regard to certain factors, no doubt. But in regard to all? Hardly likely. And on top of that, there is the matter of combining all the various factors in an all-in judgment. This can never be determined by the generalities we might have at our disposal. It involves a judgment analogous to the moral judgments of which Aristotle speaks in book 6 of the *Ethics,* to which he gives the name *phronêsis.*[7]

We find a justification of this notion of singular causal judgment in Max Weber.[8]

So there are many single causal attributions which can't be wholly grounded on inductive generalizations. But the relation may be loose in the other direction as well; that is, many such single attributions may not be combined to produce a tight inductive rule that would yield something like a law of car accidents, or of the outbreak of wars.

Induction is the paradigm case where knowledge acquired over time by experience can be formulated in a timeless proposition. We observe swans or rabbits at different times and in different places, and come to the generalizations that swans are white, and rabbits eat lettuce. (The first example illustrates that our confident assertions can be upset by the unexpected, but this doesn't fault the process itself.) But this requires that the things and properties that are related in the instances and those figuring in the concluding generalization be exactly the same (like "rabbits" and "eating lettuce"). The conclusion just sums up the instances.

Now the single causal attributions in ordinary life and history are often just too different and varied to ground any simple summation; they may

7. Aristotle, *Nicomachean Ethics,* book 6.

8. See his discussion of "historical individuals" in "'Objectivity' in Social Science," *The Methodology of the Social Sciences,* trans. and ed. Edward Shils and Henry Finch (Glencoe: Free Press, 1949), 78–80. See also the discussion in Ricoeur, *Temps et Récit,* vol. 1, 256–69. Collingwood also gives us some of the background reasoning behind this possibility of singular causal attributions. See his *Idea of History,* 213–15.

give rise to a rule of thumb, or correlation frequently encountered, but not a real inductive generalization. Inductive-type research may lead to interesting insights. We might find that a very high proportion of accidents occur, say, when drivers have just received bad news. And this may lead us to look into what it is about depressed spirits which makes people less careful or observant. The finding might make us add this psychological factor to the long list I enumerated above, but we wouldn't get to a strict induction.

3

Now our grasp of a particular account in history, or in fiction for that matter, is conditioned by our existing understanding of and familiarity with the facets of human life mentioned above. There is, however, also another response to the story; it may change and enlarge this understanding. Reading about certain historical figures may change our sense of human possibility, and of understandable motivations. And this is, if anything, even truer of our reading of literature, or seeing plays or films. They may give us new categories to understand life, a new sense of human possibility, and of the important choices which we have to make. And of course, our actual experience of life may do the same thing.

Examples from literature abound. Aristotle's account of tragedy in the *Poetics* characterizes a crucial insight this form offers. It must of necessity figure noble and not base characters. But these figures do terrible acts. The tragedy shows how this is possible, even unavoidable, thanks to the "flaw" [*hamartia*] in the hero.[9] To see such a tragedy can be to open a new window, a new mode of human possibility, unsuspected before. The modern European novel finds its origins in part in the picaresque, which usually deals with familiar types and their motivations and failings. But then it evolves in many directions, among which is the bildungsroman, which also consists of a series of adventures and experiences, but which are now seen in a new light. The hero comes through this story to an understanding of his vocation, what his life should be about; and what this consists in can't just be detached from the story, and fully expressed in its ending. The insight emerges through the story itself. A new way is offered of defining what a human life can take as its central direction.

9. Aristotle, *Poetics*; see Ricoeur's discussion in *Temps et Récit,* vol. 1, 55–84.

I return to a point I made above in Chapter 6. A novel, as a work of art, doesn't assert anything about life. It is made up of assertions, but these are about the world of the novel. Nevertheless there emerges what I called a nonassertive portrayal of human life, of its choices, issues, travails, fulfillments; and this can open new horizons for the reader. Great novelists: Jane Austen, Honoré de Balzac, Fyodor Dostoevsky, Henry James, have often done just this.

But the suspicion of narrative, which is strong in our philosophical culture, emerges in a new form. It may be conceded that the first articulation of some new avenues and possibilities of human life and understanding comes in the form of a story, either fiction or factual (as in a biography of an exceptional person, or even a meeting of such a person and hearing about his/her life). But surely, the answer comes, the lesson can be detached from this insufficiently explicit and clear form, and we can enunciate in ordinary assertive prose what we have learned.

Well we can try. And in fact, we are always trying, and a great deal of criticism and commentary does just this. *"Le symbole donne à penser,"* as Paul Ricoeur puts it.[10] (For 'symbol' here, read 'work of art'). And certainly much of this is very good and useful. But from that to the conclusion that you can entirely replace the work of art and jettison it while enjoying its insights (throwing aside the Wittgensteinian ladder after one has climbed it), there is a huge leap. No doubt very shallow and uninteresting work can be simply replaced by commentary; but for the most part, the really interesting criticism of rich works requires the text. It is a commentary on the text, which has to be constantly invoked, and which stands afterward as a continuing source of the kind of insight that commentary articulates. So that neither can the causal attributions of history be collapsed into some nomological account by a covering law; nor can the whole range of insights of the best fiction, whether into the causes of action and the gamut of possibilities of aspiration and action, be summed up in some other medium, extracted from the diachronic medium of the story and distilled in timeless assertions about human life.

This certainly fits with a common intuition shared by many of our contemporaries. But there are reasons in principle why this kind of detaching of the "moral" of a story, its translation into a timeless truth, may not be possible.

---

10. "The symbol gives rise to thought." Paul Ricoeur, *Philosophie de la Volonté, Tome 2: Finitude to Culpabilité: La Symbolique du Mal* (Paris: Aubier, 1960), 323 and ff.

Why can't our life experience lead us to a similar summing up in some timeless proposition? Why can't we extract the "moral of the story", either ours, or that of another, either real biographies or fictional portrayals?

Well, of course, sometimes we can: "Don't buy snake oil which is advertised as curing everything from the common cold to cancer" might be a safe example. Or think of well accepted adages like "God helps those who help themselves", or "become aware of your own potential". Good advice perhaps, but the relation of these adages to the biographical, historical, or literary evidence is often not the same as with the case of genuine inductions. The conclusions of these are fully justified by the cases enumerated; they just sum up what we have learned. And something of the sort holds perhaps for the warning against snake oil salesmen. But when we come to cases where we want to say that life has taught us something about important human meanings, things don't work this way. The adages don't relate to the life experiences they're drawn from in the same unproblematic manner. As with car accidents above, biographies are just too different and varied.

But something else is operative in biographies beyond what we have with road mishaps. We are dealing with human meanings. And in fact, what we grasp as an important truth through a story—be it that of our own life, or of some historical event—is so bound up with how we got there—which is what the story relates—that it can't simply be hived off, neglecting the chain of events which brought us there. Our insight is too embedded in the diachronic process which yielded the insight. Induction just sums up the instances which support it; formulations of what life has taught us require that we look back over the experiences we have learnt from to get an adequate sense of what these propositions mean, as well as a sense of their convincing power.

This diachronic embedding is a pervasive feature of human life. We can see this first in the most simple everyday cases. Someone asks you to go into the living room and check if the portrait of Grandpa is crooked (Grandpa's coming to lunch, says Mother, and I thought it looked askew yesterday). So you go in, and what do you do? You put yourself in the best position to observe, square in front, and stand where you command the best line of sight. In doing this, you are drawing on your know-how, developed from infancy, of how to get the best grasp on the situation. It's analogous to the case where you have to move some heavy object with a crowbar. You first get a firm grip on your instrument, something you know how to do from experience.

Now the judgment you make: "no, Grandpa's picture hangs straight", is made in an instant, but your confidence in this ruling draws on your sense that you have a firm grip on this scene, and that confidence is rooted in your having *achieved* this grip. In other words, it is not instantaneous; it draws on a diachronic process.[11]

This is the simplest case. More relevant to our discussion: you come after a long chain of experiences to an insight, about what's important in your life, or in human life in general. You have confidence in this insight, thanks to this chain. But the experience gives you confidence, not because it offers instances which seem to support the insight (although this may also happen), but principally because you now sense, after what you've been through, that a certain illusion, or certain superficiality of approach you used to have, has been overcome; it has been burned out of you, perhaps, by what you've suffered. Or perhaps you were previously operating under what you now see to have been a confusion; or you felt resentment because of unmet expectations, which you now see to have been unjustified.

Here we have paradigm cases of what I have called elsewhere reasoning through transitions.[12] I am confident of the conclusion because of the way I got there; I see this as involving some error-reducing move, out of a more superficial view, or a confused perception, or the interference of an irrelevant resentment, to follow the cases invoked at the end of the previous paragraph.

The analogy to the case of Grandpa's picture should be evident. The story leading up to the insight is crucial to your confidence in it, not because it offers additional "evidence" for the insight, but because it shows that you are now in a better position to see the matter in question. The diachronic basis of the conviction can be made clear in this way: my confidence in my present insight is fed not just by the immediate force of this insight, but from my classing my previous condition, in which this insight was unavailable, as an obstacle to comprehension. An overall take on a two-stage history—before and now—is an integral part of my present conviction.

If we try to look more closely at the way in which a new insight, say, comes to us embedded in our experience, we can often distinguish two interrelated facets of this diachronicity. First the insight may come to us

11. Maurice Merleau-Ponty, *La Phénoménologie de la Perception* (Paris: Gallimard, 1945). Compare the discussion in Chapter 6, section 2.

12. See my "Explanation and Practical Reason," in *Philosophical Arguments* (Cambridge, MA: Harvard University Press, 1995), especially 51–53.

in a particular episode of heightened experience. This episode lends it its convincing power while also encapsulating its meaning. We may formulate the insight in some general proposition, but the basis of our conviction, and often the nuance of meaning of the key words of our formulation, are to be found in the experience.

To convey the insight, we can't rely simply on the formulation, but must somehow convey the experience, the felt intuition. This throws us back into narrative: the narrating, first, of the episode; but then also of the key features of our preceding life against whose background the episode had the meaning and the impact that it did. These two facets are linked.

Some well-known examples from modern novels may illustrate this. The first I will take is from Thomas Mann's *The Magic Mountain,* the famous dream vision which occurs in the chapter "Snow."[13]

In the second winter of his sojourn at the mountain sanatorium at Davos, Hans Castorp becomes restless. He feels a desire to explore the great expanses of sunlit snow that surround the town. So he teaches himself to ski, and one day he sets off and goes very far afield. He recognizes that there is an element of danger; he might get lost, but this spurs him on. "Fear made him realize that he had secretly, and more or less purposely, been trying to lose his bearings."[14] His response is defiance, and he plunges on. Then a snow storm comes, he loses his way. The wind cuts through his thin clothing, and he begins to go numb; his mind wandering. He feels like lying down, and recognizes that this is what happens when one is about to freeze to death. But he is half-ready to resign himself to this. Finally he discovers a hut, leans against it in the shelter it offers, takes a drink from a bottle of port he has brought with him, becomes even more befuddled, and falls asleep.

He dreams that he is in a sunny Mediterranean landscape by the sea. He is moved by the beauty. He sees a beautiful society of young men and maidens, enjoying the sun and sea, full of "friendliness", "gentle reverence", "dignity"[15] [*Freundlichkeit, leichte Ehrerbietung, Würde*]; "all this suffused Hans Castorp with rapture" [*Entzückung*].[16]

But then he comes across something very different, a temple off to one side where horror awaits him: two half-naked old women are dismembering

---

13. Thomas Mann, *The Magic Mountain* (New York: Vintage, 1996).

14. Ibid., 471–72.

15. Ibid., 483.

16. Ibid., 484; Thomas Mann, *Der Zauberberg* (Frankfurt: Fischer Verlag, 2012), 742–43.

and eating a child. They shake their bloody fists at him. Sick and horrified, he tries to escape, and he half-wakes.[17] He ponders how to take this dream. One could conclude that the beautiful society of courteous and charming people has a terrible flaw; that it is built on respect for the horror at its center. Hans considers this, but then offers another reading: death and life are inextricably interlinked, but man is more noble [*vornehmer*] than death. Through love he can lead a life of goodness, in spite of death. "For the sake of goodness and love, man shall grant death no dominion over his thoughts" [*Der Mensch soll um der Güte und Liebe willen dem Tote keine Herrschaft einräumen über seine Gedanken*].[18] This insight fills Hans with energy and warmth. He shakes off his lethargy and finds his way home.

This is—or at least seems to be—a moment of crucial insight. This experience, the dream and the gradual awakening, has its own diachronic unfolding. But it also only makes sense against a deeper background. Hans in his period in the sanatorium has been steeped in a rarified atmosphere, far from the life as an engineer that he was fully engaged in down in the "Flatland". He has been plunged into a milieu where death is omnipresent. He has been shaken loose from the unreflecting, more or less rational liberal humanism which belonged to his bourgeois, professional life down below. The axioms on which this life was founded are the subject of fierce debate between two eloquent thinkers, Settembrini and Naphta, each with his unshakable convictions, whose intellectual jousts Hans has been following, but neither convinces him. Moreover some of the scientific studies he has engaged in seem to show that time is not something solid and objective, that substance dissolves under scientific scrutiny;[19] that life itself issues from decay. He slips toward a kind of fascination with death, in which it can seem a consummation of life, taking us beyond the bounds of time, space, and individuation—a fascination which was one of the recurring forms of Romantic thought and sensibility.[20]

This is the background to his ambivalence on the mountain, why his fear of death can turn him to recklessness, and why he recognizes without immediate alarm that he may be dying of hypothermia.

---

17. Mann, *Magic Mountain*, 485.

18. Mann, *Der Zauberberg*, 748.

19. Michael Beddow, *The Fiction of Humanity* (Cambridge: Cambridge University Press, 1982), 250.

20. "I have been half in love with easeful Death." John Keats, "Ode to a Nightingale," stanza 6, line 2.

It is this uncertainty, this inability or unwillingness to choose decisively for life, which the dream vision dispels. Hans takes a firm stand on behalf of goodness, love and life.

Or does he? Mann gives us lots of reasons to call Hans's firmness into question. Not only does the vision come in a dream, but even the reflection on it that leads to the clear stand is described at the end as part of the dream, of the process of awakening.[21] Moreover, the insight doesn't seem very solid. When he gets back to the Berghof sanatorium and its civilized atmosphere, "he did justice to his supper. His dream was already beginning to fade. And by bedtime he was no longer exactly sure what his thoughts had been."[22] On top of all that, the new insight yields no action. Hans remains many years more in the sanatorium, and he is only brought down by external events, the outbreak of the First World War.

These are indeed objections to the validity of the experience as one of insight. It can indeed shake one's claim to have a new intuition if it depends on such exceptional circumstances of diminished consciousness, and if it cannot survive very long the passing of these circumstances. But I've chosen it as an example here, because valid or not, it has the form of a new insight: first, the short chronology of the powerful experience itself, and second the longer chronology in relation to which it takes its sense; in this case, the experience of moral and metaphysical uncertainty, unmooring, and ambivalence which Hans has gone through in the Berghof, and which now seems overcome and sublated.

To recur to the discussion in Chapter 6, sections 2 and 3, such felt intuitions are essential to our acquiring or taking on ethical convictions, even though they don't have to come in momentary overpowering experiences of the kind Hans lives in his mountain dream. But these intuitions don't exhaust the role of reason in this domain. The "direct" route, where a new experiential clarity seems to come to us, can be challenged by arguments of an "indirect" kind, of which the reflections above on Hans's real convictions in this case provide an example. And there are also other such "external" arguments, to which I shall return below.

That's the step in *Bildung* lived through by Hans Castorp. But it is quite plausible that this expresses a step in learning by the author. How to describe this?

---

21. Mann, *Magic Mountain,* 487.
22. Ibid., 489.

One basic understanding of the human condition throughout Mann's life was what he drew from Schopenhauer and Nietzsche: that life, and the beautiful forms it can create and realize, were inseparable from an urge to destruction, a wild disorder, which ultimately leads to death. The Apollonian is ineluctably linked to the Dionysian in Nietzschean language, in Schopenhauer's terms, the clarity of Representation to the dark force of Will.

There are different stances we can take to this inescapable feature of our condition. We can see it as good grounds to undermine, mock, feel much wiser than Enlightenment hopes for rational improvement, and the modern bourgeois ethic which stresses constructive, rational, instrumental action. This stance can take the corollary that our capacity for artistic creation belongs to this dark side, which is thus unappreciated by bourgeois philistines, even to the point of seeing art as the fruit of disease. (An idea he found in Nietzsche.) Mann seemed to be drawn by something like this in his early career.

Or one can also appreciate the discipline and constructive achievement of bourgeois life, in which Mann's had his roots, and with which he identified, but take an ironic or tragic view of this attempt to control and limit the dark side, doomed in the end to failure; the stance which perhaps underlies *Death in Venice,* and traces certainly one possible fate which threatened Hans Castorp.

But the vision of the "Snow" chapter ends in another stance, at least for Hans Castorp. Without any hope of canceling the ineluctable link between form and destruction, life and death, the response is to espouse with all one's might the cause of life; clearly seeing the constant and irremovable menace but nevertheless engaging fully in holding it at bay.

The moment of insight comes at the point where the opposition between Form and Destruction is at its most evident and disturbing, in the stark contrast of the beautiful life by the sea, and the horrifying sacrifice in the cave temple. Precisely at this moment the insight comes through that the ineluctable doesn't mean the irresistible, that the fact that Destruction can never be vanquished doesn't mean that we can't and shouldn't combat it in the name of Life and Form.

And this insight in this context comes through as a discovery, with the ring of newly grasped truth. The supposition I'm presenting here is that the author of *The Magic Mountain* had himself gone through a similar shift, to a new position which could find expression in the thoughts of his character at this crucial juncture: "grant death no dominion." He then skillfully crafts a description of a defining moment for his character in which this thought convincingly emerges as an undeniable gain in insight.[23]

I'd like to look now at another case, that of Shatov in Dostoevsky's *Devils*. I am thinking of Shatov's moment of insight, expressed in the pithy sentence: "we are all to blame". This brings a new clarity to a facet of Shatov's outlook, but what it mainly relates to and negates is not an earlier phase of his own thought, but the views of other figures in the novel.[24]

Shatov, who is struggling to maintain (or perhaps to achieve) an Orthodox faith in God, which is in turn rooted in that of the Russian people, is responding to the outlook of the new materialist reformers. They see all ills as caused by unfavorable social conditions, and want to abolish the very idea of moral blame.

The difference between Shatov's spiritual and their objectifying perspective comes out at the moment that Shatov's son in born, aided by an unbelieving midwife. Shatov speaks in wonder of "the mystery of the appearance of a new being, a great mystery and an inexplicable one"; to which the unbelieving midwife replies: "A nice lot of drivel! It's simply the further development of the organism, there's nothing in it no mystery."[25]

But in spite of this difference, Shatov is deeply impressed by the human warmth and generosity of this same midwife. "So there's magnanimity in these people, too. . . . Convictions and the person—it seems they're two different things in many ways. Maybe in many ways I'm guilty before them! . . . We're all to blame, we're all to blame, and . . . if only we were all convinced of it!"[26]

With this new insight: we are all to blame, Shatov wants to do more than rehabilitate this concept. He is also implicitly criticizing the dominant religious, national, and hierarchical outlook of Russian imperial so-

---

23. Mann himself asserted that Castorp's words expressing his insight in the "Snow" chapter were the book's message. T .J. Reed, *Thomas Mann: The Uses of Tradition* (Oxford: Clarendon Press, 1974), 274. I have learnt a great deal from this insightful book.

24. This difference between the *Zauberberg*, and *The Devils*, is related to an important difference between the novels. *Zauberberg* is a kind of updating, tinged with parody, of the *Bildingsroman* tradition, which relates the growth and development of a single protagonist. The great novels of Dostoevsky, on the other hand, were in Bakhtin's phrase "polyphonic", see Mikhail Bakhtin, *Problems of Dostoevsky's Poetics,* trans. Caryl Emerson (Minneapolis: University of Minnesota Press, 1984), chapter 1.

25. Fyodor Dostoevsky, *The Devils*, trans. David Magarshack (London: Penguin Classics, 1954), 589.

26. Ibid., 580.

ciety, which morally condemns the reformers and revolutionaries as agents of willful destruction.

But he also sees that the revolutionaries themselves, for all their philosophical rejection of this category, want in fact to cast moral blame on the upholders of the existing order for their resistance to change.

As against these one-sided attributions of responsibility, which in one case is hypocritical and self-deceived, Shatov's vision sees how everybody, each in his or her own way, is at fault. We have all contributed to the moral debacle; and the only way in which the world can be healed and transformed is through our coming together in a common admission of guilt.

The (very Dostoevskyan, and also Christian) vision comes about in a moment of insight, through a rejection of the other reigning views, and is triggered off as a reaction to the dogmatic expression of the polar-opposite slogan of the materialists: "no one is to blame".[27] Its convincing power comes from Shatov suddenly recognizing the universal grip of the same blind spot, in the various parties in conflict, which prevents them seeing their own part in the tragedy, and reflects their need to project evil onto others so as to protect the purity of their own intentions. The insight also includes some sense of how the reconciliation based on this general admission of responsibility could contribute to healing the world.

We can see, in both these cases, an essential feature of such gains in insight, and we might say, in autobiographical self-understanding in general, that it comes, inter alia, in such comprehensive diachronic takes, linking new intuitions to the background they emerge from. The terms in which these takes are cast are internally related, in that each is defined in relation to the others. We are back in those skeins or constellations of interdefined terms which I discussed above in Chapter 6, section 8. These skeins are gestalt-like, as I said, in this interdependence of their elements or aspects. So we can speak of extended or diachronic gestalts: the meaning I'm attributing to my present course and that I attribute to my earlier goals or commitments are not independent of each other, but each only makes sense in the light of the other (in this case, in contrast to each other).

In fact, as we saw earlier, in Chapter 6, section 3, our ethical convictions have this kind of gestalt, overall character: what we recognize as a

---

27. This also echoes Stepan Trofimovitch's cry toward the end of the novel: "Let us forgive . . . : first of all let us forgive all and always. Let us hope that we too shall be forgiven. Yes, because all, every one of us have wronged one another. We are all to blame!" (ibid., 638).

worthy, or noble, activity, has this status in relation to others which are less so, and contrast sharply to still others, which we see as base or unworthy. And this gestalt take on our ethical predicament includes other elements as well. For instance, there is some sense of the moral sources which feed and strengthen this way of life, and of the sort of motivations which impede it. What I'm adding here is that these gestalts extend diachronically, so that the meaning I attribute to my present and past concerns and goals can be in a similar way internally related. The terms in which one describes the past and the present are part of a skein of interdefined descriptions.

But then why can't you just detach these terms, and the conclusion you draw from them, from the diachronic story and treat them as another synchronic gestalt of interdefined terms? Why do they have to remain in the *story*?

Because the duality of reference points that I described in Chapter 6, section 8, applies here in spades. My concluding insight constitutes a reading of the strong experience which triggered it; you can't really understand the conclusion without some sense of the experience. And this experience is inextricably diachronic: deeply colored by the sense I might have that the movement from earlier to later amounted to some gain in comprehension—or perhaps loss, or was just in the end a step sideways. This reading can be upset by later experience, or reflection (as Mann hints in the case of Hans Castorp), and my conclusion may be altered. But what I conclude at the moment is shaped by this experience.

Of course, we are dealing here with what I called in Chapter 6, sections 2 and 3, the "direct" route, where we come to a new felt intuition of what is right or good. But there remain the "indirect" arguments. My intuitive sense of this kind of diachronic gestalt can be challenged by rival interpretations of its elements. For instance, I may think that such and such an earlier concern was an obstacle or a distraction, which stopped me seeing what I know now to be really important, whereas another cherished activity was a good preparation for what I now seek; for instance, that my desire to be liked, or famous, was pulling me off what I now see as my course.

You may try to undermine my conviction that my earlier pursuit of fame was a distraction, by condemning my present goals, or talking up in persuasive terms the life of a celebrity; but if you succeed it will amount to shattering my gestalt, not simply making some punctual change in it.

What this kind of attempt shows is that autobiographical reasoning doesn't *simply* consist in perceiving gestalts. The intuitions which arise in these transitions can be supported or sapped by examining particular phases or aspects; and they can even be undermined by an inductive examination of cases. You can point out to me that I am repeatedly making this kind of reevaluation of my aim in life, at the expense of my previous concerns, and that each such shift is short-lived. Maybe I am deluding myself by the heady sense of a new departure that each new move offers me?[28] But however supported or undercut by such punctual reasons, our autobiographical understanding always incorporate such intuitive convictions.

Or again, when I am induced to give aid to people menaced by famine on the other side of the world, just because of our common humanity, the felt intuition of rightness ratifies this as an important expression of this shared humanity. But even such intuitions are not incorrigible. I may be led to doubt it later on, and learn to mistrust, even despise official, organized "humanitarian" action. In fact, the story may not stop here either. After seeing all the flaws in the action of nongovernmental organizations and governments, I may come to embrace a chastened and more discriminating form of humanitarian action.

But then my mature commitment to the value of this action will be fed by the whole process, original naïve response, and then winnowing through criticism, up to the final mature conviction. This final stance draws its force from the whole history. And we will be back once more with a (renewed and improved) diachronic take or gestalt. Some such take is inescapable, if I am to resolve my doubts and come to a new position.

But keeping this in mind, let's return to the issue raised by biographical transitions like those of our two literary examples. Is it really impossible to "detach the moral" without telling the story? "I won't tell you how I got there, but this is what I think." And I tell you that goodness and love are important, or that we are all to blame. The issue here is: is something crucial lost in the transposition?

Well clearly we lose the convincing power that comes from the transition, and the way it is read by the subject. But do we lose something of the

---

28. Here are examples of what I called in Chapter 6, section 2, the "indirect route" of argument against our felt intuitions.

conclusion as well? Yes, it seems we must. The meaning of the concluding insight: "grant death no dominion", or "we are all to blame", can't be detached from the background from which it emerges. In the case drawn from Mann's novel, the background is the view, inspired by Schopenhauer and Nietzsche, of the inseparability of life and death, beautiful form and destruction. In the foreground are different stances to this basic structural reality. What emerges from in the transition is the greater validity of a new stance.

In the Dostoevsky case, there is a deep Christian background, with a foreground of mutual imputation of blame. The transition takes us to a new deeper vision which dissolves this mutual projection of responsibility.

Now we can easily imagine someone taking up the slogans above (I'd like to adopt both), but it is clear that they will mean something rather different against different backgrounds. The would-be Christian Shatov could take up Hans Castorp's principle, but this would mean something quite different in the context of a Christian view, where the Schopenhauerian sense of the dark, destructive Will was absent, or at least would have to be seen in a different light. Recurring to the discussion in Chapter 7, section 3, about different Ethical views, we saw that they incorporated not just moral rules, but also other elements; in particular, some view of the constellation of motivations, which impede or strengthen our attempts to live up to them. These are clearly different in the two cases. Clearly there would be a large overlap in the kinds of objectively identifiable overt action which both Castorp and our hypothetical Shatov would see as flowing from the principle (and this is not unimportant), but the aspirations to ethical growth, the kind of virtues required for this, these would be very different. Without taking account of differences in background, the sense of the slogans above would remain indeterminate in crucial ways.

There is, of course, the possibility of two people with different Ethical outlooks *converging* toward a similar position, after a fuller exchange of insights about what their commonly accepted slogan means. They would try to explain to each other why certain virtues, and modes of self-change, have to be involved in realizing it, for instance a greater openness to and understanding of other groups or cultures. To the extent that they convinced each other, their positions would come closer together. But a common meaning of the slogan is not a given, but a (hoped-for) achievement.

Absent this achievement, the bland statements of their ethical views elicited from two people may be virtually identical, but some knowledge of their life histories and of the felt intuitions underlying their acceptance of these views may raise the question: are these stances really identical? The felt intuitions may be so different in force, and in their larger resonance in the lives of the two respondents, that we hesitate to put them in the same category.

What only the story can tell us is how the gestalt take, blandly laid out in answer to our question, was formed. What if any were the gestalt-forming cruces, whether instantaneous, or ripening through a protracted development, and only later recognized as such?

Perhaps my conviction that my present ethical outlook represents a gain on my past commitments is based on the sense that it resolves, or at least makes sense of, a dilemma or tension that has long troubled me. Perhaps I felt all along that my commitment to disengaged rationality was at war with some of my "gut feelings" about right and wrong or what is valuable in life; and now that I've read more Goethe (or Schelling, or Hegel), I have a different understanding of reason and instinct which reconciles the two. You can't get what the solution is all about without grasping the terms of the problem. The triad forms a gestalt where the meanings can't be dissociated from each other.

I will borrow a term from Ernst Tugendhat, which he invokes in his interesting book, *Selbstbewusstsein und Selbstbestimmung.*[29] He speaks of an "*Erfahrungsweg*", a "way of experience". My claim could be put in these terms: understanding the outlook (O) at which some agent has arrived may inseparably require that one understand the experience (E) which led her to it.

What we learn from experience biographically couldn't consist exclusively in bald statements of principle. First, there is an ineliminable role for a gestalt take on what is important, worthy or unworthy, desirable or undesirable; to get rid of any overall take altogether, any sense of what is more important than what, would be to take us to the border of an identity crisis. Secondly, these essential gestalts have a diachronic dimension; the meaning descriptions I now espouse must be understood against the background of those I have left behind. And thirdly, the convincing power

---

29. Ernst Tugendhat, *Selbstbewusstsein und Selbstbestimmung* (Frankfurt: Suhrkamp, 1979), 275.

of the new descriptions depends on my sense of how I got there, whether I see the transition as a gain in insight, or alternatively, as a puzzling loss, or just a step sideways.[30]

All this means is that the insight embedded in a story, my story, or that of someone else, or that recounted in a novel, may not be detachable in the sense described above. A biographer may have a different take from mine on the crucial issue of gain and loss. But he has to convey what my experience was, as well as indicating awareness of my illusions or blind spots. In a similar way, the novelist renders the experience of the protagonist, while often maintaining an ironic, or indulgent, or appalled distance from the character's own reading. In the latter type of case, a double reading is being offered of the transition: that experienced by the character, and that suggested by the biographer/author. In different stages of Goethe's *Wilhelm Meister*, the reader can see Wilhelm on the road to insights which he will only grasp later. But both his and our readings of his life are inseparable from the story.

So the full insight imparted by a bildungsroman can't be captured in the one-liner I might give you to sum up the book: the hero comes to see that p. Because crucial to the insight and its convincing power is the novelist's whole portrayal of the life of the protagonist as a learning, a deepening, an overcoming of illusions; (or perhaps a falling into, or continued miring in illusions). The bald statement doesn't have the same meaning outside this context and what it tells us about the illusions and errors we are heir to, and what it means to get beyond them.

But one might want to protest here: is it really impossible to "detach the moral"? Haven't I been doing just this in my account of Hans Castorp's and Shatov's transitions? I've placed their new insights against the relevant background; I've tried to explain why these new insights come across as gains in understanding. What has been left out? Of course, this is no longer giving the conclusion in a one-liner. The dialectical play of background and

---

30. There are several contrasting cases to the biographical transition which gives me confidence in my new insight. I might just experience the change as an alteration in feeling or preference without any epistemic gain or loss, like losing my taste for porridge; or I might be troubled, because the change looks like a loss: I no longer feel committed to certain goals or values, which nevertheless have going for them that people I admire subscribe to them, that they fit better with other things I still hold to, that the constellation of motivations they suppose still seems to make good sense of human life in general. I don't know what to think.

new insight is incorporated, and some description of the way the transition is experienced has been offered. But all this figures in a few paragraphs written at a sitting. There is no more diachronic *story*.

Am I checkmated? Almost. But already considerable concessions have been made to my main claim here: the dialectical picture has been accepted, and some description of the diachronic transition offered. I take these concession gladly, but in the end I don't concede refutation. And that is because of what I called above, and in Chapter 6, the "duality of reference". Yes, I offered a characterization of the transition to show why it was lived as a gain in understanding, but this was just a reading of the diachronic event. It can't simply substitute for an examination of the real diachronic passage in time, on the basis of which my, perhaps inept and certainly too summary, reading was offered. One has to be able to go back to the event. The present account can't make that recurrence otiose.

But one could imagine a last-ditch attempt to rehabilitate timeless conclusions in this area; and indeed, conclusions inductive in form. We concede that induction has no role[31] in the ethical conclusions each person reaches. But the induction is now over the biographies, say, of select wise people. And, of course, some such inductions over biographies can be and are made. I might argue that highly creative people are prey to certain kinds of anxiety, or depression, and the like. (In this I would be resurrecting some of the content of earlier notions of the "melancholic".)[32] But that doesn't mean that inductions like this will yield simply inductive generalizations about ethical outlooks, or what is important in life. Insofar as the concepts in which the lives are described include those for human meanings (and how could they not?), simple inductions can never encompass the whole story.

What the study of whole lives can yield is, of course, adages of the kind mentioned above which purport to be based on wide experience. "God helps those . . ." or "discover your potential" offer good advice, and they do reflect experience. But they can't guide as conclusions of induction do. Adages deal in concepts which are not just summations of the evidence

31. That is, no role in the "direct" development of insight; but an "indirect" role in destabilizing our putative insight is still possible.

32. See Raymond Klibansky, Erwin Panofsky, and Fritz Saxl, *Saturn and Melancholy: Studies in the History of Natural Philosophy, Religion and Art* (Nendeln, Liechtenstein: Kraus Reprint, 1979), 241–54.

they're based on. They require interpretation. What is my potential? What does helping myself mean here? They put in compressed terms certain insights, but you have to recognize that your predicament can be illuminated by them. There is a gap here which has to be bridged by this recognition.

It is in the nature of things that there should be such a gap; and that is because of the differences which exist between people, their experiences, and their self-interpretations. Adages may help; they may illuminate my situation, allow me to see it in a new, and possibly fruitful light. But this application differs from those made by others, where the same adage may be received, also with positive results, in situations rather different from mine. So there is a kind of collaboration here. I lend the adage concrete meaning, in return for which it may guide me.

Otherwise put, there is a possible fruitful interplay between two levels of language; on one side, the compressed formulation of a general insight in the adage or traditional saying; on the other, the terms I need to articulate my particular situation. Bringing them together can produce the insight I need to move ahead.[33] This is another example of the duality of reference points in play.

And we find the same kind of interplay between languages on another level in the complementary discourses of fiction and criticism. The critic often attempts to describe the view of life and of agency that a novel suggests, and this can help us to see the novel in a new light, provided we ourselves find this reading in the novel. But though there can never be a case for replacing the text with the critical summary, a great deal can be gained by the movement back and forth between text and criticism, analogous to Ricoeur's notion that I cited above, expressed in his slogan: "*Le symbole donne à penser*";[34] there is a duality of language that can never be overcome, but can be the source of continuing insight if the two are put in relation with each other.

What assures the continuation of this interplay, and prevents the definitive sidelining of text by critical commentary, is the nature of the issues involved. These concern human meanings, where the attempt to achieve

33. Michael Beddow discusses this relation between adages, or maxims, and experience in his account of Goethe's *Wilhelm Meister*: "The substantial sense of the maxims is drawn out by the represented experiences, the general significance of the represented experiences is concentrated in the maxims. Neither element alone yields a clear meaning; but the interplay of maxims and concrete representation creates a synthesis of the general and the specific, the intellectual and the sensuous, of precisely the sort that Goethe insisted on." Beddow, *Fiction of Humanity*, 78.

34. "The symbol gives rise to thought."

clarity is met by a hermeneutic which can never establish a final interpretation, invulnerable to critique and admitting of no further improvement, as we saw in the Chapters 6 and 7 above.

This means, of course, that understanding oneself or others through biography is a potentially endless process. Any interpretation we reach can be upset, challenged, or amended by a new insight, which will ramify through the whole diachronic gestalt, modifying previous takes, including the one I hold to at the present moment. Any continuities in my self-interpretation cannot amount to a simple repetition of the same take; the repetition, if there is one, must be "nonidentical", in Kierkegaard's sense.[35] I will return to this below.

4

In the previous section, I have been dealing with stories of the growth in insight, the kind of growth described in bildungsromans. But we also tell stories for many other reasons. We may be trying to explain the outcome of a passage in our lives, or those of others, or of whole societies—the kind of thing discussed in section 2 above. Here induction plays a bigger role.

And when we move from autobiography to history, we find an even greater place for induction. For instance, I might want to claim that attempts to run a modern economy without markets, through central planning alone, are bound to produce terrible consequences; and the reasons would be a number of cases, drawn from history: the Soviet Union, pre-Deng China, Eastern Europe before the Wall fell, and so on. Here history is feeding my conviction by providing evidence. But in talking about biography, argument from particular cases usually has a different logic. The goal is to confirm or upset a particular gestalt take, which may in the process acquire or lose its own convincing power; "history" here doesn't offer confirming instances, but it can show the present insight to be reliable or unreliable.

I mentioned above the critic who challenges my sense of a new departure by pointing out how frequently I repeat this claim, with a different motive each time.

35. See note 38 below.

But to recur to the case mentioned above, when I say to you: "Totally planned economies don't work", you may be unconvinced, until I can take you through a number of the individual cases. This works as an induction, because what I need to tell you to convince you doesn't alter the meaning of the proposition. The term "totally planned economies" doesn't alter its meaning from case to case. But most historical claims about what causes what cannot be confirmed in this direct inductive fashion.

The idea that story insights can always be translated into timeless truths, that the narrative form is dispensable for the pursuit of knowledge, like the Humean belief that causal attributions depend on general rules, is a powerful prejudice of modern natural science-influenced culture. In general, to learn about contemporary natural science, you don't need to know how we got there; to learn Newton, you don't need to read about Aristotle and the preinertial theory of natural places.

But things are very different when it comes to human affairs. It was a widespread view among the shallower strands of the Enlightenment to think that we can, and even should, forget about all earlier worldviews, those of cosmic orders, or gods and spirits and magic forces. The new conclusions can be "detached" from the history which preceded them. But we have to ask: how shallow would be our understanding of ourselves if we really managed to forget all that? And how shallow is the understanding which offers only a caricatural picture of these earlier outlooks?

It would seem that a proper, reflective self-understanding—of an individual, a group, or of the whole species—cannot dispense with narrative. It in fact feeds on a back-and-forth between the two forms I mentioned above, story and (philosophical-critical) commentary. It should be clear that neither can simply suffice by itself, abandoning the other.

People are prone to opt for detached distillations, because these would at least be in principle verifiable. But how can you verify the story in a work of art which is admittedly a fiction, is thus a portrayal rather than an assertion? The answer is that the understanding of the human condition offered in a story can be tested. The story tries to make sense of a life, of an historical crux. But does it succeed? This is a question of hermeneutics.

When François Furet and others challenged the mainstream historiography of the French Revolution (often influenced by Marxism), it was by examining the discourse of the revolutionaries, and asking whether certain striking features of this could be accommodated in an account of the Terror which mainly stressed the conflictual situation (invasion of the Coalition, insurrection in the Vendée) in which it arose. Was it the conjunctural necessity of radical action which explained the extreme measures, or something in the outlook and imaginary of the revolutionaries? How could one make best sense of this complex of action and discourse? This is a hermeneutical issue.[36]

5

So my plea here is to see the telling of stories in fact and fiction as a creative or constitutive feature of language. But you can only see this if you go beyond the single sentence and look at texts, complex, drawn-out accounts. This constitutive power is of the greatest importance, because it is through story that we make sense of our lives. We live across time. I have aspirations, and fears; I face opportunities and dangers. I have to understand how to realize the first of each pair and face or head off the second. I need to understand what causes what, what the possibilities are. This is looking forward. But there is also looking back. Maybe I am confident; maybe I feel inadequate. In either case, I need to understand what made me one or the other. Is it genetic fate, or irreparable damage or unalterable strength that my early background gave me? Or is there something I can alter? Or else strengthen, intensify. I read my earlier life, its crucial experiences and its turning points. This may be either to live better in the future, or to arrive at a story which I can live with, like Sophocles made it possible for his contemporaries to live with the fate of Oedipus (through the catharsis of pity and fear).

We cannot have an understanding of self and life which doesn't include some such diachronic reading of the whole through an extended gestalt.

But at any given moment, we occupy a particular place in this extended whole; we are either adolescents, youths, or aged; we are alone or in a family, active or retired; and we have to take account of this in making our assessment. We have to be conscious of who is making the judgment, and from where within the course of life.

But however I do it, through my story, I define my identity. And this is central to being a self. As Alison Gopnik argues, very young babies don't have autobiographical memory, although they may have episodic memory;

36. See above, Chapter 6, section 3.

they can't put the events in their past into a single coherent timeline. "They don't privilege events that they have directly experienced over events they have learned about in other ways. And they don't have a single 'inner biographer', a self who links past and future mental states." Not projecting themselves into the past goes with not projecting themselves into the future. At the same time that children are developing autobiographical memory they are also developing "executive control", which "requires me to care as much about my future self as my current self." These two develop together and are closely associated with consciousness.[37]

The sense that I have a story seems to be a condition of my making plans and decisions, which is integral to what we call being a self. The constitutive power of language here partakes of the two types we described in Chapter 7. It is through the power of making and understanding stories that I have access to myself as a self. But we also say that it is only in this, at first dialogical, but later potentially monological, discourse of storytelling that I *become* a self.

So making sense of our lives is something we need to do, and strive to recover where this is threatened or lost. This is not to say that any sense will do. You may say to me: "You are always negative, puncturing other people's balloons; whenever someone has a positive project, you undermine it". I may be offended and try to explain myself in different terms; or I may say to myself: "She's bang on. I have higher standards than other people. I pitilessly criticize their illusions". So the kind of sense matters. But nevertheless, the sense that my life is disjointed, or doesn't add up, is painful, something I seek to overcome. This doesn't mean that there has to be a single purpose running through the whole story. I may take pride and satisfaction in my ability to reinvent myself periodically, taking on new projects, new occupations or professions. Still being this kind of inventive-adaptive person is something I take pride in, part of my identity.

What is threatening or painful is the absence of the kind of connections that I need to make acceptable sense. For instance, in the examples of accounts of a life we discussed above, which recount the discovery of our vocation or true form, the stuff of bildungsromans, it is essential that I understand myself, at least retrospectively, as seeking. My earlier experi-

37. Alison Gopnik, *The Philosophical Baby: What Children's Minds Tell Us about Truth, Love, and the Meaning of Life* (New York: Farrar, Straus and Giroux, 2009), chapter 5, 147 and ff.

ences are seen as takes on a reality which is now for the first time really grasped. The confidence that I (or the hero of the novel) have (has) is based on the sense of having achieved something I was aiming for. Large tracts of my earlier life come together as parts or stages in this long-lasting attempt. Without this, the meaning I thought I saw falls apart.

There are other kinds of breaks or disjunctions which threaten meaning. One of the things I value in life will probably be the periodic recurrence of moments of higher, more intense, pleasurable or meaningful life: annual reunions with my family, or visits to some beautiful spot by the sea, or reunions of old friends, or visits to Bayreuth or Salzburg. But then a moment comes when I return to these meetings or festivals and the experience falls flat. It's as though I have been expelled from the place where life's meaning was most intense. This meaning was sustained in a repetition which now seems beyond reach. This is the experience recounted by Kierkegaard (or Constantin Constantius).[38] One is exiled from the life that made (livable) sense for one.

But life can break into pieces at a more micro level. I want to explore this further in the proposed companion study in connection with the "spleen" of Baudelaire, and Walter Benjamin's commentary on it.

And, on the other side, there are suddenly powerful reconnections, such as Marcel Proust recounts in *Le Temps retrouvé*,[39] where the meaning locked in a long-forgotten experience returns with all the force it gains from this reconnection, annulling the separation wrought by vast tracts of *temps perdu*.[40]

It is through story that we find or devise ways of living bearably in time.

38. Soren Kierkegaard, "Repetition," in *Kierkegaard's Writings, Vol. VI,* trans. Howard V. Hong (Princeton, NJ: Princeton University Press, 1983), 168 and ff. Kierkegaard's notion of the proper response to this kind of loss/exile is a change in the self, or a shift in the dimension in which it operates (into the religious dimension). The loss comes from an insistence on *identical* repetition, from too great a fixation on recollection; see 131–33.

39. Marcel Proust, *A la Recherche du Temps Perdu, Tome 7: Le Temps Retrouvé* (Paris: Gallimard, 1990).

40. In the later nineteenth century, philosophers started to examine the nature of lived time, as against the time of physics and cosmology. This examination has also been a kind of rehabilitation. Bergson is a major figure in this succession, as Heidegger has been. But lived time has also emerged as a new frontier for the novel: we can cite here, Joyce, Woolf, and Proust; they have multiple continuators in the twentieth and twenty-first centuries. This obviously raises issues about the relation of lived to cosmic time. See Paul Ricoeur, *Temps et Récit,* vol. 3 (Paris: Seuil, 1991).

9

The Sapir-Whorf Hypothesis

I'd like to take up here the issues around the Sapir-Whorf hypothesis, because I believe that they appear in a very different light than usually shines on them, once one takes account of the discussion in the previous chapters.

The basic idea has been described as the hypothesis "that the semantic structures of different languages might be fundamentally incommensurable, with consequences for the way in which speakers of different languages might think and act. On this view, language, thought and culture are deeply interlocked, so that each language might be claimed to have associated with it a distinctive world-view."[1]

This might be thought to be a prejudicial way of putting the matter, so we should look at some of the formulations of the two protagonists, Edward Sapir, and Benjamin Lee Whorf. First Sapir:

> Human beings do not live in the objective world alone, let alone in the world of social activity as ordinarily understood, but are very much at the mercy of the particular language which has become the medium of expression for their society. It is quite an illusion to imagine that one adjusts to reality essentially without the use of language, and

1. John J. Gumperz and Stephen C. Levinson, *Rethinking Linguistic Relativity* (Cambridge: Cambridge University Press, 1996), 2.

that language is merely the incidental means of solving specific prob-lems of communication or reflection. The fact of the matter is that the 'real world' is to a large extent unconsciously built up on the lan-guage habits of the group. No two languages are ever sufficiently similar to be considered as representing the same social reality. The worlds in which different societies live are distinct worlds, not merely the same world with different labels attached.[2]

And Whorf announced a new principle of relativity:

It was found that the background linguistic system . . . of each lan-guage is not merely a reproducing instrument for voicing ideas but rather is itself a shaper of ideas, the program and guide for the indi-vidual's mental activity, for his analysis of impressions, for his syn-thesis of his mental stock in trade.

No individual is free to describe nature with absolute impartiality but is constrained to certain modes of interpretation even while he thinks himself most free. . . . We are thus introduced to a new principle of relativity, which holds that all observers are not led by the same physical evidence to the same picture of the universe, unless their linguistic backgrounds are similar, or can in some way be calibrated.[3]

But before we can assess this hypothesis (or perhaps hypotheses), we have to be clear, first, what is being claimed, and second, for what domain of language the claim is being made. In general, the claim seems to be that different ways that languages have of encoding natural or social reality have "consequences for patterns of thought about reality."[4] But this general formulation can cover rather different theses, some of which are banal and unfrightening, and others of which are dramatic challenges to intersubjec-tively valid knowledge. The claim could just be that different ways of for-mulating some scene or state of affairs which belong to different languages

2. Edward Sapir, *Culture, Language and Personality: Selected Essays* (Berkeley: University of Cali-fornia Press, 1961), 69.

3. Benjamin Lee Whorf, *Language, Thought and Reality: Selected Writings of Benjamin Lee Whorf,* ed. John B. Carroll (Cambridge, MA: MIT Press, 1956), 212, 214.

4. John A. Lucy, "Linguistic Relativity," *Annual Review of Anthropology* 26 (1997): 294.

(Hopi and English, for instance) draw attention to different features and relations, and that this can influence the way people react to that situation, or what they will spontaneously notice in it, or what they tend to remember afterward.

But when talk turns to the "incommensurable", or "distinct worlds", or "a principle of relativity" which yields different pictures of the universe, the claim seems to be the more drastic one, that we are somehow locked within our mode of thinking, unless we can manage to rise above it, and see its contingency.[5]

These claims are on a different level of severity. We could be induced to ask: what is the real "Sapir-Whorf hypothesis"? But I don't think this is useful. That is because claims of different levels of severity are pertinent to different kinds of description. This is a point which we can now make, on the basis of the earlier chapters.

The crucial distinction here is the one that was central to Chapter 6, between the different semantic logics, and which also is relevant to Chapter 7.

Let's take, for example, descriptions of our surroundings, where the terms are governed by the "designative" semantic logic, that which aims at the accurate description of an independent reality. And we could take a difference in encoding strategies between languages, which John Lucy discusses in the article just cited,[6] the case of "number marking".

In English and most European languages, we can distinguish two kinds of terms: count nouns and mass nouns. The former can occur in the singular and the plural, and the number of instances can be marked by numerals plus the appropriate forms, singular or plural (or in archaic languages like classical Greek, singular, dual and plural). So "one horse", "two horses". Mass nouns only appear in the singular; as the term "mass" suggests, they designate kinds of stuff that can appear indeterminately in large or small amounts. Examples are "butter", "gold", "corn". If we want to count instances of the appearance of these kinds, we need a "numeral classifier". So we speak of a "pat" of butter, a "bar" of gold, an "ear" of corn.

---

5. Of course, there is a further claim, even more drastic, that we are imprisoned in our mode of thought, and can never rise above it. But I leave this aside because both Sapir and Whorf put forward their hypothesis as a way of liberating us from our narrow identification of our own outlook as the only correct one, or the only "civilized" or "rational" one. See Whorf, *Language Thought and Reality*, 218.

6. Lucy, "Linguistic Relativity," 297–98. See also John A. Lucy, *Grammatical Categories and Cognition: A Case Study of the Linguistic Relativity Hypothesis* (Cambridge: Cambridge University Press, 1992).

Now languages differ in the preponderance of these different kinds of noun. English has lots of count nouns. In Yucatec Mayan, most nouns are mass, and numerals only accompany the numeral classifiers. So pigs appear primarily as instances of an undifferentiated substance, which could be translated into English as "pig" or "pork". It can be argued that this structural difference in manner of encoding leads to behavioral differences between English and Yucatec speakers when they are given tasks like sorting and classifying objects.[7] But whatever the differences in phenomenological experience which this behavioral divergence may signal, it is clear that each language has the resources to encode the same states of affairs. Indeed, there are cases in English where one can apply either encoding strategy. "I must buy ten cows" can be expressed as "I must buy ten head of cattle", where "cattle" operates as a mass noun.

The point here is that differences in lexicon and grammar require that we pay attention to different things. Whereas a Yucatec speaker might say: "I saw bird [mass noun] on the lawn", and English speaker would have to be more precise about number; she would say "a bird", or "some birds", or just "birds". The lexico-grammatical properties of a given language may force us to encode certain features in describing a given situation.

Examples abound of such differences between languages. Some tense systems mark differences of aspect, like perfective/progressive ("he ran" vs. "he was running"), which again force precision on an issue that other languages leave aside. Or again, English tends to encode manner of locomotion as describing movement: He walked/ran/swam/fell down; while other languages tend to leave this aside or describe it with ancillary means. German and Russian don't allow you to say "he went" without indicating whether it was by foot or vehicle.[8]

What is the significance of such differences? Even Franz Boas, the inspirer of Sapir, assumed that we have in our minds a "complete concept" of the objects of experience, in the form of a "mental image".[9] And various theories of cognitive science have developed the notion of an

---

7. Lucy, "Linguistic Relativity," 297–98. See also Whorf, *Language Thought and Reality,* 140–42. When English and Yucatec people are asked to sort triads of objects to indicate the two more like each other, the English tend to associate by shape, and the Yucatec by material. See John A. Lucy, "The Scope of Linguistic Relativity" in Gumperz and Levinson, *Linguistic Relativity,* 51–52.

8. Dan Slobin, "From 'Thought and Language' to 'Thinking for Speaking,'" in Gumperz and Levinson, *Linguistic Relativity,* 70–96.

9. Gumperz and Levinson, *Linguistic Relativity,* 72.

underlying "language of thought", which different languages draw on.[10] The notion would be here that the full multifaceted reality impinges on the knowing subject, even though the verbal formulations select some aspects rather than others. "Thinking for speaking" involves selectivity, but thinking tout court may be unrestricted; we may always be taking in the facets of reality which our language tends to ignore or downplay. In which case, the Sapir-Whorf hypothesis would be simply wrong. The fact that speakers of a given language often have more roundabout means of coding the facets they don't foreground seems to point in this direction.

Another area where differences of linguistic coding have been thought to produce differences in experience is that of color categories. Languages differ in the profusion or sparseness of their color words. Does this mean that speakers of the "sparser" languages don't register differences which people with richer vocabularies do? Opponents of the Sapir-Whorf hypothesis have done research which reveals that the same basic color distinctions can be made by speakers of languages with different color vocabularies. Asked if they can discriminate, people seem to be responding to the same perceptual categories, even if the terms in current use in their respective languages seem rather divergent.[11]

All this doesn't mean that there is no content at all to the hypothesis of linguistic relativity in this domain of encoding. Plainly different lexica and grammars make different features salient. Thus there seem to be "significant language effects on memory" of differences in color terms,[12] and we should recall the way that differences in number marking make English and Yucatec speakers match samples in different ways. Nevertheless, languages of rather different lexico-grammatical structure seem either to have the linguistic means to encode the same reality—if only more indirectly and laboriously—or to be able easily to acquire them through small and punctual additions to their vocabulary.

10. See, for example, Jerry Fodor, *The Language of Thought* (Cambridge, MA: Harvard University Press, 1975).

11. Steven Pinker, *The Language Instinct: The New Science of Language and Mind* (New York: Harper Perennial, 1995), 61–67; Paul Kay, "Methodological Issues in Cross-Language Color Naming," in *Language, Culture and Society: Key Topics in Linguistic Anthropology*, ed. Christine Jourdan and Kevin Tuite (Cambridge: Cambridge University Press, 2006).

12. Lucy, "Linguistic Relativity," 299–300.

In neither of the above cases is there occasion to speak of "incommensurability", or "different worlds".[13]

But things are different when we turn to the "metaphysical" level, by which I mean the range of our most general and fundamental concepts, dealing with time, space, and the most general features of reality. This is the level on which Whorf's most important and spectacular claims were made. Whorf attributed to "Standard Average European" (SAE) languages a penchant for spatializing and objectifying time; so that we can treat different cycles in time (like day or year), and count them. We speak of "ten days", as we might speak of "ten cows". Time is seen in this construal as an abstract medium which can be filled with whatever events come to pass. In the contrast case of Hopi, this sideways-on, objectified understanding of time is impossible. Time is event, and we are in the middle of its unfolding. So the Hopi won't say: "I'll leave in ten days", but "I'll leave after the ninth day" (from now).[14] Days are numerated not in cardinals but in ordinals. Moreover, time cannot be separated from what is happening in it, from the growth, or the decay, that is occurring. There is no "homogeneous, empty time" (to quote Walter Benjamin).[15]

Now here indeed, is a deep "incommensurability", and of a mind-boggling sort. We find it hard to make sense of this view of the world. And this is partly because the development of post-Galilean natural science, that is, of a science of the physical world whose success is bound up with its eschewing of distinctions like growth/decay (at least outside biology), has accustomed us to a "bleached" view of the universe. We no longer want to speak of "cosmos" in its original sense, where the term was intrinsically linked to an understanding of proper order. We can no longer live in this cosmos, now that we are aware of the (post-Galilean) universe. And moreover, we know that the cosmos-type views that dominate earlier

---

13. The same could perhaps be said of the difference in expressions of spatial placing between English and Maya, discussed in Chapter 5, section 4, where one language says that an object is "at the top of the tree", and the other says that it is "in its head".

14. Whorf, *Language, Thought and Reality*, 140.

15. Walter Benjamin, "Theses on the Philosophy of History," in *Illuminations*, trans. Harry Zohn (New York: Schocken, 1968), 261. This is perhaps to attribute to the structures of SAE languages in general what belongs to Western modernity. Even Machiavelli uses "*i tempi*" in a way which discriminates them by the happenings intrinsic to them. See Heidegger, "The Age of the World Picture," in *The Question concerning Technology and Other Essays*, trans. William Lovitt (New York: Harper and Row, 1977), 115–54.

societies (and of which the Hopi outlook is an example) are no longer sustainable.

This is not to say that the views of order that pertain to cosmos conceptions have no more relevance for us. On the contrary, we cannot do without conceptions of order, ethical, moral, social, political. It is just that they have to be anchored differently. Their earlier cosmic anchorings are no longer credible, and in this sense the earlier understandings are wrong, and need amendment. But the new reanchored conceptions may owe much to the older ones, may transpose them to a new register.

Thus the notions of ethical order, which we saw in ancient Greek ethics, in the work of Plato and Aristotle, can be detached from their notions of cosmic order, and recur in new understandings of human nature. Political orders of equality can be detached from the old polis- or republic-contexts, and given a new basis in modern ideas of citizenship, nondiscrimination, participation.

And earlier understandings of the cosmos as the locus of signs, which can speak to us, have been transposed by writers of the Romantic period into a new register, a move that I want to explore in more detail in the proposed companion study on post-Romantic poetics.

And in parallel to all these changes, the notion of an empty cosmic time, shorn of human meaning, has led to a recognition of the ways in which lived time has distinct forms of its own, as we see in the writings, inter alia, of Bergson,[16] Heidegger,[17] Ricoeur;[18] and these forms have been explored in the works of Baudelaire, Proust, Eliot, and a host of others. This will be a theme of the proposed companion study.

Now insofar as the earlier cosmos views are shown to be inadequate and unsustainable, the fact of their incommensurability with our own categories loses some of its sting. So while the response to the different coding strategies discussed above might just be that the differences are minor and undramatic, our reply to the deep and baffling differences between English and Hopi conceptions of time could just be: "so what?" Incommensurability can easily generate incomprehensibility, but this is only troubling

---

16. Henri Bergson, *Time and Free Will: An Essay on the Immediate Data of Consciousness,* trans. F. L. Pogson (Mineola, NY: Dover, 2001).

17. Martin Heidegger, *Being and Time,* trans. John Macquarrie and Edward Robinson (New York: Harper and Row, 1962).

18. Paul Ricoeur, *Temps et Récit,* vol. 3 (Paris: Seuil, 1991).

if there is something here we need to understand in order to make sense of our world.

But of course, there still is something of this order. We don't need to study Hopi metaphysics to correct the views of Newton and Einstein, and get a better grasp on the universe qua devoid of human meanings (although Whorf seems to imply that Hopi metaphysics could better prepare us for modern relativity theory[19]). But to understand ourselves we have to grasp how we got to where we are, and this must include a grasp of where we came from. And this need to understand the other doesn't just relate to past social and metaphysical forms. We are faced today with great differences in contemporary cultures, in the skeins of meaning that they elaborate, in the forms of society that they can sustain.

And so we come to a third range of cases; beyond the modes of encoding our surroundings, beyond the deep metaphysical gulf that divides us from earlier societies, the crucial site where the Sapir-Whorf hypothesis applies is in the area of contemporary cultural differences. By the very nature of modern life, these are to be found within contemporary societies, as well as between them.

If we look at the ethical, and/or spiritual differences between people who are equally "modern", in the sense that they value and in some cases, practice, and extend modern science, depend on and apply modern technology, function within modern systems of organization—states, bureaucracies, markets, and the like—it is clear that their diverse understandings of human meanings, ethical ideals, and aspirations to self-transformation are frequently opaque to each other. And this even within the same society, let alone differences with societies which are geographically and historically more distant.

And if we look at different polities, we can see that their social imaginaries are often very different from each other. Far enough apart so that attempts to introduce "democracy" on the Western model can lamentably fail, or even lead to social disintegration (contemporary Libya?). And even polities which are alike in being democratic may be sustained by social

19. "Does the Hopi language show here a higher plane of thinking, a more rational analysis of situations, than our vaunted English? Of course, it does. In this field and in various others, English compared to Hopi is like a bludgeon compared to a rapier." Whorf, *Language, Thought and Reality,* 85.

imaginaries which are very different from each other. Witness the case of India, in comparison to countries of the Northwest.[20]

In the terms of the discussion in this book, it is those areas of our language which fall under the second semantic logic, the constitutive one, where the issues raised by the Sapir-Whorf hypothesis are most pertinent and alive: issues of human meanings (Chapter 6), and of footings and social structures (Chapter 7). It is aberrant to think that one can dismiss these issues entirely by showing that the Inuit don't have that many words for different kinds of snow, or that color vocabularies have less impact on color discriminations, than was thought.[21] These latter involve questions about different ways of encoding the *same* external reality; but when we are looking at divergent ethical or religious ways of life, or distinct political structures and social imaginaries, we are dealing with different human realities. We have, for instance, lives informed by different ethical ideals, and societies structured around different footings and social imaginaries. To treat these like differences in color vocabularies is not only aberrant but dangerous, since it reflects the unconscious projection of modern Western categories on the whole of humanity. And this situation is deeply ironical. Since it is precisely this (largely unconscious but in the end arrogant) projection that both Sapir and Whorf strove to overcome by raising the issues of linguistic relativity.[22]

Nor does recognizing this plunge us into moral uncertainty and "relativity". It means rather that the only road to mutual understanding, and perhaps ultimately agreement on moral and political principles, lies through patient mutual study and equal exchange, leading perhaps to the "fusion of horizons" of which Hans-Georg Gadamer spoke, something which is at heart an exercise in hermeneutics.[23]

I have been speaking of differences of ethical outlook and social imaginary, but there are also modes of diversity of discourse within what we rec-

20. See the illuminating work of Mukulika Banerjee, *Why India Votes? (Exploring the Political in South Asia)* (London: Routledge, 2014).

21. Pinker, *Language Instinct,* 61–67.

22. Speaking about "European dialects and heir rationalizing techniques," Whorf says: "They, and our own thought processes with them, can no longer be envisioned as spanning the gamut of reason and knowledge but only as one constellation in a galactic expanse." Whorf, *Language, Thought and Reality,* 218.

23. H.-G. Gadamer, *Truth and Method,* trans. Joel Weinsheimer and Donald G. Marshall (London: Continuum, 2004); Hubert Dreyfus and Charles Taylor, *Retrieving Realism* (Cambridge, MA: Harvard University Press, 2015), chapter 6.

ognize as languages which are incomprehensible without some grasp of their social and human meanings. Lev Vygotsky,[24] Mikhail Bakhtin,[25] and Basil Bernstein[26] have pointed to this phenomenon: different modes of discourse arise within a single society, which connect to social class, to differences in training and expertise, to particular walks of life, and the like.

On one hand, these can be "registers" that you can move in and out of.[27] If you are an English gentleman in the nineteenth century, you will speak differently before Queen Victoria (if you are ever admitted to the Presence), than you will quaffing port with your friends, than you will in Parliament, than you will addressing the local fête. On the other hand, some of these registers are unavailable to others; being able to enter them is the mark of a certain class or rank.

But these registers are defined not just by vocabulary (don't say "blimey" in front of the Queen), but also by modes of rhetoric, by stance toward the audience (de haut en bas toward the tenants gathered for the fête, with deferential respect for the Queen, toward fellow insiders when talking to Parliament); or toward the object (distanced and objectifying if we are discoursing among scientists and the learned, involved and passionate in declaring love). You can't engage in discourse in a given register without a sense of the footings and meanings it involves at all these levels. Learned speech takes its distance from emotional resonances; it speaks of "cathexis", rather than "desire", of a "dispute" occurring, and not a "flaming row". And this reflects the sense that truly objective reasoning is dispassionate. Paradoxically, all this disengaged behavior, stance and tone, is meant to embody dispassion. This register can't be properly inhabited if one doesn't "get" this.

These registers are like "dialects" which we cannot master without grasping the meanings and footings they embody and enact. These are matters which can only be articulated within the constitutive semantic logics. As dialects, they are not necessarily intertranslatable.

---

24. Lev Vygotsky, *Mind in Society: The Development of Higher Psychological Processes* (Cambridge, MA: Harvard University Press, 1978).

25. See his concept of "heteroglossia" in Mikhail Bakhtin, *The Dialogic Imagination: Four Essays* (Austin: University of Texas Press, 1992).

26. Basil Bernstein, *Class, Codes and Control: Theoretical Studies towards a Sociology of Language, Vol. 1* (London: Routledge, 1971).

27. See discussion in Chapter 7.

Of course, I have been dealing here with a narrow range of registers, register types, and register differences. The ones I've been discussing here are associated with class, or métier, or expertise, are involved in different modes of deference and hierarchy, and are relatively stable and long-lasting. In one case, that of "learned" or "scientific" language, they extend cross-nationally to whole civilizations. In fact, different natural languages have been pulled closer to each other in lexicon, grammar, and syntax by the learned, technical, administrative, objectifying, and generalizing languages developed in more powerful, formerly colonial, but now still hegemonic societies.

But there are other different kinds of register differences, for instance between those in use in smaller, more intimate milieu, and those which serve to communicate to a broader public. And this type of register difference can be repeated on many levels. There can be a marked difference between the way we communicate in the family and the kinship group, as against how we speak to outsiders; or the in-group may consist of members of a certain ethnicity or religion, within the broader multicultural society. In each case the more intimate group operates with its own modes of discourse, paradigm references (to people or events which have special resonance for us), sense of humor, and so on, which can't easily transfer into our relations with the broader society.

In addition, registers may be less fixed than some of the earlier list of examples are, or at least seem to be. In modern society, hierarchical relations are more and more challenged, and some of these involve subordinates pushing hitherto "inappropriate" modes of discourse on "superiors", as we see with the pressure to abandon hierarchically differentiated modes of address. In many European societies, the "tu/vous" distinction, and its analogues, is being breached in favor of the universalization in some cases of the "polite" form (already achieved in English with "you"), or at least the abolition of asymmetrical forms, where superiors say "tu" to inferiors who address them as "vous" (in my lifetime in Quebec, this has come about in relations of parents to children).

In addition, in multicultural societies, the boundary conditions of certain registers may be no longer so clear as they were in earlier hierarchical societies; register has to be frequently renegotiated, which in effect leads to change. Rules are creatively broken. The system is constantly in some degree of flux.

But even with fluidity and change—perhaps especially with this fluidity and change—being a speaker of a widespread modern language requires sensitivity to the meanings and footings that underlie these registers and their shifting boundaries. Just learning the language with Rosetta Stone doesn't make you fully capable of functioning in the society (and perhaps no one is truly *fully* capable of this). This is another Sapir-Whorfian effect that is part of everyday life in contemporary society.

Once one grasps the importance of the constitutive uses of language, the issues raised by Sapir and Whorf appear in a quite different light.

10

Conclusion

The Range of Human Linguistic Capacity

1

So what is the human linguistic capacity?

It doesn't just consist in encoding information, and passing it on, as I argued in Chapter 3. This encoding is indeed a remarkable capacity, which we don't fully understand, and which we might suppose follows some innately available guidelines, genetically handed on (even if the Chomsky-Pinker version has problems).

Encoding, in fact, allows us to store information and knowledge, given certain means of passing it on, if only instructing by elders, or learning the sagas of the tribe by heart. This has had immeasurable consequences in the development of human cultures and technologies. The knowledge thus accumulated makes possible informed instrumental deliberation, planning, the devising of new modes of organization and operation in the world.

But the discussion in the preceding chapters has shown that there is much more to language than this. We do indeed, observe, inform ourselves about the world of self-standing objects, and do all sorts of things with the information. But we also build ourselves landscapes of meanings, both human meanings and footings (and these are related). We make these meanings exist for us by enacting them, then expressing them, naming them, critically examining them, arguing about them, fighting (sometimes) about them (e.g., egalitarians struggling to transform a hierarchical culture).

Language here has a constructive, or constitutive, function. Not just the general constitutive power which being inducted into language gives us to invent new terms, new modes of expression; but the special ones to open us to meanings, and involve us in footings.

So we have to widen our conception of our linguistic capacity, to take in these two special modes of constitution: the first involves the mapping of human meanings: normative (ethical and quasi-ethical), and descriptive (characterizations of how things are with us), which we enact, name, describe, and argue over. The second defines the footings which we set up and sustain in discourse, while also naming and justifying and contesting them in social life.

This is a first dimension of expansion that we have to concede to the linguistic capacity. We wouldn't be able to generate the ability to encode without creating and sustaining the relationships, and identifying the meanings, that we live by.

The media of these constitutive exercises are not only (1) verbal, but also (2) enactive. But we have right away to recognize another range of media: there are also (3) what I have called portrayals, in literature, music, painting, dance which "present" [*darstellen*] meanings while neither describing them (making assertions), nor enacting them. This range of media appears to call on our abilities to enact and describe, but is distinct from them.

Looked at from another angle, the linguistic capacity is essentially more than an intellectual one; it is embodied: in enacted meanings, in artistic portrayals, in metaphors which draw on embodied experience, and also in the iconic gestural portrayal which accompanies everyday speech, not to mention the ubiquity of "body language"—tone of voice, emphasis, expressive gesture, stances of intimacy, of aloofness—which surround ordinary discourse.

From another angle again, the linguistic capacity is essentially shared: it sustains a shared consciousness of the world, within which individuals differentiate themselves by becoming particular voices in an ongoing conversation. This shared understanding develops a place for monological speech and writing, but this option is available for us only because we are inducted into speech as conversation.

So our language straddles the boundary between "mind" and body; also that between dialogical and monological. There is also a third distinction which is often invoked, that between signs which are arbitrary or "unmotivated" and those which are iconic or "motivated". Here too, I argued in

Chapter 9 that the combinatorial nature of language requires the unmotivated sign, but the iconic can't be banished, as we see in metaphor, in templates (Chapter 5), in iconic gestures; and when we come to enacted meanings, the distinction makes no sense.

It would be hard to imagine a human speech which could do without the range of features just described: for instance without enactment, body language, artistic portrayal, embodied experience, or communion. The only one of these one could "imagine away", in the sense of writing a science fiction story, would be a tribe without any art, because the damage that would do is not easily calculable.

As to embodiment, one might imagine that speech is an optional sign system, which the "mind" can use to communicate "ideas", as we use different systems of writing, or codes to get our thoughts across to others. And something like this was mooted in the eighteenth century, where some supposed with Condillac that sign language preceded speech.

And indeed, we know that sign languages are possible. But when we reflect how they become possible and even necessary, we are brought back to the original learning situation, in which they become the medium of an intense bodily exchange with others, through which our language capacity is built up. This shows how closely language is tied to (interpersonal) embodiment.

All of the above: the special modes of constitution, the three media (verbal, enactive, portrayal), the distinctions (mental/bodily, mono-/dialogical, arbitrary/iconic) that language straddles, still doesn't exhaust our theme: the nature of the linguistic capacity. There is also the nature of linguistic awareness or experience we discussed in Chapter 3. Our being a linguistic animal makes another kind of difference here, beyond what we enact, define, or communicate. Our linguistically formed experience of the world is full of liminal meanings, which invite articulation, but can easily be ignored, while we are intent in our pursuit of other ends. This is what I called, building on Heidegger's terms, our "protodwelling".

2

We might try to approach our question here from another angle. What had to evolve, through the different species of hominids, for our language capacity to develop? Our guiding thread here would be the essential features of language which we have and our primate cousins lack.

First among these is obviously our capacity for joint attention, or communion. I mean the capacity to bring out certain phenomena "for us", in shared attention, as against their being just for me and for you, severally. This is a difference which is widely recognized today by theorists of the ontogenesis of language.[1]

Sometimes this point is put by saying that we have a more adequate "theory of mind" than other primates. But this expression still privileges the case where one organism observes another and "reads" it well or badly, or in certain dimensions not at all. But this is a secondary phenomenon. The crucial condition for human language learning is *joint* attention, although it is obvious that creatures capable of this kind of communion will become much more capable of "reading" each other, even where communion is denied or out of the question.[2]

But beyond this, there is another change, which one can perhaps see already at work not just in primates, but also in mammals which are close to us. Robert Bellah has explored this in his trailblazing work, *Religion in Human Evolution*.[3] He points to the growing importance of play among these higher animals, especially among the young of the species, that is, their tendency to engage in mock fights (dogs) or mock captures (cats chasing a piece of string). There is an obvious analogy with human life, and Johan Huizinga, whom Bellah cites, has done much to bring out the importance of play in human culture.[4] Of course, one could object that this analogy anthropomorphizes the animals concerned. But we don't need to think of animal "play" as exactly like ours. We can think of it as an evolutionary step or platform, on which later developments built: a kind of protoplay.

Bellah identifies this protoplay as a platform for the human (and perhaps also hominid) development of ritual. But he recognizes that it also

1. See Michael Tomasello, *Constructing a Language* (Cambridge, MA: Harvard University Press, 2003), 22.

2. And it is probably true that the development of capacities for empathy and identifying the emotions of others among our primate relatives provided the evolutionary platform from which our joint attention emerged.

3. Robert Bellah, *Religion in Human Evolution: From the Paleolithic to the Axial Age* (Cambridge, MA: Harvard University Press, 2011), chapter 2.

4. Johan Huizinga, *Homo Ludens: A Study of the Play Element in Culture* (Boston: Beacon Press, 1950 [1938]).

has wider significance, and leaving aside much of his extremely rich discussion, I want to bring out just one facet of this here.

In "play" (or protoplay) we have behaviors which are not simply and directly related to survival: to self-preservation, acquiring the means of life, reproduction. There is something gratuitous here. Of course, play can increase survivability. Mock fights prepare for real fights, mock captures for real seizure of prey. One can readily understand how this trait, once introduced, would have survival value and would be selected for. But in the light of later (in this case, human) developments, we can surmise that this was the platform from which the corresponding human features came about.

The gratuitous: that means what is not directly required for biological survival, that which is pursued for its own sake. Of course, the animal doesn't make this distinction. The play instinct, the sexual instinct, the nest-building instinct, are equally immediate imperatives, moving the animal to action without any ulterior goal in mind. But in a linguistic being, the possibility arises for one or other of these goals to become autonomous, to be pursued for its own sake; and this sense of the independent validity of the activity is perhaps especially strong in play, which is why Huizinga singled it out for attention.[5] A certain autonomization will also accrue to sexual desire, along with a consciousness in many cultures of its analogy to play. This relates directly to language.

Now this autonomization is what occurs through the two special constitutive functions of language: the exploration and naming of human meanings on one hand, and the setting up of footings on the other, along with the contestations that arise in each domain. Through the first, normative patterns, ethical virtues, moral rules, the pursuit of truth, and the creation of beauty are established as ends in their own right. Through the second, social structures are erected which have intrinsic value. This crucial feature of human life is inseparable from the development of language and its constitutive powers. Hominization depends on language not only for the coding of information and the resultant greater efficacy of action, but also for the definition of the goals, values, and modes of relation which are essentially human. These cannot be defined by verbal formulae alone,

5. Bellah makes this point in likening play to a practice "as that term is used by Alasdair MacIntyre when he says that the good of a practice is internal to the practice, not something with an external end." Bellah, *Religion in Human Evolution,* 92. The reference is to Alasdair MacIntyre, *After Virtue: A Study in Moral Theory* (South Bend, IN: University of Notre Dame Press, 1981), 175. A converging notion of play, and its importance in human life, is to be found in Friedrich Schiller, *On the Aesthetic Education of Man,* trans. Reginald Snell (Mineola, NY: Dover, 2004).

or by objectively identifiable patterns of action.[6] They address us as embodied agents who can be moved on all levels by these human meanings.

3

On this imagined scenario, Homo sapiens emerge from the hominization process with the basic multiplicity of media that we are familiar with. Human meanings and footings can be enacted in individual and corporate behavior, for the first, and in discourse, for the second. But language is also available for the description, explanation, prediction of independent realities.

Here we reconnect with the fruitful theory of Merlin Donald. In the early stages it is likely that the capacity for mimicry played an important role. This would often occur in ritual or quasi-ritual form; as with a solemn emphatic enactment of the social order; or rituals of connection with the spirits, for instance the spirit of the deer; or rituals of connection/reconnection with the whole cosmic order. These rituals would be one way of becoming aware of the orders within which human life was set, society and its embedding in the cosmos.[7]

But this awareness was complemented by verbal accounts, particularly narrative, in the form of myths, about gods, spirits, and heroes. Later these would be supplemented, and then criticized and replaced by another kind of account, which Donald calls "theoretical"; philosophy, metaphysics, self-consciously nonmythical histories.[8]

The subsequent history of human language and culture sees the enormous expansion of the theoretical, and the growth of its rigor and critical force. The split between the mythical and the theoretical, between myth, on one hand, and philosophy, metaphysics, and what will be called "science", on the other, is the remote ancestor of the distinction I have been making between the two semantic logics, the designative and the constitutive. But in the beginning, this kind of distinction couldn't appear. All discourse about the cosmos and humans' relation to it was treated as an account of independent, free-standing realities. It took the development of post-Galilean natural science, which self-consciously brackets and sets aside

6. That is, identifiable without reference to human meanings. See Chapter 6, section 3.

7. Merlin Donald, *Origins of the Modern Mind* (Cambridge, MA: Harvard University Press, 1991), chapter 7.

8. Ibid., chapter 8.

human meanings, for the issue to arise about the status of accounts of things which do not, or cannot, operate with this kind of bracketing, such as arguments about ethics, or metaphysics; or of full accounts of human action, in daily life, society, or history. Any adequate attempt to clarify this status forces us, I have argued, to recognize the distinction between semantic logics, whether we are making a direct examination of our own felt intuitions, or engaged in an indirect attempt to defend our conclusions through appeal to human action in history, carried out inevitably in Ricoeur's "*discours mixte*".[9]

4

The upshot of all this is that we should feel the need to return to, while reexamining, Aristotle's definition of the human being as "*Zwon echon logon*". This has been traditionally translated as "rational animal"; and maybe we should bring this back to a more direct rendering as "animal possessing '*logos*'", where this Greek word is allowed its full stretch of polysemy: '*logos*' meaning in some contexts "word", in others "discourse", in others "account". In short we might render it as "animal possessing language". That this will in the end involve some notion of reason as crucial to human life is without doubt, but what this "reason" involves requires a lot of further examination.

I have tried to engage in a partial and tentative way in this examination in the preceding chapters. And the distinction of the two major semantic logics is an important step on the road. We need this in order to avoid, on one hand, the Scylla of declaring, for example, ethics a realm of purely subjective judgments or projections, and on the other, the Charybdis of imposing an alien model of rationality on them. It becomes evident that reason in this domain must take a largely hermeneutical turn; and this brings with it a certain endlessness, a resistance to completion, the impossibility of resting in some supposedly "final" and unimprovable conclusion.[10]

Much more needs to be said on this topic, but I hope that this book helps to make a start.

Because we still have a lot we don't understand in this domain. With phrases like "animal possessing language", we are trying to answer a ques-

---

9. "mixed discourse"; Paul Ricoeur, *Réflexion Faite* (Paris: Éditions Esprit, 1995), 36.

10. This is one of the points of convergence (that I mentioned in Chapter 3) of this book with Rowan Williams's *The Edge of Words* (London: Bloomsbury, 2014).

tion like: "what is human nature?" This is often conceived on analogy to other animals; something one can describe in terms of instincts and recurring behavior patterns. But the emergence of language seems to have introduced much greater flexibility, a capacity to change, even to transform ourselves, which has no parallel among other animals.

We might speak of capacit*ies* in the plural, because the flexibility comes in three dimensions, which combine in perplexing ways.

The first is the one which is evident when we look at the cultural differences between societies. Humans seem to have similar instincts everywhere, and these have mostly animal analogues: they are gregarious, like some animal species; they mate, like virtually all animals, and also care for their young, like some others; they seek the means to feed and clothe themselves and seek shelter; and so on. But the ways in which these common impulses express themselves: the kinds of societies that command loyalty, the forms of sexual and family life, the way they secure what they need for life; these are not only different from society to society, but also undergo changes, often big and dramatic, as the generations succeed each other.

This is remarkable, but by itself not upsetting. The fact that the music of one culture baffles members of another; that the sense of what's funny, or the sense of what is honorable, greatly varies; all this is not necessarily a cause for concern.

But differences which amount to incompatibility in the core ethic and basic moral rules of different societies are very troubling. Because here the background understanding is that these standards make unconditional demands. We can come to appreciate the music of another culture without denying the beauty of our own. But we can't endorse the principles of a slave society without renouncing our own; and the same goes for a society of castes, or one where women are utterly subordinate.

These clashes create an intellectual and moral pressure, a bafflement which could be relieved if we gave in and accepted some form of moral subjectivism; or if we considered this alien people as members of another species. But we are rightly reluctant to take either of these steps.

In fact, we tend to hold that there are good grounds to believe that there is a truth of the matter in each one of these clashes; that there are valid grounds which could in the best circumstances bring the intuitions of our opponents into alignment with ours (or vice versa). And there are some signs that this is happening in history; for example, there has already been some degree of convergence around a universalist ethic of human rights, equality, and humanitarian action, as I discussed in Chapter 6, section 3.

This brings us to the second dimension of flexibility; because this convergence goes against what we are tempted to identify as universal human instincts. Human gregariousness, and loyalty to the group, has from the beginning been directed toward particular societies; the sense of solidarity with insiders has as its flip side wariness, even hostility, to outsiders. In this it resembles its animal analogues. This seems an old and deeply implanted instinct.

But the universalist ethic runs against this, which is why we are not surprised that there is so much resistance to it in practice. The mystery is that it was ever adopted, and comes more and more to be endorsed. Here is a "flexibility" which involves transformation beyond—in the sense of running against—what we consider a core instinct, and one which is still operative in contemporary nationalism, for instance.

The remarkable turn in human history is the set of changes which have come to be called "Axial", transformations in religion like those we see in the preaching of the Buddha, in the teaching of Confucius, in the Hebrew prophets, and in post-Socratic philosophy.[11] These all make central some notion of a higher good, going way beyond the demands of personal and social survival and flourishing, even in some cases taking precedence over these perennial goals.[12] It is these changes that have prepared the ground for the growing universalist consensus in our day. That this ethic should have been proposed, and more and more widely endorsed, even partially put into effect, even against great resistance, shows another kind of "flexibility" than that exhibited by cultural difference. To carry through integrally on this ethic would involve a transformation, a kind of transcendence in relation to the instincts which the first humans inherited from their evolutionary ancestors. It would require an instinct of belonging, of solidarity, without the obligatory contrast case of the other, the outsider. A transformation of belonging and friendship, therefore, which transcends the need for the enemy.

So much for the second dimension of flexibility. But perhaps we can also discern a third, much more sinister. This is the one which makes possible

---

11. See Karl Jaspers, *The Origin and Goal of History* (London: Routledge, 2003), chapter 1.

12. See Charles Taylor, "What Was the Axial Revolution?," in *The Axial Age and Its Consequences,* ed. Robert Bellah and Hans Joas (Cambridge, MA: Harvard University Press, 2012), 36–37.

radical evil. This would be the case where the resistance to the ethic of universalism stems not from an anchoring in the instincts and interests this ethic wants to transform—the kind of resistance motivated by loyalty to our tribe, for instance—but rather from an excitement aroused in us by the rejection of the good itself. The motive here would be a kind of joy in destruction, a sense of heroic greatness in tearing down what the ethic of universal benevolence has tried to build. Such cases exist in literature: Milton's Satan, for instance, or Dostoevsky's "possessed". But I think there are also plausible candidates in real life: the leadership and many members of the Nazi movement, for instance, or of contemporary terrorist groups attempting to establish an "Islamic Caliphate" in the Middle East.

Whether or not this kind of evil exists depends on a hermeneutical reading of motives. But if it does (and I tend to think so), then there is a third dimension of flexibility. Moreover, its possibility seems tied to that of the second dimension. The ability to transform and transcend the instinctual heritage of nascent humanity which this move to a higher good requires would also make possible the step to what I'm calling radical evil: a drive to destroy the good which is also (largely) unanchored in this heritage.

Needless to say, much more has to be said and argued in this domain. The different forms of flexibility which the coming of language has allowed remain perplexing, even enigmatic.[13] Language remains in many ways a mysterious thing.

But approaches have been made to find a theoretical language to come to grips with the evolution of flexibility. One of these is the "philosophical anthropology" of Helmuth Plessner.

Plessner wants to treat humans and higher animals as agents. They not only exist in an environment which impinges on them, but they "position themselves" in their surroundings in order to act. They have in Plessner's terms "positionality". The mode common to all animals, and to humans a good deal of the time, is that in which the agent is the center of its environment, and things show up in their meaning or relevance to the action which

---

13. Another dimension of flexibilization is perhaps the trend toward the assertion of individual freedom and the emphasis on creativity and authenticity that we observe in the last centuries of Western civilization, but also in other societies. Is this a universal vector? Lenny Moss argues that a vector of this kind is visible in the evolution of humanity. See his "second individuation" in "From a New Naturalism to a Reconstruction of the Normative Grounds of Critical Theory" (forthcoming).

the situation calls for. But in addition to this stance, humans are also capable of an "eccentric" one; they are capable making this ordinary stance the object of a more reflexive one, to see it from outside, from another point of view, or in the eyes of another. This is what Plessner calls our "eccentric positionality", something only humans share.

This possibility makes sense in the light of our discussion in Chapter 2, which showed the primacy of joint attention, or communion, or "we-consciousness" in human ontogenesis, from which the child begins to develop a sense of discrimination, and comes to distinguish its own and others' standpoints in the conversations within which it grows. This discrimination is what underlies eccentric positionality.

Interestingly, Plessner's theory has one of its sources in Herder, who has been my inspiration throughout. One of Herder's basic theses was that humans were freed from the domination of instinct which was the rule among other animals, which imposes on them the task of finding ways of dealing with the challenges of existence. This is at the heart of what I have been calling "flexibility".[14]

5 Coda and *Renvoi*

In the previous section, I have been looking at one area where questions of what it is to be human can be explored through an understanding of language. But there are others. Another is what I called above "protodwelling", a feature of our linguistic awareness of the world. Exploring this has been largely carried out in works of art, as Heidegger intimates, and he gives a particularly central place to poetry (*"Dichtung"*, admittedly understood in a broad sense).

This brings us close to the point where the proposed companion study will take off. I would argue that Heidegger's intuitions about the nature and powers of language, and particularly poetry, owe a lot to the understanding of both which came to expression in the Romantic generation of

14. For Plessner's theory see *Die Stufen des Organischen und der Mensch* (Frankfurt: Suhrkamp 1981). See also the interesting discussion in Bernad G. Prusak, "The Science of Laughter: Helmuth Plessner's *Laughing and Crying* revisited," *Continental Philosophy Review* 38 (2006): 41–69. The Herderian idea was also developed in the twentieth century into a full-fledged anthropology by Arnold Gehlen, in ways which are different from but have some analogies to Plessner's theory. See Gehlen, *Der Mensch: seine Natur und seine Stellung in der Welt* (Wiebelsheim: Aula Verlag, 1950). An interesting contemporary theorist who is building on, inter alia, Plessner's insights is Lenny Moss; see previous note.

the 1790s, who were inspired by what I have been calling the HHH. This theory is what has informed the picture of language developed in this book. What I would like to do is show the connection between this view on language and the poetics which emerges from the Romantic era.

Now to indicate in summary, provisional fashion, what this connection amounts to, I'd like to look again at nature and role of ritual. Ritual serves to reconnect us to the whole. So I spoke above of rituals of reconnection. These not only serve to reconnect with the gods/spirits/cosmos, but also are the principal path by which this triple reality is conceived or understood, along with myth.

But in the immanent frame, does ritual disappear? I don't mean: does it disappear in the modern world? Plainly not. There are rituals within different faith communities. For instance, Christian liturgy is in some strong sense a ritual of reconnection.[15]

But can those who, beyond their diversity of faiths and nonfaiths, share only the immanent frame still have such rituals? Clearly they can; there is still the whole of society to be reconnected to, which also amounts to a reconnection with each other.[16]

But then how about our connection to the beyond-human, to the cosmos? This raises the question of disenchantment. Is it possible to live in a purely disenchanted world? This is the question posed by the Romantics, who answer this question in the negative, and pursue various modes of reenchantment.

There is in fact a streak in post-Romantic poetics which sees poetry as (potentially) ritual of reconnection. This is what I propose to explore in the companion study to this volume.

First, we can see that the Romantics were fascinated by the premodern and early Renaissance theories of languages which connect us to the deep nature of the cosmos. Either you see reality as made up of signs, waiting to be properly read; or you think of the world as modeled on the words of the Torah (Kabbalah). In either case, you see the world as the realization of a Plan; to grasp the Plan is to see the interconnections, how things relate to each other. To see this is to connect to the cosmos, and this in turn

15. Even though the Mass comes about with a sense of the (human) impossibility of beginning. See Catherine Pickstock, *After Writing: On the Liturgical Consummation of Philosophy* (Oxford: Blackwell, 1998), part 2.

16. See Chapter 7.

empowers us, in all sorts of ways, of which making gold from lead is only one, and the least exalted.

For the Romantics, the Plan is dynamic; it is growing, becoming, struggling. We need to grasp it to be what we have to be; we see our real destiny [*Bestimmung*]. But also our grasping it is part of the Plan itself, and thus helps to realize it.

This is played out differently by different thinkers/writers. For Novalis, our grasping the Plan not only helps realize it, because our full development is realized, and that is part of the Plan; but it also helps the reality which embodies the signs themselves to reach their full realization and truth. So the idealism is "magic" here.

The understanding of poetry as ritual of reconnection is strengthened by Hamann's idea that we don't simply recognize the signs of God; we translate them; "*Reden ist übersetzen.*"[17] Our creations reveal what is there, and reconnect us with it.

So we get the important post-Romantic theme of seeking the real language, the living creative one, which reconnects, as against the dead language which simply designates things that everyone can see, and allows us to manipulate them, totally ignoring their sign-character.

What does reconnection mean here? And what does it do for us?

We see how we cannot exist without certain conditions and a certain relation to the world. We need air to breathe, and things we can eat, and so on. We are biologically tied to a certain relation to the cosmos (a relation we have set about destroying in a feckless fashion). But perhaps the necessity is not just biological, but also metabiological. Perhaps certain relations to the cosmos—sun, fields, forest, mountains, wilderness, time—are essential not just biologically, but because outside of these we humans wither.

The relation to forests is a relation to our beginnings;[18] and the forests have still to be there. So our relation to forests is interwoven with our relation to deep time. And then our relation to monuments of past civilization, our seeking them out, visiting them, perhaps manifests our need to be rooted in meaningful time.

---

17. "To speak is to translate"; Johann Georg Hamann, *Sokratische Denkwürdigkeiten: Aesthetica in Nuce* (Stuttgart: Reclam, 1968), 87.

18. Robert Pogue Harrison, *Forests: The Shadow of Civilization* (Chicago: University of Chicago Press, 1992), 1.

Then in the shorter term we need to connect to sun, plants, flowers, trees. And we need meaningful lived time, here and now. Baudelaire explores this.

So this is just a fact about us? In a sense, yes, like it's a fact about us that we need food and air. But what we need in the metabiological case is to stand in a certain relationship to our world. It can only be fulfilled in the interspace. So it is more a fact of relationship than our biological needs are. We could survive in a spaceship provided nourishment were available. But the essential relational meanings can't be substituted for by anything other than the relation. And like all meaning relations it requires to be grasped, understood; we have to open ourselves to it. Hence the need for ritual, which is "poetry" [*Dichtung*].

Within this category, there are more immediate needs, the denial of which deeply disturbs and drives us into mental anguish: spleen; and then there are needs which are calmer, more long-term, but the denial of which stunts us, analogous to the way that lack of key nutrition stunts our growth.

The psychological/ontological distinction is too simple.[19] But this is obviously another domain in which the study of language can cast crucial light on what it is to be human.

What are the ontic conditions of this need and the relation which fulfills it? These are left indefinite by the Romantic tradition as a whole, though individual authors have different ideas. Ontic indefiniteness is part of the stance here. But that means that theological dimensions are not ruled out; just that they aren't already affirmed and assumed.

The proposed companion study will explore the post-Romantic tradition which distinguishes real, poetic language from routine, instrumental, designative speech, and which sees the former as operating a kind of reconnection. The link between the two, this volume and its successor, is the Romantic theory of language, called here the HHH, which underlies them both. They are two sides of the same outlook on language.

19. This whole relationship with our environment is being explored today through another approach, sociological in nature, in the interesting work of Hartmut Rosa and his associates, whose key concept is "resonance". See Hartmut Rosa, *Social Acceleration: A New Theory of Modernity*, trans. Jonathan Trejo-Mathys (New York: Columbia University Press, 2013); Rosa, *Weltbeziehungen im Zeitalter der Beschleunigung* (Suhrkamp Taschenbuch Wissenschaft 1977) (Berlin: Suhrkamp, 2012); and Rosa, *Alienation and Acceleration: Towards a Critical Theory of Late-Modern Temporality* (Aarhus: NSU Press, 2010).

Index

ÉCHÉANCE   DATE DUE